UNDERSTANDING
EVANGELISM

UNDERSTANDING EVANGELISM

BIBLICAL FOUNDATIONS,
HISTORICAL DEVELOPMENTS, AND
CONTEMPORARY ISSUES

J. D. PAYNE

Baker Academic
a division of Baker Publishing Group
Grand Rapids, Michigan

© 2025 by J. D. Payne

Published by Baker Academic
a division of Baker Publishing Group
Grand Rapids, Michigan
BakerAcademic.com

Printed in the United States of America

All rights reserved. No part of this publication may be reproduced, stored in a retrieval system, or transmitted in any form or by any means—for example, electronic, photocopy, recording—without the prior written permission of the publisher. The only exception is brief quotations in printed reviews.

Library of Congress Cataloging-in-Publication Data
Names: Payne, Jervis David, 1974– author
Title: Understanding evangelism : biblical foundations, historical developments, and contemporary issues / J. D. Payne.
Description: Grand Rapids, Michigan : Baker Academic, a division of Baker Publishing Group, [2025] | Includes bibliographical references and index.
Identifiers: LCCN 2025005508 | ISBN 9781540963581 paperback | ISBN 9781540969637 casebound | ISBN 9781493451937 ebook | ISBN 9781493451944 pdf
Subjects: LCSH: Evangelistic work
Classification: LCC BV3770 .P396 2025 | DDC 269/.2—dc23/eng/20250502
LC record available at https://lccn.loc.gov/2025005508

Scripture quotations are from The Holy Bible, English Standard Version® (ESV®), copyright © 2001 by Crossway, a publishing ministry of Good News Publishers. Used by permission. All rights reserved. ESV Text Edition: 2016

Cover design by Tobias Outerwear for Books

Baker Publishing Group publications use paper produced from sustainable forestry practices and postconsumer waste whenever possible.

25 26 27 28 29 30 31   7 6 5 4 3 2 1

*To the One who provides understanding
to make his gospel known,
and to my wife Sarah,
a woman of great understanding*

CONTENTS

List of Figures and Sidebars   ix
Preface   xi
Acknowledgments   xvii

Part 1 Introductory Issues   1

1. What Is Evangelism?   3
2. Contemporary Definitions of Evangelism   17
3. One Gospel for a Multicultural World   29
4. Global Status of Evangelization   41
5. Motives and Ethics   49

Part 2 Biblical and Theological Foundations   63

6. The Mission of God in the Old Testament   65
7. Evangelism and the Great Commission   73
8. Jesus and the Apostolic Church   83
9. Divine Sovereignty and Election   93
10. Atonement and Grace   107
11. Repentance, Faith, Conversion   114

Part 3 Historical Overview   131

12. Means of Evangelism: AD 100–300   133
13. Influencers (Part 1): AD 300–1500   147
14. Influencers (Part 2): AD 1500 to the Present   156
15. A Century of Global Evangelization Gatherings: AD 1910–2024   166

Part 4 Culture and Communication   189

16. Crossing Cultural Gaps   191
17. Apologetics and Worldview   208

Part 5 Contemporary Issues   221

18. Testimony   223
19. The Sinner's Prayer   230
20. Pastoral Leadership   234
21. Reaching Children   241
22. Overcoming Personal Concerns   247
23. Sharing and Responding   261

   Conclusion   279

   Case Study 1: Group Conversion   281
   Case Study 2: Not Being Offensive   283
   Bibliography   287
   Scripture Index   309
   Author Index   315
   Subject Index   319

FIGURES AND SIDEBARS

Figures

11.1. Bounded Centered Set   125
11.2. Extrinsic Fuzzy Set   126
16.1. The Dayton Resistance/Receptivity Scale   200
16.2. Two-Dimensional Model with Cognitive and Affective Dimensions   202
17.1. The Dimensions of Culture   215

Sidebars

Reclaiming the E Word   24
The Gospel and Digital Culture   36
The Global Reach of Evangelism Explosion   44
Ethical Methods   51
Israel as Priest, Prophet, and King   68
The Relationship Between Evangelists and Making Disciples   80
Gospel-Cultural Hermeneutics   89
Pray Like a Calvinist, Preach Like an Arminian   102
What Do We Do with Antinomies?   105
Faith and the Atonement   110
A Call for Evangelistic Collaboration   121
History and Evangelism   138
Telling Stories   149

Methodist Circuit Riders   162
Proclamation, Presence, or Power?   176
Reaching Those in Folk Islam   195
Søgaard Scale in Practice   201
Barrier to the Gospel Among Native Americans / First Nations   205
Defeaters of the Day   210
The Word Works   214
Seven Steps in Conversation   217
Explain Your Terms   224
From Pulpit to Pew   237
Evangelism: Wesleyan Way   252
Nudge Questions   267

PREFACE

Early in my faith journey, two significant factors impressed on me the significance, need, practice, and joy of evangelism. The first was the Scriptures. A simple reading of the Bible, particularly the New Testament, revealed that the church's modus operandi involved regular and intentional evangelism. The disciples were part of the continuation of God's covenantal faithfulness. His mission included both Jew and gentile in rebuilding David's tent (Acts 15:16; cf. Amos 9:11–12) before the day of the Lord. The second was my home church. My faith family, especially our church's leadership, consistently and intentionally taught, modeled, and provided helpful resources and opportunities for personal evangelism. People need exposure to the Scriptures and leaders who model it with their words and actions. This book is written with the desire to assist leaders in accomplishing such tasks in their ministries.

After becoming a Christ follower, it did not take long to realize that the gospel needs to be shared with others. The first person with whom I attempted to share the gospel was one of my high school teachers. I write *attempted* because that was all it was. I asked him what he thought about God, and he gave me an honest—and angry—answer. I despised his answer and attitude, so I decided that the conversation was over then and forever.

I was a junior and, along with a couple of friends, was invited to go on a "senior trip." He was a practical, down-to-earth kind of guy: funny, cool, friendly, and young. He loved music and was a fan of The Doors, especially Jim Morrison. He never invited juniors to go on his annual senior trips. This was an exceptional invitation.

The trip involved a three-hour drive to watch *The Nutcracker* ballet—not what most high school guys thought would be a fun trip. However, I was a guest and would enjoy hanging out with my friends and teacher. Since I had been praying for an opportunity to share the gospel with him, surely this day would allow for that opportunity.

When he arrived in the school parking lot, I called "shotgun," and the upperclassmen graciously granted the coveted seat to me. Now, I would have six hours of road trip to spend in conversation with him.

We drove to the event and watched the show. As we loaded up for our journey home, I was frustrated—a full day and no door of opportunity ... until we started the drive.

As we approached an overpass, he told me to read what was graffitied under the bridge. Seeing nothing, I returned with a puzzled look. He shared that when he was growing up in the neighborhood, someone had painted in large letters "Jim Morrison is God!"

Strange. But The Doors were my open door. Though it was just a small crack, I saw it as an answer to prayer and attempted to venture through it.

I paused, then asked, "What do you think about that?"

Uncertain as to what I meant, he asked for clarification.

"About God," I replied. "What do you think about God?"

I immediately struck a nerve and triggered a negative response. For the next few minutes, I listened to this man, whom I greatly admired, belittle the God of the Bible, inform me that Moses created the law to keep the unruly Hebrews in line in the desert, and that the way of Jesus was a myth, the Bible was filled with errors, and so on.

I was not prepared for his response. And I was not happy.

As he continued, my blood pressure increased. I was shocked and had no apologetic response. I remember biting the inside of my cheek in anger. I decided that if he was going to act that way, then I would never share the gospel with him. I remained silent for the rest of the drive and hardly said a word to him for the remainder of my high school career.

Sometime later, I read the aphorism "You will attract more flies with honey than vinegar" and reflected on that dark night. While there are times when the wisdom of not casting our pearls before swine and the principle of shaking off the dust do apply, I was in the wrong. What started as righteous indignation quickly became personal agitation and sin. My teacher may have responded the same way no matter what I said or did, but I had decided that he blasphemed my God, and I was not going to give him another opportunity.

After repenting, I learned a great deal from that horrible experience. We must be intentional when it comes to sharing the gospel. The church does not slide into evangelism; she slides away from it—especially if experiencing a teacher's negative response. The Lord works through prayer to open doors. When the apostle Paul requested prayer for opportunities (Col. 4:3), he understood that such is critical to God's Great Commission economy. I also learned that God is big enough to defend himself and does not need me to be his bodyguard. A great deal of what some people are calling apologetics and cultural engagement are little more than attempts to win arguments and the contemporary culture wars. It is assumed that God's reputation is at stake, the church's power is on the line, and we must defend them with verbal weapons. I am unconvinced that this is what Peter had in mind (1 Pet. 3:15–16), especially whenever we overlook the gentleness and respect aspect of his exhortation.

Since that road trip, I have shared the gospel countless times. I have evangelized children and adults, women and men, individuals and crowds. Though that incendiary encounter occurred over thirty years ago, I have a confession to make: I still struggle with sharing my faith—and this from a guy with two advanced degrees, and numerous publications, in evangelism! I write this book as a struggler on the disciple-making journey to assist other strugglers on the same journey.

I have shelves in my personal library filled with books on evangelism. Some address the biblical and theological foundations for evangelism and why the church is to engage in such activity. Others, though fewer in number, discuss the history of evangelism. These summarize and evaluate how the church has shared the gospel for the past two thousand years in various locations and among diverse peoples. Fewer still emphasize global strategies for evangelism. Because evangelism is the church in action, most books are methodological. They provide readers the how-to of sharing the gospel. This may come in the form of personal evangelism, "lifestyle" evangelism, servant projects, apologetics, church planting, evangelistic sermons for crowds, door-to-door canvassing, television and online evangelism, and seeker Bible studies and events. Shifting demographic and cultural dynamics have caused some authors to learn principles from the experiences of those who have done evangelistic work in other countries. Authors have been incorporating sociological and anthropological insights into the ministry of evangelism. Denominationally specific works also exist that reflect the theological foundations and methodological nuances of various church traditions. I have books by Baptists, Methodists, Lutherans, Anglicans, Presbyterians, and Pentecostals, to name a few. One may find evangelistic works written from evangelical, mainline, Catholic, and Orthodox traditions.

There is no shortage of literature on the topic of evangelism. So why add another book to the count?

Part of the answer to this question is the diversity just described. The wealth of material is overwhelming to many people. Where should one begin, as not all books on evangelism are the same? This book is an attempt to draw from the diverse and vast literature such that the reader may develop an understanding of the topic that leads to sharing the gospel both at home and throughout the world.

Another reason for this book is that large portions of the church either refuse to share the gospel, or relegate evangelism to the practices of a few leaders, or do not know how. The body of Christ is diverse with a wide array of gifts, passions, experiences, opportunities, interests, and resources (1 Cor. 12:4–7). Making disciples begins with evangelism and requires involvement from the whole body of Christ. No denomination, local church, or individual receives a pass. This book is an attempt to provide the necessary biblical knowledge, cultural awareness, and practical insights for *every* Christ follower to be part of this wonderful privilege of partnering with the Spirit in the world.

I have taught evangelism for a quarter of a century at churches, colleges, and seminaries and divinity schools. I have written articles and books on this topic. However, I am still learning and developing in my approaches to sharing the gospel. As of this writing, very few contemporary textbooks on evangelism are in print that offer breadth, depth, and engagement with contemporary global issues. This work is my attempt to provide a helpful introductory textbook to professors and students.

I also write for pastors. As of this writing, I have served in pastoral ministry for almost twenty years. Pastors are busy, very busy. And if they are single-staff, or bivocational, they are even less flexible with their time. Given the academic nature of this book, some elements are less beneficial to most church members. My hope is that elders will find this book helpful for equipping their members in evangelism (Eph. 4:11–12). But my recommendation is to approach this work as one would pan for gold. Sift through the sediment that is less helpful and collect the golden nuggets that may be applied to one's context.

The organization of this book is fairly standard for textbooks. Part 1 lays out introductory issues for the study of evangelism. Part 2 addresses biblical and theological matters related to evangelism. While I have tried to respect various theological positions by noting their relation to evangelism, some readers will want to pursue such topics to a deeper level. Since an introductory text is unable to exhaust any topic, I must point readers to the bibliography for additional information. The same is true for additional study related to any of this book's sections.

Part 3, the historical section, provides an overview of the evangelistic work of the church throughout two thousand years. At times it will be challenging to distinguish between the church's evangelization and Christianization. As will be noted, these are two different topics, with the former related to sharing the gospel for the Spirit to bring regeneration and the latter more related to sharing and developing Christian culture and worldview. I have attempted to approach this history by providing an overview of the ministry conducted throughout different epochs, including global developments in the twentieth and twenty-first centuries.

Understanding cultures and contexts is necessary for effective communication of the gospel. Faith comes by hearing a clearly communicated message (Rom. 10:17; Col. 4:4). Part 4 examines elements of intercultural study and communication. All evangelistic activity is about crossing cultural barriers, whether the church shares the gospel across the street or across the world. Apologetics, worldview and societal differences, receptor-oriented communication, and contextualization are a few of the topics addressed here.

The final section of the book, part 5, contains chapters related to questions I have encountered over the years. Here I have adjusted my writing style and limited the number of footnotes.

In order to bend this academic work toward the practical application of evangelism, I have included additional materials in the form of sidebars and numerous open-ended questions in each chapter. I end the book with two case studies. It is my hope that the reader will be able to understand how to apply principles in this book to their contexts *and* be able to equip others in the area of evangelism.

I still make mistakes in evangelism but have learned a great deal since that road trip long ago. Though I have lost contact with my former teacher, I still pray for him and ask that you would too.

ACKNOWLEDGMENTS

While the writing of a book is a solo venture, the making of one requires a great team. Limitations found in this work belong to me. However, I must recognize and thank the amazing Anna Gissing and Julie Zahm, and the outstanding team at Baker Academic for their partnership. It has been a great blessing to work with them on this project. Their long-suffering attitude toward me was so much appreciated.

I also have to express much appreciation to my students and church members over the years. The Lord used them in many wonderful ways that have influenced the contents of this book. Of course, I must add that without my wonderful wife, Sarah, this work probably would not have come to completion. Her encouragement and prayers were invaluable.

— PART 1 —

INTRODUCTORY ISSUES

We must not assume that whenever the church uses the word *evangelism* that the definition is understood. As will be noted in this section, a variety of definitions may be found. Therefore, chapters 1 and 2 attempt to show the variety and explain a working definition used in this text. The gospel and the church are found in every country of the world. Each day the word of God spreads and disciples are multiplied. Asians are sharing the gospel in Africa. North Americans are preaching in South America. Africans are evangelizing in Central America. Europeans are taking the gospel to Australia. Evangelism is occurring through the work of older and younger churches. Canadian believers are taking the gospel across the street, as are Japanese believers. Filipinos are carrying the truth of God into the Middle East. The gospel now moves in both national and transnational directions. The gospel is designed for a diverse world. This is the subject of chapter 3. Though the Christian faith is the largest religion in the world and growing, most of the world's population remains unreached. Chapter 4 introduces the reader to the global status of evangelization at the time of this writing. While much has been done in two thousand years to make disciples of all nations, a great deal of work remains. As the church has gone into the world, she has not always done so with righteous motives and a kingdom ethic. Chapter 5 examines biblical motives for evangelistic work and how such should be applied to contemporary practice.

1

WHAT IS EVANGELISM?

The defining of *evangelism* is critical to proper understanding of the contents of this book. While one may think that such is a needless task, given the widespread use and history of the word, confusion surrounds this English word and its cognates. Consider the following ways the word is used:

- Evangelism is stopping strangers on a street, interrupting their movement, and telling them about Jesus.
- She is an evangelist for her software company. Without her, their profits would decrease significantly.[1]
- Evangelism is sharing the good news about Jesus with unbelievers.
- Evangelism is sharing the good news about Jesus with believers.
- The church needs to be reevangelized.
- Jesus told us to love others through our actions—that is evangelism.
- I am not involved in evangelism because I do not have that gift.
- I do not do evangelism because I am not an evangelist.
- Evangelism is sharing the good news of Jesus and increasing our church's membership.
- Evangelism is a lifestyle.
- We evangelize by expressing our kindness to others, because people do not care what you believe until they know that you care.

1. The business world has been using *evangelism* since the late twentieth century to describe leaders responsible for communicating the value of their companies' products to the world.

- Evangelism is one needy person telling another needy person where to get their needs met.
- We evangelize when we share our testimony.
- Apologetics is evangelism.
- We evangelize all the time and, when necessary, we use words.

Notice the diverging definitions, and various underlying assumptions, for the words *evangelism*, *evangelize*, and *evangelist*. Is evangelism something done to Christians (i.e., those who are born again), or to non-Christians (i.e., unregenerate), or to both? Is evangelism an act or a lifestyle, or both? Can we do evangelism with good deeds or are words necessary? Are all Christians to engage in evangelism or only a few within the church? Is evangelism about sharing the good news of Jesus (and if so, what is that good news?) or about increasing church baptisms (and thus members)? Is evangelism exclusively limited to certain methods (e.g., street preaching, door-to-door visitation)? Is there a difference between witnessing and evangelizing?

Why the Confusion?

The answer to why such confusion surrounds evangelism is complex. The church did not arrive at this point overnight, but such has been a journey of two millennia across many geographical locations and among many cultural expressions. At least three factors have contributed to the present reality, particularly in the Western world.

Lack of Robust Theological Foundation

Though evangelism is not new, during the nineteenth and twentieth centuries the church spent considerable time defining it with clarity and examining her mission in the world.[2] Jesus told his disciples to go into the world and preach the gospel, and they went (Acts 10:42). They acted on what was commanded. Little thought was needed. While strategies and methods would develop and evolve among the unreached peoples, the "why we go" and the "what we do beyond preaching" were not given as much

2. For example, in the mid-twentieth century Roman Catholics began embracing such terminology of evangelism and evangelization. Evangelization was understood as the initial sharing of the gospel with catechesis to follow the evangelized (Gorski, "From 'Mission' to 'Evangelization,'" 35). Things began to change with Pope Paul VI's publication of *Evangelii nuntiandi* in 1975. Evangelism was not to be reduced to the initial proclamation of the gospel to the unreached, but broadened to include church members.

attention.³ Unlike debates and controversies that arose over the humanity and divinity of Jesus that resulted in much biblical study, theological conversations, and written documents, evangelism was rarely questioned.

There was no need for evangelistic congresses and councils. Evangelism creeds were unnecessary. The gospel of the kingdom was to be preached to all nations before the end (Matt. 24:14). The disciples were sent to the west, east, north, and south. Conflicts would develop over methods and strategies. Even in the twentieth and twenty-first centuries, Protestant, Catholic, and Orthodox groups would find themselves debating matters over the ethics of evangelizing in Christianized territories and proselytizing. One is hard pressed to find an argument that states that the church is not to evangelize. Even among groups that take pride in pluralistic soteriologies, Christ's command to preach the gospel is embraced.

Throughout the centuries the church faced numerous challenges both from among her members and from unbelievers. Right doctrine needed to be codified and communicated throughout what would quickly become Christendom. Theological discussions and developments surrounding evangelism were not a pressing matter and seldomly addressed. However, by the twentieth century, the growth of the Majority World church, spread of secularization, and expansion of pluralism forced the church to consider the importance of theology and evangelism.

Cultural Expectations of Church Traditions

As the church grew and developed and became intimately connected with governmental structures, expectations and traditions soon followed.⁴ Christendom became widespread. If someone was born into a particular geographical area and baptized into the church, then that person was under the jurisdiction of the church. In order to hear the gospel rightly taught, one was expected to gather with a local expression of the church on Sunday. Gospel proclamation was expected to occur every time the church gathered for worship. The good news was shared through Scripture readings, songs, homilies, and the Eucharist. In doing so, the church proclaimed the Lord's death until

---

3. By the late 1980s, David Barrett and James Reapsome estimated that more than seven hundred strategies had been developed in two thousand years to reach the world with the gospel (*Seven Hundred Plans*).

4. Judith Paulsen notes that within the church there is a bias against evangelism. In *New and Ancient Evangelism*, she attributes much of this to caricatures and stereotypes, negative experiences, assumptions about evangelists, and guilt from the pulpit (1–12). Her findings reveal that cultural and historical matters, rather than biblical ones, are generally the reason why clarification is necessary regarding evangelism.

the parousia (1 Cor. 11:26). While evangelists[5] were sent to locations where the church did not exist, under Christendom a gospel presence manifested itself within the parish's worshiping community. Unbelievers who lived in such regions simply needed to show up on Sunday, with some exceptions. Evangelism would occur within the gathered assembly of the saints and was overseen by the officiant. Though Catholic and Protestant traditions embraced such convictions, the Orthodox were clear that belief came from an experience. And what better way to encounter the divine than in the context of a worshiping community? As long as the gathering shared the good news (i.e., the Scriptures rightly taught, as stressed during the Reformation) and called people to repentance toward God and faith in Jesus (Acts 20:21), then evangelism had occurred within the walls of the building.

Added to the notion that the primary place for the occurrence of evangelism was the church's weekly gathering is the reality that the church has a history of embracing culturally defined methods and making them into sacred standards that must not be adjusted. Over time, some churches found great evangelistic success with particular evangelistic methods. Their effectiveness often resulted in an unwritten understanding: "If you want to do evangelism the right way, then our way is the way." Churches, denominations, and networks created atmospheres in which evangelism was understood and defined by the culturally preferred method of communicating the gospel. Those unwilling (or unable) to share the gospel through such means often were viewed as disobedient or not serious about the Great Commission. Someone who was unable to knock on doors in an apartment community, pass out tracts, drive a bus or van to transport kids to Sunday school, make phone calls, teach a Bible study, or memorize a lengthy presentation to share with a stranger learned "If this is evangelism, then I can't do it—so it must not be for me."

Rather than the church understanding that methods and models of evangelistic activity were birthed out of specific historical contexts and heavily influenced by the personalities, gifts, and interests of their designers, what was once unique and contextualized became universal and codified. The apostolic imagination that encouraged the customized application of biblical principles of evangelism was neglected and often substituted for a philosophy of evangelistic pragmatism.[6]

---

5. Though the word *evangelist* was used early in church history, the title *missionary* would not be developed until the sixteenth century with the Jesuits. For an excellent and concise study on the spread of the gospel and Christianization via an often-overlooked history, see Smither, *Missionary Monks*.

6. It should be noted that *pragmatism* is not the same thing as *pragmatic*. The former is an unbiblical philosophy of the end justifying the means. However, the church should be pragmatic

English Translation

The word *evangelism* does not exist in the Bible but rather comes as an adapted transliteration from Greek. What is found in the Old Testament and New Testament is a variety of words related to sharing God's good news that have come to be called *evangelism*. More will be said regarding terminology later in this chapter. It is important to understand how evangelism is frequently filtered through the cultural lens described above, especially when it comes to the words *preach* or *proclaim*.

In his extensive historical survey of the word *evangelize*, David Barrett notes that the English word and its cognates, such as *evangelizing*, *evangelization*, *evangelism*, and *evangelized*, originated in the fourteenth century and have grown in popularity since 1850 among Protestants and Anglicans and since 1965 with Roman Catholics. English translators generally translate the Greek verb εὐαγγελίζω (*euangelizō*) (and variants) with fifteen English verbs, of which the most common are *preach*, *bring*, *tell*, *proclaim*, *announce*, and *declare* instead of *evangelize*.[7]

For example, we read passages that state "and proclaim as you go" (Matt. 10:7), "the gospel I preached to you" (1 Cor. 15:1), and "preach the word" (2 Tim. 4:2). All of these are related to the concept of evangelism. However, given church history and cultural preferences, the church often reads these texts as if they were to be understood as referring to *preaching a sermon or homily* to a congregation (primarily consisting of a regenerate membership) gathered for worship. A great deal of what is related to preaching, proclaiming, heralding, and speaking the gospel in the Bible was *to be done outside a church gathering*. While it is correct to conceptualize preaching (and thus evangelizing) as taking place within a worship setting, such is a narrow and limited understanding of where, and to whom, preaching occurred in the Scriptures. The church has sanitized and privatized gospel proclamation away from the primary contexts expected in the Bible.

---

in her evangelistic work. The church has been called to bear fruit (John 15:1–11) and make disciples (Matt. 28:16–20), commands with an expectation of results. She should want to know what methods and strategies are working to reach those far from God.

7. Barrett, *Evangelize!*, 77. Barrett's work has fallen by the wayside among scholars today and must be revisited by those doing exegetical and historical studies in evangelism. Also, Bible translators should read Barrett's book not only to see how the Greek words have been translated throughout the English-speaking world but also as a case study of how translations have significant practical repercussions. Thomas Johnston noted in 2003 that the *Holman Christian Standard Bible* broke with tradition. That Bible version became the first English translation since 1382 to use *evangelize* (six of fifty-four times) for the Greek verb εὐαγγελίζω (*euangelizō*); Darby's 1884 translation of Luke 7:22 and the Douay-Rheims 1899 translation of Luke 8:1 are the only exceptions (see T. Johnston, *Motivation and Definition*, 295).

Since English translations rarely translate Greek words as *evangelize*, contemporary readers inject modern understandings of what these words mean, where such actions occur, and who is capable of executing such behaviors. Following his extensive historical and exegetical study of the translation of Old and New Testament words, Thomas Johnston concludes that the failure to use the word *evangelize* in translations reveals a theological agenda and confuses evangelizing with formal preaching known as homiletics.[8] The lack of an exegetical theology to support evangelistic practices throughout the world created a vacuum that allowed for eisegesis to conceptualize and operationalize what is described in the biblical texts.

Language of Evangelism

The examination of biblical terminology is nothing new in evangelistic literature of the late twentieth and early twenty-first centuries.[9] According to Johnston, among Old Testament passages, at least 185 proclamational verbs may be found related to the communication of the divine message.[10] Barrett notes that the New Testament uses at least forty-two Greek verbs "to cover the activities that today are called evangelism or evangelization."[11] While it is beyond the scope of this chapter to address the breadth of these lexical matters, in the next two sections I discuss some of the more prominent Hebrew and Greek terms related to the subject of communicating the good news.[12]

Old Testament Terms

סָפַר (*sāpar*). This word may be translated in numerous ways, "tell" and "proclaim" being among them. Israel was to proclaim the praise of God (Isa. 43:21). The created order declares the glory of God to all people (Ps. 19:1). Israel was to tell the glorious deeds of God to each generation (Ps. 78:4). God's glory and marvelous deeds are to be announced among the nations (1 Chron. 16:24).

---

8. T. Johnston, *Motivation and Definition*, 295.
9. See D. Watson, *I Believe in Evangelism*, 26–49; Miles, *Introduction to Evangelism*, 19–26; Drummond, *Word of the Cross*, 203–86; Klaiber, *Call and Response*, 21–27; Reid, *Evangelism Handbook*, 22–28; Beougher, *Invitation to Evangelism*, 3–4; Queen, *Recapturing Evangelism*, 93–103.
10. T. Johnston, *Motivation and Definition*, 257–388.
11. Barrett, *Evangelize!*, 77.
12. Note, particularly with Hebrew, that some of the terms may be translated in ways other than those I have identified in these sections.

לָמַד (*lāmad*). Moses "taught" Israel the words of the Lord (Deut. 4:5). The psalmist "teaches" transgressors the way of Yahweh that they may return to him (Ps. 51:13). A day will come when Israel will experience Yahweh's forgiveness because they have been "taught" his ways (Jer. 31:34).

יָדַע (*yādaʿ*). David's song exhorts Israel to "make known" Yahweh's deeds among the peoples (1 Chron. 16:8). In a similar fashion, the psalmist calls Israel to give thanks and make known Yahweh's deeds among the peoples (Ps. 105:1). Isaiah likewise calls Israel to such actions (Isa. 12:4).

דָּבַר (*dābar*). Moses is commanded to go to Egypt, for the Lord will be with his mouth and teach him what to "speak" (Exod. 4:12). The words of Yahweh are to be "spoken" to one's children (Deut. 11:19). The psalmist promises to "speak" of Yahweh's testimonies before kings (Ps. 119:46).

נָגַד (*nāgad*). Sheba was "told" of the wisdom of Solomon that resulted in her journey to Jerusalem (1 Kings 10:7). The deeds of the Lord are to be "told" to others (Ps. 9:11). In Isaiah, the Lord declares that he will send survivors to the nations who will "declare" his glory among them (Isa. 66:19).

בָּשַׂר (*bāśar*). The notion of bearing, heralding, and proclaiming good tidings and news was not lost on the ancient residents around Israel. When the Philistines defeated Saul, they "sent messengers through the land of the Philistines, to carry [*bāśar*] the good news to the house of their idols and to the people" (1 Sam. 31:9). Jeremiah notes that news of the birth of a son made people glad (Jer. 20:15). One should carry good news with speed, and the verbal proclamation of such a message was to bring delight to the hearer (2 Sam. 18:19). Johnston recommends that many of the Septuagint (Greek Old Testament) uses of εὐαγγελίζω (*euangelizō*) for בָּשַׂר (*bāśar*) should be translated as "evangelize" so as to draw attention to the Old Testament background for the New Testament uses. Isaiah 40:9, 52:7, and 61:1–2 are of special attention. He argues that translations such as "brings good tidings" and "bring good news" diminish the proclamational emphasis and should be translated as "evangelizes" and "evangelize."[13]

It should come as no surprise that the blessing of the nations through Abraham (Gen. 12:3) is connected with how Israel is to "tell of [the LORD's] salvation from day to day" and declare "his glory among the nations" (1 Chron. 16:23–24; cf. Ps. 96:2–3). The use of *bāśar* foreshadows the eschatological significance, developed in the New Testament, of the ingathering of the nations as the people of God. A "herald of good news" was to be found among Israel's communities (Isa. 40:9). Even the dirty feet of the one who "brings good news" are to be welcomed (Nah. 1:15). Such delight is because

---

13. T. Johnston, *Motivation and Definition*, 264–65.

the messenger "publishes peace," "brings good news of happiness," "publishes salvation," and verbally announces that the God of Abraham, Isaac, and Jacob "reigns" (Isa. 52:7).[14] The one of whom Scripture foretold, who delights in the will of God, "tells" the glad news to others (Ps. 40:9). This Messiah "brings" good news (Isa. 61:1), and even the nations will "bring" good news of the Lord (Isa. 60:6).

קָרָא (*qārā'*). Moses states that he will "proclaim" the name of the Lord (Deut. 32:3). Jonah is commanded to "call out" God's message of coming judgment (Jon. 1:2; 3:2). The messenger of the Lord is sent to "proclaim" the year of the Lord and freedom to those enslaved (Isa. 61:1–2).

זָהַר (*zāhar*). The language of warning is found in the Old Testament. Those who have broken the law are called to change direction. Those responsible for promulgating this message are held guilty only if they remain silent. Ezekiel was to "warn" the wicked so that they might repent and not die in iniquity (Ezek. 33:9). Certain Levites, priests, and heads of families in Israel were to settle legal matters. Their responsibilities involved "warning" others so that they might not experience guilt and wrath from Yahweh. Also, by making such declarations they too would not incur guilt (2 Chron. 19:8–10).

אָמַר (*'āmar*). God calls, sends, and commands Isaiah to "say" to the people a message that will make their hearts dull, ears heavy, and eyes sightless (Isa. 6:9–10). When the sailors confront Jonah, the prophet "utters" to them his ethnicity and the nature of the God he serves (Jon. 1:9). God's people are to "speak" of the glory of God's kingdom and power (Ps. 145:11).

New Testament Terms

εὐαγγελίζω (*euangelizō*), εὐαγγελίζομαι (*euangelizomai*). This word and its variations occur fifty-four times in the New Testament. It is often translated as "I bring the good news" and "I preach the gospel." Luke and Paul use it the most extensively.[15] In secular Greek, ἄγγελος (*angelos*) referred to a messenger who brought an εὐ (*eu* = "good") ἀγγελία (*angelia* = "message"). The Greeks connected the term with the declaration of victory, sometimes as a result of the Fates' benevolence. However, neither the Old nor the New Testament shows a connection of the good news of Jesus to serendipity or luck. In fact, an intimate connection exists between God's sovereignty and heralding the good message (Acts 10:36).

---

14. Paul supports his evangelistic ministry by drawing heavily from the prophets. The Old Testament is critical for the practice of evangelism found in the New Testament.

15. Matthew (1x), Luke-Acts (25x), Paul (21x), Hebrews (2x), 1 Peter (3x), Revelation (2x) (Kittel, Friedrich, and Bromiley, *Theological Dictionary*, 268).

The announcement of the births of the Baptist and the Messiah was good news (Luke 1:19; 2:10). The Baptist declared good news to the Jews (Luke 3:18). Jesus preached the good news, fulfilling Isaiah's prophecy (Matt. 11:5; Luke 4:18). The one who brought the good message is one who does so with great joy. The Anointed One was sent to declare the good news (Luke 4:18; cf. Isa. 61:1; Acts 10:36). The one sent brought the good news of the kingdom (Matt. 24:14; Luke 8:1; 16:16), great joy (Luke 2:10), and peace (Acts 10:36). Peter reminds believers that as a chosen race, royal priesthood, and holy nation, they are to "proclaim" (ἐξαγγέλλω, *exangellō*) the glorious matters of God (1 Pet. 2:9).

εὐαγγέλιον (*euangelion*). Used seventy-six times in the New Testament, the message, or "gospel," that was shared was a "good message," one of "good news." Secular usage understood the good news related to a victor who conquered an enemy. The Septuagint includes the plural (2 Sam. 4:10), but the New Testament uses are likely unrelated.[16] The message of good news reaches a specific zenith in the New Testament. The gospel is the good news about the Messiah (Mark 1:14) and is connected to eschatological realities of the last days (Mark 13:10; 14:9).

At times the word is paired to communicate a specificity as to what it represents, such as "the gospel of the kingdom" (Matt. 4:23), "the gospel of the grace of God" (Acts 20:24), "the gospel of the glory of Christ" (2 Cor. 4:4), "the gospel of Christ" (2 Cor. 10:14), "the gospel of your salvation" (Eph. 1:13), "the gospel of peace" (Eph. 6:15), "the gospel of our Lord Jesus" (2 Thess. 1:8), and "the gospel of God" (1 Pet. 4:17). Paul makes the most use of the word.[17]

Following Jesus's death and resurrection, the message proclaimed included references to his crucifixion, resurrection, exaltation, return, and restoration of all things.

εὐαγγελιστής (*euangelistēs*). It is a fascinating matter, for all the discussions of evangelists throughout history, that the Scriptures record this word only three times. Luke uses it once when Philip is described as an evangelist (Acts 21:8). The other two occurrences fall to Paul. The Ephesians are told that evangelists have been given to the church (Eph. 4:11). Timothy is instructed to do the work of an evangelist (2 Tim. 4:5).

μαρτυρέω (*martyreō*). Intimately connected with the church's evangelistic work, this word (including its variants) is used seventy-six times and is often

---

16. In the Septuagint, 2 Sam. 18:22 uses the rare εὐαγγελία (*euangelia*).
17. The noun is found in Matthew (4x), Mark (8x), Acts (2x), Paul (60x), 1 Peter (1x), and Revelation (1x) (Kittel, Friedrich, and Bromiley, *Theological Dictionary*, 270).

translated as "I bear witness" or "I testify."[18] John Stott notes, "Evangelism is illustrated in the New Testament both in terms of the proclamation of a herald and of the evidence of a witness. The witness must have first-hand experience of that to which he testifies."[19] John came to bear witness to the light (John 1:7). Paul gave witness to the quality of Epaphras's work (Col. 4:13) and God's work (1 Cor. 15:15). A μάρτυς (*martys*) is one who provides evidence—"testimony" or "witness" (μαρτυρία, *martyria*; μαρτύριον, *martyrion*).[20] The disciples were to serve as Jesus's "witnesses" throughout the world (Acts 1:8; cf. 2:32; 3:15; 5:32). Paul was to be a "witness" to the resurrected Lord (Acts 26:16). The Law and the Prophets bore "witness" to the righteousness of God (Rom. 3:21).

κηρύσσω (*kēryssō*). This word is translated as "I preach," "I proclaim," or "I herald," with variations occurring throughout the New Testament. It is frequently connected with εὐαγγέλιον (*euangelion*) for translations such as "proclaiming the gospel" (Matt. 9:35), "the gospel is preached" (Matt. 26:13), and "preaching the gospel" (Mark 1:14). Sometimes the content of what was proclaimed is given: "proclaimed that people should repent" (Mark 6:12), "proclaim liberty" (Luke 4:18), "proclaim the kingdom" (Luke 9:2), "proclaim Christ" (Acts 8:5), "proclaiming the kingdom of God" (Acts 28:31), "we preach Christ crucified" (1 Cor. 1:23), and "we proclaimed to you the gospel of God" (1 Thess. 2:9).

κῆρυξ (*kēryx*). This noun refers to the one who does the proclaiming. The person is a herald, preacher, or proclaimer. Paul notes that he was appointed a "preacher" (1 Tim. 2:7; 2 Tim. 1:11). Peter refers to Noah being a "herald" of righteousness (2 Pet. 2:5). The κῆρυξ (*kēryx*) had a lengthy history in Greek society. This herald or public communicator was often closely connected to royalty and made public declarations to the society at large. However, this noun is found only four times in the Septuagint and three times in the New Testament, while the verbal expression κηρύσσω (*kēryssō*) is found thirty-three times for different Hebrew equivalents and sixty-one times in the New Testament.[21]

κήρυγμα (*kērygma*). Closely connected to κηρύσσω (*kēryssō*) is the proclamation itself, or the content of the message communicated. The Synoptic

---

18. This is also the word from which the English word *martyr* is derived. However, a martyr in the New Testament was simply a witness and not necessarily one who was killed for having faith in Christ.

19. Stott, *Motives and Methods*, 17.

20. The words μαρτυρία (*martyria*) and μαρτύριον (*martyrion*) are used thirty-seven and twenty times, respectively, in the New Testament (Kittel, Friedrich, and Bromiley, *Theological Dictionary*, 566).

21. Kittel, Friedrich, and Bromiley, *Theological Dictionary*, 432.

Gospels make use of this word on two occasions (Matt. 12:41; Luke 11:32).[22] Paul uses the word several times to refer to his gospel, which consisted of "the preaching of Jesus Christ" (Rom. 16:25), "the message preached" (1 Cor. 1:21), "my preaching" (1 Cor. 2:4), "our preaching" (1 Cor. 15:14), and "the proclamation" (2 Tim. 4:17; Titus 1:3). Though this word occurs only eight times in the New Testament,[23] a great deal of scholarship has surrounded it, particularly throughout the twentieth century with C. H. Dodd's book, *The Apostolic Preaching and Its Developments*, published in 1937.[24] More will be stated regarding the message shared in chapter 3.

μαθητεύω (*mathēteuō*). This word occurs four times in the New Testament but has great influence on how the church conceptualizes and operationalizes her global work. Matthew uses it three times, with the most well-known text being "make disciples" (Matt. 28:19).[25] Luke uses it to describe the work of the apostolic team in Derbe, where they "had made many disciples" (Acts 14:21). The beginning point for making disciples is evangelism. Sharing the gospel and calling people to repentance and faith (Acts 20:21) is the tip of the Great Commission iceberg. The church must never divorce proclaiming the good news (i.e., evangelism) from teaching new disciples. The global work of the church does not end with evangelism, but rather starts there.

Practical Considerations

Contemporary evangelism must not be divorced from New Testament expressions that find their roots in the Old Testament. The first-century disciples drew from the Torah, the Prophets, and the Writings, in addition to Jesus's words and actions, for their global disciple-making labors. In view of this and before concluding, it is important to note the first-century recipients of evangelism, the primary location for evangelism, and the general means of evangelism. Recognizing these details, the church finds an excellent starting point to evaluate her contemporary understandings and expressions of evangelistic work.

Audience

It is true that Jesus's followers need to be reminded of the gospel, as it is not only the power unto salvation but also necessary for growth in the faith.

---

22. Three, counting Mark's extended ending (Mark 16:20).
23. Nine, again counting Mark 16:20.
24. For a late twentieth-century critique of Dodd and kerygmatic study, see Poe, *Gospel*, 15–55.
25. See also Matt. 13:52; 27:57.

However, Robert Webber, referencing the 1999 "International Consultation on Discipleship," is incorrect when he writes, "Evangelism brings new believers to spiritual maturity."[26] Rather, evangelism brings the unregenerate into the kingdom.[27] After his lexical study, David Barrett concludes that the New Testament made explicit the audience for evangelism: "Christians always evangelized non-Christians, either individuals, or groups, audiences in synagogues or stadiums, whole populations, villages, towns, cities, whole areas, whole regions, or even Roman provinces as large as Asia Minor."[28] These are the unregenerate. They are the ones to be evangelized.

Location

The primary location of the act of evangelism was anywhere the unregenerate may be found. Where people have not repented of sin and placed faith in Jesus as Lord, there is the proper location for evangelism. This could be a remote village in Central Asia, a city park in Paris, a coffee shop in Toronto, or our very own homes. Throughout the New Testament, the disciples engaged in evangelistic labors primarily *outside* the Christian community. While it was desired that any unbelievers present during a church's gathering would come to faith (1 Cor. 14:24–25), from a New Testament perspective, there was no such thing as the need to "reevangelize" the church.[29] By her very nature, the body of Christ is composed of regenerate individuals. Evangelism brought them into the church by the Word and the Spirit and was not an act to be repeated on this audience. The assumption was that whenever the believers gathered, the assembly consisted of members of the church, with primary evangelistic labors occurring outside the safe confines of the community.[30] If the unregenerate were present, then

---

26. Webber, *Ancient-Future Evangelism*, 13.

27. Again, the gospel is also for believers. For example, Paul made this clear when he informed the Romans of one reason for his forthcoming visit (Rom. 1:15) and told the Galatians to test all preaching (Gal. 1:8). Commenting on gospel proclamation among the believers with these texts and 1 Cor. 15:1, Walter Klaiber says that "the primary use of *euangelizesthai* also in Paul is the missionary context" (*Call and Response*, 23).

28. Barrett, *Evangelize!*, 14.

29. The reevangelizing of the church, a modern concept found throughout both Protestant and Catholic circles, is founded on a poor ecclesiology and distracts from the church's global task. I will address this matter in chap. 11.

30. While a church's weekly worship gathering is not an evangelistic crusade or rally, the gospel should always be communicated clearly to any unbelievers who may be present. During that time they should also be instructed about repentance and belief. The text of 1 Cor. 14:24–25 serves as an excellent reminder of this perennial practice. Whenever I preach a message that is directed primarily to believers, I still attempt to answer the Philippian jailer's question, "What must I do to be saved?" (Acts 16:30), which may be on the mind of someone present.

they were guests, visitors, attendees, but possibly false teachers and savage wolves (Acts 20:29–30; Rev. 2:20).

Means

The general means by which the gospel was communicated was a verbal medium. This did not rule out other means such as written expressions, for the Gospels were written that readers may know the good news about the Christ. Nor did it exclude methods of communication that have developed over the past two millennia. It is very likely that the early disciples would have embraced technological developments of the modern day. After all, they made use of the advancements of their era (e.g., Roman roads, Greek language, literature, ships, letters).

Evangelism should be done with a view toward effective communication. The one sharing the good news should be receptor-oriented in their labors, whether that is with one person, a small group, or a large crowd. Some, fearing stereotype, have attempted to discard biblical terminology and practice for a more palatable expression that sometimes portrays evangelists as those with uncertainty and still on a quest for truth. For example, David Stowe writes,

> People who characteristically talk about evangelism in terms of proclamation suggest something which is heralded, which is broadcast, which is offered to everyone. A sound truck going through the street, or the distribution of tracts on the street corner, exemplify the proclamation approach. On the other hand, the term "communication" suggests a wrestling with the problem of hearing, with emphasis not so much on the giving as on the receiving. There is an assumption that nothing is really said until it has been heard. And whereas a proclamation strategy of evangelism rests upon a great faith in the self-evidencing power of the word of God, those who think rather in terms of communication identify the need for a good deal of shrewd thought and human effort to make the message heard.[31]

While examples of those engaging in evangelism without regard for culture, context, and audience abound, Stowe creates a false dichotomy based more on cultural stereotypes than on biblical terminology and expression. His perspective is widespread, even among evangelicals. The apostle who wrote, "How are they to believe in him of whom they have never heard? And how are they to hear without someone preaching?" (Rom. 10:14), was the same person who requested prayer that he could "declare the mystery of Christ . . .

---

31. Stowe, *Ecumenicity and Evangelism*, 36.

that I may make it clear, which is how I ought to speak" (Col. 4:3–4). Whether speaking, heralding, sharing, preaching, or proclaiming the good news, all are examples of *communication*. The church should engage in such activities with an orientation toward clear transmission. An attempt to pit proclamation against communication not only is a misunderstanding of the Scriptures but also results in the church assigning more credence to contemporary language and practice than to biblical expressions and examples.

The work of defining evangelism, its intended audience, and the one doing evangelism is not a pedantic exercise. Confusion that may be found has resulted in challenges to the church's evangelistic practices at home and throughout the world. The next chapter will continue with this subject, as it will be noted that some define evangelism in terms of results produced from the gospel shared. Is a person or people evangelized when they hear the gospel or when they hear and repent and believe?

— QUESTIONS TO CONSIDER —

1. Before reading the next chapter on definitions, how do you define evangelism?
2. If contemporary understandings and practices of evangelism have little in common with the Scriptures, then what is a healthy way to respond to this divergence? If you recognize such in your ministry context, how will you lead toward healthy change?
3. How do you think your church's members would answer the following questions: Who is the expected audience for evangelism? What is the expected location for evangelism? How should the gospel be shared?
4. Do you agree or disagree with David Stowe that proclamation and communication are to be distinguished from each other? Explain.

2

CONTEMPORARY DEFINITIONS OF EVANGELISM

Priscilla Pope-Levison notes that among Protestants, Roman Catholics, and Orthodox there is no one universally accepted definition of evangelism, but if a single biblical text can be said to offer a widespread vision of evangelism, it is Isaiah 52:7.[1]

> How beautiful upon the mountains
>   are the feet of him who brings good news,
> who publishes peace, who brings good news of happiness,
>   who publishes salvation,
>   who says to Zion, "Your God reigns."

While Pope-Levison's observations are correct, and Isaiah establishes a good foundation for biblical evangelism, diversity does not mean equality or accuracy—even within the body of Christ. Definitional variance is so great that not all can be correct. It is important to consider contemporary definitions, but most importantly, to understand how the Scriptures address the concept.

John Stott approaches defining evangelism by stating three elements that should *not* be definitive characteristics. According to Stott, evangelism must not be defined by whether the unbelievers have already heard the message

---

1. Pope-Levison, *Models of Evangelism*, 6.

proclaimed. He understood this matter to be a product of his day, as some had been advocating that mission takes the message to those who had never heard, but evangelism takes it to Christianized areas. For Stott, anyone who is not a follower of Jesus, regardless of their exposure to the gospel, is in need of evangelization. Second, evangelism is not to be defined in terms of results, but faithful communication of the gospel. Evangelism could occur even if no one repented and believed in Christ. Finally, evangelism must not be understood in terms of methods. The announcement of the good news may be given through a variety of mediums. Yet, the means do not determine if evangelism has occurred. For Stott, the positive definitive characteristic is that "evangelism may and must be defined only in terms of *the message*" shared with the audience.[2]

Evangelism and Evangelization

The word *evangelism* is not found in the Scriptures. David Barrett notes that it was Francis Bacon (1561–1626) who either coined the word or first published it. Bacon, in *New Atlantis*, describes a land being saved from infidelity through the "*Apostolicall* and *Miraculous* Euangelisme of Saint Bartholomew."[3] By 1755 the word was added to Samuel Johnson's *Dictionary of the English Language*, which reads "Evangelism . . . The promulgation of the blessed gospel."[4] Barrett notes that this word, in the eighteenth and early nineteenth centuries, was viewed unfavorably because it was equated with contemptible evangelicalism or emotional and fanatical proselytism.[5] By 1850 it was seen in a positive light, but it would take an additional seventy years before it became widespread among English-speakers.[6] Though mainline Protestants and Anglicans embraced it in 1850, Roman Catholics would wait until 1962, following Vatican II.[7]

The other noun that developed over time was *evangelization*. Thomas Hobbes, in 1651, recorded its use as "The work of Christ's Ministers, is Evangelization; that is, a Proclamation of Christ, and a preparation for his second

---

2. Stott, *Christian Mission*, 37–40.
3. Bacon, *New Atlantis*, 15. I am indebted to David Barrett for his research on the early uses of the word *evangelism* (see Barrett, *Evangelize!*, 23).
4. S. Johnson, *English Language*, n.p.
5. Priscilla Pope-Levison is a contemporary example of this concern. She writes of her belief in "evangelization as the proclamation of the good news" but is "often made uncomfortable by both the content of the proclamation as well as by the person doing the proclaiming" (*Evangelization*, ix).
6. In 1851 Charles Adams published his global survey "of the present condition of evangelical religion" under the title *Evangelism in the Middle of the Nineteenth Century*.
7. Barrett, *Evangelize!*, 23–24.

coming; as the Evangelization of John Baptist, was a preparation to his first coming."[8] During the 1820s and 1850s, the word started showing up among Protestant and Anglican traditions. *A New English Dictionary on Historical Principles*, published in 1891, included *evangelization* as an entry. The term was defined as:

1. the action or work of preaching the gospel;
2. the action or process of evangelizing, or bringing under the influence of the gospel;
3. the state or condition of being evangelized or converted to the Christian faith.[9]

During the late nineteenth century, discussions occurred regarding the "evangelization" of the world. Two early publications include Benjamin Broomhall, *The Evangelisation of the World: A Missionary Band; A Record of Consecration, and an Appeal* (1889), and Robert Needham Cust, *Essay on the Prevailing Methods of the Evangelization of the Non-Christian World* (1894). However, it was through the extensive labors of John Mott, and his book *The Evangelization of the World in This Generation* (1900), that the word and concept continued to expand in use until 1908, when language and focus shifted, and it dropped from Protestant and Anglican ecumenical use. However, in 1974 the word reemerged and experienced widespread global attention.[10]

An early twentieth-century definition of evangelism was included in T. B. Kilpatrick's 1911 publication, *New Testament Evangelism*. His extensive definition did not gain widespread acceptance. According to Kilpatrick,

> To "evangelize" is to proclaim the Glad Tidings, to declare the salvation of God, wrought out by Jesus Christ, His Son, the once crucified, the now living and exalted Redeemer, to announce to men, who believingly commit themselves to the Saviour, that they will be saved from their sins, and will be restored to the privileges which God designed for them when He created them in His image, and to summon all men everywhere to turn to the God, who thus, in Christ, stretches out His hands toward sinners.[11]

Noteworthy is what is omitted from Kilpatrick's definition. Immediately following this statement, he continues, "It is certain that, in the mercy of

8. Hobbes, *Leviathan*, 365 (quotation adapted to reflect modern grammar).
9. Murray, *New English Dictionary*, 330.
10. Barrett, *Evangelize!*, 30.
11. Kilpatrick, *New Testament Evangelism*, 80.

God, great results will follow faithful evangelism. But these results are not designated or described in the term 'evangelism.' The evangelist is not burdened with the responsibility of producing them. . . . His one business is to preach the Gospel."[12]

Categories for Defining Evangelism

Of the numerous definitions of evangelism,[13] three general categories may be found: definitions based on proclamation and conversions, definitions whereby everything the church does is evangelism, and definitions based on proclamation alone.[14]

Proclamation and Conversions

Paul Chilcote and Laceye Warner observe there are some "who conceive discipleship as inseparable, even indistinguishable, from evangelism."[15] For example, one of the earliest official and popular definitions of evangelism was produced by the Church of England in 1918 and published a year later in the *Reports of the Archbishops' Committees of Inquiry*. This massive volume addresses issues related to the church's teaching office, worship, administration, industrial problem, and evangelistic work. It is in the last section (seventy-two pages) that the committee states the following: "To evangelise is so to present Christ Jesus in the power of the Holy Spirit, that men shall come to put their trust in God through Him, to accept Him as their Saviour, and serve Him as their King in the fellowship of His Church."[16]

Here is an example of a definition of the evangelistic work that is easy to understand and remember. It is trinitarian in scope, christological in soteriology, connected to God's kingdom, and ecclesiocentric in result. The service in God's church is worth consideration and was not lost on some scholars.

12. Kilpatrick, *New Testament Evangelism*, 80.
13. David Barrett estimates that in English, one may find over three hundred definitions in print of the term "evangelize" (*Evangelize!*, 77).
14. "General" is the key here. As there are exceptions, such as a 1920 cryptic definition, a category unto itself, stating, "Evangelism is the art of helping men in their quest for a complete life" (Stewart and Wright, *Personal Evangelism*, 3). For another perspective on the categorization of how evangelism is often understood, see Adeney, *Graceful Evangelism*, 2–6. Throughout the twentieth century, some have defined evangelism as manifesting a Christian presence in the world. This "presence evangelism" was defined by allowing good deeds, even without proclamation, to be the evangelistic work. It seems that presence evangelism has become consumed in the twenty-first-century category of "everything that the church does is evangelism."
15. Chilcote and Warner, *The Study of Evangelism*, 216.
16. Church of England, "Evangelistic Work of the Church," 18.

Despite its theological depth and comprehensiveness, J. I. Packer took issue with the results-oriented nature of the statement.

> It puts a consecutive clause where a final clause should be. Had it begun: "to evangelise is to present Christ Jesus to sinful men *in order that*, through the power of the Holy Spirit, they *may* come . . . ," there would be no fault to find with it. But it does not say this. What it does say is quite different. "To evangelise is *so* to present Christ Jesus in the power of the Holy Spirit, *that* men *shall come*. . . ." This is to define evangelism in terms of an effect achieved in the lives of others; which amounts to saying that the essence of evangelizing is producing converts.[17]

Everything Is Evangelism

When evangelism becomes equated with all activities in which the church engages in the world, then gospel proclamation is often compromised, and evangelism becomes limited. Having observed this problem, William Abraham provided the following warning near the end of the twentieth century:

> To be sure, we need to emphasize that by "proclamation of the gospel" we mean the *verbal* proclamation, in order to prevent evangelism from sliding into a thoroughly vague notion that stands for everything and anything that the church does in witness and service. Once we allow the latter to happen we lose sight of those distinct activities that distinguish evangelism from other activities in which the church engages, which in the long run destroys any deep sense of accountability in this area. If evangelism refers to everything the church does, then it is extremely difficult to identify; hence, it is well-nigh impossible to think specifically and carefully about the evangelistic ministry of the church. If everything is evangelism then nothing is evangelism; and we should be surprised if anyone in the church takes it very seriously.[18]

Abraham's concerns are applicable to all traditions but definitely challenge the Roman Catholic Church. Viewed as a Protestant term, *evangelization* rarely showed up in Roman Catholic writings until 1955. Throughout the 1950s and 1960s, evangelization was distinguished from catechesis, with the former directed toward unbelievers and the latter used of the faith formation of those evangelized.[19] *Evangelii nuntiandi* (*On Evangelization in the Modern World*) is Pope Paul VI's 1975 apostolic exhortation that became "the touchstone document of the modern evangelization movement in the

---

17. Packer, *Evangelism*, 40.
18. Abraham, *Logic of Evangelism*, 44.
19. Gorski, "From 'Mission' to 'Evangelization,'" 35.

Catholic Church."[20] The document notes the following: "Thus it has been possible to define evangelization in terms of proclaiming Christ to those who do not know him, of preaching, of catechesis, of conferring Baptism and the other Sacraments."[21] In other words, although a priority exists on proclamation, evangelism—or *evangelization* as noted above—includes an array of other church activities. In addition to preaching and catechesis, evangelization is understood as confirmation, Eucharist, penance, anointing the sick, ordination, and marriage. Pope Paul VI notes, "Evangelization, as we have said, is a complex process made up of varied elements: the renewal of humanity, witness, explicit proclamation, inner adherence, entry into the community, acceptance of signs, apostolic initiative."[22]

In 2012 the XIII Ordinary General Assembly of the Synod of Bishops met to address the theme "New Evangelization of the Transmission of the Christian Faith."[23] With this *new* approach, evangelization is clearly everything the church does. Although, as stated in Pope Francis's apostolic exhortation *Evangelii gaudium* (*The Joy of the Gospel*), "we cannot forget that evangelization is first and foremost about preaching the Gospel to *those who do not know Jesus Christ or who have always rejected him*," it is also about ministry to the baptized who are not walking faithfully with the Lord and to the faithful as well.[24] In other words, "the people of God, by the constant inner working of the Holy Spirit, is constantly evangelizing itself."[25]

This view is not limited to Roman Catholics. David Bosch holds to a similar understanding that evangelism "is not only verbal proclamation," but then he offers a lengthy and esoteric understanding of the concept that lacks explanation:[26]

20. Brennan, *Re-Imagining Evangelization*, 108.
21. Paul VI, *Evangelii nuntiandi*, 15.
22. Paul VI, *Evangelii nuntiandi*, 19.
23. Pope John Paul II was the first pope to use the term *new evangelization*, during the Latin American Bishops' Conference in 1983 (Grogan and Kim, *The New Evangelization*, 5).
24. Francis, *Evangelii gaudium*, 17–18 (emphasis in original).
25. Francis, *Evangelii gaudium*, 109. If conversion is understood as an ongoing process, and not a single act connected to regeneration, then Francis's desire to constantly evangelize the believers is necessary.
26. Such is no surprise, as he argues for a relativistic evangelism and gospel proclamation that lacks clarified understanding: "We cannot capture the evangel and package it in four or five 'principles.' There is no universally applicable master plan for evangelism, no definitive list of truths people only have to embrace in order to be saved. We may never limit the gospel to our understanding of God and salvation. We can only witness in humble boldness and bold humility to our understanding of that gospel" (Bosch, *Transforming Mission*, 420). While such is a noble attempt at humility toward the Scriptures, it reveals

We may, then, summarize evangelism as that dimension and activity of the church's mission which, by word and deed and in the light of particular conditions and a particular context, offers every person and community, everywhere, a valid opportunity to be directly challenged to a radical reorientation of their lives, a reorientation which involves such things as deliverance from slavery to the world and its powers; embracing Christ as Savior and Lord; becoming a living member of his community, the church; being enlisted into his service of reconciliation, peace, and justice on earth; and being committed to God's purpose of placing all things under the rule of Christ.[27]

Jan Linn, in *Reclaiming Evangelism*, offers the following statements about evangelism:

- "Evangelism is the ministry of *witnessing to Jesus Christ*."
- "Far from being something we do, evangelism is something we are."
- "As the body of Christ, everything a church does in ministry witnesses to Jesus Christ. Thus, everything is evangelism."[28]

The notion that everything is evangelism may also be observed in the Orthodox Church. Nikos Nissiotis writes, "Proclamation is the heart of evangelism and is addressed to all men," but evangelism is about "the presence, service, and witness of Christians, through their involvement in the transformation of the world for the sake of humanity."[29] Ion Bria notes that "the kerygma is not limited to the verbal proclamation," as "it seems that the heart of the apostolic proclamation is to repeat the sacramental action which corresponds with the words of Christ when he said: 'Take, eat, this is my body.'"[30] In other words, within the worship gathering, Jesus draws people to himself through the experience.

---

an evangelistic agnosticism, something that the New Testament writers did not desire for their readers (Luke 1:4; 1 Cor. 15:1–2; 1 John 2:3; 5:13). Bryan Stone, who identifies his approach as "post-liberal," seems to agree with Bosch in that "evangelism can never be only proclamation or invitation," yet also reflects esoteric language when he goes on to say that verbal proclamation in evangelism is central and should not be denigrated (*Evangelism After Christendom*, 62, 158, 249, 317).

27. Bosch, *Transforming Mission*, 420. Several years later, Bosch revised and clarified his definition of evangelism to be "that dimension and activity of the church's mission which seeks to offer every person, everywhere, a valid opportunity to be directly challenged by the gospel of explicit faith in Jesus Christ, with a view to embracing him as Savior, becoming a living member of his community, and being enlisted in his service of reconciliation, peace, and justice on earth" ("Evangelism," 17).

28. Linn, *Reclaiming Evangelism*, 21, 57, 62.

29. Nissiotis, "Modern Trends in Evangelism," 182–83.

30. Bria, "Church's Role in Evangelism," 248.

RECLAIMING THE E WORD

Bryan Stone shares the following concern about common misunderstandings of evangelism that he encountered when teaching at Boston University.

> A colleague placed in my hands a brochure introducing the Women's Interfaith Action Group. The brochure described the group as "a weekly gathering of women from all faiths, as well as those who feel drawn to the spiritual, but who do not claim a particular religion." What was especially interesting about the brochure was the following sentence, in particular its use of the word *evangelization*: "An environment of mutual respect is maintained in which members may freely share beliefs and differences without fear or disparagement or evangelization."
>
> To *evangelize* means literally to offer "good news" or a "welcome message." Isaiah 52:7 celebrates the bringer of such good news: "How beautiful upon the mountains are the feet of the messenger who announces peace, who bring good news, who announces salvation, who says to Zion, 'Your God reigns.'"
>
> But clearly, today evangelism does not always mean good news, and the feet of the evangelist are not considered so beautiful. For many people in our world, both Christian and non-Christian, evangelism is neither welcomed nor warranted. As the brochure made clear, this is especially true in the context of interfaith dialogue, where evangelism is perceived as something to be feared, as a barrier to mutual respect, careful listening, open sharing, and cooperation. But it is also the case in the wider context of an increasingly pluralistic culture, where the notion of evangelizing is automatically connected to an attitude of intolerance and superiority towards others. . . . The E-word has become a dirty word—an embarrassment to the Christian and an affront to the non-Christian.
>
> Is it possible nonetheless to reclaim the E-word as expressing something positive, vital, and beautiful about the Christian life? Might evangelism be a practice that calls forth the highest in the creative energies, intellect, and imagination of Christians rather than a crass exercise in marketing the church to consumers within a world of abundant and competing options?
>
> Stone, *Evangelism After Christendom*, 9–10.

Questions

1. Do you think that evangelism needs to be reconstructed? If so, how? If not, why not?
2. Explain what the beautiful message of the gospel would sound like to people in your context.
3. Do you think that evangelism has become the "E word"? Give examples to support your view.

Proclamation

The final category is evangelism as proclamation. William Abraham writes, "Defining *evangelism* as the verbal proclamation of the gospel provides a clear, manageable concept that is rooted in the early history of the word and that calls the church to excellence in communicating the Christian gospel to those who are prepared to listen."[31] Evangelism is not defined by whether people are converted or as anything accomplished by the church. Among his many leadership roles, D. T. Niles served as the executive secretary of the Department of Evangelism for the World Council of Churches and expressed evangelism as an aphorism. For him, "It is one beggar telling another beggar where to get food."[32] Bill Bright, founder of Campus Crusade for Christ, offers another simple, yet popular, explanation that successful witnessing is "simply taking the initiative to share Christ in the power of the Holy Spirit, and leaving the results to God."[33]

Evangelism as proclamation best represents the church for most of her history. The following are a variety of definitions of evangelism from different denominational and theological perspectives that developed in the twentieth and twenty-first centuries. The Evangelical Lutheran Church in America provides the following: "Evangelism is the simple act of sharing the good news of God's love in Jesus and inviting others to trust in this love and join in God's work."[34] The United Methodist Church defines evangelism as "the winning of persons to Jesus Christ as Savior and Lord. From the Latin word *evangelium*, meaning good news or gospel, evangelism is the proclamation of the gospel to individuals and groups by preaching, teaching, and personal and family visitation. It is the seeking by the Christian to bring others into a vital personal relationship with Christ."[35]

---

31. Abraham, *Logic of Evangelism*, 44–45.
32. Niles, *That They May Have Life*, 96.
33. Bright, *Witnessing Without Fear*, 67.
34. Evangelical Lutheran Church in America, "Evangelism."
35. United Methodist Church, "Glossary: *evangelism*." Even though this historic definition of evangelism is found on the UMC's website, so is the article "Rethinking What We Mean When We Talk About Evangelism," by Lydia Sohn, in which she writes,

> I eventually discovered progressive Christianity, a thread of Christianity I didn't know existed for most of my religious upbringing, and slowly stitched together a new understanding of God. This new understanding taught me to see prospective converts as individuals with their own rich life stories. They do not need to subscribe to mine in order to be more valuable or saved. . . . Jesus' words summoned me to a new kind of evangelism in every relationship I have: to walk alongside others, hear their stories, grieve with them when they're hurting, never push them towards one direction or another, wholeheartedly listen to what is making them come alive. And most importantly, to let them offer the same for me.

In 2012 the World Council of Churches approved a new ecumenical affirmation on mission and evangelism,[36] the first of its kind since 1982, titled "Together Towards Life: Mission and Evangelism in Changing Landscapes."[37] In this work, evangelism is understood as the following:

- "Evangelism is a confident but humble sharing of our faith and conviction with other people." (p. 6)
- "Evangelism [is] the communication of the whole gospel to the whole of humanity in the whole world." (p. 29)
- "Evangelism, while not excluding different dimensions of mission, focuses on explicit and intentional articulation of the gospel, including 'the invitation to personal conversion to a new life in Christ and to discipleship.'" (p. 29)
- "Evangelism is sharing one's faith and conviction with other people and inviting them to discipleship, whether or not they adhere to other religious traditions." (p. 30)
- "Evangelism leads to repentance, faith, and baptism. Hearing the truth in the face of sin and evil demands a response. . . . It provokes conversion. . . . It results in salvation of the lost, healing of the sick, and the liberation of the oppressed and the whole creation." (p. 30)
- "Evangelism is sharing the good news in word and action. Evangelizing through verbal proclamation or preaching of the gospel (kerygma) is profoundly biblical. However, if our words are not consistent with our actions, our evangelism is inauthentic." (p. 31)

In 1990 the United Church of Christ held a symposium on evangelism. A collection of essays was published two years later in *Affirming Evangelism: A Call to Renewed Commitment in the United Church of Christ*. This document notes,

> We affirm evangelism as the heart of God's mission and the center of the Church's life. We understand evangelism to be proclaiming the Good News of God's gift of salvation in Jesus Christ; embodying and demonstrating this Good News in acts of mercy, love, and justice; inviting others to accept Jesus Christ as risen Savior, to unite with Christ's Body, the Church, and to live as Christ's disciples in the world.[38]

---

36. The long-standing affirmation was agreed on in 1982 with a document titled "Mission and Evangelism: An Ecumenical Affirmation."
37. World Council of Churches, "Together Towards Life" (n.d.).
38. Burt, *Affirming Evangelism*, 158.

In the fourth section of the 1974 Lausanne Covenant, the following passage addresses the nature of evangelism:

> To evangelize is to spread the good news that Jesus Christ died for our sins and was raised from the dead according to the Scriptures, and that, as the reigning Lord, he now offers the forgiveness of sins and the liberating gifts of the Spirit to all who repent and believe. Our Christian presence in the world is indispensable to evangelism, and so is that kind of dialogue whose purpose is to listen sensitively in order to understand. But evangelism itself is the proclamation of the historical, biblical Christ as Saviour and Lord, with a view to persuading people to come to him personally and so be reconciled to God.[39]

Lausanne was quick to note that while Christian presence and dialogue are critical components of the church's work in the world, and *may* include evangelism, evangelism is restricted to the proclamation of the Christ. While evangelism is to be done with the desire for people to come to faith, become part of his church, and care for the world, such is not evangelism.

Evangelistic Syncretism

The church is to engage in a wide variety of actions in the world that reflect the kingdom ethic. Broad is the way of church activities, but narrow is the way of evangelism. Evangelism is the proclamation of the good news of Jesus Christ. It is a work that communicates a contextualized message of hope through judgment. The act calls people to repent of their sinful nature toward God and place their faith in the Lord Jesus (Acts 20:21). While evangelism may be connected to a plethora of kingdom actions, it must never be confused with or substituted by them. Evangelism is a very specific act, one that receives a prioritization according to the teaching and examples revealed in the New Testament. When this act is conflated with other church functions, the result is usually a syncretistic understanding of evangelism that is neither biblical evangelism, by definition, nor evangelistic practice in the world.

Evangelism is not prayer. However, prayer should go before, with, and after the evangelist. New believers should be taught to pray, particularly for opportunities to share the gospel with others (Col. 4:3–4). Evangelism is not

---

39. The entire covenant can be viewed online at https://lausanne.org/statement/lausanne-covenant.

about worship services. However, evangelism should result in new believers worshiping the Lord. The act of repentance and belief is an act of worship. And the gospel should always be proclaimed in worship gatherings. Evangelism is not caring for widows and orphans. However, evangelism should result in new believers who are taught to care for widows and orphans (James 1:27). In fact, the act of sharing the gospel is a means of caring for widows' and orphans' greatest needs, as the church provides for physical, emotional, and social needs as well. Evangelism is not social justice. However, evangelism should result in new believers who are taught to act justly and stand for righteousness and against systemic evil in the world (Mic. 6:8). Organizations and systems are not called on to repent, but the people who comprise such are called to turn from evil and to Christ. New believers are then to be taught to be salt and light. Evangelism is the greatest act of taking a stand against injustice. For the greatest injustice is sin against the holy God. Believers are to be especially concerned about eternal suffering—in addition to physical, emotional, and social suffering. When a person is reconciled to their Creator, then they have the grace to love their neighbor.

Evangelism is not doing good deeds reflecting a Christian lifestyle. However, evangelism should result in new believers taught to follow the kingdom ethic of how to live in relation to God, the church, and those outside the church. It may be argued that the greatest deed that may be done to someone is to share the good news with them—if indeed the evangel is that great of a message. Evangelism is not providing for the poor. However, evangelism should result in new believers being taught to remember the poor and share what they have with them. What would it profit someone to gain the whole world and lose their soul? Is a temporal drink from a well more beneficial than consuming living water? Would the apostles have preferred to give silver and gold to a beggar than the pearl of great price?

— QUESTIONS TO CONSIDER —

1. Review the various definitions of evangelism in this chapter. Which do you prefer and why?
2. Should evangelism be defined as (a) proclamation and conversion, (b) everything the church does, or (c) proclamation? Provide biblical support for your answer.
3. Create your own definition of evangelism. Is it consistent with biblical teaching and does it best represent what is found in the Scriptures?

3

ONE GOSPEL FOR A MULTICULTURAL WORLD

I once attended a gathering of mission agency and church leaders, authors, and popular speakers to address trends and challenges to global evangelization. After sitting in a crowded room and listening to the panel for two hours, one particular statement continues to haunt me to this day.

The topic of the moment had shifted to the role of the Western church in global work when one speaker stated, "The church in the traditionally Western countries needs to get off the field and allow the Majority World church to engage in the Great Commission task. For two centuries we have gotten in the way with our paternalistic practices and continue to interfere with the work. It is time for us to pass the baton of leadership and sit down."

I was shocked and angry, waiting for a response from the other members of the panel. As I sat in the audience, I held my breath, believing that someone from the stage would rebut this popular, yet fundamentally wrong, belief. No one responded; one person raised her eyes with surprise and noted that she did not agree. The conversation shifted to the next topic and continued without challenge.

The church in the Majority World is larger and growing at a faster rate than the church in traditionally Western countries. The church there is also experiencing growth in the number of missionaries being sent out, with an estimated 203,000 (almost half of the entire world's missionaries) in 2021. This reflects a 12 percent increase since 1970.[1] For centuries, believers in European

---

1. Zurlo, Johnson, and Crossing, "World Christianity," 17.

and North American countries, and Australia and New Zealand, went into all the world and the Spirit and the Word worked in hearts. People responded to the good news with repentance and faith. Churches were planted with new disciples. Contextualized leaders were developed. Churches were taught to obey all that Christ commanded and began to engage in evangelism at home and abroad.

Region	Evangelical Percentage	Christian Percentage	Missionaries Sent*
Africa	12%	49%	39,400
Asia	1.8%	8%	91,100
Latin America	7.6%	92%	65,300
Oceania	14.3%	65%	5,200

Source: Zurlo, Global Christianity, 6–9, 12–13, 16–17. Gina Zurlo takes a sociological and statistical approach to her study of the Christian faith, which includes groups (and their numbers) that self-identify as Christian but are not reflective of historic, orthodox Christianity (e.g., Latter-day Saints, Jehovah's Witnesses).

* Defined as "The number of long-term (two years or more) indigenous missionaries sent to other countries by the continent or country in 2020" (Zurlo, Global Christianity, xx).

When Jesus stated, "I will build my church" (Matt. 16:18), he did not dichotomize by geographical location. When he directed that his disciples be taught to obey everything he has commanded (Matt. 28:20), he did not give an exemption to disciples who had been in the kingdom longer than other disciples. His body is the one, holy, catholic, and apostolic church (Eph. 4:4–6).

The commands of Christ apply to all disciples. The Great Commission continues to apply to the church in North America as much as it applies to the church in Africa. The church's global evangelistic work is to be found among the church in Asia as it is among the church in Europe. Though for centuries the thought was "from the West to the rest," the growth of the Majority World church requires that the church now think in terms of "from everywhere to everywhere." Such is nothing new; it reflects Christ's commands. Global evangelization and disciple-making are to be on the hearts and minds of local expressions of Christ's universal body wherever she is found.

A Comprehensive Gospel

The most basic definition of the gospel is that it is the good news about the Messiah. This raises the question as to the content of the "good news." What makes this news good? And if the gospel is the message shared during the act of evangelism, then what is the content that the church is supposed to share?

A library search for books related to the gospel will reveal a large number of works, many comprised of hundreds of pages. Is the gospel a complicated message, one that it takes multiple tomes to understand? If the message of the gospel is so extensive, then how is anyone able to share it without taking days, and possibly months, to explain it to others?

Consider that the good news from God is about receiving and experiencing:

- a new kingdom
- a new ethic
- victory over the enemies of God's people
- a restored earth/cosmos
- the Spirit, who seals, indwells, and fills God's people
- justice to social injustices
- adoption into God's family
- a new community
- a life filled with wealth and poverty
- blessings and persecutions
- joy and suffering
- a hope to come for the poor, widows, orphans, and sojourners
- a hope to come for everyone
- forgiveness of sin
- righteousness from God
- the avoidance of judgment and hell
- forgiveness and heaven
- peace, freedom, and grace
- a resurrection from the dead
- friendship with God
- a new birth
- salvation

Pick any topic above, and the gospel speaks to the issue. The good news of the Messiah has implications on all these—and many other—issues.

Does the gospel speak to the topic of tithing? Yes. What about selecting a major in college? Of course. How about marriage, sex, family, work, how to study the Bible, taxes, personal budget, what car I should purchase, what entertainment I should consume, and what I should post on social media? Yes. Yes. And a thousand times, yes!

The good news affects every area of life, public and private. From God's perspective, there is no distinguishing between sacred and secular. He is Lord over everything. However, stating that the gospel is about everything is unhelpful when it comes to what is to be shared in an evangelistic message. When it comes to evangelism, the gospel becomes very specific and focused. This broad message from God becomes concentrated and offers a narrow door (Matt. 7:13–14) that opens to the fullness of joy and pleasures forevermore (Ps. 16:11). What is this gospel kernel that is to be universally communicated as the irreducible minimum? Whenever the early disciples shared the gospel with people far from God, what did they communicate, *and* were there any common threads among their messages?

Identifiable Form of the Proclamation

The search for an identifiable form of what constituted the gospel proclaimed among the nations has been part of modern scholarship.[2] Probably no one has received as much attention as C. H. Dodd and his 1935 King's College lectures published in 1937 under the title *The Apostolic Preaching and Its Developments*. Dodd drew a rigid distinction between κήρυγμα (*kērygma*), the message shared with unbelievers, and διδαχή (*didachē*), the moral instruction taught to new believers. For Dodd, the κήρυγμα was related to evangelism, and διδαχή was teaching used for the churches.

Dodd's study examines Paul, Mark, and some sermons in Acts to discern the content of the primitive preaching conducted among unbelievers. For Paul, God was pleased to save people by the foolishness of the "preaching" (κήρυγμα) (1 Cor. 1:21). And if such was what was used to bring salvation, Dodd was interested in the content of that κήρυγμα. In Corinth (1 Cor. 15:1), Paul's gospel preached (and believed by the Corinthians) included:

- Christ, who died for sins according to the Scriptures, and who was buried (15:3–4a)
- that he rose on the third day according to the Scriptures (15:4b)
- that he was seen by Cephas and others (15:5–7)

Within the context of the chapter, Paul makes it clear that the Corinthians had to respond in faith to this good news (1 Cor. 15:11). According to

---

2. Among earlier scholars interested in the kerygma are Martin Dibelius, A. M. Hunter, C. T. Craig, Floyd Filson, T. F. Glasson, Bertil Gärtner, Leil Alexander, Rudolf Bultmann, Ulrich Wilckens, Hans Conzelmann, Ernst Käsemann, Eduard Schweizer, H. J. Cadbury, and C. F. D. Moule.

additional study in Romans, Galatians, and 1 Thessalonians, Dodd argued that Paul's evangelistic message included:

1. The prophecies are fulfilled, and the new age is inaugurated by the coming of Christ.
2. He was born of the seed of David.
3. He died according to the Scriptures, to deliver us out of the present evil age.
4. He was buried.
5. He rose on the third day according to the Scriptures.
6. He is exalted at the right hand of God, as Son of God and Lord of quick and dead.
7. He will come again as Judge and Saviour of men.[3]

Dodd then turned his attention to the content of the "Jerusalem *kerygma*" as communicated in the city through speeches recorded in Acts 2–4. His summary of Peter's proclamation included:

- The age of fulfillment has dawned.
- This has occurred, according to the Scriptures, through the ministry, death, and resurrection of Jesus, a Davidic descendant.
- Jesus has been exalted to the right hand of God as Messiah over the new Israel.
- The Spirit has been given to the church as a sign of Christ's power and glory.
- The messianic age will soon reach consummation with the return of Christ.
- Those who hear are called to respond, as "the *kerygma* always closes with an appeal for repentance, the offer of forgiveness and of the Holy Spirit, and the promise of 'salvation,' that is, of 'the life of the Age to Come,' to those who enter the elect community."[4]

As a third point of comparison, Dodd examined the summary of Jesus's preaching in Mark 1:14–15, for he believed that this established a framework for the Jerusalem κήρυγμα:

- The time is fulfilled, as a reference to prophecy.
- The kingdom of God has come near, with such expanded in Jesus's ministry, death, resurrection, and exaltation.
- Repent and believe the gospel, as a means to receive forgiveness.[5]

---

3. This list is reproduced from Dodd, *Apostolic Preaching*, 18.
4. Dodd, *Apostolic Preaching*, 28–29.
5. Dodd, *Apostolic Preaching*, 30.

Dodd's work was subjected to much critique over the years. Perhaps Harry Poe best summarizes a point of relevance to evangelism: "While Dodd's critics appear to be correct that the *kerygma* did not exist as a fixed formula, Dodd was correct to the extent that the *kerygma* existed as a fixed content upon which the early Christians drew when proclaiming their faith in Christ."[6] Yet, even with a fixed gospel, why is there variation found in the primitive preaching? Such is observed in the recorded messages in the Gospels and Acts, which most likely are summaries of the most important elements of what was proclaimed.

Though the language of contextualization is a recent development, it seems that variances in evangelism may be attributed to differing situations. People, whether in the twenty-first or the first century, are not robots in need of a monolithic algorithm. As social beings created in the image of God, human diversity demands diverse expressions of communication. While the kernel of the gospel may be found in the samples of evangelistic messages throughout the New Testament, there was much versatility and variety, whether the proclamation occurred with individuals, crowds, Jews, gentiles, proselytes, or pagans.[7]

What Is the Message Shared in Evangelism?

In the Gospels, the heart of the message proclaimed is the kingdom of God.[8] However, a shift occurred with the early disciples with more attention toward the King of the kingdom. The gospel is good news. It is a message about how God's enemies become God's friends; prisoners bound by sin are set free; the spiritually dead are made alive; those under God's wrath receive mercy; those in the kingdom of darkness move into the kingdom of light; the guilty become acquitted; and those in the family of the evil one become members of the family of God. It is the message that the Creator is renewing and will renew his broken creation. It is a message about life after death and life here and now (John 10:10).

The message shared may be summarized as follows: People are separated from God because they have sinned against his standard (Rom. 3:23) and are under wrath and condemnation (John 3:18). But God loves sinners and sent Jesus to die on a cross as a sacrifice for their sins (John 3:16), to remove this separation and bring healing and blessing. The Savior was raised to life for their justification (Rom. 4:25). Now a salvation of wholeness is available to

---

6. Poe, *Gospel*, 40.
7. Green, *Evangelism in the Early Church*, 69, 70.
8. So while John Havlik is correct to state, "The *kerugma* is the proclamation that the Kingdom has come in Jesus Christ," it is incorrect for him to claim, "The church is *kerugma*" (*People-Centered Evangelism*, 53, 54).

those who repent and declare, in faith, that Jesus is Lord (Rom. 10:9). It is through belief in these truths that people are justified, and with confession of commitment they are saved (Rom. 10:10, 13).

Witnessing and Proclaiming the Gospel

The concept of witness or bearing witness (עֵד, *'ēd*; μάρτυς, μαρτυρέω, μαρτυρία, μαρτύριον, *martys, martyreō, martyria, martyrion*) runs throughout the Bible. Whether such was related to commerce, covenant, or courtroom (Gen. 21:30; 31:44, 52; Exod. 23:1), the ancient act of serving as a witness was a necessary record and declaration of truth to both a present and a future generation. False witness was a breaking of the law that harmed civilization (Exod. 20:16). Sometimes the created order bore witness to the things of God (Deut. 4:26; 30:19; cf. Ps.19:1; Acts 14:17), and God himself is even called to be a witness (1 Sam. 12:5–6; 20:12; John 15:26).

A faithful witness does not lie and even saves lives by bearing testimony or proof for the truth (Prov. 14:5, 25). However, a worthless witness is one who mocks at justice and will perish (Prov. 19:28; 21:28). The servant people of God bear witness to his character and nature (Isa. 43:10, 12). His witnesses are set in contrast to the idols of the nations that serve as "witnesses" that "neither see nor know" (Isa. 44:8–9).

The Baptist came as a witness "about the light, that all might believe through him" (John 1:7; cf. 1:15, 32, 34; 3:28). Jesus also came to bear witness to the truth through his works (John 5:36; 10:25; cf. Rev. 1:5). Both the Father and the Scriptures bore witness to the Messiah (John 5:37, 39; 8:18; cf. Acts 10:43; Rom. 3:21). The Spirit would arrive and bear witness about the Christ (John 15:26). What had been observed throughout the Old Testament and modeled before the disciples would then be replicated by the church during the last days (John 15:27). The call to follow Jesus is a call to be a witness to what one has seen, heard, and experienced (Acts 22:15; 26:16; 1 John 1:1–3).

Jesus's disciples are "to bear witness before governors and kings . . . and the Gentiles" (Matt. 10:18). Their testimonies would bring them not praise and prestige but persecution and prison. As the righteous prophets were persecuted for being Yahweh's witness, so also the disciples were to expect nothing less (Matt. 5:12; Mark 13:9; cf. Rev. 2:13; 6:9). While their witness to Jesus would be the factor that would get them in front of political leaders, the opportunity was not to be wasted on an earthly agenda. Capturing the ear of kings and governors, as a result of their capture, was to be "[their] opportunity to bear witness" (Luke 21:13).

THE GOSPEL AND DIGITAL CULTURE

Mark Appleton, vice president of internet evangelism for the Billy Graham Evangelistic Association (BGEA), notes the present global opportunities for taking the gospel into challenging contexts online.

"I read everything about Christ and I want to become a Christian." That was Zahir's [pseudonym] Instagram message to one of our Arabic volunteers. Zahir was a Muslim living in Baghdad, Iraq. Months earlier, he clicked on one of our Instagram ads and took an online course to learn about Jesus and the Christian faith. Afterward, he found a Christian and discussed the faith with him. He had a growing sense of urgency to accept Christ and finally messaged us through Instagram to take that step. Zahir has begun walking with Jesus, watching our videos on YouTube for more encouragement, and is now meeting with other believers we connected him with in his city.

Several years ago, BGEA began exploring an outreach to Arabic speakers online, and we met with many people and organizations to learn where the needs were. . . .

Over the past few years, Iraq has invested in and grown its digital infrastructure. . . . Today, the Search for Jesus Facebook page has almost half a million followers from Iraq. Several hundred Muslims in this country have come to faith in Jesus Christ through our digital presence and team of volunteers, many with powerful testimonies of courageous faith. . . .

Digital space has its own culture. It is its own place and has its own language and idioms. It has unspoken rules of engagement and social expectations. There are growing sociological similarities between teenagers in Topeka, Kansas, and those in Jakarta, Indonesia. While each group still has their ethnic culture, because of their shared experiences in the global digital space, there are aspects of their lives in which they will relate more to each other than they will to their own parents. . . .

There are a growing number of people in the world whom we will not reach simply by learning their language and traveling to their country. We will reach them by meeting them in virtual reality or their digital culture or platform of choice, and carrying the light of Christ to them within that space.

Appleton, "Digital Missionaries," 14–15.

Questions

1. Do you think that digital space is a mission field where the gospel should be shared? Explain.
2. Do you agree that "shared experiences in the global digital space" result in teenagers from diverse contexts relating "more to each other than . . . to their own parents"?
3. How would you describe "digital culture"?

Witnessing encompasses evangelism, and while the two cannot be separated, bearing witness is not to be equated with evangelism. A life that reflects the kingdom and adorns the gospel is to be set forth before the world like a city on a hill (Matt. 5:14). The church is to let her "light shine before others," so that they may see these good deeds and give glory to God (Matt. 5:16). However, salvific faith comes not from observation alone, but through hearing the word of God (Rom. 10:17). If anyone was able to live a perfect life before the world, it was Jesus. His lifestyle was without sin and was a perfect example of the good news. Yet, he verbally shared the gospel with others. He lived the message of the kingdom but knew that it was impossible for others to enter unless they were *told* how. Jesus expected his disciples' witness to include evangelism as well. Prior to his ascension, he reminds his disciples that they are witnesses, and according to the Scriptures, "the Christ should suffer and on the third day rise from the dead" (Luke 24:46). A critical component of their witness was their proclamation of "repentance for the forgiveness of sins" to all nations (Luke 24:47), not just modeling it by lifestyle. Their witness to this truth was to involve crossing cultural gaps between the nations found in Jerusalem, Judea, Samaria, and throughout the world (Acts 1:8). Their community was to reflect the power of the gospel, but their mouths were to verbalize its content to others (Acts 2:32, 40; 3:15; 5:32; 10:39). No one was transformed by the Spirit simply by watching believers. The abundant life came only from them responding to the evangelistic work of the church, not by observing and experiencing the church's lifestyle.

Translatability of the Gospel

The beauty of the gospel is that it is a message capable of being translated into every cultural context and social environment. It is not limited to a holy language but rather is effective and efficient in every language and dialect, including hearing-impaired communities. The gospel may be communicated to and embraced by the educated and the illiterate, rich and poor. Kwame Bediako notes that translatability reveals the "fundamental relevance and accessibility to persons in any culture within which the Christian faith is transmitted and assimilated."[9] Though the gospel was to the Jew first, it is God's power to bring salvation to everyone who believes (Rom. 1:16). The gospel does not know racial or ethnic boundaries, has never been restricted to Western ownership or "the white man's religion," but traces its history to Mesopotamians and exalts a brown-skinned, Jewish carpenter.

9. Bediako, "Translatability," 146–47.

This has not been, and is not, always the case with evangelism. Church history reveals evangelistic work that has often encapsulated the gospel in cultural expressions to a degree that the stumbling block of the cross (1 Cor. 1:23) was never encountered because of the stumbling block of the church's cultural preferences. Addressing the 1996 World Council of Churches Commission on World Mission and Evangelism, Musimbi R. A. Kanyoro reminded the audience of this global evangelism challenge:

> People in the cities of the South and North alike are adopting similar globalized cultural behaviour conditioned by the constraints of their context. . . . The majority have no church background and are unfamiliar with the message of the gospel, and so will not listen to the message of the church unless the church itself is significantly different and has something particular to offer. If Christianity is to make sense to them, it will have to be what Paul described as "all things to all people." In the church we speak the language of Hallelujah and Amen, but we must remember that today our world also speaks of Coca-Cola and Toyota. . . . How will the church of today and the next millennium package and market the gospel of one hope in the face of globalization and rapid transformation of a world catalyzed by information technology, the never-ending gap between rich and poor, urban and rural, those advocating ethnic unity and those seeking national unity, men and women, youth and adults?[10]

Not All Evangelism Is the Same

Part of the answer to Kanyoro's question is recognizing that though the gospel is a constant, not all evangelism is the same. Cultural issues are at play and should be considered in view of the audience.[11] This was important for the first-century heralds of the kerygma and true for every generation.

In each sermon I preached as a pastor, I included an evangelistic invitation to anyone in the crowd who was far from God. Each Sunday, at some point during my message, I would specifically speak to those who had never repented of sin and placed their faith in Christ for salvation. I also encouraged members

---

10. Kanyoro, "Called to One Hope," 144.
11. Evangelistic methods sometimes have resulted in alienation from the truth of the gospel. The "Report from the Ecumenical Conference on World Mission and Evangelization" in Salvador, de Bahia, Brazil, in 1996 included the following statement: "Because culture is constantly in flux and cultural expressions change from generation to generation, the interaction between the gospel and cultures must be a continuous process in every place. Christians must be aware of the limitations of any culture, for there is always the danger of the gospel being domesticated and made captive to that culture. Similarly, there are situations where the gospel has been abused for political purposes or to exploit people" (World Council of Churches, "Report from the Ecumenical Conference," 204).

to take any unbelieving friends with them to lunch or coffee and then discuss the worship activities experienced and use them as an opportunity to share the gospel and respond to their friends' questions.

Was I doing evangelism? Was I evangelistic? Did such acts every Sunday make our church an evangelistic church?

In one sense, the answers are yes. Since the good news of Christ's life, death, resurrection, and invitation was communicated to those present, evangelism was occurring. I had taught the church, while also attempting to create a welcoming culture, that each Sunday the gospel and an invitation would be shared with unbelievers. Members knew that while the worship gathering was primarily for the church, our prayer was that if any unbelievers were present, they would experience the power of God and come to know him (1 Cor. 14:24–25).

However, if such had been our only understanding of evangelism and evangelistic practice, then we, by limiting our evangelism to church events with people like us, would have hardly been following the expectations and examples primarily represented in the Scriptures. While we worked hard at making our Sunday gatherings as welcoming and inviting as possible, for a variety of cultural and spiritual reasons, the overwhelming majority of unbelievers in our community would not meet with us. No church, no matter how inclusive and seeker-sensitive, can be culturally neutral and will exclude some people.

This method—using a Sunday worship gathering—will fail to reach many people with the gospel. Churches who limit their understanding and practice of evangelism to worship gatherings and other church events will severely hinder the spread of the gospel throughout the world.

Os Guinness was aware of this relationship of cultural expressions and evangelism when he noted, "Some branches of the Western church have effectively abandoned evangelism, for various reasons, and others speak as if Christian truths and belief are always and readily understandable to everyone, whatever the state of their listeners' hearts and whatever the character of their audience's worldview and culture. Others again have come to rely on formulaic, cookie-cutter approaches to evangelism and apologetics as if all who hear them are the same."[12]

There is one gospel for the multicultural world, and the church must recognize that all evangelism is not the same in practice. Those created in the image of God (Gen. 1:27) are social beings and are influenced and shaped by cultures. Believers have cultures. Local churches have cultures—since they

12. Guinness, *Fool's Talk*, 17.

consist of believers. And the unregenerate have cultures. The world is a diverse place, but so are cities, small towns, and households. Paul recognized that the gospel, by its nature, is a stumbling block to some (1 Cor. 1:23). He was not willing to tamper with or compromise this message and warned others to avoid the temptation to make it more palatable (2 Cor. 4:2; 2 Tim. 4:1–5; Titus 2:1). However, he also recognized that cultural forces could place stumbling blocks in the way of those on paths to the gospel. Social dynamics in the first century could become stumbling blocks that kept people from even having the chance to hear the stumbling block of the gospel. The early apostolic teams were willing to become all things to all people in order to attempt to communicate clearly the message of the gospel (1 Cor. 9:22–23). While the message never changed, the means by which it was communicated to Jews, God-fearers, gentiles, Samaritans, Pharisees, husbands and wives, and governmental leaders varied. A one-size method designed to reach all people was insufficient and irresponsible. Toward the end of the twentieth century, evangelicals would give serious attention to crossing cultural gaps in order to take the gospel to the unreached peoples. This will be a topic of consideration in chapter 16.

— QUESTIONS TO CONSIDER —

1. Given the growth of the Majority World church, what do you think is the role(s) of the Western church in global evangelization?
2. What do you think is the irreducible minimum of the gospel that needs to be proclaimed before a person will experience God's relationship and salvation?
3. What makes the gospel a universal message to a multicultural world?
4. What is the relationship between witnessing and evangelizing?

4

GLOBAL STATUS OF EVANGELIZATION

Wise kingdom stewardship is partially a matter of knowing reality and responding appropriately. If the church is unaware of the locations of the lost, how will she know if she is a wise steward in view of the Great Commission? This chapter addresses the present status of global evangelization.

Where are the large concentrations of those peoples far from God? Statistical reports have been provided for a very long time. According to David Barrett and James Reapsome, the church has attempted to gain an understanding of her present reality at least ninety-seven times throughout history. They write, "No one can accuse the church . . . of failing to publicize the magnitude of the unfinished task of evangelizing the globe."[1] For example, beginning with William Carey in 1792 and concluding a few years following the publication of the *World Christian Encyclopedia* in 1982, at least forty-seven survey plans were promoted for the task of global evangelization.[2] Though evangelistic advances have been taking place in recent decades, their conclusion in 1988 was not encouraging, as they noted that most research had been ignored:

> It appears quire absurd—after you stand back and reflect on the list—to have surveys like these put out at the rate of eight or 10 every generation. Throughout the last 100 years the number of unreached people has hovered around one billion, virtually unchanged from one year to the next, from one decade to the next, from one generation to the next.

1. Barrett and Reapsome, *Seven Hundred Plans*, 18.
2. Barrett and Reapsome, *Seven Hundred Plans*, 18–19.

Perhaps we have studied the subject to death, or perhaps we are paralyzed by our analysis. At any rate, nothing seems to get better. With each succeeding generation, the unreached are still unreached. What has been the point of all these survey plans?[3]

At the time of this writing, Joshua Project and the Global Research Department of the International Mission Board estimate the number of unreached to be 3.4 billion and 4.8 billion, respectively.[4] Such studies help the church practice stewardship, maintain accountability, and remain diligent. Let's look briefly at these three practices.

The Church's Response: Stewardship, Accountability, and Diligence

The kingdom mindset involves knowing global realities. Paul wrote that his apostolic team should be regarded as "servants of Christ and stewards of the mysteries of God" and that stewards were to be "found faithful" (1 Cor. 4:1–2).[5] The concept of stewardship is related to one who manages or administrates an estate or household. This "building" language follows with what is found in 1 Corinthians 3:5–17. While such matters clearly applied to the apostolic band, the principle continues to be relevant as the church embraces the same gospel of God in every generation. This is especially true, given that the apostle expected the Corinthian church to imitate him (1 Cor. 4:16–17). Jesus's parable in Luke 12:42–48 of the faithful "manager" (*oikonomos*, the same word used in 1 Cor. 4:2) calls the church to wise stewardship of his resources—and of the opportunities provided—as the church awaits his return, for "blessed is that servant" who is found faithful when the master returns. If there was any confusion regarding what faithfulness entailed for the steward, Jesus clarifies that the steward "who knew his master's will but did not get ready or act according to his will" is the one who receives a "severe beating" (12:47). The master's parameters for the operations of his stewards are these: "Everyone to whom much was given, of him much will be required, and from him to whom they entrusted much, they will demand the more" (Luke 12:48). Or, as John Nolland expresses it in contemporary terms, "The gifts of opportunity create the demands of responsibility."[6]

---

3. Barrett and Reapsome, *Seven Hundred Plans*, 18–19.
4. See joshuaproject.net and peoplegroups.org. Estimates were made December 13, 2023. More will be stated in this chapter as to why these numbers are dissimilar.
5. Mark Taylor notes that this mystery (already mentioned in 1 Cor. 2:1, 7) refers to "God's plan of salvation revealed in Christ" (*1 Corinthians*, 113).
6. Nolland, *Luke 9:21–18:34*, 705.

Though there are both qualitative and quantitative limitations regarding researching populations, the church is wise to understand present realities and respond accordingly (see, e.g., 1 Chron. 12:32). Given the opportunities and resources, why would the church *not* want to understand the assigned task? Wise is the steward who understands the present *and* responds accordingly. Global research is a matter of kingdom stewardship that helps the church think about progress being made regarding the commission to make disciples of all nations.

It has been said that a person who does not know their destination will arrive there nonetheless. Likewise, a person who aims at nothing will hit it every time. Knowledge of lostness is a means of accountability. As the church engages in available research, she is faced with a decision: What next? Missiological research is a dangerous thing. It raises the bar of accountability and responsibility. If numbers are discussed, filed away, and never lead to global engagement, then such gifts of opportunity have been buried in the ground (Matt. 25:18). If it is wrong to neglect responsibilities due to ignorance, it is doubly wrong to neglect what is expected with full understanding. After two thousand years, the Lord has provided his church with numerous resources and technology for understanding peoples and locations of significant lostness and the need for the gospel and churches planted from the harvest fields. The blessings provided since Barrett and Reapsome's report in 1988 have exponentially increased. A new level of accountability now exists and must be taken captive for the kingdom. This is a wonderful matter. As the church continues to develop a better understanding of unreached peoples and least-reached places, she creates an atmosphere among church members to exhort one another to good works of proclamation.

Knowledge leads to accountability. Accountability interrupts laziness. Global research motivates and moves the church to remain diligent and take action. As denominations and networks recognize the global need for the gospel, there is no longer any room to blame ignorance for a lack of zeal or poor allocation of resources. Such findings drive the church to respond beyond herself.

Present Realities

By the time this book is published, numbers related to people groups will have changed. Such is a limitation of statistics. Yet, a chapter on the global status of evangelization would be incomplete without a snapshot taken at this moment in history and without pointing the reader toward resources for current data. In order to understand the present better, a brief digression to the past is necessary.

THE GLOBAL REACH OF EVANGELISM EXPLOSION

One of the most popular personal evangelism strategies in the twentieth century was Evangelism Explosion (EE). The following describes the global reach of EE:

> In a March morning last year, colorful flags streamed down the center aisle of Coral Ridge Presbyterian Church carried by delegates celebrating the establishment of Evangelism Explosion International (EE) ministries in all 211 nations of the world. . . .
>
> EE was founded in 1967 to teach pastors the methods that Coral Ridge Presbyterian Church used to build its membership from 17 to more than 8,000. EE offers a system of church-based training that includes both a carefully developed, effective, simple-to-administer evangelism and discipleship ministry, and a means of developing lay leaders. In other words, EE not only helps churches develop "soul winners" but "trainers of soul winners" as well.
>
> From its beginning, we felt that EE had the potential to be a means for overcoming barriers to worldwide evangelism and achieving the Great Commission. Within seven years of its founding, EE was launched internationally. From a base of 66 nations in 1988, we set our goal of reaching all the nations of the world by the end of 1995. Our plan was to have at least one EE-trained individual actively making disciples in each country through the EE ministry. Our recently revised purpose statement recognizes our international focus: "to glorify God by equipping the body of Christ worldwide for Friendship, Evangelism, Discipleship and Healthy Growth!" . . .
>
> All of us at Evangelism Explosion recognize that reaching the nations is not an end, but a beginning. The next step of reaching all people groups is an enormous and expensive task. We have much left to do in training, developing leadership, and translating materials. It is a task we cannot do alone. It will require partnerships with many other mission organizations.
>
> But these challenges should not cause us to overlook the accomplishments of the many dedicated evangelists and missionaries who worked to bring EE to all the nations. Nor should they keep us from giving praise to the Savior who is truly responsible.
>
> Kennedy, "Evangelism Explosion."

Questions

1. Do an online study of Evangelism Explosion. Why do you think that it became global in its reach?
2. What are the strengths and limitations of the model developed in Coral Ridge Presbyterian Church in Fort Lauderdale, Florida, during the 1960s?

At the Lausanne Congress on World Evangelization in 1974, Ralph Winter gave a plenary address in which he spoke of the "hidden peoples" who would remain without the gospel unless the church started crossing cultural gaps to share the gospel. By the Lausanne II gathering in Manilla in 1989, Patrick Johnstone and John Robb coordinated "Track 310—Unreached Peoples," in which they provided a summary report that contained a number of goals and action steps to challenge the Lausanne movement. Among these, they wrote of the need to "provide a listing of all the known peoples of the world as soon as possible, clearly defining those still unreached" and to "facilitate the establishment of research and information function in every region and country where possible to serve the body of Christ in conducting national surveys of all areas, peoples and cities. This information can then be used to mobilize the church nationally and worldwide."[7]

It was recommended that cooperation occur to establish global databases that would be part of

- facilitating the setting up of regional and national research functions where none exist
- producing a simple yet comprehensive explanation of definitions and numbers relating to all the peoples and people groups of the world
- refining and locally verifying the current list of ethno-linguistic peoples by December 1990
- relating to regional and national research bodies for updating database information
- sharing and disseminating information (within the limits of security considerations) with research bodies and mission agencies
- producing an annual global update on progress
- retaining a regularly updated list of global prayer coordinators for specific peoples, cities, and so on
- presenting research information in a style and form that will give grass-roots/frontline workers the means to plan and work strategically[8]

Years later, research was conducted, compiled, and disseminated for global evangelization and church planting. Two of the global data sets are housed with Joshua Project and the Global Research Department of the International Mission Board.[9] In order to interpret the information related to the global

---

7. Johnstone and Robb, "Track 310," 413, 414.
8. Johnstone and Robb, "Track 310," 415.
9. The World Christian Database is the third set, housed with Gordon Conwell Theological Seminary, and accessed for a fee. See https://worldchristiandatabase.org/. For the Joshua Project,

state of evangelization, it is necessary to understand how each organization defines terminology.

Of the eight billion people alive today, Joshua Project divides them into 17,286 people groups, while the Global Research Department count is 12,114.[10] Such divisions serve strategic purposes for evangelization. The reason for the difference is related to how each organization categorizes the groups. Joshua Project observes that different categorizations have different strengths and serve different purposes, noting, "An ethno-linguistic peoples list has a somewhat quantifiable criterion, namely language, and serves as a helpful target for language-oriented ministries such as radio broadcasting, Jesus Film production, Bible translation, etc. An ethnic peoples list considers non-language distinctives which create significant barriers."[11]

A second definition needed to understand the global reality is related to what constitutes an unreached people group. It is important to note that missiologists have been discussing the strengths and limitations related to present terminology and definitions.[12] Fifty years of research has resulted in encouraging progress, but global and cultural shifts are pressing for a paradigm shift. Though it is too early to address the details of such conversations, it should be known that such discussions will result in future changes to understanding global lostness and the development of evangelistic strategies. Until then, it is important to recognize the present global realities as understood to date.

Joshua Project estimates that there are 7,250 unreached people groups in the world, while the Global Research Department estimate is 7,251. Joshua Project defines an unreached people group as one that is "less than or equal to 5% Christian Adherent *AND* less than or equal to 2% Evangelical."[13] An evangelical is generally understood to be one who believes in Christ alone for salvation, that the Scriptures are God's word to be obeyed, that the gospel is to be shared with others, and that Jesus is returning with both rewards and judgment. However, Global Research Department defines an unreached people group as one "in which less than 2% of the population are Evangelical Christians."[14] Those who claim to be Christian, even if they are nominal, are

see https://joshuaproject.net/ and Global Research at https://grd.imb.org/ and https://peoplegroups.org/.

10. For a discussion on the history of people groups and evangelization, see Datema and Bartlotti, "People Group Approach."

11. Joshua Project, "How Many People Groups?"

12. See McMahan, "Ferment in the Church"; Nguyen, "Globalization"; Bartlotti, "People Groups"; Bartlotti, *People Vision*; Scribner, "Making of Lists"; Gill, "Church for Every People"; Courson and Geisler, "Changing Landscape"; Courson and Geisler, "Status of the Task."

13. https://joshuaproject.net/help/definitions#unreached.

14. https://peoplegroups.org/294.aspx#309.

counted in Joshua Project's reporting. Global Research Department's concern has little to do with cultural values, family history, and religious tradition, and focuses on the theological by defining groups as regenerate or unregenerate.[15] Therefore, Joshua Project estimates the unreached to be about 3.4 billion people, or 42 percent of the world's population. Global Research Department's estimation is 4.8 billion people, over half of the global demographic.

Regardless of the statistic used, a great imbalance remains among countries, even fifty years since Lausanne I. Those with the most Christians receive the largest number of missionaries. It has been estimated that for every one missionary sent to unreached peoples, thirty are sent to reached people groups.[16] Another perspective on the global realities is to consider the number of unevangelized people in the world. According to Gina Zurlo, Todd Johnson, and Peter Crossing, "Evangelized persons are those who have had an adequate opportunity to hear the Christian message and to respond to it, whether positively or negatively. Evangelization among a language or people group is measured by a series of variables including presence of Christians, availability of Christian media (film, radio, Scriptures in print and online), missionary presence, and level of religious freedom."[17]

The estimated number of unevangelized people is 2.3 billion, a number expected to rise to 2.7 billion by 2050, or about 28 percent of the global population. It is also estimated that 81 percent of the population do not know a Christian.[18]

An examination of the status of evangelical Christianity among the world's population reveals:

- 336 people groups with a population of 12 million who have no known evangelical Christians or evangelical churches among them, and no access to evangelical print, audio, visual, or human resources
- 6,492 people groups with a population of 3.4 billion who are less than 2 percent evangelical and have some evangelical resources but no active church planting within the past two years
- 220 people groups with a population of 512 million who are less than 2 percent evangelical and have active church planting reported in the past two years[19]

---

15. It is beyond the scope of this book to discuss the history and reason why percentages of 5 percent and 2 percent are used when identifying unreached people groups. I discuss these details in Terry and Payne, *Strategy for Missions*, 186–89.

16. Lewis, "Frontier Mission Task," 159.

17. Zurlo, Johnson, and Crossing, "World Christianity," 17.

18. Zurlo, Johnson, and Crossing, "World Christianity," 23.

19. GSEC Presentation, with data as of January 2024 (https://grd.imb.org/map-resources/). It should be noted that Global Research Department defines an evangelical Christian as "a person who believes that Jesus Christ is the sole source of salvation through faith in Him, has

Though the gospel has advanced throughout the world for two thousand years, a great task remains. Cultural shifts, population growth, isolation of people groups, and internal church issues are a few of the reasons as to why so many people remain unreached and unengaged. The command to make disciples of all nations must continue to be the priority related to the church's global task.

— QUESTIONS TO CONSIDER —

1. What significance is found in a global estimate of the status of evangelization?
2. Given all the research, why do you think, according to Barrett and Reapsome, that the evangelistic outcomes have been poor?
3. What should stewardship and accountability look like for most churches in light of the present status of global evangelization?

---

personal faith and conversion with regeneration by the Holy Spirit, recognizes the inspired Word of God as the only basis for faith and Christian living, and is committed to biblical preaching and evangelism that brings others to faith in Jesus Christ" (https://peoplegroups.org/294.aspx #305). While it should be noted that the regenerate are found among non-evangelical traditions (with the unregenerate found among evangelical traditions), when we study the world's population, evangelical measurements provide the simplest tool to estimate the number of followers of Christ.

5

MOTIVES AND ETHICS

Mention the word *evangelism* in certain Western contexts and an array of negative images come to mind of people driven by poor motives. There's the angry street preacher shouting at passersby, telling them that they are going to hell unless they repent. Or there's the televangelist with the Hollywood hair in his recording studio sharing the gospel just before he makes a passioned plea for more money so he can purchase a private jet for "ministry" purposes. Maybe the mental picture appears of a group of Christian "headhunters" as they strive to get another convert so their church will become larger or so they can get another notch in their Bible belts.

Why do evangelism? What should drive the church in her global disciple-making activities? What are healthy motives? Are there any unhealthy motives for doing evangelism? After all, if the outcome is another person in the kingdom, should our motives matter?

Closely related to the topic of motives is ethics. Are the church's actions in a pluralistic world above reproach when it comes to sharing the gospel? There are so many faith traditions. Is it not unethical to claim that Jesus is the only way to God? What about Protestant evangelization done in locations that have a substantial number of Catholic or Orthodox communities? Is proselytizing acceptable? Is unethical evangelism even a thing? If so, what is ethical evangelism?

Motives

Bad motives have existed in the church since the first century. While some evangelized from good will, others preached Christ "from envy and rivalry"

(Phil. 1:15). These people were motivated to trouble Paul while he was imprisoned (Phil. 1:17). The apostle was quick to note that his team was "not, like so many, peddlers of God's word," but rather they were "men of sincerity, as commissioned by God" (2 Cor. 2:17).

Though poor motives remain, the church, like Paul, must make certain that her drives are appropriate. Desires are related to actions in the world and should not be overlooked. Michael Green notes that Jesus's "motivation was paramount" and observes how the word "must" governed his life and ministry (Luke 9:22; John 9:4; 10:16). He was "totally constrained by this 'must.' His ministry did not spring from duty but from passion, passion to do the Father's will."[1] His attitude and actions shaped the motives of his followers. The following are some of those motives observed in the Scriptures.

Gratitude

The disciples' gratitude for the Lord's accomplishments drove their labors. They loved him and would keep his commands (John 14:15). Paul noted that the love of Christ compelled him in his life and ministry (2 Cor. 5:14). The church loves much because she has been forgiven much and has received much from the Lord. Hearts that overflow with gratitude motivate the church to sacrifice and take the gospel across the street and throughout the world. Green states that of all the motivators for evangelism, the primary one for the first believers was gratitude to God.[2]

Glory of God

Ultimately, all that the church does is to work toward God being glorified (1 Cor. 10:31). When people are called to faith, God receives the glory (2 Pet. 1:3). The Chronicler urged God's people, "Declare his glory among the nations, his marvelous works among all the peoples!" (1 Chron. 16:24). The psalmist desired that all the nations would praise God (Ps. 67), and one of the prophets foretold that the earth would be filled with the knowledge of the glory of God (Hab. 2:14). Paul stated that a day is coming when all will confess that Jesus is Lord to the glory of God (Phil. 2:11). Whenever the gospel changes people's hearts, it gives "the light of the knowledge of the glory of God in the face of Jesus Christ" (2 Cor. 4:6). As Jesus builds his church through the gospel (Matt. 16:18), God receives the glory (Eph. 3:21).

---

1. Green, *Evangelism: Learning from the Past*, 8.
2. Green, *Evangelism in the Early Church*, 236.

ETHICAL METHODS

Charles Kelley addresses the importance of ethical methods of evangelism. He also provides thoughts on evaluating such methods.

> Ethical methods of evangelism are those which allow the gospel, not the method or the witness, to be the stumbling block. The gospel itself is a barrier to belief for many. Paul noted that the call to trust a crucified Savior for deliverance from sin was foolishness to some and a scandal to others (1 Cor. 1:18–29). The Christian witness must be certain that those who reject the message are not rejecting the messenger or his method of witness before they hear about the Savior. He was willing to vary his approach based upon the unbeliever's point of receptivity. Paul presented the gospel differently to Jews and to Gentiles (cf. Acts 13:14–43 and 17:22–33).
>
> In both cases some believed and some did not, but the stumbling block for his hearers was the message of the gospel, not the manner of presentation. . . .
>
> Paul's guideline is to allow the possibility of rejection from the hearers. He was willing to use all means in order to save *some*. Ethical evangelistic methods are those methods which allow people the freedom to say no and walk away from Jesus. Any approach to evangelism that always succeeds is questionable. If all who are approached with an evangelistic method or presentation say yes to Jesus, they either do not understand the message or they are not allowed to say no. Neither Jesus, nor Paul, nor Peter, nor any New Testament witness saw total success with their methods of evangelism. If there is not resistance to and rejection of the gospel, there is manipulation and coercion in the method.
>
> Evangelism is ethical which results in both believers and unbelievers. The ethical evangelist and witness allows persons to say no as well as yes. To evaluate evangelistic methods, consider the responses they generate. Ethical evangelists want all to say yes to Jesus and receive eternal life, but they allow those who so desire to say no without coercion.
>
> Kelley, "Ethical Issues in Evangelism," 37–38.

Questions

1. How can we work to avoid becoming the stumbling block in our evangelism? Give examples.
2. What are some contemporary examples of stumbling blocks that are not the stumbling block of the cross?
3. Do you agree that "any approach to evangelism that always succeeds is questionable"? Why?
4. In light of your response to question 3, should we expect people to come to faith whenever we share the gospel?

Joy of the Lord

In Pisidian Antioch, Paul and Barnabas observed the excitement produced in the gentiles who came to faith (Acts 13:48). Though their conversions led to the team's persecution and departure from the city, "the disciples were filled with joy and the Holy Spirit" (Acts 13:52). The church is most engaged with the *missio Dei* when co-laboring with God in evangelism (1 Cor. 3:9) and engaged in completing a portion of John's eschatological vision (Rev. 7:9). Such delight is a motivator as one understands that one's efforts result in a heavenly party (Luke 15:7, 10). Experiencing fellowship and life with new believers brings joy to those who share the gospel (2 Cor. 7:4; 1 Thess. 2:20; cf. 2 John 4).

Fear of the Lord

Fear is not always a bad thing. Though irrational fear is a poor motivator, righteous fear is a godly motivator. A distorted theology advocates that the church should never be motivated by fear. Does not the Bible state, "Perfect love casts out fear" (1 John 4:18)? And what about the numerous times when the Bible commands, "Do not fear"? While such is true in its proper context, a whole-Bible theology reveals that there is another aspect to fear. Paul writes, "We must all appear before the judgment seat of Christ, so that each one may receive what is due for what he has done in the body, whether good or evil. Therefore, knowing the fear of the Lord, we persuade others" (2 Cor. 5:10–11). The follower of Jesus is secure in the hands of the Lord, but this blessed assurance is not to result in a lackadaisical attitude toward life. We will not be judged for our sins, but we will be judged in regard to our stewardship. The Lord has saved his church and has blessed her by calling her to engage in his mission. Jesus is building *his* church (Matt. 16:18), and the church gets the wonderful privilege of being the means by which he does his work. A day is coming when each disciple will give account of what they did with all that was received in this life. And, as Paul notes, this judgment will include matters related to evangelism.

Judgment of God

In addition to the judgment experienced by believers, based on their stewardship in this life, the judgment of God rests on those outside the kingdom. Though the topic of judgment is unpleasant for many in contemporary settings, it is a biblical doctrine that must not be overlooked, explained away, demythologized, or discarded as a social construct of ancient societies. The writer of Hebrews notes that people are destined to die once, "and after that comes judgment" (Heb. 9:27). The next major event on the divine calendar is what the prophets described as the day of the Lord. This day of judgment and restoration was to follow the outpouring of the Spirit that occurred at Pentecost. Understanding the gravity of the moment after being told that Joel's prophecy was being fulfilled before their eyes and ears, unbelieving Jews in Jerusalem knew that judgment was to follow, and in light of this reality they cried out, "What must we do?" (Acts 2:37). Peter's response was simply, "Repent and be baptized every one of you in the name of Jesus Christ" (Acts 2:38). The church is motivated to share the gospel because she knows a time of judgment is coming for those who have not found salvation in Jesus, and the result is a horrible, eternal separation from the merciful, loving, and forgiving judge.

Transformation of Societies

An evangelist motivated only by the kingdom to come falls short in motivation. The gospel and its implications are practical and affect life in the present. Generally, an improvement and positive changes occur in the lives of individuals, families, and societies following redemption. Husbands stop abusing wives and children. Parents make wise choices with their finances. What used to be wasted on frivolous and foolish things is now used to provide food and clothing for children. Work ethics improve. Employees stop stealing from employers. Business owners begin to treat employees with respect and fairness. Neighbors cease fighting and strive for peace and resolution to conflicts. People turn from drugs, crime, and violence whenever the gospel is embraced, and the kingdom ethic transforms communities. Such is not a utopia on earth, but rather a display of coming attractions. The kingdom ethic is a foreshadowing of what is to come when the day of restoration occurs. Wherever the church is found in the world, she is to work toward the transformation of societies. And the *primary* means by which the church is to engage in such action is by making disciples of all peoples, and such begins with evangelism.

Improper Motives

If evangelism is what brings people into the kingdom and into relationship with God, provides escape from coming judgment, and helps others to experience abundant life, are there improper motives that drive evangelistic actions in the world? While the outcome of people moving from the domain of darkness into the kingdom of the beloved Son (Col. 1:13) is a wonderful matter that brings rejoicing in heaven, the end does not justify the means. A strong warning exists for those who do amazing kingdom work that is not according to the will of the Father (Matt. 7:21). The sanctification of the church should not be compromised for the redemption of the lost.

The church's attitude and actions are critical to the disciple-making process. Paul's exhortation, "Be imitators of me, as I am of Christ" (1 Cor. 11:1), is just as relevant and important today as it was in the first century. The world, and new believers, are watching Christ's followers. *What* we say and do, and *how* we communicate and act reveal life in the kingdom and reflect our God. The church must not exclude the fruit of the Spirit from her evangelistic practices. While the church is to be pragmatic (we want to know what works), the ungodly specter of pragmatism is never to be part of her labors. An "anything goes" or "reach the lost at any cost" approach may rally the troops, but it is dangerously close to relieving the Spirit of his desired work in and through the church.

While churches should desire conversion growth and increase in baptisms, they must not be motivated to share the gospel to get more money, gain a reputation as the largest church in the community, or for pastoral prestige. Evangelistic motives must be pure and not for selfish gain. "Pride goes before destruction, and a haughty spirit before a fall" (Prov. 16:18). Improper motives can easily result in ungodly evangelistic practices.

Manipulation

Evangelism should never be done in a manner that manipulates people to make false decisions for Christ. Psychological tactics and peer pressure should not be used to "get decisions" for the Lord. Evangelism is not about high-pressure sales pitches. It is not about coercion or guilt trips.[3] Ethical evangelism must be done without attempting to make the gospel more palatable. Watering down the message to gain more converts or avoid conflict produces a false gospel. Jesus never manipulated someone into making a profession of faith. He was willing to allow people to reject him. When a wealthy man asked him what he had to do to have eternal life, Jesus gave him a difficult answer: he must sell his possessions and give the money to the poor (Matt. 19:16–30; Mark 10:17–31; Luke 18:18–30). Even though Jesus loved him (Mark 10:21),

---

3. A guilt trip is not to be confused with the feeling of guilt over one's sin. Godly sorrow brings repentance and results in salvation (2 Cor. 7:10). The Spirit convicts the world about sin, righteousness, and judgment (John 16:8). Manipulating people with a guilt trip provokes a false feeling and does not result in genuine conversion.

the man said no and departed "disheartened" and "sorrowful" (Mark 10:22). The decision was his to make without being manipulated.

False Promises

Although evangelism is never to be done with a combative attitude of unkindness, the whole picture must be revealed to hearers. The gospel is *good news*, but this message is one of blessing through judgment on self in light of God's standard. Those who desire to follow Jesus are to deny self (Luke 9:23) and not look back after putting their hands to the plow (Luke 9:62). The church should never attempt to talk about the good and easy things of Christ while avoiding the good and difficult things of Christ. Sharing about faith and blessings both now and to come is great, but what about repentance? May it never be said that the church fails to communicate the lordship of Christ to others in her attempts at evangelism. Matthew wrote, "Then Jesus told his disciples, 'If anyone would come after me, let him deny himself and take up his cross and follow me. For whoever would save his life will lose it, but whoever loses his life for my sake will find it'" (Matt. 16:24–25). Easy-believism is from the pit of hell and has no place in evangelism. While the Lord does provide health and wealth, there is no guarantee of these blessings in this life. It is unethical and ungodly to make promises that might not come to new believers. Although the church should never elevate discussions about the challenges, persecutions (2 Tim. 3:12), and sufferings to an inappropriate height, communicating the good news does include challenging others with the cost of discipleship (Luke 14:25–33), for nothing lost in this life is more valuable than what is gained both now and in the age to come (Mark 10:29–31).

Ethics

Discussions about motives in evangelism are closely related to the topic of ethics in evangelism. Motives drive strategies and methods. The church has not always operated from godly motivations. Evangelistic ministry must be governed by a kingdom ethic. Few scholars in the twenty-first century have written as much on the ethics of evangelism as Elmer John Thiessen.[4] After examining Paul's writings, Thiessen concludes, "Paul is clearly very concerned about the ethics of evangelism. That is why he found it necessary to defend himself again and again against a variety of criticisms against his own person.

---

4. Bryan Stone has also produced a serious study on evangelism and ethics: *Evangelism After Pluralism*.

One way to summarize Paul's many reflections on the ethics of evangelism is to introduce the notion of personal integrity. Paul knew the verbal witness of the followers of Jesus must be undergirded by Christian character and lifestyle. Christian character and lifestyle are necessary ingredients of embodied ethical witness."[5] Though history contains examples of unethical evangelistic practices, the church should not use past mistakes as an excuse to avoid present evangelistic labors. Rather, the church should repent, reform her theology, and practice an ethical witness moving forward. As she does, two particular issues arise related to ethical evangelism.

Treatment of People

Jesus and the first-century disciples were follow-up oriented. The Great Commission is about making disciples. While this begins with evangelism, it includes teaching obedience (Matt. 28:18–20). Thiessen notes that the treatment of new believers must include teaching them to obey all that Christ commanded. It is "a betrayal of love and a denial of the dignity of the person" if evangelism is divorced from discipling new believers in the faith.[6]

Christlike treatment of others also extends to unbelievers. One may not agree with another person's views or lifestyle, but respect may be extended to the individual. Jesus was denounced as a friend of tax collectors and sinners (Matt. 11:19; Luke 7:34; 15:2). Sam Chan notes that because people are sinners, such as Levi and his friends, priority was given to spend time with them. Jesus showed that "it's possible to associate with sinners without approving of their lifestyle. Association and approval are not the same thing."[7] People are not the enemy (Eph. 6:12). The church is frequently described as intolerant and disrespectful of others. Ethical evangelism seeks to overcome this accusation. Sharing the gospel with gentleness and respect is part of the plan (1 Pet. 3:15). Knowledge of the gospel and the kingdom should lead to humility. People should not be viewed with dishonor and disgust.

Ajith Fernando draws attention to cultural imperialism, force, and manipulation as three disrespectful ways that have no place in the church's evangelism.[8] History shows how powerful "Christians" have sometimes imposed

---

5. Thiessen, *Scandal of Evangelism*, 93. After surveying the New Testament, Thiessen developed thirty guidelines for ethical evangelism (110–33).
6. Thiessen, *Scandal of Evangelism*, 50.
7. Chan, *Talk About Jesus*, 31. Chan also notes that we demonstrate inclusiveness and unconditional love whenever we make room for disagreement with others. "After all, if we only eat with those who agree with us, we're practicing exclusion by turning away those who disagree with us" (117–18).
8. Fernando, *Sharing the Truth*, 42–43.

on others to surrender their cultures and be Christianized, but such practices are most ungodly and a denial of the gospel proclaimed. Paul also noted the importance of an ethical approach to his work. In his defense before Felix, he said, "I always take pains to have a clear conscience toward both God and man" (Acts 24:16). His correspondence with the Corinthians reveals an intentional effort to avoid "disgraceful, underhanded ways," to not "practice cunning" (2 Cor. 4:2), and to refrain from being "peddlers of God's word" but rather to be "men of sincerity" (2 Cor. 2:17). Paul's apostolic team was willing to make great sacrifices and endure anything and everything so that others may come to faith (1 Cor. 9:12; 2 Tim. 2:10).

Proselytism

The world *proselyte* is found in the New Testament and had positive connotations. A gentile who had converted to Judaism was considered a proselyte (Acts 2:11).[9] Historically, proselytism was equated with evangelization. Such is no longer the case among evangelical, mainline, Catholic, and Orthodox churches. The word has come to mean "sheep-stealing," taking one church's members to become members of another church,[10] and fails to communicate anything positive.[11]

A joint working group of the World Council of Churches (WCC) and the Roman Catholic Church saw the need for all Christians to provide a common witness to the world. As long as members of WCC and the Roman Catholic Church were switching membership, unity could not be achieved. The group produced "Common Witness and Proselytism: A Study Document" in 1970 to bear common witness to Christ, provide mutual support for effective witness, and to avoid anything contrary to the gospel. Proselytism was defined as "improper attitudes and behavior in the practice of Christian witness."[12] Included within the term *proselytism* was anything that violated human rights

---

9. Nicolaus, one of the seven chosen to serve, is descried as a "proselyte of Antioch" (Acts 6:5). He apparently experienced two conversions, one to Judaism and later one to the Christian faith.

10. The World Council of Churches defined proselytism as "the encouragement of Christians who belong to a church to change their denominational allegiance, through ways and means that 'contradict the spirit of Christian love, violate the freedom of the human person and diminish trust in the Christian witness of the church'" ("Towards Common Witness," 467).

11. For a modern defense of proselytizing, see Thiessen, *Ethics of Evangelism*. Thiessen in his later book, *The Scandal of Evangelism*, notes that it is better to distinguish between ethical and unethical evangelism as "talking about evangelism and proselytism within the same context creates confusion. It is all too easy for Christians to say they are opposed to proselytism when what they really mean is they are opposed to evangelism" (219).

12. World Council of Churches, "Common Witness and Proselytism," 11.

or coerced others (Christian or non-Christian) to convert. In a footnote, the document acknowledges that in some contexts the word still referred to "zeal in spreading the faith," but now should be used in "the pejorative sense" or with "some phrase which denotes defective attitudes and conduct."[13] They produced a study "to encourage all Christians to pursue their calling to render a common witness to God's saving and reconciling purpose in today's world and to help them avoid all competition in mission."[14]

In 1997 the Central Committee of the WCC gathered in Geneva to approve a statement on partnership and proselytism. The title of the document expressed a clear perspective on the topic: "Towards Common Witness: A Call to Adopt Responsible Relationships in Mission and to Renounce Proselytism." The WCC was clear that proselytism was a "scandal and counterwitness," as churches had been engaged in sheep-stealing. The concept was synonymous with the encouragement of Christians who belong to a church to change their denominational loyalty.[15]

Evangelicals were well aware that accusations of proselytizing had been directed their way. The Evangelical-Roman Catholic Dialogue on Mission consisted of three meetings that occurred between 1977 and 1984. The discussions emerged from a new zeal for evangelization that developed among both groups and to address where both groups converged in their understandings of the nature of evangelism since Lausanne I (1974) and the publication of Pope Paul VI's 1975 exhortation, *Evangelii nuntiandi* (*On Evangelization in the Modern World*). From these discussions, Basil Meeking and John Stott published *The Evangelical-Roman Catholic Dialogue on Mission, 1977–1984* to make the final report available to all. It was expressed that there are examples of proselytism—and not evangelism—that both groups were opposed to in theory and practice, but differences were clearly noted:

> Evangelicals see nominal Christians as needing to be won for Christ. Roman Catholics also speak of "evangelizing" such people, although they refer to them as "lapsed" or "inactive" rather than as "nominal," because they do not make a separation between the visible and invisible Church. They are understandably offended whenever Evangelicals appear to regard all Roman Catholics as *ipso facto* unbelievers, and when they base their evangelism on a distorted view of Roman Catholic teaching and practice. On the other hand, since Evangelicals seek to evangelize the nominal members of their own churches, as well as of others, they see this activity as an authentic concern for the gospel, and not as

---

13. World Council of Churches, "Common Witness and Proselytism," 11.
14. World Council of Churches, "Challenge of Proselytism," 213.
15. World Council of Churches, "Towards Common Witness," 463, 467.

a reprehensive kind of "sheep-stealing." Roman Catholics do not accept this reasoning.[16]

Such theological differences resulted in an impasse. Evangelicals were opposed to identifying someone—or an entire nation—as Christian because of history, tradition, or political influence. If such had been the case, many European and Central and South American countries would have been off-limits for evangelism. Countries under the auspices of Orthodox churches would have been omitted too. The world was the parish, and anywhere the unregenerate may be found—regardless of church membership—evangelicals were there to share the gospel.

Times had shifted. Now, calling, including coercing, others to give up religious ways inherited from ancestors was viewed as a hangover from colonialism and ethnocentrism. Tolerance and acceptance had become dominant values. By the turn of the twenty-first century, Lawrence Uzzell believed that proselytism "was most often invoked by those who ultimately oppose all forms of Christian evangelism."[17] The understanding of the word had broadened so much that "if the Apostles had refrained from everything that today is lumped under the term, there would have been no carrying out of the Great Commission and the Church might have died in its infancy. Precisely because it labels all missionary activity pejoratively, the term is no help."[18]

Ethical evangelism soon became a topic of discussion. Though it did not gain widespread acceptance among evangelicals, some called attention to the matter. The World Evangelical Alliance, World Council of Churches, and the Pontifical Council for Interreligious Dialogue partnered to produce, in 2011, "Christian Witness in a Multi-Religious World: Recommendations for Conduct." The work attempts to establish an ethical approach to mission, drawing from both the Great Commission and kingdom ethics. It was clear that any deceptive or coercive means in mission betrays the gospel. Though the document did not have widespread acceptance among evangelicals in the United States, Thomas Schirrmacher notes that by 2014 it had become a standard reference in interreligious dialogue and mission.[19] The five-page document took five years to produce and says more about respecting other people and standing up for religious freedom than it does to encourage evangelism.[20] Stanko Jambrek drew attention to the fact that the document hardly used the

16. Meeking and Stott, *Evangelical-Roman Catholic Dialogue*, 90.
17. Uzzell, "Don't Call It Proselytism," 16.
18. Uzzell, "Don't Call It Proselytism," 16.
19. Schirrmacher, "Code," 83.
20. See World Council of Churches, "Christian Witness."

word *evangelism*, and when it did, it was in a negative context. His critique was that an impression had been given that evangelism had been sacrificed for ecumenical cooperation and "on behalf of the humanistic greater good of mankind."[21]

Evangelicals gave serious thought to ethics and evangelism. By 1983 the International Conference for Itinerant Evangelists in Amsterdam produced a fifteen-point standard known as the "Amsterdam Affirmations."[22] The sixth affirmation explicitly stated evangelism was to be done in love and "without coercion or manipulation." Commenting on this matter, Billy Graham wrote, "We must be careful that coercion does not enter into that persuasion."[23] Noting that biblical urgency can be abused by evangelists, Graham stated there was no place for one "to excite emotions and manipulate people," or "use dubious means, such as threats, scare tactics, and psychological pressure" to produce converts.[24] By 1986 an article appeared in *Cultic Studies Journal* titled "A Code of Ethics for the Christian Evangelist," but it did not receive lasting attention. The "Manilla Manifesto," produced at Lausanne II in 1989, included the statement that the church was to "renounce unworthy methods of evangelism," "be sensitive to those of other faiths," and "reject any approach that seeks to force conversion" on anyone.[25] The Lausanne III gathering at Cape Town in 2010 published "Cape Town Commitment," which included statements about proselytization under the section "Living the Love of Christ Among People of Other Faiths." Here the document noted, "We are called to share good news in evangelism, but not to engage in unworthy proselytizing. . . . We wish to be sensitive to those of other faiths, and we reject any approach that seeks to force conversion on them. Proselytizing, by contrast, is the attempt to compel others to become 'one of us,' to 'accept our religion,' or indeed to 'join our denomination.' We commit ourselves to be scrupulously ethical in all our evangelism."[26] These brief statements focused on the relationship of the church to non-Christian religions. Evangelicals wisely noted that while they will engage in evangelism, they will not participate in forced efforts to Christianize others. The good news of Jesus is to be shared with conviction and persuasion, but not with coercive and manipulative methods.

---

21. Jambrek, "Christian Witness," 203.
22. For the fifteen affirmations, see Graham, *Biblical Standard*. See also, in the bibliography in the present volume, "The Amsterdam Declaration."
23. Graham, *Biblical Standard*, 60.
24. Graham, *Biblical Standard*, 60–61.
25. In Douglas, *Proclaim Christ*, 38.
26. Lausanne Movement, "Cape Town Commitment," 76.

Sharing the gospel is a good thing; however, poor historical examples cause one to question this assumption. It seems little attention is given to evangelistic motives and ethics, for such is taken for granted. The drives behind zeal and reasoning for evangelistic methods are to be questioned and evaluated. This is a matter of faithful stewardship.

— **QUESTIONS TO CONSIDER** —

1. What are your motivators for evangelism?
2. Are there other motives not addressed in this chapter? If so, explain.
3. Have you observed improper evangelistic motives? If so, explain.
4. How would you describe ethical evangelism?
5. What are your thoughts about proselytism?

— PART 2 —

BIBLICAL AND THEOLOGICAL FOUNDATIONS

Unless evangelism is derived from a biblical and theological foundation, it risks becoming that which it was never intended to be according to God's expectations. Beginning with the Old Testament, this section addresses God's mission, the relationship of evangelism to the Great Commission, and principles related to Jesus's and the apostolic church's practices. Doctrines such as sovereignty, grace, atonement, repentance, faith, and conversion are discussed. Various theological traditions related to these topics will be summarized.

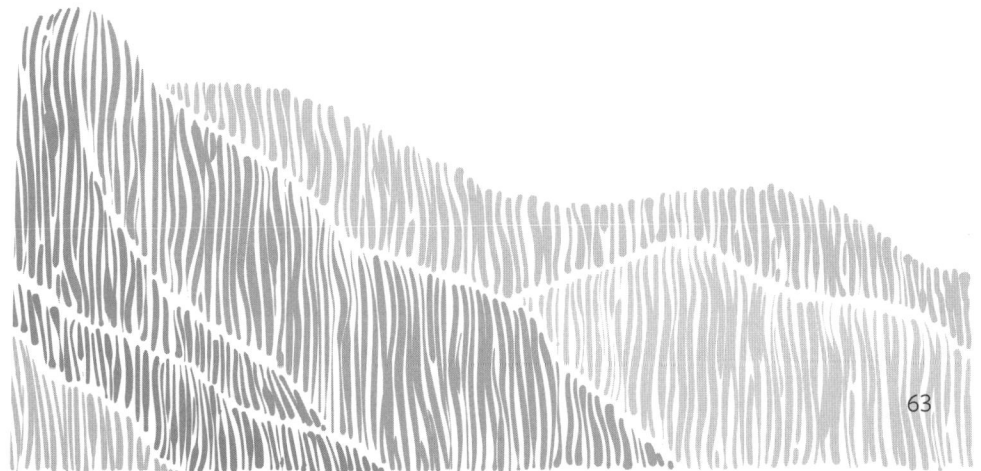

6

THE MISSION OF GOD IN THE OLD TESTAMENT

It is impossible to understand the gospel, the command to preach the good news to all nations, and global disciple-making apart from the Hebrew Scriptures. The mission of God begins there, and a great deal of the church's lack of evangelism and discipleship can be traced back to a failure to understand this and the continuity between the Testaments. There is no theology of evangelism without the Old Testament.

The Baptist was the good news messenger before the arrival of the Lord's servant (Mark 1:1–9; cf. Isa. 40:3; Mal. 3:1). God sent forth his son in "the fullness of time" (Gal. 4:4), not into a first-century vacuum. Jesus came not to create a new religion called Christianity but to continue everything from eternity past and manifested in Genesis 1:1. Jesus's public ministry was revealed with a reading from Isaiah (Luke 4:17–19; cf. Isa. 61:1–2). Drawing back to Daniel's vision, Jesus told his disciples that he will always be with them and that all authority has been given to him (Matt. 28:18–20; cf. Dan. 7:13–14). With his presence, power, and commission, they were to make disciples of all nations. The kingdom was already, but not yet. The disciples were living between the first and second comings of the Messiah. During this time, Joel's prophecy would be fulfilled such that they would receive the power to go into the world (Acts 1:5–8; 2:16–21; cf. Joel 2:28–32). The last days as foretold by the prophets had arrived; now was the day of good news, repentance, forgiveness, and healing as judgment day was approaching.

The gospel as preached by Jesus and the first disciples clarified the storyline and themes of the Old Testament. The church was not an afterthought in God's plan, nor did they believe they were distinct from God's historic work in and through Israel.[1] Ethnic and cultural practices nearly caused the church to split during the first century. Until reports were heard from the field and James cited Amos for theological support, one party believed that gentiles could not be saved by faith alone (Acts 15:13–19; cf. Amos 9:11–12). Paul and Barnabas pointed to Isaiah for the rationale for turning attention toward the gentiles (Acts 13:47; cf. Isa. 49:6). Paul also noted that his apostolic work of taking the gospel to those who never heard was found in the Torah, the Prophets, and the Writings (see Rom. 10:18–20; cf. Deut. 32:21; Ps. 19:4–5; Isa. 65:1). In order to understand New Testament evangelism for contemporary practice, we must see the mission of God starting in the Old Testament.

Protomissio and *Protevangelium*: Hope Through Judgment

The Old Testament describes an apostolic God who reveals himself by *intentionally* sending himself into the created order. From the beginning of Genesis, this God reveals himself to be both transcendent and immanent. He is intimately acquainted with what he brought into existence from nothing. He speaks to the man and woman. He engages them with his presence (Gen. 2:15–23).

Readers are quickly told that this couple was made in God's image (Gen. 1:27), but more is then said about their reason for being: They also had a mission from God. As image-bearers, they were to multiply and fill the earth, enjoying their Creator and his blessings and engaging in the developing of culture and civilization (Gen. 1:28–30). This *protomissio*, or first declaration of God's mission, set in motion a plan that would not change. Even after the fall, God's mission remained the same. Noah and his family, again, created in God's image, were to depart from the ark, multiply, and populate the earth (Gen. 9:1). Though sin had entered into the created order, God was to be glorified throughout the world, and the good news was that those honoring him could enjoy relationship with him.

The effects of the fall hindered people from experiencing the blessings of God and glorifying him throughout the world. Darkness and death entered the cosmos, which now groans (Gen. 3:6; Rom. 8:19–23). Yet, God sent himself

---

1. I recognize that some will take issue with select words in the latter part of this sentence. However, it is beyond the scope of this chapter to address my concerns with certain elements of dispensationalism. For a more developed treatment of my theology, see Payne, *Theology of Mission*.

into the garden with a message of hope through judgment. Death was here, but it was not ultimate. It was possible for God's face to shine upon people and not be hidden by people's sin nature. The *protevangelium*, or first declaration of the gospel, was revealed in Genesis 3:15. A descendant from the woman would be the one to deliver the deathblow to the serpent. Hope would now be found through judgment. God's grace would manifest itself as the population multiplied and filled the earth with their presence.

Blessing Through a Man: Abraham

The Genesis narrative takes a dark turn with Cain's murder of Abel. Instead of the woman's offspring (i.e., Cain) being the one who crushes the serpent's head, he crushes his brother's head. Seth's descendants are offered as a ray of hope, but sin's effects multiply, and soon the reader is introduced to Noah and the judgment to follow. Again, God *intentionally* sends himself into creation to tell the preacher of righteousness about the only hope in view of the coming deluge. After the waters recede, matters do not improve, as the descendants of Adam and Eve continue with the effects of sin.

With Abraham, God's mission becomes very specific and remains so until the fulfillment of Joel's prophecy at Pentecost. The good news is that God now begins working through a particular person and family—Abraham and his descendants—to bring about his blessing to the nations.

God's promise to Abraham of blessings and greatness is a clear example of God's grace upon people, given only by his divine prerogative. Yet, as Johannes Blauw notes, "election is not primarily a privilege but a responsibility."[2] With blessing comes stewardship. Readers should not be quick to overlook God's mission here. Along with God's favor and blessings, the promise is that "in you all the families of the earth shall be blessed" (Gen. 12:3).[3] Rather than Abraham and his descendants consuming God's blessings for themselves, their story was to be intimately connected to God blessing the nations created in his image. God's universal blessing would reach the nations, but it would occur through his particular blessing upon Abraham and his family.

---

2. Blauw, *Missionary Nature of the Church*, 23. See also Braaten, "Meaning of Evangelism," 159.

3. Grammarians have discussed whether in this text the verb *bless* should be translated as passive, reflexive, or as a middle voice, with passive being the traditional approach. Derek Kidner notes that the New Testament (i.e., Acts 3:25; Gal. 3:8) follows the Greek of the Septuagint (i.e., Gen. 22:18; 26:4) and views the verb as passive (*Genesis*, 114). After an extensive treatment, Kenneth Matthews concludes that the passive "probably suits the context of the passage best" (*Genesis 11:27–50:26*, 117).

ISRAEL AS PRIEST, PROPHET, AND KING

Israel was to reflect a kingdom ethic that explained to them, and the world, how to live in relation to God, others within Israel, and the nations. As God's "treasured possession among all peoples," who were to be a "kingdom of priests and a holy nation" (Exod. 19:5–6), Israel was to represent and reveal Yahweh to the nations he had created. Robert Martin-Achard, in his early twentieth-century work on God's mission in the Old Testament, draws attention to Israel's functions.

> We have indicated that the encounter of the heathen with Yahweh, effected by the agency of the Chosen People gathered together at Jerusalem, depends upon the divine initiative alone. It is grounded not in any independent intervention by Israel but in a Yahweh-theophany. The God of Israel reveals Himself to the world which He summons to Jerusalem. Israel is a tool in the hands of its God who uses His People in order to make Himself known to mankind. By the mediation of His faithful who are gathered at Jerusalem, Yahweh bring the nations into communion with Himself.
>
> Finally, Israel has no other mission to the heathen than to be the Chosen People. It is in so far as it is the Holy Nation, consecrated to its God, that it will reflect His glory and testify to His holiness, and in this way, by its very existence in the world, it will assume its mediatorial function: it is through Israel that Yahweh will manifest His sovereign power and utter His Word. The duty devolving upon the Chosen People assumes three complementary aspects: its task is to communicate the divine oracle, to speak in the name of Yahweh, and to testify to His kingship over the whole of creation: in short, *the eschatological mission of Israel to the world consists in its taking upon itself the offices of priest, prophet and king. What Moses was for Israel at the decisive hour in its history, Yahweh's People will be for mankind when God brings in the Messianic Age.*
>
> Martin-Achard, Light to the Nations, 75
(emphasis in original).

Questions

1. Do you agree with Martin-Achard that Israel's mission was to be the chosen people? Explain.
2. How would you explain the mission of Jonah and Isaiah 66:18–23 in light of Israel's overall mission? Do you think that Israel was to "go" to the nations with Yahweh's message? Explain.
3. How is the church's mission to take the gospel to the nations both similar and dissimilar to Israel's mission in the Old Testament?

Blessing Through a People and Land: Israel

Following four hundred years of slavery, the Hebrews were delivered by Moses and given the covenant at Mount Sinai. Faithful to his covenant with Abraham, God elevated Israel to a global position whereby they could share and show how life was to be lived in relationship with the Creator. He called them to be his "treasured possession among all peoples," and to be "a kingdom of priests and a holy nation" (Exod. 19:5–6).[4] They would represent God to the nations and represent the nations to God. Christopher Wright notes that Israel "will neither be the *agent by whom* nor the *source from which* blessing will come, but they will be the *means through which* God (the true agent and source) will extend his blessing to the universal scope of his promise."[5] As they obeyed the statutes, they would find wisdom and understanding "in the sight of the peoples, who, when they hear all these statutes, will say, 'Surely this great nation is a wise and understanding people'" (Deut. 4:6).

The blessing of the nations was connected to Israel's obedience. Michael Goheen observes that Israel's location in the land and walk with God were to set a visible example to the nations. Israel was to extend an invitation to those around them: "This is where history is going—come and join us."[6]

Blessing Through a Person and Place: Land, Tabernacle, and Temple

The promised land served as a bridge connecting three continents. Nations passing between these locations would travel and stay in Israel and be exposed to this nation of priests and their ethical monotheism and God. The tabernacle, and ultimately the temple, served as the epicenter of the divine and human interaction. God encountered his people, and the nations, here.

The Davidic covenant builds upon the Abrahamic and Mosaic covenants to provide greater specificity as to how God will bless the nations. David's name will be great, Israel will be established in the land, rest will be provided from enemies, and an eternal dynasty will follow with one of his descendants (2 Sam. 7:1–17). Solomon's dedicatory prayer for the temple reveals the universal relevance for the place. It is a prayer filled with good news. His request was for God to bless greatly the foreigner for a purpose related to God's mission: "When a foreigner, who is not of your people Israel, comes from a far country for your name's sake (for they shall hear of your great name and your mighty

---

4. Peter applies these words to followers of Jesus (1 Pet. 2:9).
5. C. Wright, *Mission of God*, 253 (emphasis in original).
6. Goheen, *Light to the Nations*, 51.

hand, and of your outstretched arm), when he comes and prays toward this house, hear in heaven your dwelling place and do according to all for which the foreigner calls to you, in order that all the peoples of the earth may know your name and fear you, as do your people Israel" (1 Kings 8:41–43).

The prayer also concludes with this universal purpose. Solomon pleaded for God to hear his words and maintain his mission with Israel "that all the peoples of the earth may know that the LORD is God; there is no other" (1 Kings 8:60). Again, Goheen's thoughts are helpful here:

> The temple nourishes Israel's missional identity and role by holding before Israel the goal of God's redemption: to fill the whole earth with his glorious presence. The temple provides the sacrificial system as a way to repair the people's failure and set them on the right path again; it provides worship to nurture faithfulness, celebrates an alternative worldview to that of paganism, stands as a witness to the true God and the real world, and exhorts Israel to exercise a universal vision. To miss the missional significance of the temple is to misunderstand profoundly the role of the temple in Israel's life.[7]

Blessing Through a Person: Servant and Spirit

Sadly, Israel failed to walk faithfully with God. Though the prophets called Israel to repentance, the people refused and continued to scorn their blessings in acts of idolatry. God promised that if such unrepentance continued, he would raise up nations to serve as a sword in his hand (Deut. 28:25). His promises would be kept; the nations would be blessed even if a remnant had to go through atrocities. In exile, Israel was to be a blessing to the nations around them (Jer. 29:4–7). If God's people would not bear witness to the good news of their God in their land, he would use them in exiled captivity to manifest his glory.

Assyria defeated the ten northern tribes in 722 BC, followed by the destruction of the two southern tribes by the Babylonians in 587 BC. Even during Israel's dark days, a message of hope was proclaimed by the prophets. However, judgment would precede rest and restoration. After Persia destroyed the Babylonians, Cyrus allowed those captured by Babylon to return to the land and rebuild (2 Chron. 36:22–23; Ezra 1:1–11).

Joel told of an unusually great outpouring of God's Spirit on his people. Ezekiel understood that once this occurred, they would be a great nation with God's indwelling Spirit and with hardened hearts replaced with fleshy

---

7. Goheen, *Light to the Nations*, 59.

ones containing God's law and bent toward obedience (Ezek. 36:22–32; 37:1–14). Jeremiah described a new and everlasting covenant to come that would also be connected to the hearts of the people (Jer. 31:31–40; 32:36–41).

Isaiah addressed the servant of God as a "light for the nations" and said that the nations were a gift to the servant (Isa. 42:1–7; 49:1–7; 50:4–9; 52:13–15; 53:1–12). The prophets foresaw a time when the nations would come to Israel to serve God (Isa. 2:2–3; Mic. 4:1–2). People of the nations would be so excited that on hearing of someone traveling to Jerusalem, they would "take hold of the robe of a Jew, saying, 'Let us go with you, for we have heard that God is with you'" (Zech. 8:23). In a scandalous statement, it was said that God would bless Egypt and Assyria and count them as equivalent to Israel (Isa. 19:23–25). The temple was to be called a "house of prayer for all peoples" (Isa. 56:7).

As the Old Testament closed with Israel restored to the land (2 Chron. 36:22–23) and the anticipation of Elijah before the day of the Lord (Mal. 4:5–6), one wonders if the words of the psalmists continued to echo in their memories:

> All the ends of the earth shall remember and turn to the Lord, and all the families of the nations shall worship before you. For kingship belongs to the Lord, and he rules over the nations. (Ps. 22:27–28)

> Say among the nations, "The Lord reigns!" (Ps. 96:10)

> May God be gracious to us and bless us and make his face to shine upon us, that your way may be known on earth, your saving power among all nations. Let the peoples praise you, O God; let all the peoples praise you! (Ps. 67:1–3)

Four centuries would expire before the births of the Baptist and Jesus. Persia would be defeated by the Greeks. Hellenization would spread throughout the world. The Greeks would fall to the Romans, who would keep many aspects of Hellenization. The *pax Romana* (Roman peace), road systems, Greek language and thought, numerous cults searching for fulfillment, Judaism, and the Jewish diaspora all helped create a fertile soil for the coming of David's son, the promised Spirit, and rapid, widespread dissemination of the gospel.[8] The time was fulfilled, the kingdom had come near; God's image-bearers were to repent and believe the good news (Mark 1:15).

---

8. Green, *Evangelism in the Early Church*, 13–28. God's timing was so precise, Green notes, that "the spread of Christianity would have been inconceivable had Jesus been born half a century earlier" (13).

— QUESTIONS TO CONSIDER —

1. What has been your understanding of the Old Testament in relation to evangelism? Why?
2. What is the significance of finding the *protomissio* and *protevangelium* in God rather than the church in the New Testament?

7

EVANGELISM AND THE GREAT COMMISSION

A global survey conducted by the Lausanne Movement solicited responses from fifteen hundred leaders about matters related to the Great Commission. Leaders in Africa, Asia, and Latin America perceived that 30 to 40 percent of Christians in their regions viewed the Great Commission as optional. This percentage rose to 50 percent in North America, Europe, and Australia. In all regions, no more than 16 percent perceived that local churches were "very much united" by a shared commitment to the Great Commission. The majority of survey participants stated that less than half the Christians in their regions would be able to define the Great Commission. In all regions, no leaders believed that more than half of Christians felt prepared to share the gospel.[1]

The church exists by evangelism, just as a fire exists by burning. Where there is no evangelism, there is no church. I recognize that some will take issue with these sentences, if for no other reason than I have revised one of the most famous mission-related statements of the early twentieth century. In 1931 Emil Brunner wrote, "The Church exists by mission, just as a fire exists

---

1. Lausanne Movement, "Great Commission Discipleship." While a limitation of the survey methodology is related to leaders' perceptions about a wide range of people in their areas, the findings are important and troubling. They reveal a likely reality throughout the world, even where the church is the largest and growing the fastest. The Lausanne study seems to reveal a fundamental limitation in disciple-making throughout the world. When regional leaders were asked, "What percentage of members in your local church would say they feel prepared to share the Gospel with others?," the responses were: Africa, 40 percent; Asia, 46 percent; Europe, 44 percent; Latin America, 47 percent; North America, 37 percent; Oceania, 36 percent.

by burning. Where there is no mission there is no Church; and where there is neither Church nor mission, there is no faith."[2] Brunner's words are important, but they were produced during a time when many people assumed that all church activities were considered "mission." Almost three decades later, the confusion reached such a height that Stephen Neill produced another famous statement: "If everything that the Church does is to be classified as 'mission,' we shall have to find another term for the Church's particular responsibility for 'the heathen,' those who have never yet heard the Name of Christ; and that, in 1959, means half of the people now living on the earth."[3] Both Brunner's and Neill's words attempted to change the tide. However, the language of mission has come to mean a variety of matters. Definition is in the eye of the beholder. Even within the church, we now must ask one another for definitions when we speak.[4] Even among evangelicals, the church can engage in "mission" activities and the gospel never be shared. Two millennia after Jesus's words to the first disciples, evangelism and teaching obedience have become two activities among a plethora of ecclesiastical endeavors. Everything is now equivalent. In several traditions there is no longer a prioritization, including for global engagement. In response to Neill's concern for terminology related to unbelievers, we should hold that *evangelizing* and *discipling* are two classic terms that should remain, with the former referring to sharing the gospel with the unregenerate and the latter to teaching obedience to those in the faith—in this case, new believers.

The church's global task involves activities in addition to evangelism. The church is called not to make converts but rather to make disciples. But what is a disciple, and how is one made? In brief, a "disciple" (μαθητής, *mathētēs*) is a follower, pupil, learner. One becomes such when they become a follower of Jesus. With Christ, there was no spectrum of disciple. A person did not progress into redemption as if they were only 80 percent in the kingdom and making progress. Either a person had received the seal of the Spirit and was thus a disciple, or they had not and remained outside the kingdom (2 Cor. 1:22; 5:5; Eph. 1:13; 4:30).

But if the church is not called to make converts, how are disciples made? People become disciples through evangelism and grow in the faith as they are

---

2. Brunner, *Word and the World*, 108.

3. Neill, *Creative Tension*, 81–82. Interestingly, with no reference to Neill, David Larsen provided a related view on evangelism with this statement: "If everything the church does is evangelism or an equivalent to evangelism, we have obviously lost evangelism in any significant sense.... Thus the meaning of evangelism is skewed and distorted beyond recognition" (*Evangelism Mandate*, 13–14).

4. For more on this matter, see Payne, *Apostolic Imagination*.

taught to apply the Scriptures to life.⁵ Disciple-making begins with regeneration and continues throughout life as a process of sanctification. However, it is beyond the scope of this book to address the details of actions after conversion. For now, it must be emphasized that the global task of the church, at home and abroad, is not simply evangelism—but begins with evangelism.

To return to my revision of Brunner, the church came into existence with Jesus's call to follow him (John 1:43). Coupled with the call to be a disciple is the call to reach other people with the blessing one has received (Matt. 4:19; Mark 1:17). Jesus builds his church as people make the same great confession that Peter made (Matt. 16:16; cf. Rom. 10:9). If disciples do not reproduce by bearing fruit (John 15:1–5), the church on earth will cease to exist. The church came into existence by Jesus's evangelistic activity (John 1:14; 3:16). The church grows and multiplies through evangelism (Acts 2:41; 6:1, 7; 9:31; 19:8–10; Col. 1:5–7; 1 Thess. 1:8–10; 2 Thess. 3:1).

As we consider the church's global task, conversations quickly turn to what is referred to as the Great Commission, usually a reference to Matthew 28:18–20. We will look at this passage below; however, note that Jesus's statements about his disciples' global task may be located in all four Gospels and Acts. In each of these books, the disciples are informed that they will be sent into the world to engage in work that Jesus modeled during his three years with them. Each writer approaches the content of the commission from a slightly different angle. When taken together, the passages outline the global approach of evangelizing and discipling that was to be used following the ascension of Jesus.⁶

Proclaiming the Gospel to All (Mark 13:10; 14:9)

Mark twice references the global scope of the dissemination of the gospel. In both instances, Jesus's words foreshadow a coming day when the good news would be proclaimed beyond the borders of Israel. During the Olivet Discourse, four of the disciples inquire as to the time of the destruction of

---

5. For an influential twentieth-century perspective on the Great Commission and evangelism, see McGavran, *Bridges of God*. McGavran believed that "make disciples" (Matt. 28:19) was evangelism, and the "teaching" (Matt. 28:20) was what he called "perfecting," which was related to growth in the faith.

6. Marvin Newell has written a couple of helpful books examining these different commission passages. In his research, he finds significance in the chronological order and different emphases. I deviate from Newell's passages by substituting Mark 13:10 and 14:9 for Mark 16:15, which was not found in the earliest manuscripts. See Newell, *Commissioned*. Another excellent and thorough work on the Great Commission is Akin, Merkle, and Robinson, *40 Questions*.

the temple. After giving a warning about false prophets, wars and rumors of wars, earthquakes, and persecution, Jesus states, "The gospel must first be proclaimed to all nations" (Mark 13:10).[7] The disciples' arrests will allow for them to bear witness to Christ during such difficult times. This global activity serves as an eschatological marker, for until the nations hear and times of tribulation unfold, the parousia will not occur (Mark 13:24–27). Not even the angels know when the Son of Man's coming will take place, so the disciples are to be alert and endure to the end (Mark 13:13, 32–36).

The second Markan account is found a few verses later, describing Jesus's anointing by the woman in the home of Simon the leper. Observers viewed the use of the ointment on Jesus's body as a waste, saying it should have been sold to provide for the poor (Mark 14:3–6). Jesus commended her sacrifice to prepare him for his burial. Her "beautiful thing" done for the Messiah would be told in her memory "wherever the gospel is proclaimed in the whole world" (Mark 14:9; cf. Matt. 26:13; John 12:1–8).

Covering the whole world would have been a daunting task for the first-century disciples. How much more so if their knowledge of geography matched that of the twenty-first century! Only one with all authority in heaven and earth could enable the disciples for such work. As the Son had been sent into the world for the world, soon the disciples would be sent as well to continue the global task.

Sending That All May Be Forgiven (John 20:21–23)

On the evening of the resurrection, Jesus visited his disciples in a room locked away from the threat of the Jews. During this moment of fear, Jesus spoke peace to the few present. Though they were huddled in this space, he shared, "As the Father has sent me, even so I am sending you. . . . If you forgive the sins of any, they are forgiven them; if you withhold forgiveness from any, it is withheld" (John 20:21, 23). This sending and the provision of the Spirit showed a continuity between Jesus's mission and that of his disciples.[8] Commenting on this passage, Johannes Blauw writes, "Man is, as it were, the arm of God by which He directs His saving acts, man is taken up actively in God's

---

7. Debate surrounds whether this text advocates that the parousia will occur only after all the nations have heard. For a recent discussion see Hesselgrave, *Paradigms in Conflict*, 279–314. Johannes Blauw held to the belief that global evangelism was a sign of the end and not a means to fulfillment (*Missionary Nature of the Church*, 106). Regardless, at the time of this writing, Jesus has not returned—and many people groups remain unengaged.

8. Köstenberger, *Missions of Jesus*, 192.

design of salvation."⁹ The forgiveness of sins was intimately connected with the disciples being sent from the room into a dangerous context where sinners would cause them harm. Yet, the sinners could not experience forgiveness until the forgiven had been sent with the same message that they had received.[10]

Martin Erdmann's engagement with this text led him to conclude:

> Jesus' activity as the one sent by the Father serves as the definitive example for his followers as they seek to fulfill their mission. Jesus was always obedient, striving to complete the Father's work and to communicate the Father's message. . . . Likewise, the disciples of Jesus must respond with faithful obedience, regardless of the cost. They continue to witness to the truth of God's message in order that others may find life and forgiveness in Jesus. . . . Their ministry is to tell the world that forgiveness of sins is available in Christ.[11]

Jesus's promise was not that his disciples would be sent in the *same* fashion as he had been sent. They were not to die for the sins of the world. Their sending, though grounded on the apostolic nature of the coming of the Messiah, would be reflective but not an exact replication of his ministry.

Anyone who sins is a slave to sin. However, only the Son could redeem the enslaved (John 8:31–36). Eternal life comes to those who manifest faith in the Son (John 3:16). Without knowledge of such truth, people remain separated from the Creator. If the disciples were not sent into the community with the message of hope through judgment, no sins would be forgiven. If the disciples withheld this message of forgiveness, no one would be forgiven. The trust they had received was to be passed along to those without it.

Making Disciples of All (Matthew 28:18–20)

Marvin Newell notes that the Matthean account of the Great Commission emphasizes the method by which the peoples of the world would be reached.[12] As the disciples were to go into all the world, the command given was for them to "make disciples." Three years prior, Jesus's hearers were not his followers. What they had experienced, what they had become and were growing into, was what they were to share throughout the world among all the peoples. John Harvey

---

9. Blauw, *Missionary Nature of the Church*, 88.
10. Köstenberger, *Missions of Jesus*, 193. D. A. Carson notes that while John's text reminds readers of the parallel statement in Matt. 18:18, there the attention is on church discipline. However, with John 20:23 the context is mission and "the focus is on evangelism" (*John*, 655).
11. Erdmann, "Mission in John's Gospel," 222.
12. Newell, *A Third of Us*, 18.

notes that Matthew's use of μαθητεύω (*mathēteuō*, "make/become a disciple") is limited to four instances in the New Testament, three of which are exclusive to Matthew and should be taken in context:[13] "For Matthew, the focus of the disciples' mission is less one of public proclamation than one of intensive instruction. This perspective, of course, is in accord with Matthew's portrait of Jesus as a teacher who repeatedly instructs his disciples at length and in depth. Such intensive instruction would be viewed by Matthew's Jewish readers as natural for any disciple, but as especially necessary for Gentiles coming into the church."[14]

While the emphasis is ongoing instruction, the initial audience would have understood that no one embraces baptism without embracing the gospel—a matter foreign to later church traditions. For disciples to be made and experience baptism and teaching, they first had to be initiated into the kingdom. Though baptism marked their declaration of faith, the discipleship journey began with hearing, understanding, and owning, by faith, the good news.

Jesus preached, "Repent, for the kingdom of heaven is at hand" (Matt. 4:17). Though a message similar to the Baptist's (Matt. 3:2), its roots extended back to the Davidic covenant and Daniel. David had been promised an eternal kingdom (2 Sam. 7:1–17). The prophet foresaw a day in which "the God of heaven will set up a kingdom that shall never be destroyed"; this kingdom would be such a mighty foe that "it shall break in pieces" all other kingdoms "and bring them to an end" (Dan. 2:44–45) and was given to the "one like a son of man" (Dan. 7:13–14).

Though the Great Commission concludes the First Gospel, an understanding of what it means to see people become disciples of Jesus may be found only by returning to the beginning of the book. Immediately following Jesus's preaching, Matthew notes that he called his disciples to follow him (Matt. 4:19). Anyone who wanted to "follow" Jesus had to "repent" of the direction in which they were going with their lives. This change of thought and action was the beginning of a lifelong process of growing as a disciple through understanding and applying the teachings of Jesus to life.

Matthew's Great Commission was not given to the disciples for them to go and find people who had been in the kingdom for a lengthy period and then to go deeper in the faith. That is part of the disciple-making process. The context, however, was that the disciples were to go to people *outside the kingdom*, sharing with them the message of repentance of sin and belief in the Messiah for entrance into the kingdom. Following baptism, they were to be taught to obey all that Christ commanded. Apart from the evangelistic

---

13. Matt 13:52; 27:57; 28:19. The fourth occurrence is in Acts 14:21.
14. Harvey, "Mission in Matthew," 131–32.

work of the disciples, there is no teaching obedience.[15] The unregenerate are unable to grow and develop into something they are not. Unless the good news is proclaimed, non-disciples will not become disciples, and the command of Christ will be neglected.

Proclaim to All: Repentance for Forgiveness of Sins (Luke 24:44–49)

Luke makes clear that of all the things Jesus could have done, he came "to seek and to save the lost" (Luke 19:10). After the two from Emmaus shared their encounter with the resurrected Jesus, the Lord appeared among the disciples. He explained that his resurrection had been foretold in the Torah, the Prophets, and the Writings. His exhortation to the believers was emphatic and specific. All nations should hear a message proclaimed of "repentance for the forgiveness of sins" (Luke 24:47). As the disciples engaged in evangelism, they were participating in the fulfillment of Scripture.[16] Luke was no stranger to the theme of the gentile in both his Gospel and Acts.[17] The disciples were to remain in Jerusalem until the coming of the Spirit (Luke 24:49). They would not be alone or abandoned in the work. They were to begin in the city with the good news of forgiveness and then move beyond its borders.

Their proclamation would mark an early stage of the conversion process. The Messiah's exaltation would allow for Israel to experience repentance (Acts 5:31). In a short period of time, Peter would proclaim the gospel during Pentecost. His message would include a call to commitment. Hearers were to "repent . . . for the forgiveness of your sins" (Acts 2:38).

This μετάνοια (*metanoia*, "repentance") is a change of mind or heart. It is a turning from one direction toward another. This transition was accompanied with a change of lifestyle and mindset and moved one to the way of the Messiah. For those deciding to come after Christ, they would be required to deny self, take up their cross, and follow him (Luke 9:23) who came to create division on earth (Luke 12:51). Those who fail to repent are those who will perish (Luke 13:3), but those who repent bring great rejoicing to the angels of God (Luke 15:10). Embracing this message was costly (Luke 14:25–33), for "no one who puts his hand to the plow and looks back is fit for the kingdom of God" (Luke 9:62). But those who "hear the word of God and keep it" are indeed "blessed" (Luke 11:28).

---

15. Roland Leavell refers to Matthew's Great Commission as the "*Magna Carta* of evangelism" (*Evangelism*, 3).
16. Larkin, "Mission in Luke," 168.
17. Polhill, *Acts*, 67.

THE RELATIONSHIP BETWEEN EVANGELISTS AND MAKING DISCIPLES

In 1994 Charles Crabtree, of the Assemblies of God, spoke on the topic "Disciples Are Our Number One Goal" to the attendees of the North American Council of Itinerant Evangelists. The following is taken from his presentation noting the important relationship between the evangelist and disciple-making.

> Why should we, as evangelists, become involved in the process of making disciples? The obvious answer is in the fact that our Master commanded us to make disciples. That one fact alone should be enough to make the task of discipleship a personal mandate and responsibility. . . .
>
> Why did Christ make disciples? He knew His work would be relatively short on earth (as is ours). He knew it was important for the ministry He established to continue when He finished His earthly sojourn. He knew the only way to effectively build His church was to pour His life into others (as should we). Discipleship was the mechanism to perpetuate His life and ministry. . . .
>
> Why should we make disciples? Because the leaders of the New Testament church commanded and modeled discipleship on every level. They did not exclude discipleship from the office of the evangelist. . . .
>
> Unless the evangelist, and for that matter the whole church of Christ, begins to demand discipleship from every convert, and provide for it, decisions for Christ will become statistics for disaster rather than a growing potential for a victorious church. . . .
>
> The future of the church as we see it in America is at stake around the issue of discipleship and the subsequent quality of the Christ-life. . . .
>
> When an evangelist does not believe he has the responsibility to make disciples, a subtle change takes place which leads to a self-centered ministry rather than a Kingdom ministry. This shift results in diminishing effectiveness. . . .
>
> The evangelist is a gift to the entire body. . . . The evangelist should give his life to proclaiming the Gospel, training others in evangelism, and studying the principles which lead to conserving the spiritual harvest he has been called to gather. He should become an expert in evangelism and discipleship for the purpose of being an effective resource to the Kingdom of God.
>
> Crabtree, "Disciples," 640, 642, 643, 645.

Questions

1. Do you agree with Crabtree's conviction that the evangelist should be involved in disciple-making? Why or why not?
2. What do you think Crabtree means when he notes that it is possible for "decisions for Christ" to "become statistics for disaster"?
3. What is the difference between converts and disciples?

The good news to be shared among the nations was a message of hope through judgment. Forgiveness and entrance into God's kingdom required one to consider the claims of the Messiah in light of one's essence. People were called to examine themselves from a divine perspective. Hope for the present and future was possible, but such examination drove listeners to a declaration of agreement with God. They were sinners in need of repentance. Acknowledgment of this judgment call was to lead to life.

Witness to All (Acts 1:8)

The last of the global-commission-related passages is found in the beginning of Acts. Following the outpouring of the Spirit, marking the last days, the disciples were to be Jesus's μάρτυρες (*martyres*, "witnesses"). Again, Luke begins with the Jews in Jerusalem and notes that this bearing of testimony was to be in regions throughout the world. A global witnessing movement marked the lives of the disciples. Though they thought that the time had arrived when the Messiah was to set up his kingdom in full and overthrow Israel's enemies, a lacuna was necessary. The kingdom would come, but the disciples were to bear witness to what they had observed, heard, and experienced. An examination of the remainder of Acts reveals how these initial believers understood what it meant to be witnesses.

A significant theme in the book is message over messenger as the gospel triumphs over any attempts to thwart its advancement.[18] The witnesses believe that they have a message to share with their words and demonstrate with their lifestyles. Though they are threatened, arrested, imprisoned, and killed, the message of the gospel continues to spread. The movement advances as more and more people become disciples through the witnessing of the believers. The book concludes with Paul under house arrest as he serves as a witness by "proclaiming the kingdom of God and teaching about the Lord Jesus Christ," and, though in such a restricted setting, he does so "without hindrance" (Acts 28:31).

The church is known as a worshiping community and one that cares for its members (Acts 4:34; 6:1). They quickly develop appellations of identity, being called followers of the Way (Acts 9:2; 19:9, 23; 22:4; 24:14) and Christians (Acts 11:26). But the primary way they manifest what it means to be witnesses is with the unique message they verbally share in the marketplace, among households, and before kings. The believers do not get into trouble with those outside God's kingdom because of their good deeds in society. They are not faulted for upright living and incarcerated for wanting to teach

18. Polhill, *Acts*, 71.

their children their beliefs. They are not seen organizing political rallies to overthrow ungodly systems and bring about transformation to the Roman society. As a minority group, originally seen as a sect of Judaism, they encounter problems when they refuse to remain silent about a resurrected Jesus sitting in heaven and returning to judge the world. As they proclaim his message of hope through judgment and teach his ethic, the Spirit works to transform societies. Those found to be against Christ turn up the fires of persecution.

Variations of the Great Commission are found in each Gospel and Acts. The disciples were informed of the message they were to share and the audience to whom they were to go. The gospel would be proclaimed to all nations before the end. Though entrance into Christ's church began with evangelism, kingdom life was not to end with conversion. A lifetime of learning obedience to the commands of Christ was necessary for both the church's sanctification and witness in Jerusalem, Judea, Samaria, and to the ends of the earth.

— QUESTIONS TO CONSIDER —

1. Have you considered the Great Commission to include passages in each of the Gospels and Acts? If not, why?
2. How would you summarize (in one sentence) the Lord's expectations in each of the Great Commission texts?
3. Do you agree or disagree that the church exists by evangelism as a fire exists by burning? Explain.

8

JESUS AND THE APOSTOLIC CHURCH

An examination of the evangelistic practices of Jesus and the early disciples, as described in the Scriptures, is a worthy task. This act is not an attempt to replicate first-century cultures and worldviews; rather, it is an opportunity to imitate that which is godly (1 Cor. 11:1) and was worthy of their time and attention. Unless we are willing to pull them down from their lofty position, we must grant to their approaches some degree of universality throughout the ages. It should be noted that the authors of the texts did not write to teach subsequent generations how to evangelize. Their primary purpose for writing was not to give a model to the world. However, wisdom is found in the history of those who have gone before us. Methods should not be cloned; rather, principles should be discerned and applied to the multitudinous settings throughout the world. As will be noted in this chapter, their evangelistic approaches were not the same in every context. There was never a one-size-fits-all method of evangelism. Rather, the individuals in the Scriptures understood God's message and their audiences, and they attempted to communicate most effectively to such groups.

Several books related to this topic have been published.[1] This chapter outlines eight principles of evangelistic practices found in the New Testament.

---

1. An early and thorough work is Bruce, *Training of the Twelve*. The most popular study, with millions of copies in print, is Coleman, *Master Plan of Evangelism*. Other similar books include Calkins, *How Jesus Dealt with Men*; Hobbs, *New Testament Evangelism*; Scarborough, *How Jesus Won Men*; Coleman, *The Master's Way*; Miles, *How Jesus Won Persons*; Barrs,

These are offered not as an exhaustive list, but rather as a starting point for understanding some of the governing elements related to Jesus and the early disciples. They used a variety of different evangelistic methods, some unique to their day and settings and some translatable to other times and contexts.[2]

They Proclaimed an Exclusive Gospel[3]

The message of Jesus and the apostolic church was not just another message (1 Cor. 1:23). It was good news, but an exclusive type of good news. Salvation was found in no one other than Christ, and people had to place explicit faith in him (Acts 4:12). Jesus was seen as the only way to the Father (John 14:6). Repentance toward God and faith in the Lord Jesus were proclaimed to Jew and gentile (Acts 20:21). Herschel Hobbs draws attention to this matter: "These early evangels did not regard a man's sincerity as the sole criteria of the validity of his religion. All had sinned, and come short of the glory of God."[4] This gospel was proclaimed to those following the Jewish religious ways (John 3) and Samaritan faith traditions (John 4; Acts 8). It was proclaimed also to the extremely religious (Acts 17:22–34) and to God-fearers (Acts 10). It was news of love, hope, freedom, healing, deliverance, reconciliation, and forgiveness. It was a message of God incarnating himself among people, dying as atonement for the sins of the world, and rising from the dead (1 Cor. 15:1–4)

They Were Intentional in Sharing the Gospel

Evangelism did not happen by coincidence. The first Christians were intentional in their efforts. Evangelism was not a backup plan in case the other good deeds of the church did not work. John records, "And he had to pass through Samaria" (John 4:4). Though it is easy to miss the gravity of these seven simple English words, it should be remembered that no decent, right-minded Jew would ever pass through Samaria when traveling from Judea to Galilee. Rather than journey through that region, Jewish people would circumvent the entire area. Jesus, however, intentionally entered this location and encountered a Samaritan woman, who along with her village became believers (John 4:39–42).

Learning Evangelism; Paulsen, *New and Ancient Evangelism*. Michael Green broadens his research field to include not only the evangelistic labors in the period of the apostolic church but also the early church until about the fourth century in *Evangelism in the Early Church*.
  2. Terry, *Evangelism*, 14, 24–26.
  3. Portions of this section are from Payne, "Eight Principles of New Testament Evangelism."
  4. Hobbs, *New Testament Evangelism*, 80.

Following this account, Jesus leaves the area. Apparently, the primary reason he traveled through this community was to reach these people with the gospel.

Connected to such intentionality was the eschatological reality of God's mission in the world. The kingdom was breaking in *now* and transforming lives, families, and communities (Luke 17:20–21). The kingdom was also yet to come (Matt. 6:10), as a day of judgment was the next event on God's calendar (Acts 2:20). Between the now and the not yet was the reality that human lives are a vapor (James 4:14). Death draws nigh and then the judgment (Heb. 9:27). Timothy Beougher argues that part of a balanced approach to evangelism is that it be done with sensitivity, integrity, and *urgency*.[5] Such urgency was reflected in their intentionality. Time was short. The captives needed to be set free (Luke 4:18). Now was the moment of salvation (2 Cor. 6:2).

They Were Spirit-Led

Writings regarding the relationship between the Holy Spirit and missions developed significantly in the twentieth century. One early pioneer on the topic was an Anglican missionary-priest, Roland Allen, who wrote extensively on the role of the Spirit in the growth and expansion of the church. In his 1917 groundbreaking work *Pentecost and the World*, he wrote, "At His first coming, the Holy Spirit revealed His nature and His work as world-wide, all-embracing. He revealed His nature as a Spirit who desired the salvation of all men of every nation; He revealed His work as enabling those to whom He came to preach Christ to men of every nation."[6]

The acts of the Spirit recorded in Acts are extensive and saturate the stories in the book. From the beginning (Acts 1:8), the Spirit was the one who enabled the church to witness effectively throughout the world. The church today must understand that this miraculous work of God remains absolutely necessary. Robert Webber, reflecting on contemporary societal shifts in the West from a high value on intellectual arguments to a prioritization on experience, writes, "In the post-Christian world in which the rational methods of modernity are suspect, the reliance on the Holy Spirit to bind a person to Christ has emerged as a primary factor in evangelism."[7] This is not a novel truth but one that the church must recognize as vital. The Spirit was the one who provided boldness to share the gospel (Acts 4:13, 31, 33; 7:55–56; cf. 2 Tim. 1:7). He worked through the apostles to perform signs and wonders

---

5. Beougher, *Invitation to Evangelism*, 176–78.
6. Allen, "Pentecost and the World," 22.
7. Webber, *Ancient-Future Evangelism*, 65.

(Acts 2:43). He called out the apostolic team that was sent from the church in Antioch (Acts 13:1–3).

Following a great awakening in a Samaritan city (Acts 8:4–8), Philip received word from an "angel of the Lord" (Acts 8:26) to go to a southbound road leading from Jerusalem to Gaza and await further instructions. On his arrival, the Spirit told him to go up to the chariot of an Ethiopian who was ready to come to faith (Acts 8:29). Also, the Spirit led Peter to evangelize the household of Cornelius (Acts 10:19–20).

The advancement of the gospel was always coupled with the Spirit's ministry. The church received wisdom from God to know how to speak clearly (John 16:13; 1 Cor. 2:13). As the gospel was communicated, the Spirit would bring conviction of sin, righteousness, and judgment (John 16:8). J. B. Lawrence writes, "Missionaries would preach the gospel in vain to men who are dead in trespasses and in sins if the Holy Spirit did not quicken the perception of these men and make available to them the life-giving, redeeming gospel."[8] The church did not have to manipulate people or create a false sense of guilt to make them respond favorably to the good news. It was with the Spirit's power that people entered the kingdom through evangelism (1 Cor. 2:4; 1 Thess. 1:5; cf. 1 Pet. 1:12). The Spirit's leadership was an absolute necessity in the church's ministry in the first century.

They Understood the Importance of Culture

Jesus and the apostolic church knew about the value of culture in the communication of the gospel. Though the church is not called to be anthropologists and sociologists, there is much value in studying cultures and societies. History contains examples where evangelists, believing themselves to be culturally superior, presupposed that certain cultures were unsuitable for receiving the gospel. Instead of working with the cultural vessels, evangelists wrote off any value or positive leverage they would provide for the good news.[9] David Gustafson writes, "The missional task of communicating the gospel to people who see reality through a different lens requires that we understand their perception of reality and the vocabulary that explains it."[10] For example, in Paul's address on Mars Hill, he begins his message by stating what would have been a compliment to the Athenians, that they were very religious people (Acts 17:22). Continuing, he decides to connect with his Athenian hearers, not with a passage from the Old Testament, but instead quoting freely from

---

8. Lawrence, *Holy Spirit in Missions*, 9.
9. Mugambi, "Evangelism in Africa," 354–59.
10. Gustafson, *Gospel Witness*, 54.

their own poets (Acts 17:28–29). Later, in his defense before Agrippa, Paul made certain to conduct himself appropriately as any proper orator would have before such a statesman by stretching out his hand before proceeding to speak (Acts 26:1). Being aware of the various expectations, mannerisms, and mores of the people to whom they were speaking allowed the early evangelists to connect with their audiences and gain a hearing.

Showing deference to others, especially those with whom one disagrees, reveals humility, respect for them as image-bearers of God, and concern. If the church cares enough to understand a people's traditions, values, and social expectations, then she reveals a care for people. Relating to others with appropriate demeanor, without compromising the gospel message, is a way to love one's neighbor. If the gospel is the good news of God's gift, then the church should do all she can to avoid packaging it in offensive wrapping.

They Were Sensitive to the Context

In the middle of the twentieth century, Lesslie Newbigin brought attention to the shifts occurring in the West that were posing challenges to the advancement of the gospel. For centuries, the church had great social influence under the auspices of Christendom. But the winds of change had been blowing and wearing away the height of the steeple. Newbigin's question, of what would be involved in a missionary encounter between the gospel and the West, is one about understanding and adapting to contexts.[11]

One of the beautiful elements of the power of gospel is its ability to flow into any setting, worldview, or ideology and transform it. Oftentimes the problem in evangelism is not the gospel but rather the adaptability of the church in her methods of engagement and communication. Methods, the how-tos of evangelism, must be held loosely. Unfortunately, like strategy, methods take time to learn and come with the temptation to believe that they are to be universally applied, especially if the Lord used them in powerful ways in some contexts to bring people to faith. Though the message is a constant from the Creator to those created in his image, the messengers must constantly adjust to the people with whom they speak. Flexibility, rather than rigidity, is vital.

Closely related to their understanding of the value of culture was the fact that the methods and gospel presentations of Jesus and the apostolic church

---

11. Newbigin, *Foolishness to the Greeks*, 1. The missional church movement would be birthed from the thoughts and writings of Newbigin and would influence a large number of churches and denominations in traditionally Western countries in the areas of witness and evangelism. The publication that launched this movement in North America is Guder, *Missional Church*. For a concise summary of the movement, see Payne, *Kingdom Expressions*.

varied from situation to situation. Jesus did not speak to Zacchaeus as he did to Nicodemus. Paul did not present himself in the same manner to Agrippa as he did to Lydia or the Philippian jailer. Jesus's encounter with the Gerasene demoniac required a different approach than how he engaged the Samaritan woman.

Methods are developed in specific contexts, in specific moments in history, and reflect the personalities, passions, talents, gifts, experiences, and interests of the evangelist. While methods are important and should be learned, they are best seen as tools to be added to one's Great Commission toolbox. A hammer is a great method for putting a nail in a board. But if the board needs to be cut, a saw is the appropriate means for the task. Sensitivity to context means that the church is always to be developing methods and refining older ones as she goes into all the world.[12] The church's toolbox is to be ever expanding because contexts are ever changing.

They Began Where People Were in Their Spiritual Journeys

Jerram Barrs observes that Jesus "varied his approach according to his understanding of the place each person had reached in his or her journey either toward or away from the Lord: some needed only a gracious invitation to come and lay the burdens of their failures and sorrows, or the beauty of their lives, at his feet; others needed a gentle push; others a firm challenge; still others had to be sent away to face the idols of their hearts, or the self-righteousness of their attitudes to God and to their fellow human beings."[13] In many evangelistic encounters, Jesus and the apostolic church began with the people's felt needs at the moment. Finding common ground is critical to clear communication. Mark McCloskey notes the value of a point of contact: "Many people reject or remain indifferent to the gospel not so much because they disagree with it, but because it is alien to their world of thought and outside of their realm of comprehension."[14] Since Nicodemus believed that his genealogical account was sufficient to earn God's favor, Jesus spoke of being "born again" (John 3:3). The Samaritan woman was concerned not with her heritage, but rather with getting water from a well; Jesus used the felt need as an opportunity to speak of "living water" (John 4:10). Philip did not begin sharing with the Ethiopian a discourse about Adam and Eve but rather started preaching from the passage about which the man had questions (Acts 8:35).

---

12. Michael Green provides an extensive treatment of the evangelistic methods used in the first three centuries of the church (*Evangelism in the Early Church*, 194–235).
13. Barrs, *Learning Evangelism*, 249.
14. McCloskey, *Tell It Often*, 34.

GOSPEL-CULTURAL HERMENEUTICS

Sam Chan's approach to connecting the gospel with an audience is threefold: (1) Enter—find a cherished "cultural text" and explain it from a kingdom perspective; (2) Challenge—speak using language and expressions from the people's point of view; (3) Fulfill—show how Jesus fulfills their cultural story line. Here, Chan reflects on Paul's time in Athens:

> One of the best biblical examples of gospel-cultural hermeneutics is found in Acts 17:16–34, when the apostle Paul visits Athens. . . . In Athens, the cultural texts were the idols, and these idols fulfilled the Athenians' existential cry for transcendence. In their storyline, the Athenians wanted blessings from the gods, and the idols would appease the wrath of the gods. Notice how Paul empathizes with this desire: "I see that in every way you are very religious."
>
> Paul's understanding and empathy are evidence that Paul has entered their culture. That's the first step. Now that he has entered, he next challenges it: "You are ignorant of the very thing you worship." Paul describes to the Athenians their own storyline. They want to worship the gods, to get their blessing and appease their wrath. But they won't find their happy ending because they don't know the name of the Unknown God.
>
> Finally, Paul fulfills their storyline. He gives them Jesus as the happy ending that their culture's storyline is looking for: "This is what I am going to proclaim to you." He gives them Jesus as the Unknown God that they want to worship, but whose name they do not know. The Unknown God can now be the Known God.
>
> Chan, Evangelism, 158–59.

Questions

1. What are some cultural texts in your community?
2. How would you describe those texts from a kingdom perspective?
3. How does Jesus satisfy the cravings that those texts seek to fulfill?

They Were Sensitive to the Fears, Hurts, and Concerns of Others While Speaking the Truth in Love

Evangelistic practice has developed the stereotype of being more like a salesperson attempting to win a consumer to a new product.[15] While there are

---

15. Richardson, "Will to Power," 94–95. Some of the negative reputation can be attributed to book titles and practices based on Prov. 11:30: "The fruit of the righteous is a tree of life; and he

examples of such caricatures, they are not reflective of the biblical example. Within the text, the thread of truth-telling is intertwined with the thread of sensitivity. Conviction and compassion are wed together. It appears that the first evangelists responded accordingly to the attitudes and actions of the people. Those interested and open were approached differently than the hostile and opposed. Though Jesus could have spent much time speaking about the evils of adultery and fornication to the Samaritan woman, he instead acknowledged her wickedness and continued the conversation (John 4:17–18). Jesus could have scolded and severely rebuked Zacchaeus for having wicked business practices (Luke 19:7). He decided, however, to stay at his house, bring salvation (Luke 19:9), and develop the reputation as a friend of tax collectors and sinners (Luke 7:34). Jesus and the apostolic church never denied wickedness. They called people to repentance out of love (Mark 10:21), even when they spoke rebuke to the self-righteous (Luke 13:3).

The call to follow Christ is a call to die to self and take up the cross (Luke 9:23–24). The cost is to be counted (Luke 14:25–33). For some people, the cost is greater than for others. Some idols have blinded the minds of people to such a degree that the fear, heartache, loss, and destruction are more than they wish to bear. The abdication of relationships, identities, lifestyles, worldviews, prestige, honor, responsibilities, finances, and career platforms may come at tremendous sacrifice. Those sharing the gospel must be concerned with what weighs on the hearts and minds of unbelievers. A good practice is to place oneself in the other person's shoes. We may know the value of the pearl of great price (Matt. 13:45–46) and the peace of Christ that passes all understanding (Phil. 4:6–7), but such is unknown to the unregenerate. A failure to be sensitive to their fears, hurts, and concerns is a hindrance to evangelism.

They Were Postconversion Oriented

As noted in the previous chapter, evangelism is the first step of the Great Commission; the mandate to the church included making disciples (Matt. 28:19). Priscilla Pope-Levison brings attention to this matter, noting that conversion is the beginning of the relationship: "Remember, too, that when your friends decide to follow Christ, your interaction with them is not done. They are not

---

that winneth souls is wise" (KJV). Though the nomenclature is unpopular today, publications may be found with "winning," "winner of souls," and "soul winning" in their titles, from the respected C. H. Spurgeon's *The Soul Winner* to the methodologically questionable C. S. Lovett's *Soul Winning Made Easy*. An exception to this use of language is the recent publication of Medders and Logan, *Soul-Winning Church*.

projects to be completed, a means to an end. An important part of following up includes connecting them with a church, a small group, a Bible study, or online resources to help them deepen and strengthen their fledgling faith. Another often overlooked aspect of follow up is to mentor your friends in personal evangelism so they can become evangelists to others."[16]

The New Testament was not written to provide its readers with every detail of the historic events. It is easy to wonder what happened to those first-century people who were evangelized but are not mentioned again in the Scriptures. Despite this silence, Jesus and the apostolic church were concerned with what occurred in the lives of people after they came to faith. A simple reading of the book of Acts and the New Testament Epistles reveals that the new believers were gathered together in new churches. Church planting was (and still is) a major part of fulfilling the Great Commission. Following the conversion of the Gerasene demoniac, the man begs Jesus to allow him to get into the boat and accompany him. Rather than agreeing to the man's plea, Jesus immediately calls the man to obedience and to bear fruit for the kingdom by sending him back to his region to proclaim the works of God (Mark 5:19). The result? The man obeyed and "everyone marveled" (Mark 5:20). Delos Miles comments on this passage, noting that the one thing the man had "which qualified him to be a witness was that God had done some things for him."[17] Philip made certain that the Ethiopian received baptism (Acts 8:36–39). Paul and his team did likewise; they planted local expressions of the body of Christ (Acts 13–14; 16:11–34), followed up to appoint leaders (Acts 14:23; Titus 1:5), returned to visit and teach, and wrote letters with instructions as well. As noted earlier, evangelism is the tip of the Great Commission iceberg. It is what brings one into the kingdom of God and his church. Evangelism is the beginning, not the ending. It addresses the initial phase of sanctification known as regeneration. Though this book is focused on this topic, biblical evangelism is done with a concern that new believers will become fruit-bearing disciples in local churches.

Though the New Testament was not written primarily to instruct in evangelism, it is possible for the church to learn from what is described in the texts. A study of Jesus and the first disciples reveals a variety of approaches used when they encountered individuals and groups of people. The call to turn from the gods of this world was a constant in their message, but the means by which they delivered this truth varied from context to context.

16. Pope-Levison, *Models of Evangelism*, 25.
17. Miles, *How Jesus Won Persons*, 39.

— **QUESTIONS TO CONSIDER** —

1. Are you aware of any additional evangelism principles in the New Testament not mentioned in this chapter? If so, describe them.
2. Which of the eight principles do you feel most comfortable applying to your life? Least comfortable? Why?

9

DIVINE SOVEREIGNTY AND ELECTION

A theology of biblical evangelism is a trinitarian theology. Disciple-making was not an afterthought in God's heart. He was involved in his mission before the world was established (Eph. 1:4; Rev. 13:8). This chapter, as well as those remaining in this section, addresses theological issues related to evangelism. Though such study often results in lively debates, without expressions of God's sovereignty and omniscience no one would experience eternal life. Regardless of one's theological camp, election brings blessing *and great responsibility*. This is an important reminder whenever the church is tempted to substitute evangelism for debating matters of divine mystery. There is a good and rightful place for study and respectful and passionate dialogue, but not to the neglect of making Christ known that others may enter the kingdom. Election does not negate evangelism as the divine means to bring people to salvation (1 Thess. 1:4–5; 2 Thess. 2:13–14; James 1:18). Rather, it makes evangelism a certain necessity.

Sovereignty

God acts according to his will among the nations and the hosts of heaven (Dan. 4:35). He speaks everything into existence (Gen. 1:1), sustains everything through the Son (Neh. 9:6; Heb. 1:3), brings people into his kingdom by the Spirit (John 3:5), and will restore the groaning creation (2 Pet. 3:12–13; Rev. 21). He is described as a sovereign king over the entire world by both his people (2 Kings 19:15; Pss. 47:2; 103:19; 1 Tim. 6:15) and pagan rulers (Dan. 4:34–37). His reign is eternal (Exod. 15:18; Lam. 5:19; Mic. 4:7) and comprehensive (Rev. 11:15). He not only created all things but also owns all things (1 Chron. 29:11; Ezek. 18:4). The Ancient of Days has authority over all and is capable of extending that might to the Son of Man (Dan. 7:13–14; Matt. 28:18; cf. 2 Sam. 7:12–16).

מָשַׁל (*māšal*), often translated as "rule, reign, have dominion over," is related to sovereignty particularly among the nations of the world. Scriptures note that "kingship belongs to the Lord, and he rules over the nations" (Ps. 22:28; cf. 47:8; 96:10; 97:1) and all creation (Pss. 8:6; 89:9). It is good news to announce God's sovereignty to the peoples of the earth (Isa. 52:7).

In the New Testament, the kingdom of God is a central theme. Whereas God is the מֶלֶךְ (*melek*), "king," in the Old Testament (Deut. 33:5; Ps. 145:1), the New Testament applies this appellation to Jesus. He is the βασιλεύς (*basileus*), "king" (Matt. 2:2; 21:5; Luke 19:38; John 1:49; 1 Tim. 6:15; Rev. 17:14; 19:16). The kingdom arrives with Jesus's ministry (Matt. 12:28) but is yet to come in full (Matt. 6:10; Rev. 11:15). He is sovereign over sin (Mark 2:5), Satan (Matt. 12:28; Col. 2:15), sickness (Mark 2:10–12; Luke 10:9), and nature (Mark 4:39). All things were created through him, for him, and are held together by him (Col. 1:15–17). Now is the time to bow before the Son (Ps. 2:12; Rom. 14:11), for a day will come when everyone will pay homage to the Son as righteous judge (Matt. 25:31–32; James 4:12). He will put his enemies under his feet (1 Cor. 15:25). His kingdom is both eternal and comprehensive (Rev. 11:15).

Jesus promised to build his church (Matt. 16:18), which takes place when people move from the kingdom of darkness into the kingdom of Christ (Col. 1:13–14). Nothing escapes the jurisdiction of God's sovereignty, especially how people come to faith and are united to the body of Christ.

God's sovereignty is a wonderfully liberating factor in evangelism. The church's witness will result in disciples made only because God is sovereign over his creation, church, and processes. His sovereignty guarantees that the mission will be accomplished. Nothing can thwart his plan. Though we may decide not to participate in his kingdom mandate, our inaction will not prevent the nations from gathering around his throne (Rev. 7:9–10). He will achieve his purpose. The question we must ask is, will he accomplish it through us?

The church takes great rest in the knowledge that nothing happens apart from God's will and authority. The church is able to proclaim the message of good news and rest in the fact that the results are not dependent on her skills. Such is no excuse for poorly contextualized strategies and methods, but God frees the church from guilt and worry when she shares the gospel and rests in the power of the Spirit. The seed is cast broadly and without prejudice in boldness and wisdom while the farmer waits for germination, growth, and gleaning (Matt. 13:1–9; Eph. 6:19–20; Col. 4:3–5).

Predestination, Election, Reprobation

A highly individualistic society that prioritizes equality often balks when considering the doctrines of predestination, election, and reprobation. Some fear that such discussions may lead to fatalism. However, on examination of the Scriptures, one must acknowledge numerous passages that relate, directly or indirectly, to these topics. In addition to the evidence, one must also note the biblical support that describes God as omnibenevolent, compassionate, gracious, and manifesting loving-kindness. Rather than avoid biblical teachings, the church must seek to understand them and how they affect evangelism. Lewis Drummond is correct in stating, "Whatever the Bible means by predestination, it is God's way of saving the most people possible."[1] The church would be wise to keep his words in mind as she considers a theology of evangelism.

In the New Testament, προορίζω (*proorizō*, "determine beforehand, foreordain, predestine") refers to two matters in relation to God. First, the wider understanding of predestination refers to God ordaining everything that comes to pass. Nothing happened in history, happens in the present, or will happen in the future that escapes the boundaries of his sovereignty. God decided that Abraham would be the one to bring blessing to the nations (Gen. 12:1–3). He decided that Israel would be the people for his plan to bless the nations (Deut. 7:6; 14:2). He makes declarations and brings them to completion (Isa. 48:3–5). Old Testament prophecy is filled with his decisions decades and centuries before they came to pass. The psalmist recognized God's position and acknowledged his ability to do whatever he pleases (Ps. 115:3). Nothing in heaven or earth is capable of overriding his will (Dan. 4:35). Jesus was crucified "according to the definite plan and foreknowledge of God" (Acts 2:23), as was "predestined to take place" (Acts 4:28). Luke notes that during the evangelistic work of Paul and Barnabas in Pisidian Antioch, "as many as were appointed to eternal life believed" (Acts 13:48). Paul wrote to the Romans, "Those whom he foreknew he also predestined to be conformed to the image of his Son. . . . And those whom he predestined he also called, and those whom he called he also justified, and those whom he justified he also glorified" (Rom. 8:29–30). The apostle gives the reason for the great

1. Drummond, *Word of the Cross*, 278.

salvation obtained by the Ephesians: "In love he predestined us for adoption to himself as sons through Jesus Christ, according to the purpose of his will" (Eph. 1:4–5). And if such a statement did not make the point, he repeats the truth by noting that their obtained inheritance was because they had "been predestined according to the purpose of him who works all things according to the counsel of his will" (Eph. 1:11).

Second, the narrow understanding of the topic relates to election and reprobation. If predestination is a general category, then election and reprobation are subcategories. Reprobation is the notion that God grants some unbelievers their desire to go away from him and continue as their own lords. While the cause of election is found within God, the cause of reprobation is found within the sin of unbelief. Reprobates deserve justice, and God grants that to them through judgment. There are differing views on whether God directly chose the reprobate or simply passed over them, in their sin, allowing them to continue without him for eternity.[2]

In the Old Testament, the notion of being selected or chosen is represented by בָּחַר (*bāḥar*) and בָּחִיר (*bāḥîr*). In the New Testament, ἐκλέγομαι (*eklegomai*), ἐκλεκτός (*eklektos*), and ἐκλογή (*eklogē*) are found. The usage is generally plural and refers to all God's people or to those comprising a local church. The use of the plural may be related to the audiences of most New Testament letters, or more likely is related to the calling out of a people and not individuals divorced from community.[3] Election includes Israel (Deut. 14:2; 1 Kings 3:8; Isa. 42:1; Ps. 135:4), individuals (Rom. 16:13; 1 Pet. 1:1–2), and angels (1 Tim. 5:21). This choice is based on God's love (Deut. 4:37; 7:6–8; Ps. 47:4; Ezek. 16:1–14). Individuals are chosen for certain tasks (2 Sam. 6:21; Ps. 106:23). The Messiah is described as a chosen one (Matt. 12:15–21; cf. Isa. 42:1–7; Luke 9:35; 23:35; 1 Pet. 2:4–6). The disciples are chosen (Luke 6:13; Acts 1:2) to follow Christ.

No one deserves salvation. Election is God's choice (Exod. 33:19; Isa. 65:1; Jer. 18:1–12; John 15:16; 17:6; Rom. 9:10–24; 11:1–6; Eph. 2:10; 1 Pet. 2:9). It is not based on human merit (Deut. 9:4–6; 1 Cor. 1:26–31). The elect are made manifest by their reception of the gospel (Acts 15:7). This is the doctrine that in eternity past God chose some unbelievers to be spared from judgment and experience his eternal grace. The object of election is the individuals who will become believers through repentance and faith when presented with the gospel. Though they deserve judgment, God extends to them grace for salvation.

---

2. The term *double predestination* is often used to refer to some Reformed teachings by those who do not subscribe to Reformed theology. It is the notion that God predestines the elect to heaven and the reprobate to hell by the same direct method.

3. Elwell and Beitzel, "Elect, Election," 682.

Jesus did not shy away from the topic of the elect (Mark 13:20; Matt. 24:22, 24, 31). Romans 9–11 contain some of the strongest statements on election in the New Testament (Rom. 9:11; 11:5, 7, 28). Paul wrote to the Ephesians that God "chose" them in Christ "before the foundation of the world" (Eph. 1:4), and to the Colossians that they were "God's chosen ones" (Col. 3:12). In his correspondence to the Thessalonians, he states that God "has chosen you" (1 Thess. 1:4), and "God chose you as the firstfruits to be saved" (2 Thess. 2:13). Paul notes that God's election occurred in eternity past, for he "saved us and called us . . . not because of our works but because of his own purpose and grace . . . before the ages began" (2 Tim. 1:9; cf. Eph. 1:4). Paul was willing to endure "everything for the sake of the elect, that they also may obtain the salvation that is in Christ Jesus" (2 Tim. 2:10). Peter exhorts his readers to confirm their "calling and election" (2 Pet. 1:10).

Theological Traditions

Augustine (354–430), during his debates with Pelagius (born c. 354), revealed his belief that the fall prevented people from choosing Christ's salvation. All deserve death and condemnation. God's sovereign will is to elect some and pass over others. This act has come to be known as unconditional election and results in people turning to Christ, persevering in the faith, and glorifying God.[4] Because of the effects of the fall on the volition, God elects some people to receive grace that they may repent and believe the gospel. Grace and faith are a gift from God and necessary for salvation. Everyone else is granted permission to continue in their own directions according to their desires, which separates them from God for eternity.

Thomas Aquinas (1225–1274) argued that predestination is God's direction of a rational being toward eternal life. Just as God ordains some to eternal life, he permits others to go their own way apart from his goodness. Reprobation is his will to allow a person to fall into sin, judgment, and damnation. For Aquinas, foreknowledge of human actions is not the cause for electing anyone to salvation.[5]

These matters were also part of the thoughts and writing of the Reformers. Martin Luther (1483–1546) argued that election is not based on a person's response to the gospel. Rather, it is unconditional. The elect are predestined according to matters only known by God. John Calvin (1509–1564) explained predestination as "the eternal decree of God, by which he determined with

---

4. Allison, *Historical Theology*, 456–57.
5. Allison, *Historical Theology*, 460–61.

himself whatever he wished to happen with regard to every man."[6] For Calvin, election is unconditional and set in eternity past. Gregg Allison notes that for Calvin, predestination "is not something that God makes up as time and history move on."[7] Rather, Calvin wrote regarding the elect that God's plan was "founded on his free mercy, without any respect to human worth, while those whom he dooms to destruction are excluded from access to life by a just and blameless, but at the same time incomprehensible judgement."[8] Wayne Grudem's Reformed understanding of election is described as *"an act of God before creation in which he chooses some people to be saved, not on account of any foreseen merit in them, but only because of his sovereign good pleasure."*[9] Election is seen as being unconditional, not based on any divine foreknowledge of a person's response to the gospel for salvation. There are differing views as to whether election took place before or after the fall (see the Canons of Dort for the classic expression of Calvinism).[10]

Jacob Arminius (1560–1609) argued that election is based on divine foreknowledge of how a person would respond when confronted with the gospel. If the individual chose Christ, then they would be chosen by God to be the elect; if the person rejected the gospel, then they were not elected and were left in sin condemned. The faith God foresaw within them comes not from God, but rather from their free will to believe as they would cooperate with the Spirit's work in their lives. This is described as conditional election. Arminius wrote of election and reprobation as having their "foundation in the foreknowledge of God, by which he knew from all eternity those individuals who would, through his prevenient grace, believe, and, through his subsequent grace would persevere . . . and, by which foreknowledge, he likewise knew those who would not believe and persevere"[11] (see the Remonstrance for the classic expression of Arminianism).[12]

Jesuit theologian Luis de Molina (1535–1600) advocated an approach that he believed to be neither Calvinism nor Arminianism. His system of thought became known as Molinism and developed from his teachings. This perspective related to sovereignty, predestination, and free will was an attempt to protect human freedom in salvation, thus offering a middle ground between Calvinism and Arminianism. Kenneth Keathley writes, "Molinism

---

6. Calvin, *Institutes* 3.21.5, 610.
7. Allison, *Historical Theology*, 463.
8. Calvin, *Institutes* 3.21.7, 613.
9. Grudem, *Systematic Theology*, 670 (emphasis original).
10. Read the Canons of Dort online at https://prts.edu/wp-content/uploads/2016/12/Canons-of-Dort-with-Intro.pdf.
11. Arminius, *Writings*, 248.
12. Read the Remonstrance online at https://www.ccel.org/ccel/schaff/creeds3.iv.xv.html.

simultaneously holds to a Calvinistic view of a comprehensive divine sovereignty and to a version of free will (called *libertarianism*) generally associated with Arminianism."[13] Molinism argued for God's "middle knowledge" as one of three elements in his omniscience. God has "natural" knowledge, which represents his understanding of everything past, present, future, *and* possible things as well—if they could have occurred. God also has "free" knowledge, which is all that he has predetermined to occur. However, a knowledge (i.e., middle) exists between the two.[14] According to Allison, "*Middle* knowledge is the knowledge God possesses of all things that can take place involving an act of human will before God freely chooses to decree something about them."[15] Keathley attempts to clarify by comparison to other theological systems: "In the Calvinist understanding of foreknowledge and predetermination, the future is the product of the will of God. . . . In the Arminian formulation God looks forward into a future made by the decisions of free creatures and then makes His plans accordingly. . . . By contrast Molinism contends that God actively uses His foreknowledge. Among the many possibilities populated by the choices of free creatures, God freely and sovereignly decided which world to bring into existence."[16]

John Wesley (1703–1791) did believe in election and reprobation but was staunchly opposed to the Calvinist understanding of such teachings. Concerning the former, he wrote, "God did decree from the beginning to elect or choose, in Christ, all that should believe to salvation. And this decree proceeds from his own goodness, and is not built upon any goodness in the creature." And concerning reprobation, he stated, "God did from the beginning decree to reprobate all who should obstinately and finally continue in unbelief."[17] Wesley viewed the Calvinist understanding of predestination of the reprobate as a great evil, arguing that it was counter to God's love and justice.[18]

In a sermon on free grace, Wesley clarified his perspective: "I hold only the election of grace. What I believe is no more than this,—that God, before the foundation of the world, did elect a certain number of men to be justified, sanctified, and glorified. Now, all these will be saved, and none else; for the rest of mankind God leaves to themselves: So they follow the imaginations

---

13. Keathley, *Salvation and Sovereignty*, 5.
14. Keathley acknowledges, "Scripture never states explicitly that God utilizes middle knowledge to accomplish his will. But when all the disparate components of the biblical witness are brought together it becomes clear that Molinism is a reasonable proposal" (*Salvation and Sovereignty*, 41).
15. Allison, *Historical Theology*, 221.
16. Keathley, *Salvation and Sovereignty*, 155–56.
17. Wesley, *Works*, 10:266.
18. Olson, *Arminian Theology*, 187.

of their own hearts, which are only evil continually, and, waxing worse and worse, are at length justly punished with everlasting destruction."[19] Election for salvation was understood as being conditional, based on divine foreknowledge of a person's positive response to the gospel for salvation.[20] However, God's foreknowledge does not determine people's decisions.[21] The condition of the reprobate is based on their rejection of Christ.[22] Wesley explained his rejection of unconditional election: "But unconditional election I cannot believe; not only because I cannot find it in Scripture, but also . . . because it necessarily implies unconditional reprobation."[23]

Karl Barth (1886–1968) argued that God neither chose some for salvation nor passed over others. Such was a radical departure from nineteen hundred years of theological development. Rather, in Jesus, all humanity is rejected by God and elected by God. All people, in Christ, experience God's judgment for sin, and all people are elected. Therefore, the elect one is Jesus. Barth rejected the idea that this resulted in universalism and believed that people could reject Christ.[24]

God Is Mystery

Scripture affirms both God's sovereignty and human responsibility for choices made. Perhaps R. B. Kuiper's words should be kept in mind: "As we seek to relate to evangelism this phase of what is usually termed 'the secret will of God,' it behooves us to remember that we are dealing with profound mystery, that we are here on holy ground where angels fear to tread, that finite man cannot begin to comprehend the infinite God, and that therefore we must be sober, scrupulously avoiding human speculation and abiding strictly by the sure Word of God."[25] Nothing happens apart from God's will, and individuals (and nations) are accountable for their actions before him. God's sovereignty and human responsibility do not need reconciliation. God is mystery. He has not chosen to reveal all truth to the church (Deut. 29:29). This is not a cop-out

---

19. Wesley, *Works*, 7:374.
20. Wesley argued that if the doctrine of reprobation, which he viewed as the same as unconditional election, were true, then "the whole Scripture must be false" (*Works*, 10:256).
21. Olson, *Arminian Theology*, 188.
22. Wesley, *Works*, 10:210. He wrote, "Sin only, not the decree of reprobation, hinders thy being accepted" (10:211).
23. Wesley, *Works*, 10:210–11. Wesley noted, "But if every man be unalterably consigned to heaven or hell before he comes from his mother's womb, where is the wisdom of this; of dealing with him, in every respect, as if he were free, when it is no such thing?" (10:233).
24. Elwell and Beitzel, "Elect, Election," 683.
25. Kuiper, *God-Centered Evangelism*, 30.

or an attempt to avoid doing the difficult work of systematic theology or philosophical theology. It is biblical reality.

Without striving to hold these matters in tandem, the church usually elevates one above the other. Instead of resting in the silence of Scripture, rationalism cries out for the removal of tension. The result is that theological systems run beyond the text to make either God or people responsible for undisclosed matters. Logically, philosophically, propositions and conclusions make sense, but sometimes they extend beyond the realm of biblical clarity. Mystery is found in God's character, the created order, and the atonement. It would be wise to accept mystery in soteriology as well, especially when such does not hinder evangelism.

At the turn of the twentieth century, Handley Dunelm acknowledged the tension. He encouraged the church to remember the character of God: "The doctrine passes upward to the sphere where antinomies live and move, where we must be content to hear what sound to us contradictions, but which are really various aspects of infinite truth. Let us be content to know that the Divine choice is sovereign; and also that 'his tender mercies are over all his works,' that 'He willeth not the death of a sinner,' that 'God is love.'"[26]

J. I. Packer, in his influential work *Evangelism and the Sovereignty of God*, helps to explain the relationship between God's sovereignty and human responsibility, not as a paradox or contradiction, but, like Dunelm asserted, as an *antinomy*: "It is an *apparent* incompatibility between two apparent truths. An antinomy exists when a pair of principles stand side by side, seemingly irreconcilable, yet both undeniable. There are cogent reasons for believing each of them; each rests on clear and solid evidence; but it is a mystery to you how they can be squared with each other. You see that each must be true on its own, but you do not see how they can both be true together."[27] It is important to consider the derivative practical matters, regardless of theological positions. The following should be kept in mind when considering the relationship between sovereignty, election, and evangelism.

God Desires the Salvation of All People

While it is important to understand theological systems related to the topics of this chapter, regardless of whether one is a Calvinist, Arminian, Molinist, or Wesleyan, one matter is clear to all: God desires the salvation of all people (1 Tim. 2:3–4; 2 Pet. 3:9; cf. Ezek. 18:23).

---

26. Dunelm, "Election," 926.
27. Packer, *Evangelism*, 18–19 (emphasis added).

PRAY LIKE A CALVINIST, PREACH LIKE AN ARMINIAN

In his work *Evangelism Through the Local Church*, Michael Green reflects on God's sovereignty and human choice as related to evangelism. The following draws from theology and history with application toward the practical.

> The Christian world is sadly divided on this matter. Calvinists stress the sovereignty of God in salvation and tend to be quietest. Arminians stress the responsibility of man and tend to be activist.
>
> A candid look at the Bible shows that there is truth in both positions. Salvation flows from God alone. He devised it. He revealed it. He purchased it at immense cost on the cross. He applies it by His Spirit to the human heart. That is fundamental. On the other hand, God does not force His will upon His creatures. That is the surpassing glory of our humanity. We have the ability to choose. Throughout Scripture we see men and women exercising that right, sometimes for God and sometimes against Him. . . . To be sure, men and women cannot repent and believe unless it is given them by God, but then we cannot do anything without His enabling capacity and the life that he alone gives us. Nevertheless, we are called to make the response that He enables. There is a human strand as well as a divine strand in evangelism.
>
> One particular saying of Jesus embodies this paradox very clearly. "All that the Father gives me will come to me," He says in John 6:37. You could not have divine election more clearly spelled out than that. But the verse continues, "And him who comes to me I will not cast out." That speaks very directly of the human choice we have, to come or not to come. . . . The two strands are not incompatible but profoundly congruent. . . . It was that celebrated Anglican divine Charles Simeon of Cambridge who, when reflecting on this matter, observed: "The truth lies neither at one extreme nor at the other, nor yet in a mean betwixt the two. It lies in holding both extremes at the same time." He would advise the evangelist to be a Calvinist in his prayers and an Arminian in his preaching. The evangelist is called to pray as if it all depended on God and to preach as if it all depended on him. I, for one, seek constantly to be a Calvinist on my knees and an Arminian in the pulpit.
>
> Green, *Evangelism Through the Local Church*, 385–87.

Questions

1. Why do you think Green describes Calvinists as "quietist" and Arminians as "activist"?
2. Do you agree or disagree that "men and women cannot repent and believe unless it is given to them by God"? Explain.
3. What are your thoughts on the expression "be a Calvinist in prayer and an Arminian in preaching"?

Salvation Is to All Who Come to Christ

God's love is so extensive that he sent his Son for salvation to all who believe in him (John 3:16). Jesus was very clear that all who the Father gives to him will come to him and be received into the kingdom (John 6:37). His call extends to "all who labor and are heavy laden," and his promise is to give them rest (Matt. 11:28). Anyone who confesses Christ and has faith in the resurrection will be saved (Rom. 10:9). Whoever calls to the Lord for salvation will be granted such grace (Rom. 10:13; cf. Joel 2:32; Acts 2:21).

Election Encourages and Motivates the Church

A biblical understanding of the doctrine of election should bring encouragement and motivation to the church in her evangelistic activities and not division. God's election is the means by which people will come to faith. The massive number of unbelievers in the world could cause some to despair, especially when sharing the gospel among resistant populations. However, knowing that the preaching of the gospel will accomplish what God decided would happen in eternity past is a strong motivator when faced with global realities. Fields abound and will result in a harvest because of the doctrine of election.

As the church engages in evangelism, she does not go alone. Global disciple-making is done in conjunction with God, with the church being a co-laborer (1 Cor. 3:9). It is God's mission, and he will accomplish his desired outcome through the Spirit. The church knows that she is on the winning side. As the church engages in sharing the gospel, the elect will hear and come to faith. God has determined not only the end but also the means to accomplish the end. Knowledge of election provides a motivator of what will come. Just as the church received the gospel, so also will others as a result of her ministry in the world. John's vision of the glorious gathering around the throne reveals the elect from every nation, tribe, and language (Rev. 7:9–10). The church in every age is motivated by that vision, understanding her privilege of being part of the process of seeing the kingdom of God populated by those whom God chose before the foundation of the world (Rev. 13:8; 17:8).

Election Liberates the Church

Successful evangelism is when the church shares the gospel and allows the Spirit and the Word to work in the hearts of others. Success is not defined by the number of people who come to faith. The elect are known only to God. The church is not called to discern who is or is not the elect. The church has not received the ability to save anyone and grant eternal life. The church's responsibility is to proclaim repentance toward God and faith in the Lord Jesus (Acts 20:21). The fact that no one is responsible for regeneration is a liberating reality. The church cannot transform the unregenerate (whether they are the elect or not). Knowing this truth frees people from the burden of feeling guilty whenever they do not observe a conversion. While the church is to manifest a wise stewardship by being certain of executing contextualized methods and strategies, the results of her evangelism are left to the Sovereign, who elects the peoples of the world.

Election Is No Excuse to Avoid Evangelism

If one's view of election results in refraining from sharing the gospel, then such is not a biblical teaching, but rather is something akin to a doctrine of demons. Though God's sovereignty is a wonderfully liberating truth in evangelism, it was never meant to result in laziness. Could it be that God has revealed this doctrine to motivate the church when it is easy to find discouragement in an age of persecution and resistance to the gospel? Any tradition that does not burn with an intentionality and urgency for sharing the gospel is one that fails to have roots in the first-century church.

The church would be wise to remember these words of Drummond: "The Sovereignty of God does not preclude human instrumentality in effecting His sovereign will. God does not simply act upon a person without means; sovereignty does not mean that. God uses people in effecting His purpose. So believers call people to Christ's kingdom. One day they will understand it all. In the meantime, in their theology of evangelism, believers realize the truth that salvation is of God, and they herald to the unbeliever the wonderful truth that 'whosoever will' can be saved."[28]

Mark McCloskey perhaps says it best: "Does my philosophy and practice of evangelism make me effective in getting the gospel out to as many as possible, as soon as possible and as clearly as possible?"[29] The doctrines of God's sovereignty and election are deep, profound, and enshrouded in mystery. Such is a wonderful and blessed matter, and comforting and freeing for contemporary evangelism. Sovereignty and election, rather than being hindrances to gospel advancement, are something in which the church is to delight and rest. Both the biblical text and great evangelists from a variety of theological persuasions recognize the importance of God's sovereignty and election in the church's Great Commission task.

28. Drummond, *Word of the Cross*, 283.
29. McCloskey, *Tell It Often*, 186.

WHAT DO WE DO WITH ANTINOMIES?

J. I. Packer argues for the importance of living with tension between God's sovereignty and human choice in soteriological matters. Though not original to him, he developed and popularized the concept of antinomy as a way of understanding election and evangelism.

> An antinomy is neither dispensable nor comprehensible. It is not a figure of speech, but an observed relation between two statements of fact. It is not deliberately manufactured; it is forced upon us by the facts themselves. It is unavoidable, and it is insoluble. We do not invent it, and we cannot explain it. Nor is there any way to get rid of it, save by falsifying the very facts that led us to it.
>
> What should one do, then, with an antinomy? Accept it for what it is, and learn to live with it. Refuse to regard the apparent inconsistency as real; put down the semblance of contradiction to the deficiency of your own understanding; think of the two principles as, not rival alternatives, but, in some way that at present you do not grasp, complementary to each other. Be careful, therefore, not to set them at loggerheads, nor to make deductions from either that would cut across the other (such deductions would, for that very reason, be certainly unsound). Use each within the limits of its own sphere or reference (i.e., the area delimited by the evidence from which the principle has been drawn). Note what connections exist between the two truths and their two frames of reference, and teach yourself to think of reality in a way that provides for their peaceful coexistence, remembering that reality itself has proved actually to contain them both. This is how antinomies must be handled, whether in nature or in Scripture. This, as I understand it, is how modern physics deals with the problem of light, and this is how Christians have to deal with the antinomies of biblical teaching.
>
> Packer, *Evangelism*, 21–22.

Questions

1. Do you agree or disagree with Packer's view of antinomy? Explain.
2. What is the difference between antinomy, contradiction, and paradox?

— QUESTIONS TO CONSIDER —

1. What are your views on sovereignty and election? Are they supported by biblical texts or by emotion and logic?

2. Do you agree or disagree that the doctrine of election is liberating for the church? Explain.
3. Do you identify more with a Reformed or Arminian tradition? If so, why?

10

ATONEMENT AND GRACE

Just three chapters into the Scriptures, the reader quickly encounters the fall of Adam and Eve. Death, conflict, and loss of fellowship and paradise have now entered humankind. If God is holy, how might a sinful person be forgiven and brought into intimacy with the Creator? The answer is related to atonement.[1] The Torah refers to making atonement on numerous occasions and serves as an important soteriological background throughout the rest of the Old Testament. "Atone, cover, expiate" shows up as כָּפַר (*kāpar*) and relates to the covering of or payment for sin.

Sin must be addressed and atoned for because it is a grave offense. It is a transgression, a trespass, against God's person and standard. Everyone has sinned, and its wages bring death (Rom. 3:23). A sacrificial offering is the divine means for remedying the effects of sin (Lev. 1:4). Sin results in separation and broken relationship. Paul notes that the Father's love actively works to reconcile the world to himself (2 Cor. 5:19; Eph. 2:16). This is accomplished through the willing, loving sacrifice of the Son as the propitiation for sin (Rom. 3:25).

The traditional language used to describe the Arminian and Calvinistic understanding of the extent of Christ's atonement is that of *unlimited* and *limited*. Some theologians, however, do not prefer these terms and instead use the language of *general redemption* and *particular redemption*. The Arminian view is that Christ's atonement was for everyone. It was universal and not limited to the elect. However, his atonement did not secure salvation for every person. It was not guaranteed. His work on the cross enabled God to

---

1. It is beyond the scope of this book to address theories of the atonement. For those interested, a good starting point is John Stott's classic work *The Cross of Christ*.

forgive sinners, but only if they believe. John Wesley viewed the atonement as available to all, though not everyone would receive the salvation it provides. The Calvinist view was that Christ's atonement was only for the elect. In this way, it was a limited atonement. It also secured the gift of faith for the elect to believe when the Spirit worked within them providing the gift of faith. Salvation is guaranteed for the elect.

Efficacious Grace

Reformed and Wesleyan-Arminian traditions articulate views of grace differently when it comes to salvation. This is related primarily to how and when people experience grace from God. A Calvinistic view states that though the external call for repentance and belief is extended to the world through evangelism, the Spirit extends a special (i.e., efficacious) call to the elect that brings them to salvation. While the external call is rejected by many, the special call is accepted by the elect. Wayne House writes, "By means of this special call the Spirit irresistibly draws sinners to Christ. . . . The Spirit graciously causes the elect sinner to cooperate, to believe, to repent, to come freely and willingly to Christ. God's grace, therefore, is invincible; it never fails to result in the salvation of those to whom it is extended."[2]

The Reformed tradition makes a distinction between common grace and saving grace. The former is extended to all people as God blesses his creation. However, common grace is not salvific. There is a grace that accomplishes the work of salvation as God effectively calls and regenerates people who then respond in saving faith.[3] Augustine spoke of God's operative grace. Conversion is a divine act in which God's grace "operates" on the unbeliever without their cooperation.[4]

Oftentimes the grace that brings salvation is described as irresistible (i.e., efficacious) grace. As R. C. Sproul explains this: "What the unregenerate person desperately needs in order to come to faith is regeneration. This is the necessary grace. It is the *sine qua non* of salvation. Unless God changes the disposition of my sinful heart, I will never choose to cooperate with grace or embrace Christ in faith. . . . *Irresistible grace* means that the sinner's resistance to the grace of regeneration cannot thwart the Spirit's purpose. The grace of regeneration is irresistible in the sense that it is invincible."[5]

---

2. House, *Charts of Christian Theology*, 100.
3. Grudem, *Systematic Theology*, 700.
4. McGrath, *Christian Theology*, 378.
5. Sproul, *Grace Unknown*, 188–89 (emphasis in original).

Prevenient Grace

Wesley was opposed to the Reformed perspective of irresistible grace. Though he agreed salvation is by God's grace, he was unable to locate the teaching in the Bible. He challenged, "Show me any one plain scripture for this,—that 'all saving grace is irresistible.'"[6] How, then, could the unregenerate be made alive? For Wesley, the answer was related to a different kind of grace. He further noted, "The condition of man after the fall of Adam is such, that he cannot turn and prepare himself by his own natural strength and good works to faith and calling upon God. Wherefore we have no power to do good works, pleasant and acceptable to God, without the grace of God by Christ preventing us, that we may have a good-will, and working with us when we have that good-will."[7]

Centuries before Wesley, Augustine spoke of God's grace in people's lives before they come to faith in Christ. This grace went ahead to prepare the will for conversion.[8] According to Roger Olson, "Prevenient grace is simply the convicting, calling, enlightening and enabling grace of God that goes before conversion and make repentance and faith possible. Calvinists interpret it as irresistible and effectual. . . . Arminians interpret it as resistible."[9]

Mildred Bangs Wynkoop notes from a Wesleyan-Arminian perspective "the results of grace in man are limited to man's grasp of God."[10] The Arminian view argues that a common grace has been provided to every person. This grace enables them to repent and place faith in Christ, but they can resist it and reject the Lord's kindness.

Dimensions of Salvation

One of the most basic understandings of the gospel reveals that it addresses fundamental issues that are both present and eternal realities for people. The gospel shared during evangelism is not a privatized and individualistic concept that is kept between the person's private life and God. Rather, it is a message that transforms and unites the person to God and his people. Mark McCloskey notes that the message of salvation addresses forgiveness, gift of the Spirit, and need for completion and fulfillment.[11] The gospel reveals the extent of the sinfulness and brokenness of people, need for healing, and love of a holy God.

6. Wesley, *Works*, 10:254.
7. Wesley, *Works*, 8:52–53.
8. McGrath, *Christian Theology*, 378.
9. Olson, *Arminian Theology*, 35.
10. Wynkoop, *Wesleyan-Arminian Theology*, 98.
11. McCloskey, *Tell It Often*, 20.

FAITH AND THE ATONEMENT

In *The Heart of the Gospel*, Robert Coleman addresses the efficacy of the atonement and a person's belief in Christ. Regardless of one's theological perspective, evangelism and faith are necessary in the application of salvation to the person.

> That Jesus died for the world seems clear, but whether everyone can benefit from it has been a subject of contention in the church through the ages. Basically Arminians believe that the atonement extends to all people who ever lived and therefore, through God's grace, everyone can be saved. On the other hand, Reformed theologians argue that Christ died for everyone but that does not mean that he paid the penalty for everyone. The Gospel is offered to all but only the elect will be moved by God to accept it. What appears to be an irreconcilable contradiction, however, need not be an impediment to evangelism.
>
> Whether Arminian or Reformed, the Gospel must be received by faith for the atonement of Christ to be efficacious. "To all who did receive him, who believed in his name, he gave the right to become children of God" (John 1:12). So in either system of thought, the Gospel is freely offered to every person, and whosoever will may come to Christ. Only those who respond to the invitation will be saved, and in that response their election is known, whether Arminian or Calvinist. Without evangelism neither system of theology has any practical value.
>
> Coleman, Heart of the Gospel, 109.

Questions

1. What difference does it make when inviting people to Christ whether one is a Calvinist or Arminian? Or is there no difference?
2. If only the elect will be saved, do Calvinists and Arminians differ over how many people will be in heaven? Explain your thoughts.
3. What are the similarities and differences between Calvinists and Arminians when it comes to the atonement, grace, and faith?

This salvation provided by a gracious God is a complex matter, one that addresses all aspects of life. For one to receive it, by receiving Jesus as Lord (John 1:12), results in being ushered into an abundant life (John 10:10) filled with blessings (Eph. 1:3) that know no end (John 11:25). McCloskey provides a helpful summary of seven dimensions of salvation provided by Christ's atonement.[12]

---

12. McCloskey, *Tell It Often*, 21–26.

Regeneration = From Death to Life

Evangelism is about good news. However, there is no good news without bad news. Paul noted that everyone is dead in trespasses and sins (Eph. 2:1). There is no life, nothing can be done to please God and earn salvation (Eph. 2:8–9). The gospel is a message of life—a second birth. Peter wrote that, according to God's great mercy, he enables people to be "born again" (1 Pet. 1:3). Jesus, during his conversation with Nicodemus, a pious man who was a descendant of Abraham, shared that religion and pedigree were insufficient to see the kingdom of God. One had to be "born again" (John 3:3), or from above, as a divine work of the Spirit (John 3:5–8).

Reconciliation = From Enemies to Friends

The gospel is a message that transforms God's enemies to God's friends (Rom. 5:10). Everyone is already condemned because of lack of belief in the gospel, related to the sin nature (John 3:18). Jesus's atonement occurred that he "might reconcile us both to God" (Eph. 2:16; cf. Col. 1:22). Shame has now been replaced with the honor of being friends (John 15:15). The gospel proclaimed is a call to be reconciled to God (2 Cor. 5:20), for God works to reconcile the world to himself in Christ (2 Cor. 5:18–19).

Propitiation – From Wrath to Mercy

The notion of atonement looms large in the New Testament. It is a concept found within words such as ἱλαστήριον (*hilastērion*) and ἱλάσκομαι (*hilaskomai*), often translated as "expiation" and "propitiation," which reflect movement from being under God's wrath to receiving his mercy. Jesus is the "propitiation" put forward by God to show his righteousness (Rom. 3:25; Heb. 2:17). He is the "propitiation for our sins, and not for ours only but also for the sins of the whole world" (1 John 2:2). Even though fallen creatures did not love God, he manifested his love toward them by sending his Son "to be the propitiation for our sins" (1 John 4:10). Fear has been replaced with peace (John 14:27; 1 John 4:18). Regarding this element of the gospel brought about by the atonement, Robert Coleman writes, "God is seen as both the subject and the object of propitiation. His wrath is removed, not because we do something, but because he did something. From beginning to end, it is a display of his sovereign grace."[13]

---

13. Coleman, *Heart of the Gospel*, 103.

Sanctification = From Being in the Kingdom of Darkness to Being Set Apart for the Kingdom of Christ

Sanctification can refer to the process of growth in the Christian faith that continues until glorification (Acts 26:18; 1 Thess. 5:23; Heb. 10:14). However, at the moment of conversion it denotes a transfer of ownership. One moves from the domain of darkness to a life under the jurisdiction of the kingdom of Christ (Col. 1:13). This change of ownership is a cleansing (1 Cor. 6:11) and involves an inheritance to come (Acts 20:32).

Redemption = From Slavery to Freedom

God's liberation of captives is found throughout the Scriptures. This is explicit in the Old Testament where Israel is redeemed from Egyptian captivity (Exod. 6:6; Deut. 15:15), but also reflects a more fundamental matter that extends beyond literal chains and owners. The prophet Isaiah noted that God's redemption is connected to the removal of transgressions and sins (Isa. 44:22). The Messiah comes to "give his life as a ransom for many" (Matt. 20:28; Mark 10:45), for "everyone who practices sin is a slave to sin" (John 8:34). He comes to set people free through the truth of his word (John 8:32). God's redemption is provided by the blood of his Messiah (Acts 20:28) to redeem those "under the law" (Gal. 4:5) "from all lawlessness and to purify for himself a people" (Titus 2:14).

Justification = From Guilt to Acquittal

The doctrine of justification runs throughout the Scriptures and is connected to law in God's economy.[14] Lawbreakers are unable to stand before the holy as innocent. Because of this reality, justification is necessary. J. I. Packer explains the meaning of "justify" as "to pronounce, accept, and treat as just, i.e., as, on the one hand, not penally liable, and, on the other, entitled to all the privileges due to those who have kept the law."[15] Through Christ's sacrifice, God is able to remain righteous while justifying guilty sinners (Rom. 3:26). Christ pays the penalty for breaking God's law while enabling lawbreakers to "become the righteousness of God" (2 Cor. 5:21). Everyone who believes in the Messiah and his work receives the freedom that cannot not be provided by the law (Acts 13:38–39). This justification is a gift that comes from God's grace (Rom. 3:24). Justification comes not from works, but by faith (Rom. 4:2–5; 10:10; Gal. 2:15–3:29) in the faithfulness of Jesus

---

14. Morris, *Apostolic Preaching*, 293.
15. Packer, "Justification," 593.

(Rom. 5:19). Those who are predestined for salvation are called and justified (Rom. 8:30).

Adoption = From Being Orphans to Being Part of the Family of God

The gospel brings people into a kingdom community. There is no privatized faith. The faith of the individual supernaturally yokes them to those in God's family (Matt. 12:48–50). Those who claim the name of Jesus are no longer "children of wrath" (Eph. 2:3) or considered of the family of the evil one (John 8:44; 1 John 3:10). Redemption results in adoption into God's family (Rom. 8:14–17; Gal. 4:6–7; Eph. 1:4–5).

Atonement and grace may be found throughout the Scriptures. They are integral to the message of good news. Without them, people remain dead in trespasses and sin. They remain separated from their Creator. Relationship and restoration are impossible apart from God's grace. "Without the shedding of blood there is no forgiveness of sins" (Heb. 9:22).

— QUESTIONS TO CONSIDER —

1. What is the relationship of the atonement to evangelism?
2. Explain the meaning of Ephesians 2:8–9. What is the "gift" mentioned in the text?
3. Does your approach to evangelism generally emphasize one dimension of salvation above another one? Why?

11

REPENTANCE, FAITH, CONVERSION

The word *conversion*, even within certain circles of Christendom, has developed a negative reputation. A convert is sometimes understood to be one who was manipulated to turn from their religion to a new faith.[1] And one who converts others is seen as a scoundrel, lurking around dark corners waiting to pounce on some unsuspecting passerby, blitzing them with a tirade on why hell is their destination while stuffing gospel tracts into their hands. However, in relation to biblical evangelism, three introductory matters should be kept in mind.

First, conversion is good. Conversion reveals that someone has entered the kingdom of God. Conversion results in a new relationship with God (Gal. 3:26–29; 1 John 3:1). Converts have come out of the kingdom of darkness and into Christ's kingdom. Whenever someone converts, they have given up the idols of this world and are now serving the true and living God (Acts 26:20; 1 Thess. 1:9).

Second, conversion is connected to regeneration, justification, and repentance. Although conversion is a human act in the salvation process, it is wed to the divine working of the Spirit. While providing a definition of conversion, J. L. Nuelsen writes, "Conversion denotes the human volition and act by which man in obedience to the Divine summons determines to change the

---

1. For an example in contemporary India, see Shah, "Saving the Soul of India." Shah notes that conversion in India, whether to Christianity or Islam, is viewed as a rejection of Indian identity and a betrayal of Indian loyalty (14).

course of his life and turns to God. Arrested by God's call man stops to think, turns about and heads the opposite way."[2]

Third, conversion cannot be forced. John the Baptist came to turn people to the Lord (Luke 1:16), and James said that it is possible to turn the wanderer back to the truth (James 5:19–20), but such actions are indirect. The church has an important role to play in the conversion process, but she cannot force someone to convert. A forced conversion is a false conversion, based not on the miracle of the Spirit but rather on the manipulation of the sinner. A child cannot be forced to eat. Parents can place food before a child with an empty stomach, tell the child to eat, and note how delightful it is, but the child has to chew and swallow it on their own.

Both Testaments address the matter of conversion. An examination of the concept requires a study in regeneration, repentance, and faith. If Nuelsen is correct, conversion is where the Spirit and a person's response meet in the presence of the gospel.

Old Testament

Conversion is related to the work of the Spirit in the life of the nation or individual (Ezra 6:26–27; Jer. 24:7; 31:18; Lam. 5:21). Moses reminded the people that a day would come when they would wander from God. Once this is realized, the response is a call to "return to the LORD your God and obey his voice" (Deut. 4:30). Israel's history is filled with prophets calling them to return to the Lord (e.g., Isa. 55:1–9; Jer. 3:1–4, 12–13; 4:1–4; Joel 2:12; Zech. 1:3; Mal. 3:7; cf. James 5:19–20; 1 Pet. 2:25). Israel's sins will lead to judgment unless a change of thought, heart, and action occurs. A remnant was predicted to turn from wickedness and return to the Lord (Isa. 10:21). Conversion is connected with healing and pardon (Isa. 6:10; 55:7).

Gentiles were allowed to become part of Israel and were exhorted to make this decision. Conversion usually involved circumcision and adherence to Torah. It is believed that baptism was included as well during certain points in Jewish history. The Old Testament reflects a future hope when the nations convert to the God of Abraham, Isaac, and Jacob (Ps. 22:27). By the first century, a προσήλυτος (*prosēlytos*, "proselyte") was one who converted to Judaism (Matt. 23:15; Acts 2:11; 6:5; 13:43).

Related to conversion is the notion of turning away (i.e., repentance) from sin and turning toward (i.e., faith or belief in) God. Judgment awaits the unrepentant (Jer. 26:3; cf. Matt. 11:20–24), but blessing comes to the faithful.

2. Nuelsen, "Conversion," 707.

The use of שׁוּב (*šûb*) refers to a turn, change of direction, or repentance. A significant portion of the prophets' messages involves its use while they called Israel to return to God (Jer. 3:12–24; Hos. 5:15–6:5; Joel 2:12; Amos 4:6–13). As preachers of Torah, prophets understood what sin meant for them in both the present and the future. God was always faithful to his word. He would provide great blessings as Israel walked in covenantal faithfulness. Curses would follow with habitual, ongoing sin. Yet, healing, rest, and forgiveness were found in returning to the Lord (cf. Pss. 51; 130).

Repentance involved regret or sorrow for sin and a confession to God that his standards are correct.[3] Though the notion of repentance developed slightly from the Old Testament period to the first century, there is a continuity between the Testaments with the expectation that it involved not only a change of thought but also a change in behavior. Whether Israel is called to turn back (Jer. 3:12) from its rebellious direction or the gentiles are called to turn toward God before the day of judgment (Acts 17:30–31), repentance is a grace that brings relationship, favor, and the avoidance of judgment.

New Testament

As Latin's influence dominated Western Christianity, the Greek nouns *epistrophē* and *metanoia* were translated into *conversio* ("turning over"), with "conversion" becoming the English expression.[4] In the New Testament, the concept of conversion includes the understanding of repentance and faith and signifies a change in belief and practice. It entails a submission to Christ as Lord as one turns from sin to follow him.[5]

During the first century, the Christian faith was viewed as a sect of Judaism. Ethnic tensions reached such a fevered pitch that a gathering was called in Jerusalem to address the question of whether gentiles could be saved *without* becoming Jewish proselytes. In the book of Acts, Luke provides extensive evidence that circumcision was unnecessary, but faith was the determining factor. Reports of Samaritans, the Ethiopian eunuch, Cornelius and his household, and extensive accounts from Barnabas and Paul note that gentile conversion was possible by faith alone. An examination of the prophets confirmed what the church had been experiencing (Acts 15:15–17). Through evangelism, the

---

3. DiFransico, "Repentance."
4. Kling, *Christian Conversion*, 1.
5. Thomas Watson describes repentance as a "spiritual medicine" that consists of recognition of sin, sorrow for sin, confession of sin, shame for sin, hatred for sin, and turning from sin (*Doctrine of Repentance*, 18).

Spirit and Word were at work to bring about a greater circumcision that was not done by hands (Col. 2:11–12).

Three New Testament terms are of particular significance to the doctrine of conversion. Πίστις (*pistis*), often translated as "faith, belief, trust," must be present and directed toward a specific object, that being Christ (Mark 1:15; Acts 20:21). The change and turning are related to μετανοέω (*metanoeō*) and ἐπιστρέφω (*epistrephō*), which we will look at below.

Faith

John wrote, "But to all who did receive him, who believed in his name, he gave the right to become children of God" (John 1:12). A woman's faith saved her (Luke 7:50). People are sanctified by placing faith in God (Acts 26:18). Jews and gentiles have their hearts cleansed by faith (Acts 15:9). Paul declared to everyone the need to place faith in the Lord Jesus (Acts 20:21; 24:24). The writer of Hebrews notes, "And without faith it is impossible to please him, for whoever would draw near to God must believe that he exists and that he rewards those who seek him" (Heb. 11:6). For belief to be salvific faith, the object of that faith must be in the one capable of providing salvation.

Object of Faith

Jesus claimed, "I am the way, and the truth, and the life. No one comes to the Father except through me" (John 14:6). Speaking to religious leaders about Jesus, Peter and John declared, "There is salvation in no one else, for there is no other name under heaven given among men by which we must be saved" (Acts 4:12). Paul, quoting the prophet Joel, wrote, "Everyone who calls on the name of the Lord will be saved" (Rom. 10:13; cf. Joel 2:32). He reminded the Corinthian church that they were sanctified and justified in the name of Jesus (1 Cor. 6:11).

Saving Faith Involves the Intellect

There is a cognitive aspect related to faith. While knowing facts alone about salvation is insufficient for conversion, as even demons exhibit this kind of belief (James 2:19), some knowledge is necessary. Historical facts about Christ's life and work must be understood. At the least, this involves his relation to the Father, the reason for the incarnation, atonement, and resurrection.

Saving Faith Involves the Emotions

While emotions are involved in the process, having an emotional sensation alone about the truth of Jesus is insufficient. It is not wise to base salvation on a feeling. Saving faith is not always accompanied by emotional outbursts. However, emotions related to godly fear, shame and guilt for sin, gratitude, peace, and joy on account of God's love should be expected to some degree.

Saving Faith Involves the Will

Saving faith involves a commitment to follow Jesus as Lord. It includes the decision to put one's hand to the plow and not look back (Luke 9:62). Regardless of one's theological tradition, volition is involved whenever a person believes.

Repentance and Conversion

Prior to the first century, μετανοέω referred to a change of mind. In the New Testament, this word, used thirty-four times, includes this meaning, but also turning toward God (Acts 3:19; cf. 20:21). The related word μετάνοια (*metanoia*) occurs twenty-two times in the New Testament and often is translated as "repentance." Closely connected, ἐπιστρέφω refers to turning, repenting, changing direction, and converting. Peter declared, in Solomon's portico, "Repent [μετανοέω] therefore, and turn back [ἐπιστρέφω], that your sins may be blotted out" (Acts 3:19).[6] During his defense before Agrippa, Paul noted that his declaration to Jews and gentiles was "that they should repent [μετανοέω] and turn [ἐπιστρέφω] to God" (Acts 26:20). Connected to such language is the notion of transitioning from unbelief to "belief" (πίστις). When the gospel arrived in Antioch, "a great number who believed [πιστεύω, *pisteuō*] turned [ἐπιστρέφω] to the Lord" (Acts 11:21). Paul's discussion with the Ephesian elders included a reminder that his testifying to both Jews and gentiles included a call "of repentance [μετάνοια] toward God and of faith [πίστις] in our Lord Jesus Christ" (Acts 20:21). The language of μετανοέω looks to past sins, while ἐπιστρέφω and πιστεύω look forward to the Lord of salvation.[7]

The New Testament opens with the Baptist calling Israel to repent and show evidence of such repentance by their actions (Matt. 3:7–10; Luke 3:3, 7–9). Jesus followed this pattern of preaching repentance (Matt. 4:17; Mark

---

6. The words *conversion* and *convert* are not frequently found in English translations. In the New Testament, the noun ἐπιστροφή (*epistrophē*) occurs only in Acts 15:3, where the apostolic team shared about "the conversion [ἐπιστροφή] of the Gentiles."

7. Peace, *Conversion*, 348–49.

1:15). His messages told of people who turned from their ways of destruction and death (Luke 15:11–32). Adults were expected to turn and be like children (Matt. 18:3). Luke's account of Paul's conversion is told three times (Acts 9:1–19; 22:6–16; 26:12–18) in addition to other conversion stories (Acts 8:26–40; 9:35; 10:1–11:18).

The book of Acts shows that belief was tied to conversion (2:41–42; 4:4; 9:42) as well as repentance and having one's sins "blotted out" (3:19). Conversion was not limited to Jews (2:22–41); it included Samaritans (8:5–25) and gentiles (10:44–48). God commands all people to turn away from unrighteousness and toward him (17:30; cf. Isa. 45:22). All the residents of Lydda and Sharon turned to the Lord (9:35). The turning is described as being one "from darkness to light" (26:18) and "from vain things to a living God" (14:15). Belief in Jesus as Lord was connected to the conversion experience (11:21). Those who heard the gospel received a message communicating that "they should repent and turn to God, performing deeds in keeping with their repentance" (26:20).

Only a few references to repentance may be found in the Pauline corpus. God's kindness leads people to repentance (Rom. 2:4), and he alone provides the gift of repentance that leads to an understanding of truth (2 Tim. 2:25). Conviction for sin that results in godly grief leads to repentance and salvation (2 Cor. 7:9–10). Paul describes his change of mind and actions (1 Cor. 15:8–10; Phil. 3:5–8). He reminds readers of God's initiative that brought them to faith (1 Cor. 1:2; 6:20). Conversion is described as an act of grace (Rom. 3:21–26; Eph. 2:8–9) that brings liberation from sin (Rom. 6:18). The believers in Thessalonica heard the gospel and turned from idols to God (1 Thess. 1:4–9). Paul warned the Galatians not to turn back (Gal. 4:9), a warning issued also by the author of Hebrews (Heb. 6:4–6; 10:36–39). According to Peter, God does not desire that "any should perish, but that all should reach repentance" (2 Pet. 3:9).

Repentance and Christ's Followers

It is true that the life of the believer is a life of turning from sin. A person who comes to faith in Jesus remains at war with Satan, the flesh, and the world. There will be ongoing temptations in this life. At times, the believer will give into those and sin, but will not, however, lose the salvation God has provided. Believers cannot be snatched from the Son's hand (John 10:28), as nothing can separate them from God (Rom. 8:31–38). Unconfessed sin hinders fellowship, both with God and the church (1 John 1:5–10). It grieves the Spirit (Eph. 4:30). Therefore, the life of the believer is one of repentance (Luke 22:32; 1 John 1:9; Rev. 2:4–5; 3:19).

Scripture warns believers not to return to their old ways. The church is told to restore to fellowship anyone who does wander (James 5:19–20). It is incorrect to refer to the "reconversion of Christians" as if it related to regeneration. Not only is such language theologically incorrect; it is a contradiction. One who has been sanctified by the name of Christ cannot be reconverted, unless one never was converted in the first place (Heb. 10:10).

Regeneration

The effects of the fall on humanity were so extensive that only a miracle by God could bring any healing and restoration. Sin brought not only death (Gen. 3:19; Rom. 6:23) but also the inability of humans to experience a relationship with God and experience his rest and peace. A "regeneration" (παλιγγενεσία, *palingenesia*) was necessary to transform the entire person. In the Old Testament, the notion of regeneration is related to a work of God on behalf of his people. With this monergistic act, God changes their hearts to love, know, and serve him (Deut. 30:6; Jer. 31:31–34; 32:39–40; Ezek. 11:19–20; 36:25–27). This renewal is a supernatural work of the Spirit (Ezek. 36:27) that brings the dead to life. Paul notes, "He saved us, not because of works done by us in righteousness, but according to his own mercy, by the washing of regeneration and renewal of the Holy Spirit, whom he poured out on us richly through Jesus Christ our Savior, so that being justified by his grace we might become heirs according to the hope of eternal life" (Titus 3:5–7). Prior to the planting of the church in Antioch, Luke recorded that some who left Jerusalem traveled to Antioch preaching Jesus: "And the hand of the Lord was with them, and a great number who believed turned to the Lord" (Acts 11:21).

Though the process of sanctification occurs throughout life, it begins with regeneration (Heb. 10:14). This one-time, instantaneous event moves a person from the kingdom of darkness into the kingdom of Christ (Col. 1:13). The regenerate transition is from death to life, separation to reconciliation, hostility to peace, strangers to fellow citizens, and under wrath to becoming members of the household of God (Eph. 2:1–22). Those born of God walk in righteousness (1 John 2:29), love their neighbor (1 John 4:7), and overcome the evil world system (1 John 5:4).

Regeneration is connected to the new birth, or when the individual is "born again" or "born from above" (γεννηθῇ ἄνωθεν, *gennēthē anōthen*) and brought into a right relationship with God (John 3:3–7). Those who are slaves to sin

(John 8:34) are set free and brought to life, even though they were dead in trespasses and sin against God (Eph. 2:1). The Lord provides the gift of repentance and forgiveness to Israel and the gentiles (Acts 5:31; 11:18) and opens hearts to belief (Acts 16:14–15). He saves "by the washing of regeneration and renewal of the Holy Spirit" (Titus 3:5). Peter notes that God "has caused us to be born again" (1 Pet. 1:3) through his Word (1 Pet. 1:23). Those who experience this regeneration are a new creation (2 Cor. 5:17).

A CALL FOR EVANGELISTIC COLLABORATION

Robert E. Coleman, recognizing the scope of the church's Great Commission task, writes with a plea for disciples to recognize their common beliefs. The views of Reformed and Arminian traditions have many similarities and should unite rather than divide the church in evangelistic outreach.

> Certainly, the truth that binds Reformed and Arminian together in the Gospel is far stronger than our differences. Both agree that there is a divine purpose and providence in God's creation. Both agree that God has a perfect knowledge of himself and all that he has made. Both agree that God's sovereign will is exercised in consistency with his personal moral nature. Both recognize that the permissive will of God is resolved in his perfect will. Both understand that God respects the integrity built into this creation of man and woman, including their freedom of choice. Both affirm that sin is the result of human refusal to accept God's will. Both agree that God's foreordination does not take away human liability resulting from the fall. Both realize that God must himself take the initiative in our redemption from sin. Both believe that only by response to the Gospel can a person be saved by grace. And as faith is defined, both agree that Christians are eternally secure.
>
> Coleman, *Heart of the Gospel*, 244.

Questions
1. Do you think that Calvinists and Arminians can partner in evangelistic activities? Explain your answer.
2. How do you think Calvinists and Arminians engage in evangelism differently?
3. If you believe these theological camps can collaborate, what evangelistic methods do you anticipate being points of conflict?

Conversion Perspective of the Individual

A question that frequently occurs during discussions related to evangelism involves the timing of conversion. Is conversion a punctiliar or a progressive event? Does a person become a follower of Jesus at a moment in time or is this something that takes place over a period of days, weeks, months, or years? Theology shapes method. Nearing the conclusion of his serious study on conversion in the New Testament, Richard Peace is correct when he says, "I have come to believe that *how we conceive of conversion determines how we do evangelism.*"[8] Is conversion an event or a process?

David Larsen claims that the Scriptures do not provide a uniform type of experience that is to be expected.[9] Following the 1976 Fifth Assembly of the World Council of Church in Nairobi, the Commission on World Mission and Evangelism was tasked to produce a document on mission and evangelism. The result was "Mission and Evangelism: An Ecumenical Affirmation," which notes, "While the basic experience of conversion is the same, the awareness of an encounter with God revealed in Christ, the concrete occasion of this experience and the actual shape of the same differ in terms of our personal situation."[10] David Kling sees conversion as a multifaceted phenomenon that is both an event and a process, even arguing for a continuum rather than a punctiliar event.[11]

The answer to the question of whether conversion is an event or process depends on the perspective. The seventeenth-century Puritan theologian Richard Baxter describes conversion as a process but distinguishes between two stages: the moment of turning to Christ in faith ("closing with Christ") and everything else as preparatory for that moment.[12] On the one hand, from a theological perspective, it is a punctiliar event whenever someone crosses the line of faith—though the Spirit may have taken a period of time to bring a person to this point. On the other hand, from an anthropological perspective, the conversion process appears to occur over time. It is worth briefly examining conversion from these different angles.

Regeneration Is Instantaneous

Conversions described in the New Testament were in the moment, evidenced by turning from sin, belief, and sometimes an outward manifestation

---

8. Peace, *Conversion*, 286 (emphasis in original).
9. Larsen, *Evangelism Mandate*, 39.
10. Stromberg, *Mission and Evangelism*, 18.
11. Kling, *Christian Conversion*, 668–69.
12. Beougher, *Richard Baxter and Conversion*, 90.

of the Holy Spirit. For example, Luke recorded that the God-fearers such as Cornelius (Acts 10) experienced a clear event of conversion (Acts 10:44–48). Peter's account given in Jerusalem resulted in the disciples declaring that the Cornelius encounter confirmed God had granted to the Gentiles "repentance that leads to life" (Acts 11:18).

Though the Scriptures reveal conversion as punctiliar, different theological camps debate the order of salvation, when repentance and faith happen within the heart. Regardless, a person does not gradually move out of the kingdom of darkness and, over a period of time, arrive in the kingdom of Christ. Someone is not one-third born again today, two-thirds next year, and fully born again five years later. A person does not ooze into the kingdom of God. Repentance and faith occur simultaneously at a specific moment.

The Mind May Not Recall the Moment

It is possible that one's memory may not include when salvation occurred. According to one Puritan tradition, a failure to remember the moment of conversion was the rule among Christians, not the exception.[13] Consider children raised in homes where families teach them the ways of the Lord at young ages. Parents model the life of a disciple by their words and actions. Bible stories and prayers occur each night for years and worship attendance is a regular part of life. They are taught to love and fear the Lord. For the individual with a history of swimming in the Christian milieu, conversion moments may be imperceptible. The cognitive abilities to remember when they turned from their sin to Jesus for forgiveness may not be present. I have frequently heard conversion stories whereby individuals could not remember a specific time of their initial belief, but only a history of fearing God and following Jesus. Though the mind was unable to recall that moment of regeneration and conversion, the Spirit made a moment possible when the person turned to the Lord.

Conversion Perspective of Set Theory

Consider an agnostic. Friends have shared the gospel with him many times. He has watched a few television preachers and even tried reading the Bible—but gave up when he got to Leviticus. A friend invites him to her church's

---

13. Beougher, *Richard Baxter and Conversion*, 96. For a contrasting view, I recall one pastor who regularly told his congregation that if they were unable to note the date of their spiritual birthday, then it was likely they were not saved, as conversion was dramatic and happened in the moment.

Christmas Eve worship gathering, to which he agrees to go. That night, over dinner, they discuss what he experienced, and he declares, "Jesus is Lord." He is able to mark the moment on the calendar. He knew what he was wearing, eating, and feeling when he repented and believed. Did his conversion occur at a moment in time or was it a process?

Though he recalled hearing the gospel and knew the moment of his repentance and prayer of confession, we may be quick to conclude that his conversion was a process. Though the Spirit had a lengthy history of working in this man's life, which indeed was a process of preparing him for conversion, the process was not his conversion moment. It was definitely a lengthy and necessary journey of moving him from agnosticism to an openness to attending a gathering, to repentance and belief as his friend shared the gospel over dinner.

Near the end of the twentieth century, Paul Hiebert began to apply and popularize anthropological set theory to evangelism and conversion.[14] Hiebert showed how cultural expressions and worldview issues affect the way the church identifies what it means to become a Christian. Set theory became influential among mainline and evangelical scholars when it came to considering the timing of conversion.[15]

According to Hiebert, people form categories based on Scripture, cultures, and church traditions as to how they define "Christian" and "church." These categories are four in number: intrinsic bounded sets, intrinsic fuzzy sets, extrinsic centered sets, and extrinsic fuzzy sets. Hiebert discusses these at length with application to the church and mission, but our focus is on the latter two.

Extrinsic Centered Set

While the church should be inclusive and allow people the time to investigate the claims of Christ, such welcoming should not be equated with a "we're all in this together" journey. It is tempting to state that the church should *not* view people as Christian or non-Christian, but instead view people as relative to the Center, which is Jesus. Again, this is a noble desire, but it is not reflective of biblical ecclesiology or kingdom theology. Stanley Jones notes that Jesus "divided humanity into just two classes—the unconverted and the converted, the once-born and the twice-born."[16] It is true that the centered set is the best option for understanding evangelism and conversion, but it must not be forgotten that the centered set is a *bounded* set. It has a

---

14. Hiebert, *Anthropological Reflections*, 107–36.
15. Two influential works that seek to apply this theory to practice are Guder, *Missional Church*, 201–20; and Frost and Hirsch, *Things to Come*, 47–51, 206–10.
16. E. Jones, *Conversion*, 15.

line of demarcation. Those who have moved across the border into the set have experienced the regenerative work of the Spirit. They have been born again (John 3:16). There will be progress in sanctification as they move in the direction of the Center. And there will be times when temptations and sin will occur. But these individuals should not be confused with those outside the boundary *moving toward the center*. Those outside are the ones counting the cost and pondering the possibility of following Jesus. Regardless, there is a theological, ecclesiological, and kingdom distinction between them and those who have crossed the boundary. On one side are the unregenerate, not part of Christ's church and outside the kingdom. The regenerate are found inside the bounded set (see fig. 11.1).

FIGURE 11.1
BOUNDED CENTERED SET

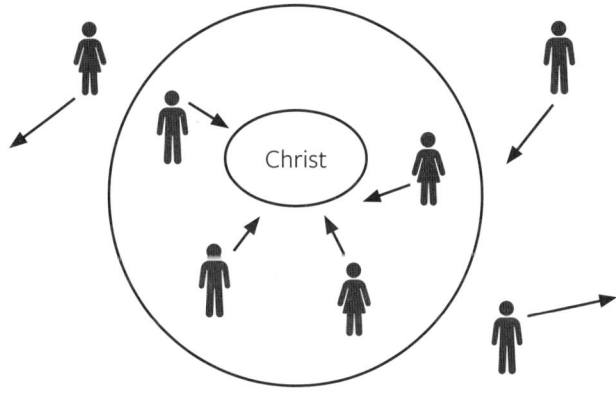

Adapted from Hiebert, *Anthropological Reflections*, 112.

Extrinsic Fuzzy Set

Hiebert notes that the boundary for a group reflective of an extrinsic fuzzy set is that the boundary is fuzzy as far as who is considered in or out. Everything is based on how people move in relation to what is the center (see fig. 11.2). With an extrinsic fuzzy set, "things range from full membership to nonmembership and all points between." Conversion is "a process of changing directions, not an instantaneous about-face." Such sets result in relativism as everyone moves in their own direction; "even things moving in the direction of the center may move independently from that center and pass by it on their own trajectory to some higher goal." When the extrinsic fuzzy set theory is applied to conversion, there is no dividing line between Christians and non-Christians. Jesus is related to all—for some Lord, for others a guru, and for others just a good example to follow. Conversion becomes a "series of decisions, as a process of turning around and moving toward Christ." The church then becomes a "loose collection of people with varying degrees of commitment to Christ and to one another." Members are viewed as "partly converted and in need of further conversion." Taken further, all paths lead to God, as the exclusivity of Christ is dissolved into the pluralistic mass.[17]

FIGURE 11.2
EXTRINSIC FUZZY SET

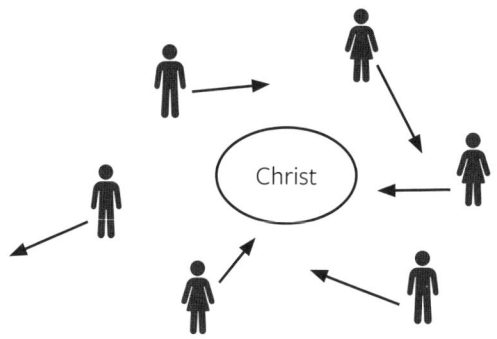

Adapted from Hiebert, *Anthropological Reflections*, 112.

Hiebert's reflections on the application of set theory to conversion draw attention to the divine-human relationship. He writes, "To us conversion often looks more like a process than a point, and the church more like a fuzzy body made up of people with different degrees of commitment to Christ. The problem here is not the true nature of spiritual realities, but the limits of our human perception."[18] Such may be what Baxter meant when he described conversion as a process with two stages.

While it is not wrong to consider the process of conversion, or a person's journey to faith, the church should distinguish between the theological and the anthropological. Clarity of language, and not confusion, is needed. For example, David Wells explains conversion as follows:

> A significant part of the evangelical world encourages us to think of a simple, all-embracing, momentary crisis as the standard form of conversion. But

---

17. Quotations in this paragraph are from Hiebert, *Anthropological Reflections*, 131–33.
18. Hiebert, *Anthropological Reflections*, 134.

conversion, our turning to God, is better understood if we view it as a complex process. The process involves thinking and rethinking, doubting and overcoming doubts, soul-searching and self-admonition, struggle against feelings of guilt and shame, and concern as to what a realistic following of Christ might mean, whether or not it culminates in a personal crisis that will afterward be remembered as "the hour I first believed." Sometimes, of course, it does so culminate, outside as well as inside revivalist circles. . . . But sometimes the process does not climax in a single conscious crisis, even for those who attend evangelistic crusades. God is Lord in conversion, as elsewhere, and our experiences of his dealings with us differ.[19]

While Wells's language is helpful in addressing the journey, or process, of someone coming to faith in Christ, conversion proper is punctiliar and not a process. Conversion and the process leading up to conversion should not be confused.

Recognizing conversion as a moment in time and the process leading up to conversion as a series of steps appears congruent with the findings that Don Everts and Doug Schaupp observed after listening to over two thousand conversion stories. There was clearly a path, a sojourn, to entrance into the kingdom of God, but journeying along that path did not make people converts; rather, it resulted in their conversions.

Everts and Schaupp discern five shifts that occur in people before coming to faith in Christ. These "five thresholds of postmodern conversion" begin with friends moving from distrust to trust. Second, people shift from complacency to curiosity about the person and work of Christ. Third, people move from being closed to change to open to experiencing change in their lives. The fourth threshold is a movement from meandering to purposefully seeking God. Finally, people must cross the threshold of the kingdom by repentance and faith in Christ.[20]

Revisiting How Peoples Become Disciples

Most evangelism books, particularly those written to an individualistic Western audience, approach evangelism and conversion as an individualistic

---

19. Wells, *Turning to God*, 63.
20. Everts and Schaupp, *I Once Was Lost*, 23–24. At the turn of the century, George Hunter and others noted that people in the United States were experiencing Christian gatherings and contexts *before* believing in Christ. They were first *belonging*, and then *believing* for salvation, as opposed to belief preceding belonging to the Christian community. See Hunter, *Celtic Way of Evangelism*.

experience.[21] Jesus is emphasized to be a personal savior, and unbelievers are challenged to make a personal decision for him. While this is theologically true and methodologically helpful much of the time in the West, the church must understand that the majority of the world's population is more collectivistic. Decisions, especially major life decisions, are made in conjunction with others in the family, clan, or tribe (see Case Study 1 on group conversion at the end of this book). The church needs to understand that this reality also exists within Western neighborhoods and learn from the last century of related missiological studies.

Donald McGavran studied evangelism and conversion among people groups in India, where he served as a missionary for more than thirty years. He learned that a one-by-one approach to evangelizing individuals *and* extracting converts from their ungodly communities had both hindered the new believer's growth in Christ and the urgent and widespread dissemination of the gospel across the people group. Social bonds were severed. The natural networks through which the gospel was designed to travel were removed. The individual was now a Christian, regardless of what their family and friends thought.

McGavran challenged the church to recognize that the Majority World is not as individualistic, and evangelizing people and teaching them obedience to Christ should focus on reaching *"the entire fabric which is the people,* or large enough parts of it that the social life of the individual is not destroyed."[22] Where the church fails to focus on starting people movements to Christ in such communities, *"it will be walled off and confined to an ineffective and expensive conversion of individuals here and there."*[23]

Communities observing converts ostracized from family because of their new religion labeled them as rebels and disrespectful. Though McGavran did not argue for a mass movement or group conversion, he did advocate a multi-individual, mutually interdependent conversion.[24] He argued that rather than conversion being "the decision of a solitary individual taken in the face of family disapproval,"[25] a group of people should take time to discuss and consider the claims of Christ. While conversion occurs at an individual level, each individual considers the cost of following Jesus in light of the decisions of others in the group. Repentance and belief take place. The new believers

---

21. For example, Wardle, *One to One*.
22. McGavran, *Bridges of God*, 16 (emphasis original).
23. McGavran, *Bridges of God*, 98 (emphasis original).
24. McGavran comments, "There is no such thing as group conversion. A group has no body and no mind. It cannot *decide* anything whatever" (*Understanding Church Growth*, 340, emphasis added).
25. McGavran, *Understanding Church Growth*, 340.

are then gathered and discipled as a group with the unrepentant seen as those still in need of evangelizing.[26] For the church in the West, significant theological and methodological shifts will need to occur before she is able to engage in evangelism beyond the individual.

Conversion: The Beginning of Sanctification

Conversion should not be equated with the whole of sanctification, which begins with regeneration and culminates in glorification. Throughout life, a believer will remain in a state of growth, confession, and repentance. However, such experiences are subsequent to coming to faith (i.e., conversion). All of life is a turning from sin and reorienting of self toward the Center. However, such reorientation comes *from* one who is already adopted into the family of God (John 1:12; Gal. 4:1–7). One's maturity in the faith changes over time. In this way, it is true that sanctification is a spectrum; not everyone resides at the same point and grows at the same rate. But all are within the boundary, not because of church and family traditions but because of a gospel embraced. The language of being a pilgrim people was applied to those who had already embraced the Christ at the Center (Heb. 11:13; 1 Pet. 2:11), not to the unrepentant, still considering the way of Jesus. Sanctification is a spectrum; regeneration is not. No one is somewhat or partially born again.

There are serious implications for evangelism and disciple-making when viewing conversion this way. If churches and denominations apply the traditional language of conversion to everyone, then everyone is in an ongoing state of conversion and in need of being evangelized over and over again. The primary audience for evangelism is no longer the lost (i.e., ungenerate); they simply become one group among many. *Reevangelizing* Christians takes priority because it is the most convenient task and least costly ministry to engage in, giving a false sense that one is completing the Great Commission.

— QUESTIONS TO CONSIDER —

1. How would you explain conversion, repentance, and saving faith in your own words?
2. What is your conversion story? How did you become a follower of Jesus?
3. What is the difference between repentance for the unbeliever and repentance for a follower of Jesus?

26. McGavran, *Understanding Church Growth*, 340–41.

— PART 3 —

HISTORICAL OVERVIEW

The following section provides a glimpse of the past two thousand years of evangelism. Four chapters to cover two millennia of history are insufficient for the task, but one can address only so much in an introductory textbook. Excellent book-length treatments on the history of evangelism, though few in number, should be consulted (see bibliography).

The two centuries following the close of the New Testament witnessed a variety of methods and social circumstances that contributed to the gospel's advancement. Many of these methods remain with the church today and are used in her evangelistic work throughout the world. Particular attention will be given to this epoch.

Church history is filled with the names of men and women who took the gospel to the nations. These, along with events such as awakenings, are worthy of mention and discussion. Two chapters provide a glance into the history of evangelism across the centuries by focusing on these influencers. The final chapter in this section considers some of the most significant global gatherings on world evangelization, beginning with the Edinburgh Conference in 1910 and ending with the Lausanne Congress in Seoul-Incheon 2024.

12

MEANS OF EVANGELISM

AD 100–300

The Christian faith is a global faith. It is multiethnic and multinational. It is not constrained by racial or geographical boundaries. Followers of Jesus may be found in every country, even those where government officials and locals attempt to extinguish its light. The gospel is fluid. It is able to travel to remote locations and take root among any people's cultural contexts. Prosperity and plague cannot stop its advance. Peacetime and persecution are unable to bring it to an end.

Many would agree with Cleveland Coxe: "For who does not close the records of St. Luke with longings to get at least a glimpse of the further history of the progress of the Gospel?"[1] By the end of the first century, disciples had been made and churches started in numerous cities of the Roman Empire. Michael Green observes, "Probably no period in the history of the world was better suited to receive the infant Church than the first century AD."[2] God had sent his Son in the fullness of time that was ripe for a global movement. Elements such as the *pax Romana* (Roman peace) created a massive

---

Portions of this chapter were adapted from J. D. Payne, "Methods of Evangelism: The First 300 Years," paper presented at the Annual Meeting of the Evangelical Theological Society, November 16–18, 2005, Valley Forge, Pennsylvania, and "Means of Evangelistic Growth: The First Three Hundred Years," *Journal of the American Society for Church Growth* 18 (Winter 2007): 55–77.

1. Coxe, "Introductory Notice," vii.
2. Green, *Evangelism in the Early Church*, 13. For cultural and religious developments in the first century that served as a catalyst for gospel advancement, see Green's chapter "Pathways for Evangelism" (13–28).

geographical region that would allow for the gospel to spread on the wings of merchants, military, slaves, and other travelers. Rome's road system, with artifacts remaining to date, allowed for easier and faster travel along land routes. Centuries of Hellenization had created cultural contexts open to the ethical monotheism of the good news. Greek had become a trade language spoken throughout the empire. This common tongue allowed for people to pass along the gospel with ease. Greek philosophers, and thought, for centuries had been taking swipes at the pantheon. The divine was as immoral, corrupt, and limited as humans. Various enthusiastic cults had developed that attempted to help people address cleansing from sin and guilt, security from fate, and immortality. The Jewish diaspora, with its synagogues and Septuagint, modeled to watching gentiles an exclusive faith of ethical monotheism. It was in this location in the fullness of time that the incarnation occurred, the promise of the Spirit was fulfilled, and the disciples were sent to preach the gospel to all nations before the day of the Lord.

My approach in this chapter is to provide an account of the evangelistic methods of the expansion of the faith during the two centuries that followed the days of the apostles. This epoch is often overlooked in evangelism studies; however, many of the evangelistic methods that developed in the early centuries remain today with their contextualized variations.

By the second century, most of the churches were in urban contexts.[3] During this period, churches spread and continued to develop in Arabia, Persia, North Africa, Armenia, Asia Minor, Pontus, and Rome. Eusebius's account of what developed in Rome since the first century had resulted in forty-six presbyters, seven deacons, seven subdeacons, forty-two clerks, and fifty-two exorcists, readers, and janitors by the mid-third century.[4]

Though Christianity was initially understood as a sect of Judaism (Acts 24:5), within roughly three hundred years it became a government-sanctioned religion. Even by the mid-third century, the influence of the gospel could be felt in the highest offices in the land. For example, Cyprian's (AD 200–258) comments about the persecution of the believers reveals this widespread impact. Writing to the bishop Successus, he noted,

> But the truth concerning them is as follows, that Valerian had sent a rescript to the Senate, to the effect that bishops and presbyters and deacons should immediately be punished; but that senators, and men of importance, and Roman knights, should lose their dignity, and moreover be deprived of their property;

---

3. For sociohistorical studies, see Malherbe, *Social Aspects of Early Christianity*; Harnack, *Expansion of Christianity*, 1:1–39; Green, *Evangelism in the Early Church*, 29–75.
4. Eusebius, *Ecclesiastical History* 6.43.11.

and if, when their means were taken away, they should persist in being Christians, then they should also lose their heads. . . . Moreover, people of Caesar's household, whoever of them had either confessed before, or should now confess, should have their property confiscated, and should be sent in chains by assignment to Caesar's estates.[5]

Ramsay MacMullen has argued that the growth of the early church was quite slow and that the faith was not as widespread as many post-AD 312/313 writers believed.[6] His reason for this assumption is that there are too few Christian inscriptions before AD 313 to offer substantial historical evidence for a widespread expansion of the faith and a large number of believers. According to MacMullen, not only were the writings few in number, but their publication ceased for approximately a half a century prior to the early fourth century. When the Christians returned and took up the pen, it was post-AD 313, and then the Christians were prominent among the writings. "What happened?" MacMullen asks. "Merely, A.D. 312/313—that is, the prominence of Christians postdates and is explained by the grant of toleration."[7] According to MacMullen, for the most part, Christians "kept quiet" for the two centuries comprising the early church epoch.[8] The early believers were not very evangelistic, were not successful in spreading their apologetics, participated little in open-air preaching, and little in open advertising of the faith.[9] Though MacMullen is correct that there was much growth post-AD 313, I am not ready to dismiss the evangelistic work of the church for two hundred years except for the isolated and sporadic situations.

Reidar Hvalvik, agreeing that the early church did grow, also does not see a widespread passion for evangelism. According to Hvalvik, "There is very little evidence for the assertion that every Christian in the early church saw it as a duty to take active part in evangelism. And what we would think of as the main motivation for missionary work, the Great Commission, was thought to have been fulfilled."[10]

Adolph Harnack, however, offers a different perspective: "The literary sources available for the history of primitive Christian missions are fragmentary. But how

5. Cyprian, *Epistle* 81.1 (Roberts and Donaldson, *Ante-Nicene Fathers*, 5:408).
6. MacMullen notes, "Nothing counts for more than the year 312, which brought Constantine's conversion, or 313, with the Edict of Milan. The toleration of the latter simply made manifest the meaning of the former date" (*Christianizing the Roman Empire*, 102).
7. MacMullen, *Christianizing the Roman Empire*, 103.
8. I am defining the apostolic church years as ending in about AD 100, and the early church years as AD 100–300.
9. MacMullen, *Christianizing the Roman Empire*, 104–11.
10. Hvalvik, "In Word and Deed," 279.

extensive they are, compared to the extant sources at our disposal for investigating the history of any other religion within the Roman Empire! They not only render it feasible for us to attempt a sketch of the mission and expansion of Christianity, which shall be coherent and complete in all its essential features, but also permit us to understand the reasons why this religion triumphed in the Roman empire, and how the triumph was achieved."[11]

Other scholars have commented on a strong militant zeal in the lives of the early believers.[12] Another view comes from Kenneth Scott Latourette, who is in clear disagreement with MacMullen and Hvalvik: "One of the factors to which is attributed the triumph of Christianity is the endorsement of Constantine. But, as we have suggested, the faith was already so strong by the time when Constantine espoused it that it would probably have won without him. Indeed, one of the motives sometimes ascribed to his support is his supposed desire to enlist the cooperation of what had become the strongest element in the Empire, the Christian Community."[13]

Even the writers of the early church offered their commentary on the number of believers. Tertullian (c. 155–220), in his *Apology*, noted the large number of believers during his days: "We are but of yesterday, and we have filled every place among you—cities, islands, fortresses, towns, market-places, the very camp, tribes, companies, palace, senate, forum,—we have left nothing to you but the temples of your gods."[14]

The gospel spread and the church grew. But the question that remains unanswered is, how? The rest of this chapter will address nine particular means.[15]

Martyrdom

Though persecution of the early church is believed to have been sporadic and parochial, history does record the death of many believers and the

---

11. Harnack, *Expansion of Christianity*, 1:xii.
12. Hinson, *Evangelization of the Roman Empire*, 31.
13. Latourette, *History of Christianity*, 105.
14. Tertullian, *Apology* 37 (Roberts and Donaldson, *Ante-Nicene Fathers*, 3:45). In his writing *To Scapula*, Tertullian specifically mentioned by name the wife of one authority figure, noting to what social heights the gospel had spread: "Claudius Lucius Herminianus in Cappadocia, enraged that his wife had become a Christian, had treated the Christians with great cruelty: well, left alone in his palace, suffering under a contagious malady, he boiled out in living worms, and was heard exclaiming, 'Let nobody know of it, lest the Christians rejoice, and Christian wives take encouragement'" (*To Scapula* 3 [Roberts and Donaldson, *Ante-Nicene Fathers*, 3:106]).
15. In this chapter I draw heavily from early source material. Though the accuracy of some writings may be questioned, there are elements that may shed light on the means by which the gospel spread. Even writers of fiction are influenced by their culture.

impact of their testimonies on unbelievers.[16] While offering his apology to Diognetus, the author of the *Epistle to Diognetus* (AD 130), wrote of the growth of the church coming through the means of persecution: "Do you not see them exposed to wild beasts, that they may be persuaded to deny the Lord, and yet not overcome? Do you not see that the more of them are punished, the greater becomes the number of the rest? This does not seem to be the work of man: this is the power of God; these are the devices of His manifestation."[17]

Eusebius (ca. AD 260–339), referencing Clement's record of the martyrdom of the apostle James, described the resulting conversion of an unnamed guard: "He said that the man who led James to the judgment seat, moved by the way James bore his testimony to the faith, confessed himself Christian. Both therefore, said he, were led away to die. On their way, he entreated James to be forgiven of him, and James considering a little, replied, 'Peace be to thee,' and kissed him. Then both were beheaded at the same time."[18]

Eusebius also wrote of the martyr Agapius, who was led into an arena to be thrown to wild beasts. Reflecting on this situation, Eusebius noted that apparently this believer was supposed to have been executed on another occasion, but for some reason his martyrdom was delayed. Noting that the emperor was present, Eusebius speculated, "He seemed to have been purposely reserved for that time and that also the declaration of our Savior might be fulfilled which he declared to his disciples in his divine foreknowledge that they would be led before kings for the sake of confessing him."[19] Describing the story, he wrote,

> But this wrestler of piety was first summoned by the tyrant, then demanded to renounce his purpose with the promise of liberty. With a loud voice, he declared that he would cheerfully and with pleasure sustain whatever he might inflict on him, not indeed, for any wickedness but for his veneration of the God of the universe. Saying this, he combined actions with his words and rushing against a bear let loose upon him, he most readily offered himself to be devoured by the beast, after which he was taken up yet breathing and carried to prison. Surviving but one day, he had stones bound to his feet and was plunged into the midst of the sea. Such then was the martyrdom of Agapius.[20]

16. Latourette, *History of Christianity*, 106–7.
17. Mathetes, *Epistle to Diognetus* 7 (Roberts and Donaldson, *Ante-Nicene Fathers*, 1:27–28).
18. Eusebius, *Ecclesiastical History* 2.9.2–3 (Cruse, *Eusebius' Ecclesiastical History*, 44).
19. Eusebius, *The Book of Martyrs* 6 (Cruse, *Eusebius' Ecclesiastical History*, 314).
20. Eusebius, *The Book of Martyrs* 6 (Cruse, *Eusebius' Ecclesiastical History*, 314–15).

HISTORY AND EVANGELISM

Evangelism is ministry in action. It is supposed to be practical. Then why study the history of evangelism? This is a question addressed by Timothy Beougher. In the following, he raises four important matters related to the value of understanding the past when it comes to our Great Commission labors in the present.

> Why study history? The oft-quoted phrase "Those who fail to learn from the mistakes of history are doomed to repeat them" reminds us of the benefits of learning from those who have gone before. We could also reformulate that phrase in a more positive way: "Those who learn from the successes of history have an opportunity to repeat them." Let me suggest four benefits to studying church history, specifically the history of evangelism.
>
> First, we are helped to become more aware of our own presuppositions. We all bring to our study of the Bible (or any other material) a perspective that is influenced by the historical and cultural situation in which we find ourselves. Often, even without being aware of it, we screen all we consider through the filter of our own understanding. As we study different historical perspectives, we learn that there are alternative ways of viewing the matter. Studying history can sensitize us to the manner in which culture affects one's thinking and one's practice of evangelism.
>
> Second, we are encouraged to make our own formulations with a little more humility. Other believers throughout history may have viewed things differently. I remind my students, "When you enter the gates of heaven, you are not going to be met by a gauntlet of the great theologians of the past, cheering your entrance, exclaiming, 'Finally! The person who got it all right! Welcome!'" Studying history reminds us that faithful believers have differed on various means of communicating the gospel message.
>
> Third, we can learn from what others before us have done and not done, both good and bad. We can observe common threads that contribute to evangelistic movements. We can see how each generation sought to be faithful to the Great Commission in its own particular context. We can learn lessons from the experiences of others. Wise people learn from their experiences; really wise people learn from other people's experiences.
>
> Fourth, we can gain inspiration for Christian ministry. The church has a remarkable heritage of faithful believers throughout the centuries!
>
> Beougher, *Invitation to Evangelism*, 59–60.

Questions

1. Can you think of any additional benefits to studying the history of evangelism? Describe them.

2. What is the value of learning from past successes and mistakes?
3. Do you think that future generations (Lord willing) will learn from our successes and mistakes? If so, how should knowing that we will make mistakes influence our present evangelism?

Personal Evangelism

One of the most famous critics of the church was Celsus. Though the original writing has been lost, Origen (c. 185–c. 254) included portions of Celsus's attacks in his own writings. Noting Celsus's disgust with the Christians, Origen recorded the role of the personal witness of the believers in the spread of the gospel:

> We see, indeed, in private houses workers in wool and leather, and fullers, and persons of the most instructed and rustic character, not venturing to utter a word in the presence of their elders and wiser masters; but when they get hold of the children privately, and certain women as ignorant as themselves, they pour forth wonderful statements, to the effect that they ought not to give heed to their father and to their teachers, but should obey them; that the former are foolish and stupid, and neither know nor can perform anything that is really good, being preoccupied with empty trifles; that *they* alone know how men ought to live, and that, if the children obey them, they will both be happy themselves, and will make their home happy also. And while thus speaking, if they see one of the instructors of youth approaching, or one of the more intelligent class, or even the father himself, the more timid among them become afraid, while the more forward incite the children to throw off the yoke, whispering that in the presence of father and teachers they neither will nor can explain to them any good thing, seeing they turn away with aversion from the silliness and stupidity of such persons as being altogether corrupt, and far advanced in wickedness, and such as would inflict punishment upon them; but that if they wish (to avail themselves of their aid,) they must leave their father and their instructors, and go with the women and their playfellows to the women's apartments, or to the leather shop, or to the fuller's shop, that they may attain to perfection;—and by words like these they gain them over.[21]

Eusebius notes the evangelistic practices of Origen:

> But in presenting such specimens of his ascetic life to the beholders, he naturally induced many of his visitors to pursue the same course; so now many,

---

21. Origen, *Against Celsus* 3.55 (Roberts and Donaldson, *Ante-Nicene Fathers*, 4:486).

both of the unbelieving heathen, some of the learned, and even philosophers of no mean account, were prevailed upon to adopt his doctrine. Some of these, also, having been deeply imbued by him with the sound faith in Christ deeply implanted in the soul, were also eminent in the midst of the persecution then prevailing, so that some were taken and finished their course by martyrdom.[22]

The Octavius of Minucius Felix is an argument between the unbelieving Caecilius and the believing Octavius. Minucius Felix (died c. 250), the supposed author, serves as an arbitrator between the two. By the end of the writing, Caecilius becomes a believer:

> While, therefore, I was silently turning over these things in my own mind, Caecilius broke forth: "I congratulate as well my Octavius as myself, as much as possible on that tranquility in which we live, and I do not wait for the decision. Even thus we have conquered: not unjustly do I assume to myself the victory. For even as he is my conqueror, so I am triumphant over error. Therefore, in what belongs to the substance of the question, I both confess concerning providence, and I yield to God; and I agree concerning the sincerity of the way of life which is now mine."[23]

Open-Air Preaching

Through the writings of Origen, Celsus may have revealed a common public preaching approach of the early believers while expressing his opposition to the gospel. He accused them of being like the charlatans who "in the marketplaces perform the most disgraceful tricks, and who gather crowds around them, would never approach an assembly of wise men, nor dare to exhibit their arts among them; but whenever they see young men, and a mob of slaves, and a gathering of unintelligent persons, thither they thrust themselves in, and show themselves off."[24]

In his introductory comments to the *Recognitions of Clement*, Thomas Smith writes, "The *Recognitions of Clement* is a kind of philosophical and theological romance. The writer of the work seems to have had no intention of presenting his statements as facts; but, choosing the disciples of Christ and their followers as his principal characters, he has put into their mouths the most important of his beliefs, and woven the whole together by a thread

---

22. Eusebius, *Ecclesiastical History* 6.3.13 (Cruse, *Eusebius' Ecclesiastical History*, 195).
23. *The Octavius of Minucius Felix* 40 (Roberts and Donaldson, *Ante-Nicene Fathers*, 4:197).
24. Origen, *Against Celsus* 3.50 (Roberts and Donaldson, *Ante-Nicene Fathers*, 4:484).

of fictitious narrative."[25] Despite the fictitious nature of the narrative, the writer may have left behind a clue to open-air preaching as an early method used by the church.

It is here that the writer tells the story of a certain Barnabas, a believer, who arrived in Rome to share the gospel. The author notes, "When I heard these things [that he had come to preach], I began, with the rest of the multitude, to follow him, and to hear what he had to say. . . . For he did not confirm his assertions by the force of arguments, but produced, from the people who stood round about him, many witnesses of the sayings and marvels which he related."[26]

As Barnabas began to speak, hecklers began their opposition and the educated and more philosophically minded attacked with "grappling-hooks of syllogisms." Undaunted, he responded to the crowd:

> We have it in charge to declare to you the words and the wondrous works of Him who hath sent us, and to confirm the truth of what we speak, not by artfully devised arguments, but by witnesses produced from amongst yourselves. For I recognise many standing in the midst of you whom I remember to have heard along with us the things which we have heard, and to have seen what we have seen. But be it in your option to receive or to spurn the tidings which we bring to you. For we cannot keep back what we know to be for your advantage, because, if we be silent, woe is to us; but to you, if you receive not what we speak, destruction.[27]

Itinerant Evangelists

Eusebius shared the traditions where the apostles traveled throughout the world spreading the gospel.[28] In another account, he told of Pantaenus, a philosopher turned evangelist:

> The tradition is that this philosopher was then in great eminence, as he had been first disciplined in the philosophical principles of those called stoics. But he is said to have displayed such ardor and so zealous a disposition respecting the divine word, that he was constituted a herald of the gospel of Christ to the nations of the East and advanced even as far as India. There were even there many evangelists of the word, who were ardently striving to employ

---

25. T. Smith, "Recognitions of Clement," 73. The *Recognitions* are part of the Pseudo-Clementine literature.
26. *Recognitions of Clement* 1.7 (Roberts and Donaldson, *Ante-Nicene Fathers*, 8:78–79).
27. *Recognitions of Clement* 1.8 (Roberts and Donaldson, *Ante-Nicene Fathers*, 8:79).
28. Eusebius, *Ecclesiastical History* 3.1.

their inspired zeal after the apostolic example to increase and build up the divine word.[29]

In *Against Celsus*, Origen revealed the itinerant nature of many believers of his day. He articulated, "Christians do not neglect, as far as in them lies, to take measures to disseminate their doctrine throughout the whole world. Some of them, accordingly, have made it their business to itinerate not only through cities, but even villages and country houses, that they might make converts to God."[30]

Cleveland Coxe, in his introductory note to Irenaeus's *Against Heresies*, comments on the evangelistic thrust behind some of the leaders of the early church. For example, "We reach the banks of the Rhone, where for nearly a century Christian missions have flourished. Between Marseilles and Smyrna there seems to have been a brisk trade, and Polycarp had sent Pothinus into Celtic Gaul at an early date as its evangelist."[31] Later, specifically referring to Irenaeus, he writes, "The Episcopate of Irenaeus was distinguished by labours, 'in season and out of season,' for the evangelization of Southern Gaul; and he seems to have sent missionaries into other regions of what we now call France.[32]

Signs and Wonders[33]

Ramsay MacMullen refers to the role of signs and wonders in the growth of the apostolic and early church as "the chief instrument of conversion."[34] Origen argued that the Holy Spirit who empowered Jesus to accomplish the miraculous was the same Spirit who worked in some believers in his day to accomplish likewise.

> They expel evil spirits, and perform many cures, and foresee certain events, according to the will of the Logos. And although Celsus, or the Jew whom he has introduced, may treat with mockery what I am going to say, I shall say it nevertheless,—that many have been converted to Christianity as if against

---

29. Eusebius, *Ecclesiastical History* 5.10 (Cruse, *Eusebius' Ecclesiastical History*, 166).
30. Origen, *Against Celsus* 3.9 (Roberts and Donaldson, *Ante-Nicene Fathers*, 4:468).
31. Coxe, "Irenaeus Against Heresies," 309.
32. Coxe, "Irenaeus Against Heresies," 310.
33. As a historical note, the relationship between signs and wonders and evangelism received revived interest among evangelicals in the United States in the late twentieth century. Numerous resources and publications were produced. One of the most significant is Wimber, *Power Evangelism*.
34. MacMullen, *Christianizing the Roman Empire*, 27.

their will, some sort of spirit having suddenly transformed their minds from a hatred of the doctrine to a readiness to die in its defense, and having appeared to them either in a waking vision or a dream of the night."[35]

Irenaeus (c. 120/140–c. 202) argued that believers received grace to perform signs and wonders in relation to evangelism. He commented, "For some do certainly and truly drive out devils, so that those who have thus been cleansed from evil spirits frequently both believe [in Christ] and join themselves to the Church."[36]

Public Discussion and Debate

In the *Recognitions of Clement*, the author described a time when, after arriving in Caesarea Stratonis, he met Peter, "a most approved disciple of Him who appeared in Judaea."[37] This Peter entered into an intentionally planned public discourse with a certain Simon Magus about the truth of the gospel. Before going to the location for the debate, Peter requested prayer from the believers, revealing the evangelistic drive behind the debate: "'Brethren, let us pray that God, for His unspeakable mercy through His Christ, would help me going out on behalf of the salvation of men who have been created by Him.' Having said this, and having prayed, he went forth to the court of the house, in which a great multitude of people were assembled."[38]

Later, Peter arrived in Tripolis and through his connections with a believer named Maro was able to locate a place in his home to address another crowd of people:

> "But enough has been said of these things; for time presses, and the religious devotion of the people invites us to address them." And when he had thus spoken, he asked where there was a suitable place for discussion. And Maro said: "I have a very spacious hall which can hold more than five hundred men, and there is also a garden within the house; or if it please you to be in some public place, all would prefer it, for there is nobody who does not desire at least to see your face." Peter said: "Show me the hall, or the garden." And when he had seen the hall, he went in to see the garden also; and suddenly the whole multitude, as if someone had called them, rushed into the house and thence broke through into the garden, where Peter was already standing, selecting a fit place for discussion.[39]

---

35. Origen, *Against Celsus* 1.46 (Roberts and Donaldson, *Ante-Nicene Fathers*, 4:415).
36. Irenaeus, *Against Heresies* 2.32.4 (Roberts and Donaldson, *Ante-Nicene Fathers*, 1:409).
37. *Recognitions of Clement* 1.12 (Roberts and Donaldson, *Ante-Nicene Fathers*, 8:80).
38. *Recognitions of Clement* 2.19 (Roberts and Donaldson, *Ante-Nicene Fathers*, 8:102).
39. *Recognitions of Clement* 4.6 (Roberts and Donaldson, *Ante-Nicene Fathers*, 8:136).

Church Planting

Glenn Hinson comments, "Individual missionary endeavor most of the time either took place in relation to churches or resulted in the planting of churches which would continue the task of witnessing to others and incorporate them into their membership."[40] Throughout the New Testament the pattern for church planting usually resulted from the church planters entering a city, evangelizing and then congregationalizing the new believers, and finally appointing elders over the new congregation.

Eusebius, writing on the evangelism and church planting work following the first apostles, noted:

> Of those who flourished in these times, Quadratus is said to have been distinguished for his prophetic gifts. There were many others also noted in these times who held the first rank in the apostolic succession. These, as the holy disciples of such men, built up the churches where foundations had been previously laid in every place by the apostles. They augmented the means of promulgating the gospel more and more and spread the seeds of salvation and of the heavenly kingdom throughout the world far and wide. . . .
>
> After laying the foundation of the faith in foreign parts as the particular object of their mission, appointing others as shepherds of the flocks, and committing to these the care of those who had been recently introduced, they went again to other regions and nations with the grace and cooperating of God.[41]

Also, according to Eusebius, it was Mark who traveled to Egypt and first "proclaimed the gospel there which he had written and first established churches at the city of Alexandria."[42] Reflecting on the growth of the church, the early historian also noted that "inspired evangelists and apostles had gone throughout all the earth and their words to the ends of the world. Throughout every city and village, like a replenished barn floor, churches were rapidly found abounding and filled with members from every people."[43]

Writings

Origen's evangelistic labors were evident in his writings. In his work against Celsus's ideologies, he wrote, "We . . . at first invite all men to be

---

40. Hinson, *Evangelization of the Roman Empire*, 40.
41. Eusebius, *Ecclesiastical History* 3.37 (Cruse, *Eusebius' Ecclesiastical History*, 102).
42. Eusebius, *Ecclesiastical History* 2.16 (Cruse, *Eusebius' Ecclesiastical History*, 50).
43. Eusebius, *Ecclesiastical History* 2.3.1–2 (Cruse, *Eusebius' Ecclesiastical History*, 39).

healed, and exhort those who are sinners to come to the consideration of the doctrines which teach men not to sin, and those who are devoid of understanding to those which beget wisdom, and those who are children to rise in their thoughts to manhood, and those who are simply unfortunate to good fortune, or—which is the more appropriate term to use—to blessedness."[44]

In his introductory note to *Exhortation to the Heathen* by Clement of Alexandria, Cleveland Coxe comments on the purpose of the publication as "to win pagans to the Christian faith."[45] It is here Clement makes the call for repentance: "But it has been God's fixed and constant purpose to save the flock of men: for this end the good God sent the good Shepherd. And the Word, having unfolded the truth, showed to men the height of salvation, that either repenting they might be saved, or refusing to obey, they might be judged. This is the proclamation of righteousness: to those that obey, glad tidings; to those that disobey, judgment."[46]

It was said of Justin Martyr (c. 100–c. 165) that "he acted as an evangelist, taking every opportunity to proclaim the gospel as the only safe and certain philosophy, the only way to salvation."[47] At the conclusion of his *Second Apology*, Justin wrote, "And I despised the wicked and deceitful doctrine of Simon of my own nation. And if you give this book your authority, we will expose him before all, that, if possible, they may be converted. For this end alone did we compose this treatise."[48]

The writer of the *Epistle to Diognetus* was obviously writing to share with Diognetus about the Christian faith. Throughout this brief epistle he describes the truth of the gospel: "He Himself took on Him the burden of our iniquities, He gave His own Son as a ransom for us, the holy One for transgressors, the blameless One for the wicked, the righteous One for the unrighteous, the incorruptible One for the corruptible, the immortal One for them that are mortal. For what other thing was capable of covering our sins than His righteousness? By what other one was it possible that we, the wicked and ungodly, could be justified, than by the only Son of God?"[49]

44. Origen, *Against Celsus* 59 (Roberts and Donaldson, *Ante-Nicene Fathers*, 4:487–88).
45. Coxe, "Clement of Alexandria," 167.
46. Clement of Alexandria, *Exhortation to the Heathen* 11 (Roberts and Donaldson, *Ante-Nicene Fathers*, 204).
47. Coxe, "First Apology of Justin Martyr," 160.
48. Justin Martyr, *Second Apology* 15 (Roberts and Donaldson, *Ante-Nicene Fathers*, 1:193).
49. Mathetes, *Epistle to Diognetus* 9 (Roberts and Donaldson, *Ante-Nicene Fathers*, 1:28).

Family Units and Homes[50]

Reidar Hvalvik discussed the importance of the role of the family in the spread of the gospel. He observes, "The early Christians were part of families and other social networks. At the very outset it is reasonable to think that this became an important factor in the spreading of the Christian faith, maybe *the* most important factor."[51] For example, in the brief, anonymous writing *The Martyrdom of the Holy Martyrs*, the author clearly revealed the importance of the family in the spread of the gospel: "And Paeon stood up and said, 'I too am a Christian.' Rusticus the prefect said, 'Who taught you?' Paeon said, 'From our parents we received this good confession.' Euelpistus said, 'I willingly heard the words of Justin. But from my parents also I learned to be a Christian.'"[52]

The tradition in Torah of passing along the faith (Deut. 6:7–9) was continued by the early believers. The home was the place where the gospel was shared with family, acquaintances, servants, or anyone receiving hospitality from those called Christians. In some contexts, early churches met in homes.

It is estimated that by the year 300, 7 percent of the world was Christian, with 17 percent of the global population evangelized, and the Scriptures had been translated into ten languages.[53] What started as a persecuted group became one of the recognized religions of the Roman Empire by the fourth century. Disciples used a variety of methods to communicate the good news that they had received. Though the church would innovate and develop other approaches, many of these evangelistic methods would continue into the twenty-first century.

— QUESTIONS TO CONSIDER —

1. Why do you think that some of the means of evangelism used during this period are still being used today?
2. Were you surprised by any of the means by which the gospel spread? If so, why? Which one was the most interesting? Explain.

---

50. For more details on the role of the family and households with the early church, see Carolyn Osiek and David L. Balch, *Families in the New Testament World: Households and House Churches* (Westminster John Knox, 1997). Roger W. Ghering has produced a serious study of the relationship of families and the expansion of the gospel in *House Church and Mission: The Importance of Household Structures in Early Christianity* (Hendrickson, 2004).
51. Hvalvik, "In Word and Deed," 282.
52. *The Martyrdom of the Holy Martyrs* 3 (Roberts and Donaldson, *Ante-Nicene Fathers* 1:306).
53. Barrett and Johnson, *World Christian Trends*, 114.

13

INFLUENCERS (PART 1)

AD 300–1500

Before continuing with this survey of the history of evangelism, we must note three limitations. First, while women have had an extremely important role in evangelism, scholarship is lacking (though growing) in this area.[1] I have included a few names, but more must be added to future histories. Laceye Warner brings attention to this limitation in scholarship in *Saving Women: Retrieving Evangelistic Theology and Practice*, where she examines the lives of seven women.[2] Second, only a few Majority World evangelists, from the past two centuries, have been included in my overview. Again, names and stories from Asia, Africa, and Central and South America must be part of the church's history of evangelism, especially in the modern epoch. Herein is another area ripe for scholarship and publication.

---

1. Michael Green was quick to note that the gospel and kingdom ethic elevated women to a place of significance and involvement that was unknown in first-century Roman society. Beginning with Jesus's ministry, women were involved in the advancement of the gospel (Green, *Evangelism in the Early Church*, 118). Also, examples such as Perpetua and Felicity (early third century) revealed the powerful testimonies of women who gave witness to the gospel while facing great persecution.

2. Warner, *Saving Women*. Jiang Peifen also raises awareness of this issue in "Women and Evangelism," and Richard Douglass-Chin draws attention to the matter in *Preacher Woman*. Walter Liefeld, in "Women and Evangelism," traces the topic, in seven pages, from the first through the fourth centuries. Note also Pope-Levison, *Old Time Religion*; Epstein, *Politics of Domesticity*; Liptak, "Bible Women." However, a few books have been published on the topic of women in missions, including Beaver, *American Protestant Women*; Robert, *American Women in Mission*; Dzubinski and Stasson, *Women in the Mission*; Doyle and Doyle, *Women Who Risk*; Zurlo, *Women in World Christianity*.

Finally, church history contains a multitude of examples of the gospel encountering people who then confess Jesus as Lord. Women and men traveled across the street and across the known world to proclaim the message of the hope of Christ. The Spirit worked in conjunction with the word preached and brought people into the kingdom. However, such should not be equated with Christianization, whereby people embrace a novel religion for political, material, or survival reasons. When a ruler declares to his people that they are now a Christian kingdom and will be baptized or face retaliation, such should not be considered evangelism. When a military authority leads troops into mass baptism, the church is right to question if such persons have heard the gospel and been born again.

Historians often equate biblical conversions with cultural conversions. Jesus did not commission the church to make Christians, civilize people, or produce converts. Since historical records have not always been kept by evangelists, sometimes it is difficult to distinguish between people who became followers of the Way and people who became followers of the way of their authority figures.[3]

Another related challenge when studying church growth across two thousand years is that history is filled with heroes and heretics. Oftentimes, heroes of the faith strive to communicate orthodoxy, and we read of the church's expansion in a certain part of the world. Other times, heretics teach a message that is a syncretistic expression of biblical doctrine, and we read of the church's expansion in that part of the world too. Just because the church grows does not mean that such is healthy growth reflected by biblical evangelism and discipleship.

By the fifth century, the faith had spread in a variety of directions. Patriarchates existed in Rome, Alexandria, Constantinople, Antioch, and Jerusalem. From the fourth through the ninth centuries, the faith continued to spread in an eastwardly direction to areas in Arabia, Yemen, Persia, and India.

In his important work on the church's expansion in the East, Philip Jenkins notes that "Christianity became predominantly European not because this continent had any obvious affinity for that faith, but by default: Europe was the continent where it was not destroyed."[4]

---

3. Clovis, king of the Franks, requiring his soldiers to receive baptism with him (496) and Charlemagne's invasion and forced baptisms of the Saxons (772–97) are a couple of infamous examples of widespread Christianization without regeneration. Milton Rudnick attempts to resolve the problem faced by the historian, stating that he uses "evangelism" in his study to refer to the ways the church has tried to "Christianize" other people. While his language is unhelpful and theologically problematic, his clarity of historical method is appreciated, for many authors fail to acknowledge the challenge of producing a history of evangelism. See Rudnick, *Speaking the Gospel*, 9.

4. Jenkins, *Lost History of Christianity*, 3.

TELLING STORIES

One method used by those who preached the gospel in the centuries following the apostles is that of storytelling. Though many who were officially sent by the church were literate and even provided Bible translations, oftentimes those to whom they ministered were illiterate. Preachers discovered that there is power in telling the grand stories in the Old and New Testaments. This method of evangelism has not been lost with time, as Tom Steffen recalls the power of storying the gospel.

> I thought that I had finally learned enough of the Ifugao language and culture (Philippines) to allow me to do some public evangelism. I developed Bible lessons that followed the topical outline we received in pre-field training: the Bible, God, Satan, humanity, sin, judgment and Jesus Christ. I began by introducing my Ifugao listeners to the authority-base (the Bible). Then I quickly moved on to the second part of the outline (God), and so forth, culminating with Jesus Christ. I presented the lessons in a topical, systematic format. My goal was not only to communicate the gospel, but to communicate it in such a way that the Ifugao could effectively articulate it to others.
>
> But as I taught, I soon realized that the Ifugao found it difficult to follow the topical presentations and found it even harder to explain the content to others. I was perplexed. Something needed to change, so I added a number of stories from the Old Testament to illustrate the abstract (theoretical) concepts in the lessons through pictorial (concrete) characters and objects. I told stories about Creation, the Fall, Cain and Abel, the Flood, the escape from Egypt, the giving of the Ten Commandments, the Tabernacle, Elijah and Baal, all of which would provide foundation for Jesus's story. Their response was phenomenal. Not only did the evangelistic sessions come alive, the recipients became instant evangelists, telling the stories to friends enthusiastically and effectively. From then on, I integrated stories in all my evangelistic efforts. . . .
>
> Is it not time for today's Christian workers to revitalize one of the world's oldest, most universal and powerful art forms—storytelling? I believe so. I also believe that Christian workers, with training and practice, can effectively communicate the finished story of Jesus Christ and connect it to the target audience's unfinished story. Presenting an overview of Old and New Testament stories that unveils the history of redemption will highlight for the listeners the Storyline (Jesus Christ) of the sacred Storybook (Bible). Should this happen, the gospel will be much more easily understood, and more frequently communicated to family and friends.
>
> Steffen, "Gospel Through Stories," 6, 10.

Questions

1. What do you think Steffen means by "abstract (theoretical) concepts"?
2. Why do you think such change occurred among the Ifugao after Steffen used stories as a method?

The first Christian kingdom was beyond the Roman Empire. The king of Osrhoene, whose capital was Edessa, accepted the Christian faith in about AD 200. During the second century, Christianity reached India.[5] By AD 300, Armenia, and soon thereafter Georgia, declared Christianity the official religion.[6] In Africa, Nubia remained a Christian kingdom from the sixth century until the fifteenth. Ethiopia (Abyssinia) was recognized as a Christian context before Constantine's fourth-century conversion. By the third century, a strong Christian presence was felt in Persia. Central and East Asia were encountering missionaries by the fifth and seventh centuries. By the eighth century, plans were made to expand into the lands of the Turks and Tibetans.[7] The following are names of a few significant individuals who labored extensively in spreading the gospel from the third to the fifth century.

Gregory Thaumaturgus (b. 213?). Gregory, born in Pontus, had studied under Origen in Caesarea and became an evangelist and bishop in his hometown. Tradition has it that only seventeen Christians lived in the city when he became bishop, but after thirty years there were only seventeen pagans.[8] He also co-opted pagan festivals and renamed them after martyrs.

Ulfilas (311–380). Among the northern peoples, the Goths were the first to be significantly influenced by the Christian faith.[9] It is thought that this people initially encountered Christians whom they took as captives. One particular Goth, Ulfilas, converted and eventually became a missionary to his own people, north of the Danube River. His work involved producing a written form of Gothic and then providing scriptural translation into the language. This innovative method would influence missionaries in years to come as they ventured to other peoples.

Martin of Tours (316–397). Martin was born into a pagan family, but he chose the Christian faith at ten years of age. He became a missionary in the provinces of Pannonia and Illyricum (Balkan Peninsula). Martin served as a bishop during the fourth century and pioneered the use of monasticism in Gaul. He served as a missionary in Touraine, France. Martin spent much

---

5. If church tradition is correct about Thomas's arrival in the country. According to Kenneth Scott Latourette, it is probable that by the fourth and fifth centuries, Christians were located in India and Ceylon (*History of Christianity*, 104).

6. Stephen Neill notes that with Armenia, this was the first known case where a king's conversion was the initial step in the conversion of a whole country. He writes, "Tiridates accepted Christianity as the religion of his state; willy-nilly the aristocracy had to follow him, and then the Gospel spread among the common people" (*History of Christian Missions*, 48).

7. For historical details on these matters, see Jenkins, *Lost History of Christianity*, 45–70.

8. Neill, *History of Christian Missions*, 47.

9. Most Gothic Christians embraced Arianism (Latourette, *History of Christianity*, 100).

time with Hilary of Poitiers, protested against heresy, razed pagan temples, developed a reputation as an exorcist, and saw many conversions.

Ambrose of Milan (339–397). Ambrose was another early figure associated with the rise of monasticism. Born in Gaul, Ambrose served as the bishop of Milan and was known for his oratory skills as a preacher, saw many conversions, and sent preachers to the Alps. Augustine of Hippo was converted under his ministry.

Monica (331–387). The prayers, lifestyle, and proclamation of the gospel by a mother to her children, and even a wife to her spouse, is a story that has been told countless times throughout history. One of the most influential witnesses to the gospel was Monica, mother of Augustine of Hippo. Most of what is known about her comes from Augustine's pen. It was her witness that was used by the Lord to bring her husband, Patricius, to faith and her witness and the preaching of Ambrose to bring Augustine to faith.

Augustine of Hippo (354–430). Ordained as a priest and soon thereafter consecrated as bishop, Augustine would become one of the church's most influential theologians. He was a preacher but was mostly known for his prolific and weighty writings and apologetic treatises, which address a variety of issues, including heresy.

John Chrysostom (345–407). Chrysostom became a monk and was an eloquent preacher in Antioch. The emperor appointed him as bishop of Constantinople. While serving in this role, he had a vision for reaching the pagans. He was able to send missionaries to such, particularly the Goths. He was also engaged in destroying pagan temples and repurposing structures for churches. Paganism continued in the Roman Empire but began to wane after the fifth century.[10]

Patrick (389?–461). A great deal of what can be known about Patrick comes from his two writings: *Confessions* and *Letter to the Soldiers of Coroticus*. Beyond these extant records, much is speculative and myth. Patrick was a native of Britain, raised in a Christian family, but was kidnapped and carried off to Ireland, where he remained a slave for six years. As a sixteen-year-old, he was given charge over flocks. Through a dream (vision?) he found guidance and courage to flee from his captors and find passage home. Sometime later, through dreams, he heard the Irish calling to him to return and be with them. Understanding this as a call from the Lord, he returned as a bishop and baptized thousands and ordained many clergy. Though he was not the first to introduce the faith to the Irish, nor was he the only missionary who influenced the people, he did have the most extensive and lasting impact.

---

10. Latourette, *History of Christianity*, 99.

His work had little connection with Rome, resulting in an Irish expression of the faith.

In their work on mission history, John Mark Terry and Robert Gallagher note that several social factors contributed to the growth of the church throughout the fourth and fifth centuries. With societies disintegrating, the church provided an element of stability and security that was appealing. Paganism was spiritually bankrupt, and monotheism met religious needs. Christian morality provided a standard of superiority to other lifestyles. The missionary zeal of certain bishops and others resulted in activities to advance the faith. Miraculous events sometimes accompanied preaching that revealed the power of Christ over other divinities. By this time, Rome had embraced the Christian faith and created a favorable environment for its advancement. Monasticism developed to become an influential method to spread the faith.[11] A momentum of successful growth had occurred for a lengthy period, and such success bred success. As Germanic tribes migrated into Roman territory, they were exposed to the new Roman religion.[12]

The next thousand years revealed a variety of individuals engaged in a wide array of kingdom practices. Monks and educators were some of those who carried the church's message to the highways and hedges of both familiar and foreign societies. Some engaged in ministry endorsed with the blessing of church leaders. Others defied ecclesial orders of their day and suffered greatly at the hands of such leaders.

Benedict of Nursia (480–547). Benedict founded the Benedictine monastery at Monte Cassino in central Italy and is considered the father of Western monasticism. The area around Cassino was largely pagan, and many were converted through his ministry. He is also known for the Benedictine Rule, which was written to provide governance for his monastery as well as its spiritual and material support. Others throughout Europe began to apply the Rule to their abbeys.

Columba (d. 597). Columba was an Irish missionary who ventured beyond his country and established a monastery on the island of Iona to reach the Picts. From here, many other missionaries were sent to parts of Scotland and England.

Columbanus (543–615). Near the end of the fifth century, Clovis, king of the Franks, accepted baptism. With many of his military following suit, a

---

11. Originally, monastic life was cloistered from society, but by the sixth century monks were engaged in reaching pagan communities (see Rudnick, *Speaking the Gospel*, 67–73). Of course, if Patrick is considered a monk, then the timeline is moved back to the fifth century. For a list of reasons why Patrick was a monk, though the best surviving documents on his life never make that claim, see Smither, *Missionary Monks*, 61–63.

12. Terry and Gallagher, *History of Missions*, 18–19.

cultural context was set for the Franks. The Irish monk Columbanus and a team of monks sought favor with Frankish king Guntram and were granted permission to establish a monastery. Throughout his life, he was responsible for establishing monasteries in France, Italy, and Switzerland.

Augustine of Canterbury (d. 604/5). Augustine was sent by Pope Gregory I with forty monks to pagan England. King Ethelbert I of Kent welcomed them and provided a place for them to live and preach. The king and others converted under the ministry of Augustine. Augustine founded the church in southern England and was the first archbishop of Canterbury.

Boniface of England (d. 754). The English scholar, priest, and monk (later bishop) Boniface (also named Wynfrith) was assigned by Pope Gregory II to the area of Germany. He worked with political leaders, established monasteries throughout the country, and developed missionary efforts in Bavaria, Saxony, and among the Frisians of the Netherlands. Unlike the Celtic monks, Boniface translated a Roman form of the Christian faith where he served. He was martyred in 754 while serving among the Frisians.

Ansgar (801–865). Ansgar, a French monk who became archbishop of Bremen, received the title "Apostle of the North," and his move from France to the north began with two kings. The Frankish king Louis the Pious and Danish king Harald Klak collaborated to develop a mutual alliance. Louis exhorted Klak to take missionaries with him to his land so that the people could be instructed in the Christian faith. Klak and his court had recently received baptism. Ansgar and a team were selected to relocate and serve in the Scandinavian region among the violent Vikings. His work involved working with political leaders, preaching, establishing schools, founding churches, and sending missionaries.

Cyril (826–869) and **Methodius (815–885).** The first significant advancement of the faith among the Slavs is credited to the work of two brothers. Born to a prosperous family in Thessalonica, Cyril and Methodius were selected by the emperor to venture into the land of the Slavs. Their work included developing local leaders and producing an alphabet to express the Slavonic language. From this, scriptural translations would be provided. People would have an opportunity to hear, read, and understand the Christian faith in their heart language. The brothers endured hardships and opposition. Following Cyril's death, Methodius was appointed by the pope to be the archbishop over the Slavonic regions of Pannonia and Moravia. Their work provided a foundation for future Eastern Orthodox missionary labors. Missionaries would eventually travel into areas of Bulgaria, Serbia, and Russia.

Peter Waldo (d. 1218). Born in France, and also known by the name Valdes, Waldo became a wealthy merchant. Waldo was an itinerant preacher who advocated voluntary poverty. His numerous followers called themselves the "Poor in Spirit" or the "Poor Men of Lyons"; many were known as the Waldenses.[13] He founded an order of lay preachers who traveled in twos, preaching repentance wherever allowed. He preached that salvation was by faith through Christ alone. He expressed his numerous frustrations and opposition toward the Catholic Church and eventually was excommunicated along with the Waldenses.

Francis of Assisi (1182–1226). Francis's simple lifestyle and labors among the poor won many converts. He is well-known for the monastic order that took his name: Franciscans. The monks moved beyond the monastery and traveled extensively, begging, serving others, and preaching.

John Wycliffe (1330–1384). Wycliffe was an English professor and rector who had been influenced by Augustine and Aquinas. He was outspoken against the corruption within the Catholic Church and what he believed were false teachings. He argued that the Bible was to be the authority for the church, and he translated it from the Latin into English for the common person. He was responsible for sending itinerant and lay preachers to do evangelism. A large number of followers developed with the name Lollards. Both they and Wycliffe experienced a great deal of persecution for the faith, mainly from the Catholic Church.

Jan Hus (1373–1415). Hus became a priest and later dean and rector of the University of Prague. He preached in both Latin and Czech. He openly spoke against corruption that he observed within the Catholic Church, among both priests and popes. He was burned at the stake, but his death fanned the flames of an even greater movement.

An examination of the life and ministries of Waldo, the Waldenses, Wycliffe, the Lollards, Hus, and the Hussites reveals a connection to evangelism. These forerunners of the Reformation emphasized the centrality of the Bible and preaching in local languages. They preached wherever an opportunity arose, be it a sanctuary, public meeting place, or in the open air. Their example would be imitated for centuries to follow. They opposed church corruption and false teaching and emphasized holy living while giving attention to the laity in ministry.[14]

The fourth century saw the decline in obedience to the commands of Christ as the church and the state strengthened their relationship. During

---

13. Latourette, *History of Christianity*, 451. Scholars debate the origins of the Waldensians and Waldo's influence on them. Most argue for a connection between the two with Waldo's influence.

14. Terry, *Evangelism*, 57–69.

this time, Christians wanted to get away from the impurities of society (and church corruption) and observed the rise of monastic communities that likely had origins with Saint Anthony the Great in 285. Monasteries would develop throughout the East and West for the next millennia. At the start of the fifth century, the estimated Christian population was 13 percent, with 24 percent of the global population evangelized. However, it is estimated that eleven hundred years later world population had increased to 18 percent Christian, but the total percentage evangelized had decreased to approximately 20 percent.[15]

— QUESTIONS TO CONSIDER —

1. What is the difference between evangelization and Christianization?
2. What are some of the evangelistic methods mentioned in this chapter that are still being used today?
3. What were common evangelistic practices from the fourth century until the fifteenth?

---

15. Barrett and Johnson, *World Christian Trends*, 116, 128.

14

INFLUENCERS (PART 2)

AD 1500 TO THE PRESENT

The Reformation, led by Martin Luther, Huldrych Zwingli, John Calvin, John Knox, and Anabaptists, brought about seismic theological, ecclesiastical, and cultural shifts. While gospel proclamation generally occurred within the confines of church gatherings, several times a week, some preachers were sent to audiences who were not cultural Christians: Paulus Scharpff states that evangelistic work was almost exclusively pointed toward Roman Catholics.[1] Reforms during this time started a chain reaction that eventually resulted in increased evangelistic zeal and practice throughout the world.

Pietism was a movement that developed among German Lutherans in the seventeenth century. The emphasis on the authority of the Bible and personal faith and holiness was seen as a more excellent expression than an orthodoxy that lacks commitment and zeal. Justo González claims that the most significant contribution of Pietism to the faith was the birth of Protestant missions.[2] While various social forces and individuals influenced this movement, it was a Frankfurt pastor, Philipp Jakob Spener, whose concerns, messages, and writings catalyzed the growth of Pietism.

Philipp Jakob Spener (1635–1705). Through his ministry in Frankfurt, particularly home prayer and Bible study, Spener collected his thoughts in a 1675

---

1. Scharpff, *History of Evangelism*, 10. Scharpff also notes that Luther periodically traveled and addressed outdoor crowds (11) and advocated for periodic church gatherings that were focused on evangelism (12). However, the "first traveling evangelist of the Reformation period" was Kaspar Schwenkfeld von Ossig (1489–1561) (13).

2. González, *Reformation*, 207–8.

publication, *Pia Desideria*. This work addressed his concerns with the church and points of reformation. They included Bible study, emphasis on lay involvement, personal holiness and godly lifestyle, and evangelism. He eventually moved to Berlin and had great influence at the University of Halle. This institution became the epicenter for Pietism and resulted in much missionary activity.

Milton Rudnick notes the evangelistic connection: "Out of Pietism came evangelistic motivation, skills, and agencies. Like the Anabaptists before them, Pietists assumed that most people around them, both laity and clergy, although externally connected with the church, were not authentically Christian. Therefore, they were lost and in need of conversion—a vast mission field. The Pietists, on the other hand, having deeply experienced their own lostness and God's saving grace, realized that they had something vital to share."[3] Spener's example resonated with many people. However, it was his relationship with a particular professor that resulted in great dissemination of his views.

August Hermann Francke (1663–1727). Francke encountered Spener and became a Pietist. His newfound views resulted in his departure from teaching at Leipzig but moved him to Halle, where he both served a church and taught at the university. He was significantly engaged in social ministries throughout the city but also did extensive training of evangelists to be sent throughout the world.

Count Ludwig Nickolaus von Zinzendorf (1700–1760). The University of Halle influenced many for the advancement of the gospel. However, it was a young Lutheran who studied at the school who would change the course of global Protestant evangelization. Zinzendorf was ordained a Lutheran and used his family's Saxony estate (Herrnhut) to provide refuge to Bohemians and Moravians fleeing persecution. Though Zinzendorf wanted to incorporate the new community into the Lutheran Church, Lutheran leaders did not agree. The community of "Moravians," under Zinzendorf's leadership, sent teams of evangelists to some of the most remote places on the planet to preach the gospel.

Those influenced by Pietism made significant contributions to the advancement of the gospel throughout the world. Wherever they traveled, they attempted to learn the language and culture of the people. This way, the gospel could be communicated more effectively, and Bibles could be translated into the local languages. Pietists frequently established schools to teach literacy so the Scriptures could be read. Their preaching emphasized personal conversion based on repentance and faith. Evangelism was also connected to small groups and at times involved social ministry.[4]

---

3. Rudnick, *Speaking the Gospel*, 116.
4. Terry, *Evangelism*, 85–95.

Great Awakenings and Revivals. The terms *awakening* and *revival* are often confused with each other.[5] Scholars, often more concerned with historical and sociological attributes, are guilty of equating the two, as theological and spiritual matters are not their primary concerns. An awakening, as opposed to a revival, is generally characterized by a large ingathering of unbelievers into the kingdom of God. A widespread movement of the Spirit and evangelistic preaching results in many people coming to faith. A revival is focused on believers. It represents a reviving of what is already regenerated.[6] While evangelism and conversion growth are found during times of revivals, awakenings find their identity in the dead being raised to life.

The First Great Awakening occurred in the American colonies during the eighteenth century (1734–70).[7] It resulted in many conversions and social transformation, during a time when morality had sunk to a low depth. Baptist and Methodist churches began to grow in number, with pastors, members, and circuit riders eventually moving to the western frontier to preach and plant churches. Jonathan Edwards (1703–58) was a theologian and pastor of the Congregational Church in Northampton, Massachusetts, when the awakening began and swept through the congregation and beyond. His preaching, scholarship, and writing were used by God during this unique period.

The Second Great Awakening occurred in New England in the 1790s and concluded in the 1840s.[8] This would result in the founding of several colleges, seminaries, and tract societies, as well as mission societies such as the American Board of Commissioners for Foreign Missions (1810) and Bible societies such as the American Bible Society (1816). In 1801 the Cane Ridge Revival in Cane Ridge, Kentucky, began, organized by James McGready, a Presbyterian pastor. An invitation was extended to many people to gather for a "camp meeting." Thousands arrived in what became an interdenominational gathering to hear a variety of preachers over a few days. It was here that uncontrolled emotional outbursts were observed, with people weeping, laughing, running around, and barking like animals. A large number of people were converted during the gatherings. In years to follow, whenever the

---

5. As an example of this, see the article "Great Awakening" on the website *History* (https://www.history.com/topics/european-history/great-awakening). Unfortunately, many Christian scholars equate the two terms.

6. Revivals have also been connected with revivalism, a practice to revitalize churches and reach the lost.

7. Scholars frequently disagree over the exact dates of awakenings and revivals. It should also be noted that such events were not limited to North America. For example, Europe has a history of similar works of the Spirit, and Pyongyang (now part of North Korea) experienced a revival in 1907.

8. Carwardine, "Second Great Awakening," 84. Milton Rudnick dates the beginning and ending of this awakening as 1796/97 to around 1830 (*Speaking the Gospel*, 172).

words *evangelism* or *revival* were mentioned, audiences equated such with the Cane Ridge Revival.[9] It has been argued that a Third Great Awakening occurred in 1857–58. Some have postulated that a Fourth Great Awakening in the United States occurred during the mid-to-late twentieth century with the Jesus Movement.

George Whitefield (1714–1770). Whitefield was one of the most famous evangelists in England and North America, often drawing massive crowds to hear him preach. He, along with his friends John and Charles Wesley, innovated evangelistic methods that resulted in many coming to faith in Jesus and continued to be used throughout the twentieth and twenty-first centuries. Though not the first to conduct open-air preaching throughout Europe, his approach to preaching outside church gatherings in public spaces allowed him to connect with unbelievers and horrified many church leaders and members. He was a Calvinist in his theology. As an evangelist with the Church of England, Whitefield was involved in awakenings both in Britain and the British American colonies.

John Wesley (1703–1791) and **the Methodists.**[10] Wesley, along with his brother **Charles,**[11] did not set out to establish a new denomination.[12] Rather, as a minister of the Church of England, he desired an internal reformation. As with Whitefield, many came to hear Wesley preach. Wesley was influenced by Pietism and Jacob Arminius. He eventually modified his views, which were later described as Wesleyan-Arminianism. Because other ministers did not appreciate his messages, he (like Whitefield) took to open-air preaching. His travels took him to many locations and required innovative approaches. He established societies (overseen by lay people) that served as weekly small groups for accountability and encouragement in the faith. If a society outgrew its meeting place (usually a home), a chapel was constructed. This approach to organizing believers' growth in holiness, worship, ministry, and the development of circuit preachers was a significant means to the development and expansion of Methodism through evangelism. Wesley's organization and leadership training catalyzed a disciple-making movement that continued long after his death.

---

9. González, *Reformation*, 246.

10. The title "methodists" was given by outsiders who observed the movement's advocacy for the use of methods related to growth in Christ.

11. Charles Wesley (1707–88) was also a minister in the Church of England, known for his extensive and influential hymns. His use of music, in partnership with his brother, was a novel and effective method of doing evangelism and strengthening societies in the faith. Charles was also an evangelist, traveled extensively, and preached to multitudes.

12. By 1790 Wesley's religious societies numbered 117 with 77,000 members and 313 preachers (Scharpff, *History of Evangelism*, 76).

The evangelistic work of Whitefield and the Wesleys often dominates historical discussions of evangelism in Europe and North America during the eighteenth century. However, other individuals were significantly involved in such labors as well. The following are a few from the period.

Countess Selina Huntingdon (1707–1791). Though connected to the Anglican Church, Huntingdon was Calvinistic and had a zeal for evangelism and eventually joined with the Methodists to form a group of Calvinist Methodists. She leveraged her prosperity to facilitate evangelism. She was a strong advocate for Whitefield's ministry. Huntingdon provided a retreat for itinerant evangelists and also traveled with others, sometimes providing the funds necessary for preaching venues.

Theodore Frelinghuysen (1691–1747). Frelinghuysen was a German pastor who was sent to New Jersey to oversee four Dutch Reformed congregations. The plague of unregenerate church membership had already taken hold in the colonies a generation after the first settlers. Influenced by Pietism, his preaching warned against nominal Christianity and church membership as means of salvation. He preached evangelistic messages and was a significant leader in the First Great Awakening in the colonies that resulted in many people coming to faith.

Gilbert Tennent (1703–1764). Tennent, a Presbyterian pastor in New Jersey, was influenced by Frelinghuysen's example and counsel. His preaching shifted to calling church members to salvation in Christ, and for them to not rest in their Christian heritage. His ministry influenced extensive revival among Presbyterians in New Jersey and New York that resulted in many people experiencing salvation in Christ.

John Marrant (1755–1791). Marrant was born a freeman in New York and later moved to the South. He became known as a Methodist missionary in North America, specifically a Calvinist Methodist. He developed a relationship with Whitefield. After the American War for Independence, he pastored in Nova Scotia. He preached to slaves in the United States, Blacks in Canada, white American communities, and Native Americans. Marrant was North America's first Black ordained minister and early American missionary.

Evangelists in the United States would leverage the method of mass evangelistic gatherings and continue to innovate. What manifested itself by the numbers of attendees through the ministries of Whitefield, Wesley, and other evangelists on the American frontiers was embraced and modified for suburban and urban contexts. It was during this time that evangelism met business and marketing principles that resulted in large-scale evangelistic gatherings.

Many evangelists throughout the world would build upon the methods and strategies of the eighteenth century. Developments in technology, particularly in communication and travel, would be embraced and modified for urban, and eventually suburban, contexts. The next two centuries would observe much progress in taking the gospel to all nations. In addition to new approaches, the number of evangelists would greatly increase, both in the West and throughout Majority World countries. The following is a brief list of names representing differing theological, methodological, gender, and ethnic perspectives on global evangelistic ministry of the nineteenth through the twenty-first centuries.

Charles Finney (1792–1875). Finney served as a lawyer, professor (Oberlin College), and pastor, but he was known mostly for his evangelistic preaching and approaches to revivalism. He preached to many, including those in England and Scotland, in the nineteenth century and developed a method for hosting public revival gatherings, which had become a popular evangelistic method in the United States. Finney was strongly opposed to Calvinism and embraced Arminianism. He was able to influence many preachers with the publication of his *Lectures on Revivals of Religion*. He was a master innovator in evangelistic methodology. Believing that revival could be produced by the use of the right means, Finney developed protracted (three or four weeks) evening meetings of mass evangelism in American urban contexts. A music director, using contemporary music and choirs, was employed. Women were allowed to lead in public prayer. Prayer and marketing campaigns took place before the scheduled gatherings. Door-to-door evangelistic visitation was included in the preparation. Locals were trained to provide spiritual counseling to people under the Spirit's conviction. Those who felt themselves in such a state knew to walk forward, during the preaching, to sit in the front of the room on "anxious benches."[13]

Phoebe Palmer (1807–1874). Born in New York and raised in an American Methodist family, Phoebe Palmer was an evangelist and leader in the nineteenth century Holiness Movement. During the 1850s, she traveled in the eastern United States and Canada to attend camp meetings and host Holiness revival gatherings. During her lifetime she preached at over three hundred camp meetings. In addition to her ministry in the United States, she and her husband served in England for four years. She has been called the mother of the Holiness Movement and one of the founding mothers of American Methodist missions.[14]

Amanda Berry Smith (1837–1915). Born a slave in Maryland, her father was able to buy Smith's freedom three years later. She started itinerant preaching as a Holiness evangelist and was closely connected to African Methodist Episcopal churches. In addition to preaching throughout the United States, by the time she was in her forties, global preaching tours took her to England, West Africa, and to India, where she served as a missionary for a few years. Many people came to faith through her evangelism.

13. Terry, *Evangelism*, 141–46.
14. For more on Palmer, see https://www.cbeinternational.org/resource/phoebe-palmer.

METHODIST CIRCUIT RIDERS

The Methodist movement greatly expanded through the evangelistic work of circuit riders along the American frontier. Paulus Scharpff, in his work *History of Evangelism*, sheds light on some of the details related to this method of Great Commission labors.

> Because their pastors customarily trekked along with their congregations to some new location, it was the Baptists who established the first churches in the new settlements. Presbyterian and Congregational pastors as well moved beyond the Allegheny Mountains for longer or shorter periods of time to visit their dispersed membership. It was especially the Methodists, however, who best kept pace with the vast westward movement. To divide the country into circuits, as organizationally gifted Wesley had done in England, was an excellent technique in the new states.
>
> All Methodist preachers at that time were traveling preachers and evangelists. Pressing ever forward with the vanguard of settlers, they exerted spiritual oversight on the ever-moving border areas as well as over the settled communities. Their working areas stretched from the Atlantic to Pacific Oceans, and from Canada to the Gulf of Mexico. One man's preaching circuit often comprised 500 square miles; to cover his area he often traveled four to six weeks on horseback. These circuits were under the watchful supervision of a district overseer, the so-called presiding elder, who obviously also traveled many miles for many weeks. In supreme command over all were the bishops, also constantly on the move. The reason for the success of Methodism rested upon far more than excellent organization, however; basic to everything was a religious fervor and evangelistic zeal that had not been seen since apostolic times.
>
> Day and night these circuit preachers preached in log cabins, barns, school houses, court houses or even in the open fields. Those won to Christ in the first visit would be united into a "class" by the preacher and placed under the care of a leader with whom the group met once or twice a week for spiritual help. When the circuit preacher returned after several weeks, he carefully checked the condition and progress of the classes.
>
> Scharpff, *History of Evangelism*, 98–99.

Questions

1. Why do you think Scharpff says that the Methodists brought "evangelistic zeal that had not been seen since apostolic times"?
2. What was the difference between the methods used by the Methodists and those of the Baptists?
3. What do you think were some of the sacrifices made by the circuit-riding preachers?

Dwight L. Moody (1837–1899). Another evangelist who focused on urban contexts and launched what would become "crusade evangelism" was D. L. Moody—described by some as the "greatest evangelist" in the nineteenth century.[15] Over the course of his lifetime, Moody preached to large multitudes and innovated evangelistic methods. Paulus Scharpff refers to Moody as "the greatest evangelist of his generation and one of the most fruitful soul-winners in Kingdom History."[16] He was born in Massachusetts, spent years in Chicago, was involved in establishing a Sunday School, and directed the YMCA. He also served as an itinerant evangelist throughout the United States, England, and Scotland with musician Ira Sankey, and founded educational institutions, with the most popular being the Moody Bible Institute. Moody preached simple evangelistic messages, extensively promoted his campaigns, built special tabernacles for gatherings, made use of appealing music, implemented "decision cards" for use during campaigns as a means for local pastors to follow up, and introduced the "inquirers' room" as a private place where people could obtain counsel on matters regarding spiritual questions.[17]

Billy Sunday (1862–1935). Finney and Moody used business principles to promote their evangelistic rallies, and Sunday followed their example. A professional baseball player for the Chicago White Stockings, Sunday eventually gave up sports and became an itinerant evangelist. He traveled extensively throughout the Midwest to small towns. His messages often incorporated elements of the gospel, social evils (e.g., alcohol), and American patriotism. Large crowds would come to see the former baseball player turned preacher in his portable tents whose floors were covered with sawdust. When Sunday would extend an invitation to receive salvation from Christ, attendees were to walk the aisle, take his hand, and complete a commitment card. Those who came forward received follow-up literature. Sunday's work was extensive and made him a wealthy man—an opulence that eventually led to a loss of credibility among the middle class who supported his ministry financially.[18]

Bakht Singh (1903–2000). Bakht Singh was born and raised Sikh in India, became an atheist while studying in England, and came to faith in Christ as an engineering student in Canada. He preached numerous revival gatherings in India for over six decades as an evangelist and Bible teacher, and his influence and leadership resulted in thousands of churches planted in India, Pakistan, Sri Lanka, Australia, and the United States.

---

15. Green, *Evangelism: Learning from the Past*, 123. For an excellent biography on Moody, see Dorsett, *Passion for Souls*.
16. Scharpff, *History of Evangelism*, 177.
17. Terry, *Evangelism*, 147–54.
18. Terry, *Evangelism*, 159–65.

D. T. Niles (1908–1970). Niles was born in Ceylon (Sri Lanka) to a Christian family. He served in a variety of ministerial roles throughout his life, notably as chair of the Youth Department and executive secretary of the Department of Evangelism with the World Council of Churches. A Methodist, Niles was committed to ecumenism and considered his primary calling to be an evangelist. His popular description of witness as "one beggar telling another where to find bread" remains in the minds of many to this day. He was a prolific writer and defined evangelism as "the proclamation of an event, it is also an invitation to an encounter—an encounter with the risen Christ."[19]

Billy Graham (1918–2018). With advances in transportation and telecommunications, it is likely that Billy Graham preached the gospel to more people than anyone in church history. Graham pastored a church in Chicago for a few years, and he later devoted himself to serve with Youth for Christ as an evangelist. Following his 1949 evangelistic crusade in Los Angeles, Graham's popularity increased. A year later, he founded the Billy Graham Evangelistic Association (BGEA). His gatherings where he preached evangelistic messages were often held in major cities in the United States and throughout the world. Graham was also an innovator with his methods. In addition to putting accountability and safeguards in place to protect Graham and members of his team from scandals, the BGEA produced movies, radio and television programs, numerous books and training resources, and *Decision* magazine. Graham was responsible for sponsoring international gatherings for world evangelization, most notably the Lausanne Congress on World Evangelization, and helped found *Christianity Today*. His "crusades" gathered thousands, engaged the music of Cliff Barrows, provided testimonies from notable celebrities, used a time of invitation where people walked to the stage to commit themselves to Christ, and partnered with local churches for follow-up with the new believers.

Gottfried Osei-Mensah (1934–2016). Osei-Mensah, born in Ghana, served as the executive secretary of the Lausanne Committee for World Evangelization from 1975 to 1984. He also served as a pastor, was instrumental in developing evangelistic work on universities in West Africa through the Pan-African Fellowship of Evangelical Students, and gave particular attention to discovering, understanding, and evangelizing unreached people groups. He also was a special representative on staff with the BGEA.

Billy Kim (1934–). Described as the "Billy Graham of Asia," Kim was born in Korea and came to faith in Christ while a student in the United States.[20] He is known for his evangelism and humanitarian efforts. In addition to his global

---

19. Niles, *That They May Have Life*, 25.
20. For more on Kim, see https://www.moodypublishers.com/authors/k/billy-kim.

preaching events, he has served as a pastor, with Youth for Christ, as president of the Baptist World Alliance, as chair of the Far East Broadcasting Company (Korea), and with the BGEA as a translator and preacher.

The history of evangelism is a story of great diversity. Beginning in Jerusalem, the gospel has traveled to every country on the planet. Women and men, from north, south, east, and west, approached the task of preaching the gospel to all nations with a variety of methods. Many developed important innovations that remain in the twenty-first century. Sacrifices were made for Christ and his kingdom. Though history books provide a glimpse of some names and activities, countless others will never be known in this life. However, their faithfulness to gospel advancement during their respective days continues to bear eternal benefits that will only be fully recognized by us in the kingdom to come.

— QUESTIONS TO CONSIDER —

1. How did Pietism influence the church's interest in evangelism?
2. What are some of the methods mentioned in this chapter that are still being used today?
3. Are there any dangers in using marketing, media, and musical innovations in relation to evangelism?

15

A CENTURY OF GLOBAL EVANGELIZATION GATHERINGS

AD 1910–2024

Conversations related to world evangelization took on a new level of complexity with the development and growth of multinational, multidenominational, multiday gatherings. These events were critical to the development of the Roman Catholic, ecumenical (conciliar), and evangelical movements related to the Great Commission.[1] This chapter addresses some of the most significant meetings. Readers will have to excuse obvious omissions, as space does not allow for an exhaustive treatment of all such gatherings. The following is a summary noting the location of the event, reasons for the occasion, participants, main topics addressed, and outcomes.

World Missionary Conferences

The world missionary conference is thought to have begun in 1854 when Alexander Duff visited New York and held a two-day gathering of 150 participants. A second, two-day conference followed that same year in London.

---

1. For a collection of documents from conciliar, Roman Catholic, Eastern Orthodox/Oriental Church, and evangelical gatherings during the latter twentieth century, see Scherer and Bevans, *Basic Statements*. This work contains many excerpts, providing good representation of the views reflected during this period.

Other gatherings would occur in 1860 (Liverpool) and 1878 (London).[2] In recognition of the forthcoming centenary of the Protestant mission movement, leaders attempted to host a worldwide gathering in 1888. Though the ten-day London gathering was viewed as a success, it did not have the desired global representation. A New York conference was scheduled for 1900 and described as "ecumenical," for it represented missionary work in all areas of the inhabited world. The multiday event brought together fifteen hundred delegates from across the United States and Canada, two hundred European delegates, and six hundred missionaries. The final count revealed representation from 115 mission societies and forty-eight countries.[3]

Edinburgh 1910

The Edinburgh World Missionary Conference was the culmination of the great century of missions. Eight main subjects were studied and reported during the gathering. Each subject was researched by twenty commission members. Their subjects were (1) Carrying the Gospel to All the Non-Christian World, (2) the Church in the Mission Field, (3) Education in Relation to the Christianization of National Life, (4) the Missionary Message in Relation to Non-Christian Religions, (5) the Preparation of Missionaries, (6) the Home Base of Missions, (7) Missions and Governments, and (8) Co-operation and the Promotion of Unity.[4] The attendees included 1,356 delegates: 594 from the United States and Canada, 560 from Great Britain, 175 from the continent of Europe, and 27 from British territories. Reports were shared of the work of the Spirit and church throughout the world during the nineteenth century. The entire world was understood to be the mission field. Doors for the gospel were opening. Mission was understood primarily as evangelism and the task of the whole church. The concern was finding ways to get the gospel to the world, and how the church must remain unified in this task. Or, as John Mott famously stated, the guiding principle should be "the evangelization of the world in this generation."[5]

After Edinburgh, three organizations formed that produced particular streams of conferences related to a global ecumenical movement: Life and Work, Faith and Order, and the International Missionary Council (IMC).[6] In 1921, under the leadership of John Mott, Joseph Oldham, and A. L.

2. World Missionary Conference, *History and Records*, 3–4.
3. World Missionary Conference, *History and Records*, 5.
4. World Missionary Conference, *History and Records*, 10–12.
5. Bassham, *Mission Theology*, 15–20.
6. Briggs, "World Council of Churches," 1026–27.

Warnshuis, the IMC was constituted and sponsored several global gatherings to assist churches in the advancement of the gospel. In 1958 the IMC merged with the World Council of Churches. In 1961 the IMC became the Commission of World Mission and Evangelism of the World Council of Churches.[7] Prior to the merger, the IMC was focused on evangelism through churches. After this event, attention shifted to the global struggle related to humanization connected to topics such as injustice, racism, loneliness, and poverty.[8] The IMC stream will receive particular attention throughout this chapter.

Jerusalem 1928

This was the first significant meeting of the IMC that developed after its 1921 constitution. The growth of industrialization and secularization was a major concern for the participants. A widening of the definition of mission occurred. Mission was to be broad and challenge unjust economic and social structures.[9] Half of the 231 delegates came from Majority World contexts. Conservatives were concerned about theological differences and a growing concern for social issues. Materials related to Jerusalem were published in

---

7. According to the World Council of Churches, the Commission of World Mission and Evangelism exists to foster

> conferences, consultations, seminars, study processes, publications and visits, correspondence or other forms of contacts, for the sake of mission and unity of all Christians. Missional formation and theological education are important dimensions of the work. The main concern is to empower churches, mission bodies and other agencies to be united in common mission and to do it in Christ's way, i.e., linking the methods used with the content of the gospel. The CWME has always wanted to experience and to live the prayer of Jesus Christ "that they may all be one . . . that the world may believe" (John 17:21). (https://www.oikoumene.org/what-we-do/commission-on-world-mission-and-evangelism#what-we-do)

8. Rudnick, *Speaking the Gospel*, 211. By 1979 Harvey Hoekstra would publish his critique of the World Council of Churches and their redefining mission and evangelism. In his introduction to the book *The World Council of Churches and the Demise of Evangelism*, he wrote,

> This study grows out of a concern that the present understanding of mission with the WCC, and its programs to carry out that understanding, do *not* provide the churches the support they need for this task. A definition of mission has emerged that many feel is too horizontal—and too closely associated with other ideologies. Those who subscribe to this wider definition seem primarily concerned to work for a better society; they place their emphasis on human dignity and human rights. Such participation in the social struggle is a worthy objective as long as it does not lead to the eclipse or neglect of the churches' responsibility to win others to faith in Christ. (*World Council of Churches*, 10)

Arthur Johnston traces the "demise of evangelism" long before the merger of the IMC and WCC to the Edinburgh 1910 gathering (*Battle for World Evangelism*).

9. Bevans and Schroeder, *Constants in Context*, 257.

an extensive eight-volume work that addressed (1) the Christian Message, (2) Religious Education, (3) Younger and Older Churches, (4) Missions and Race Conflict, (5) Missions and Industrialism, (6) Missions and Rural Problems, (7) International Missionary Co-operation, and (8) Addresses and Other Records. The focus of this gathering was the content of the Christian message shared. During one particular discussion, D. T. Niles emphasized that "missionaries should not import Christianity, but preach the gospel."[10] The desire at Jerusalem was that national churches, wherever they were found, would carry out the Great Commission task. Matters related to evangelism and social problems were addressed.[11] One influential matter that emerged from Jerusalem was the 1930 initiative related to interreligious dialogue.[12] This began with a method of engaging Jewish communities, but the focus was broadened with some advocates discarding proclamation for discussion.[13]

Tambaram 1938

Nearly five hundred people from sixty-nine countries gathered around the theme "The World Mission of the Church," with a special focus on developing younger churches throughout the world. Global evangelism was understood as a task for the church. A major topic addressed was the relationship of Christianity to non-Christian religions. Though some called for syncretism, the council reaffirmed the truth and exclusivity of Christ for the entire world. The IMC noted that the answers to the problems of the world were found in the "saving power of Jesus Christ."[14] While missionaries may enter pioneer areas with this message, as soon as possible they should plant local indigenous churches and pass future evangelistic work to them. Attention was given to the social ramifications of the gospel, noting that churches have a responsibility to engage in social ministries too.[15]

---

10. International Missionary Council, *Life of the Church*, 279–80.
11. Bassham, *Mission Theology*, 20–21.
12. Briggs, "Jerusalem Conference (1928)," 516.
13. Seventy years later, after observing this trend among the WCC, evangelicals would note, "We live in a multi-faith world, and understanding the religious belief of those we seek to evangelize can help us to reach out to them with both clarity and sensitivity. Interaction with non-Christians can help us develop this understanding and must involve honest listening, with mutual respect that must be maintained even in debate. (Unfortunately, interfaith discussion has often been marred by the assumption that all religions are equally valid—an assumption evangelicals cannot share.)" (Packer, "Theologians Task Group," 480).
14. Hoekstra, *World Council of Churches*, 32.
15. Bassham, *Mission Theology*, 23–24.

Whitby 1947

The gathering of 112 delegates from forty countries following the Second World War was held at a time for reuniting for world evangelism. The theme for the Canadian gathering was "Christian Witness in a Revolutionary World." Emphasis at this event was on the unity of the church for the task of evangelism. Partnership—as well as loyalty—was pledged to Christ first, rather than any nation or denomination. Both younger and older churches throughout the world were called to partner together in the Great Commission. The need for evangelism to be connected to social involvement was emphasized as the church stands up for social justice and caring for the destitute and needy.[16] However, Ken Mulholland notes that Whitby "downplayed the structural difference between mission societies and church bodies," and because of this, "responsibility for mission initiative was placed in the hands of established national churches to the neglect of vast unevangelized populations beyond the influence of existing church bodies."[17]

Willingen 1952

One hundred and ninety delegates gathered in Germany around the theme "The Missionary Obligation of the Church." The twentieth century's quest for mission theology and policy would be influenced greatly by Willingen. The voice of Johannes Hoekendijk called the church to recognize that mission belongs to God, and the focus of his work is not in the church but in the world. While many countered his views, he was persuasive in various circles. Willingen called the church to recognize the trinitarian nature of mission. Theological shifts were occurring, and traditional mission fields were closing to traditional methods. The vision for evangelizing the world dimmed at Willingen.[18] Willingen also called attention to the necessary unity of the church for effective witness in the world.[19] The influence of neoorthodoxy resulted in a low view of the Scriptures and the need for individual conversions. Attention was shifted toward the salvation of society. Eschatological views argued for a "realized evangelism" that understood the atonement as having "already saved Christians and non-Christians alike." Shifts resulted in evangelism being separated from a forthcoming eternal damnation to the present reign of Christ.[20]

16. Bassham, *Mission Theology*, 26–27.
17. Mulholland, "Whitby Conference (1947)," 1014.
18. Hoekstra, *World Council of Churches*, 34.
19. Bassham, *Mission Theology*, 33–36. Ken Mulholland believes that emphasis on partnership and unity received higher priority than reaching the unevangelized peoples of the world ("Willingen Conference [1952]," 1017).
20. A. Johnston, *Battle for World Evangelism*, 86–87.

Accra 1958

From the beginning, the IMC was focused on world evangelization. At Accra, the IMC voted to integrate into the World Council of Churches (WCC). The organizational shift would not occur until 1961. Accra opened the door for Majority World churches to join the WCC and reduced the dominance of churches from the West.[21] However, several voices spoke in opposition to the integration. Fridtjov Birkeli stated that with Accra, they "arrived at the funeral of the I. M. C."[22] The broadening to focus on other noble activities beyond evangelism continued to be brought to the forefront. M. M. Thomas's assembly paper drew attention to this in particular:

> There is a need to define more clearly than we have done before in the lands of the so-called Missions and the younger Churches: (a) Christ's relation to Creation which can do justice to the creative aspects of the social humanism and nationalism and give the creation of structure of social and political existence a status in relation to Christ; (b) the relation of *Kerygma* (proclamation) to *Diakonia* (Service) in the life and mission of the Church which again will give social action an independent stand and status in the essential mission of the Church and not merely as an instrument or appendage of evangelism. This theological clarity is most necessary as it alone can provide us the basis for common loyalty of Christians and non-Christians to human values and co-operation in working for the realization of social goals which express them.[23]

Accra was organized to evaluate the IMC and the relationships between church and mission, partnerships, and new forms of mission. Sizable shifts were about to occur that would lead to an evangelical movement for world evangelization.

New Delhi 1961

It was here that the IMC officially merged with the WCC. Evangelicals raised concerns, noting that the move would result in a loss of focus on frontier evangelism and disciple-making efforts for the sake of conserving and developing established church structures. Proclaiming the gospel was starting to be eclipsed by the church's presence in the world.[24] The New Delhi report noted the following about the church's witness, strongly emphasizing social and material blessings:

---

21. Briggs, "Accra Conference," 33.
22. World Council of Churches, *International Missionary Council: Ghana*, 133.
23. Thomas, "Christian Witness," 24.
24. A. Johnston, *Battle for World Evangelism*, 80.

> When the Church recognizes that it exists for the world, there arises a passionate concern that the blessings of the Gospel of Christ should be brought to every land and to every man and woman. These blessings include the alleviation of poverty, disease and hunger, and the creating of a true fellowship that relieves the loneliness of modern mass society. Christian evangelism is therefore a joyful privilege, being sustained by the knowledge that all the world is the object of God's love and is even now under the lordship of Christ. . . . The evangelistic task of the Church is to give the whole Gospel to the world, not merely those parts of it which we find congenial.[25]

Unbelievers needed to observe the good deeds and actions of Christians, even if this meant that the church remain silent about the gospel. The New Delhi report concludes,

> Witness to the Gospel must therefore be prepared to engage in the struggle for social justice and for peace; it will have to take the form of humble service and of a practical ministry of reconciliation amidst the actual conflicts of our times. The wholeness of the Gospel demands a corporate expression since it concerns every aspect of men's lives. Healing and the relief of distress, the attack upon social abuses and reconciliation, as well as preaching, Christian fellowship and worship, are all bound together in the message that is proclaimed.[26]

By the mid-1960s, liberal and neoorthodox perspectives greatly influenced views on global evangelism. Harvey Hoekstra wrote, "Missionaries and those directly committed to world evangelization were no longer in control. It was a new era in world mission. The new understanding about mission presumed that man had come of age: that secularization was setting him free. He no longer needed God. There was great confidence in man's ability to reap the benefits of science."[27]

Unfortunately, such views not only had become part of the warp and woof of mainstream Western societies but also had infected and spread throughout the theological academy and into mission agencies and churches. Whereas the global task had been focused on redemption and then the lifting of society to the benefits of the kingdom's ethic, it was now about attempting to redeem social structures, according to the kingdom's ethic, without the redemption of the peoples comprising those structures. The growing concern among evangelicals was that evangelism had not only been redefined but also reallocated. The best case was that it was now only one among a variety of

---

25. Visser 't Hooft, *New Delhi Report*, 85–86.
26. Visser 't Hooft, *New Delhi Report*, 86.
27. Hoekstra, *World Council of Churches*, 57.

very important activities related to God's mission in the world. There were so many needs in the world that the kingdom ethic addressed, and redemption was just one among the multitude. The worst case was that evangelism was discarded; after all, it was an embarrassing, narrow-minded hangover from a superstitious epoch when hell was real and God was a condemning monster.

Berlin 1966

As a leader among evangelicals, Billy Graham was concerned over what he viewed as a lack of global clarity and agreement on evangelism. He was not alone, and the result was an international gathering in Berlin. Carl Henry stated that the event convened "for an evangelistic and soteriological purpose, and not for epistemological and philosophical considerations."[28] What had occurred among the WCC was troubling. In an effort to rectify matters, the World Congress on Evangelism met in Germany with the theme "One Race, One Gospel, One Task." Graham's opening greetings set the tone and clarified the reason for the event. He noted, "Our purpose is important because we hold the conviction that evangelism—the proclamation of the Gospel of Christ—is the only revolutionary force that can change our world." A few days later, Stanley Mooneyham would conclude the gathering by reminding delegates, "Our goal is nothing short of the evangelization of the human race in this generation, by every means God has given to the mind and will of men." Lest there remain any confusion, "Evangelism is the proclamation of the Gospel of the crucified and risen Christ, the only Redeemer of men, according to the Scriptures, with the purpose of persuading condemned and lost sinners to put their trust in God by receiving and accepting Christ as Savior through the power of the Holy Spirit, and to serve Christ as Lord in every calling of life and in the fellowship of his Church, looking toward the day of his coming in glory."[29] Twelve hundred delegates from 120 countries met with the event chaired by Henry. Discussion was on biblical foundations for evangelism and the most effective methods. More than two hundred people from nearly one hundred countries presented papers. A pledge was made to complete the evangelization of the world. A challenge was extended to the WCC to return to the vision and zeal for global evangelism that existed in the 1910 Edinburgh gathering where they traced their heritage. Some attendees expressed frustration that no consensus was achieved on the relationship of evangelism to social responsibility.[30]

28. Henry, *Evangelicals*, 10.
29. Henry and Mooneyham, *One Race*, 1:8, 5, 6.
30. Glasser, "World Congress," 1023.

Uppsala 1968

The fourth assembly of the WCC, at Uppsala, revealed to evangelicals what they feared was approaching: Mission should be everything the church does. The theme of the gathering was "Behold, I Make All Things New," with six main topics related to the theme: (1) Holy Spirit and the Catholicity of the Church, (2) Renewal in Mission, (3) World Economic and Social Development, (4) Justice and Peace, (5) Worship of God, and (6) Toward a New Style of Living. Uppsala was the largest WCC gathering at that time, with 704 delegates and approximately 2,700 participants. The meeting resulted in a de-emphasis on evangelism and evangelistic prioritization among missionaries. After reviewing preassembly documents, Donald McGavran, representing an evangelical perspective, published a fiery article, "Will Uppsala Betray the Two Billion?" This work challenged the direction of the Commission on World Mission and Evangelism (CWME) in light of the unevangelized peoples in the world. Concerns were about mission including humanization, maintaining a Christian presence, and engaging in dialogue, without a prioritization on evangelism.[31] Uppsala had been influenced by Hoekendijk's attention to humanitarian efforts rather than salvation. This was shown in the second main topic: Renewal in Mission. The report states, "The crying needs of the world for justice and peace, development and rescue, which have been so vitally brought home to us in this Assembly, must be the context of all our thinking about mission and evangelism. . . . Only as we start serving the fellow man do we discover the hardness of our hearts and our common need of salvation."[32] According to McGavran, Uppsala "deliberately omitted any reference to conversion mission in its program for the next decade"; following the theological and methodological emphases of Uppsala, "discipling the nations disappears in a multitude of urgent local tasks."[33] Though tensions between evangelicals and the WCC had existed for decades, Uppsala brought matters to a climax.[34] Since Berlin, evangelicals had been discussing a global gathering in the early 1970s to build on what they had already set in motion. Just as Uppsala was the largest WCC gathering to date, evangelicals were about to convene a meeting that set a new goal for themselves. This one would not only break records but also begin a movement that continues long into the twenty-first century.

31. Glasser, "World Council of Churches," 1024–26.
32. Goodall, *Uppsala Report*, 25.
33. McGavran, *Momentous Decisions*, 141–42.
34. Bevans and Schroeder, *Constants in Context*, 261.

Lausanne 1974

The International Congress on World Evangelization gathering in Lausanne received much support and leadership from the Billy Graham Evangelistic Association (BGEA). Over 2,700 participants gathered from 151 countries under the theme "Let the Earth Hear His Voice." Participants were provided plenary papers in advance and divided into National Strategy and Theology study groups. The former were asked to answer how they could best evangelize their own country together with others and what they could do to cross the cultural gaps to evangelize the two billion who had never heard the gospel.[35] Plenary sessions, Bible studies, discussions, and debates occurred related to theology, strategy, and methods of evangelism.[36] Lausanne worked toward practical outcomes such as producing the Lausanne Covenant; discussions, research, and strategy on hidden peoples; evangelism and social responsibility; and the development of partnerships. It was the Lausanne Covenant that would unite evangelicals throughout the world, become the most significant statement on evangelization, and launch the Lausanne Movement.[37] At least twenty-five new evangelistic organizations or missions were developed following Lausanne.[38]

International Conferences for Itinerant Evangelists

Amsterdam 1983, 1986, 2000

The Amsterdam conference consisted of three international gatherings for evangelists. Billy Graham's vision to equip those called to such ministry sparked gatherings over a seventeen-year period. Though 6,000 possible participants had to be turned away due to capacity matters, 3,827 attendees came from 133 countries. Seventy percent came from Majority World nations. Over half had no formal training. It is estimated that during this meeting at least 10,000 itinerant evangelists were serving throughout the world. Graham addressed the crowd during the opening session. He stressed the need to maintain the purity of the gospel, follow biblical standards with ethics and morality, partner with local churches, and provide effective evangelistic invitations. The primarily purpose of Amsterdam 1986 was to offer encouragement, equipping, and motivation for evangelists. The attendance included 8,160 evangelists and 2,000 other participants from 173 countries.[39]

35. Hoke and Little, introduction to Douglas, *Let the Earth Hear His Voice*, vii.
36. See https://lausanne.org/gathering/lausanne-1974.
37. See https://lausanne.org/statement/lausanne-covenant.
38. See https://decisionmagazine.com/evangelism-conferences/.
39. Glasser, "International Conferences," 496–97.

PROCLAMATION, PRESENCE, OR POWER?

In the 1970s Leighton Ford addressed an issue that influenced evangelistic thought and practice. Was the church to just verbally speak the gospel or be visible in communities as a reflection of the kingdom? In the following, Ford shares his thoughts on the matter.

> There seem to be three different groups within the church, each pushing and shoving, trying to get to the door and saying, "We've got the key. Just let *us* get at the door. We've got the key to an effective witness for the church!"
>
> One group says the key is *proclamation*. Just preach the simple gospel of Christ; it's the power of God to salvation. Another group says the key is *presence*—Christian presence in the world. We're to be salt; we're to be light; we're to be involved in the world. Just be there. That's the key to witness: presence. Then there is a third group, especially active in the last four or five years, which says, in effect, the key is *power*. "You shall receive power after the Holy Spirit has come upon you. We need to open ourselves to the Holy Spirit and as he moves into our lives, takes us and uses us, we will be able to have an effective ministry. We've got the key."
>
> The irony is that the lock on the door is a triple lock. One key will not open it. It takes three keys to turn the lock and open the door. I believe that our Lord, in his grace and his sovereignty, is saying to the church in our day, "Take these keys, all of them, and use them." . . .
>
> I don't think God is saying, "Each of you do your own thing." I think he is saying, "It's time to turn and start doing *my* thing." Take a gospel that is true. Take a love that has presence, and take the power that belongs to God alone. Turn the keys. Open the lock. Go through the door, and he will be with you.
>
> Ford, "Evangelism Adequate for Today," 72, 84.

Questions

1. Why do you think that the three groups that Ford describes developed by the 1970s?
2. Can evangelism be done without proclamation? Presence? Power? Explain.
3. Do you agree or disagree with Ford that "the lock on the door is a triple lock"? Explain.

Following on the momentum of Amsterdam 1983 and 1986, the BGEA sponsored Amsterdam 2000. This nine-day event brought together 11,300 evangelists and other leaders from 211 countries and territories. The theme was "Proclaiming Peace and Hope for the New Millennium," and the event was an opportunity for Graham and others to address younger evangelists. The purpose of the gathering was fivefold: (1) celebrate God's work through his evangelists from around the world, (2) equip evangelists for better ministry, (3) affirm evangelical distinctives, (4) strategize to reach multitudes with the gospel, and (5) communicate together how to accomplish more effective evangelism. Three special task groups—for evangelism strategists, theologians, and church leaders—met repeatedly to discuss evangelism in the twenty-first century. Over nine hundred meetings were scheduled during the gathering. The meeting included a covenant for evangelists and "The Amsterdam Declaration: A Charter for Evangelism in the 21st Century."[40]

Manilla 1989

What began at Lausanne continued for ten days in Manila. Also known as Lausanne II, the second International Congress on World Evangelization occurred with 4,300 in attendance from 173 countries. Fifty percent of the participants were under the age of forty-five. One-fifth were women. Though the Graham organization was instrumental in launching Lausanne I, Lausanne II was the result of numerous churches, organizations, and individuals throughout the world.[41] The format and structure were somewhat different from Lausanne I, with attention given to motivation and showing the diversity of the global church. Plenary sessions and 425 workshops provided resources for evangelism. Over three hundred partnerships and new initiatives developed from Manilla. The event had a two-part theme: (1) Proclaim Christ Until He Comes and (2) Calling the Whole Church to Take the Whole Gospel to the Whole World. These culminated with the congress's publication of the Manila Manifesto, which provided a declaration of "convictions, intentions, and motives."[42]

Cape Town 2010

Touted as the "most representative gathering of Christian leaders in the two-thousand-year history of the Christian movement," Cape Town 2010 (also known as Lausanne III) brought together 4,000 delegates from 198 countries.

---

40. Akers, Conard, and Coutu, *Amsterdam 2000*. The Amsterdam Declaration and Covenant are printed in *Evangelical Review of Theology* 25, no. 1 (2001): 5–16. *Christianity Today* also posted it on August 1, 2000, in the article "The Amsterdam Declaration" (see the bibliography).
41. Ford, "Proclaim Christ," 50.
42. In Douglas, *Proclaim Christ*, 25. For the Manila Manifesto, see https://lausanne.org/statement/the-manila-manifesto.

For the first time, Lausanne went "wired" to the global community. Plenary sessions were broadcast online to 650 sites in ninety-one countries. A network of bloggers was created as well as a website for dialogue regarding matters leading up to and during the gathering. The purpose of the Third Congress on World Evangelization "was to re-stimulate the spirit of Lausanne, as represented in The Lausanne Covenant, and so to promote unity, humility in service, and a call to active global evangelization."[43] The gathering limited the percentage of Western Christians attending in order to better represent the global church and attempted to strengthen the connection between evangelism and social action. The congress also gave attention to numerous global issues facing gospel advancement in the twenty-first century.[44] The congress released the Cape Town Commitment as a contemporary confirmation of the Lausanne Covenant and was to "act as a roadmap for The Lausanne Movement over the next ten years."[45]

Crete 2012

The WCC central committee held a meeting in Crete before the WCC's Tenth Assembly in 2013 in Busan. Since the integration of the IMC and the WCC in 1961, only one official position statement on mission and evangelism had been produced. This was in 1982 under the title "Mission and Evangelism: An Ecumenical Affirmation." At Crete, a new affirmation was unanimously approved to be presented the following year in Busan. "Together Towards Life: Mission and Evangelism in Changing Landscapes" served as a document to offer guidance to member churches.[46]

Numerous statements were made regarding evangelism. It is defined by the report as "a confident but humble sharing of our faith and conviction with other people."[47] Later, the report notes that "evangelism is sharing the good news both in word and action." Witness "takes concrete form in evangelism," which is described as "the communication of the whole gospel to the whole of humanity in the world." The goal of such action is to glorify God as the church "seeks to share this good news with all who have not yet heard it and invites them to an experience of life in Christ."[48] "Together

---

43. See https://lausanne.org/about-the-lausanne-movement.
44. In addition to my involvement as one of the members of the bloggers' network, conversations and writings resulted in my publication *Pressure Points: Twelve Global Issues Shaping the Face of the Church.*
45. Birdsall and Brown, "Foreword," 8.
46. World Council of Churches, "Together Towards Life" (2012).
47. World Council of Churches, "Together Towards Life" (2012), 252.
48. World Council of Churches, "Together Towards Life" (2012), 273.

Towards Life" acknowledges that while there are different aspects to mission, evangelism "focuses on explicit and intentional articulation of the gospel, including 'the invitation to personal conversion to a new life in Christ and to discipleship.'"[49] Proselytism is illegitimate evangelism and should not be practiced, and neither should any methods that attempt to force conversions.[50] The document is explicit in that evangelism "leads to repentance, faith, and baptism" and drives toward conversion that results in personal, social, and cosmic transformation.[51]

Evangelism was to be done in humility and with respect toward others.[52] While evangelism may naturally take place in the context of interfaith dialogue, "evangelism is not the purpose of dialogue." Both actions are distinct from each other but interrelated.[53] When engaging those of other faith traditions, attention is not given to being God's ambassador; the church is to "witness to the God who is already there," as Paul did in Athens (Acts 17:23–28).[54]

Arusha, Tanzania 2018

The Conference on World Mission and Evangelism was "in the tradition of the International Mission Council and the World Council of Churches (WCC) Commission on World Mission and Evangelism (CWME)" and occurred with the theme "Moving in the Spirit: Called to Transforming Discipleship." It was the first global conference since the WCC's adoption of the affirmation statement "Together Towards Life" in 2012. The gathering understood mission as a "multivalent activity," focused on witness to Jesus and his gospel, justice and reconciliation, and participation in dialogue with others for mutual understanding and witness. This conference celebrated the unity that all people have in common. Participants included mainline Protestant, Orthodox, Roman Catholic, evangelical, Pentecostal, and African Instituted churches. The gathering "celebrated the unity of all peoples" and "reflected thoughtfully on issues of missionary practice and sought new ways of being faithful to God's mission with the leading of the Spirit."[55]

---

49. World Council of Churches, "Together Towards Life" (2012), 271. Though the affirmation states (in the body and a footnote) such regarding evangelism, it goes on to acknowledge some churches disagree in theology and practice (272).
50. World Council of Churches, "Together Towards Life" (2012), 271–72.
51. World Council of Churches, "Together Towards Life" (2012), 272, 275.
52. World Council of Churches, "Together Towards Life" (2012), 273.
53. World Council of Churches, "Together Towards Life" (2012), 275, 276.
54. World Council of Churches, "Together Towards Life" (2012), 275, 280.
55. See https://www.oikoumene.org/what-we-do/commission-on-world-mission-and-evangelism/conference-on-world-mission-and-evangelism. Such mission conferences are held approximately every decade.

If the documentation published in the *International Review of Mission* provided a summary of the gathering, it is worth noting the understanding of evangelism advocated: "Evangelism is from everyone to everyone, extending to all the invitation to personal conversion to a new life in Christ." However, what was meant by "conversion" is something that was to be applied to both the unregenerate and the regenerate, for "it means a change in the evangelist as well as the evangelized."[56] Nowhere is this understanding clearer than when disciples reach out to those of other religions. The article noted, "It is time to disown the model of evangelism as conquest and instead promote partnership, dialogue and collaboration with believers of other religious traditions. It is time to redraw the boundary lines of religious differences, so that they become way marker to peace, not battle lines for violence."[57]

Arusha was clear that it wanted to separate itself not only from any stereotype or caricature of evangelism but also from that which was advocated by the first-century disciples.

Seoul-Incheon 2024

The Fourth Lausanne Congress gathered in Seoul-Incheon for seven days under the theme "Let the Church Declare and Display Christ Together." The desire was to bring together ten thousand people, both in South Korea and online, to engage in advancing a fourfold vision: "the gospel for every person, disciple-making churches for every people and place, Christ-like leaders for every church and sector, and kingdom impact in every sphere of society."[58] There were 5,394 gathered in the city from 200 countries and territories, with virtual participants numbering around 2,000.[59] Emphasis was placed on the polycentric nature of mission, church unity, and collaboration for kingdom work. Tensions continued between those advocating for a more integrated approach to missions and those desiring a greater emphasis on evangelism. Three important documents were produced related to the event: the "State of the Great Commission Report," the "Collaboration and Action Commitment," and the "Seoul Statement."[60]

---

56. "Conference on World Mission," 554.
57. "Conference on World Mission," 555.
58. See https://congress.lausanne.org.
59. Evi Rodemann, "5,394: The Exact Number of Participants at the Seoul Lausanne Congress," *Evangelical Focus*, October 13, 2024, https://evangelicalfocus.com/feature/28584/data-seoul-l4-lausanne-statistics-lausanne-congress-evi-rodemann.
60. Joseph W. Handley Jr., "Reflection on the Fourth Lausanne Congress," *Evangelical Review of Theology* 48, no. 4 (2024): 293–301. At the time of my writing, it is too early to determine the impact of the Lausanne 2024 gathering on world evangelization. The original

Roman Catholic Gatherings and Documents

The Roman Catholic Church engaged in several global events and produced important documents related to global evangelization. The Second Vatican Council took place from 1962 to 1965 and brought a great deal of changes to the church. Prior to this time, Catholics rarely used terms such as *evangelism* and *evangelization*, lest they appear to follow the example of Protestants.[61] While Avery Dulles overstates reality that with such changes the church "became in a true sense evangelical," the language of evangelism and evangelization received much attention with Vatican II referring to *evangelium* 157 times and evangelization 31 times and stressing that "every Christian has a responsibility to evangelize."[62] However, the 1968 Second General Conference of Latin American Bishops served as a catalyst to move the church in the direction of what would become known as the "new evangelization."

The bishops emphasized that "evangelization is the main task of the Latin American Church" because of what was stated during Vatican II and the changing dynamics in the Latin American context. It was declared that evangelization in Latin America was incomplete. They were clear on their understanding that "evangelization announces the Gospel of Christ as kerygma, as good news of salvation, ordered to the establishment of a Christian community by means of conversion that leads to baptism."[63] In addition to unbelievers, the audience for the church's evangelistic ministry included "the baptized," the "non-practicing Catholics," the "non-initiate practicing adults," and "baptized children and adolescents who need to ratify their faith as adults."[64] In other words, everyone—the faithful regenerate and the unregenerate outside the church—needed the gospel because

---

priority on global evangelization has been lost. A shift has occurred over the decades to a focus on "global mission," which has become for evangelicals (in general) everything the church does in the world. Broad is the way of mission. Narrow is the way of evangelism. Local churches are to be engaged in a wide array of kingdom activities. Lausanne no longer has the 1974 laser focus. While acknowledging her historical foundation in global evangelization, the church has allowed many important and good things to move to the forefront. Evangelism remains, but now among a multitude of other activities. After fifty years, the movement has diversified and generalized.

61. Hater, "Catholic Evangelization," 15. Hater also notes that Cardinal Suenens connected evangelization to the process of Christianization in the 1956 publication *The Gospel to Every Creature*. John Gorski observes that, among Vatican II documents, "evangelization" and "evangelize" are used most frequently in *Ad gentes* ("From 'Mission' to 'Evangelization,'" 35).

62. Dulles, "Evangelizing Theology," 27.

63. Latin American Episcopal Council, *Position Papers*, 156.

64. Latin American Episcopal Council, *Position Papers*, 158.

"the process of conversion never ends for a Christian."[65] This understanding of soteriology represents a failure to distinguish between the regenerative work of the Spirit that brings one into the kingdom and his sanctifying work that *indeed* never ends for a Christian.[66] The difference between first-century believers and the twentieth-century Roman Catholic Church was clear: "If the task of the primitive Church was to baptize the converted, our task today is to convert the baptized."[67] This theological shift required a new way of thinking and practice. Hence, the "new evangelization" would soon be advocated.[68]

Following the bishops' gathering, Pope Paul VI published his apostolic exhortation *Evangelii nuntiandi* (*On Evangelization in the Modern World*) in 1975. This brief work would become the Magna Carta of Catholic evangelization throughout the world.[69] The document states that "the task of evangelizing all people constitutes the essential mission of the Church," and that everyone who had been evangelized is expected to evangelize others.[70] Evangelization is portrayed as a complex ministry consisting of "proclaiming Christ to those who do not know him, of preaching, of catechesis, of conferring Baptism and the other Sacraments," and "the Church evangelizes when she seeks to convert."[71] Pope Paul VI was clear in his brief that though proclamation was often equated with evangelism, it was only one part of the ministry.[72] "Evangelization," he wrote, "is a complex process made up of varied elements: the renewal of humanity, witness, explicit proclamation, inner adherence, entry into the community, acceptance of signs, apostolic

---

65. Latin American Episcopal Council, *Position Papers*, 168.
66. Catholic priest Robert Hater provides an honest assessment: "Biblical evangelists say that conversion, a once-and-for-all event, happens when a person is 'saved.' While Catholic evangelization admits that one event . . . may trigger conversion, it teaches that conversion is a lifelong journey to God, not a single isolated event" ("Catholic Evangelization," 25).
67. Latin American Episcopal Council, *Position Papers*, 168.
68. Though the Roman Catholic Church was referring to the reevangelization of the church at this time, Protestants, and eventually some mainline evangelical groups, would begin to advocate for such practice and the need for even those of other religions to evangelize the church, as everyone needs to find truth in their faith tradition. Another noteworthy matter is that the bishops emphasized their belief that the whole of Latin America did not have possession of the faith and that they were committing to "a serious re-evangelization of the various human groupings on the continent" (Latin American Episcopal Council, *Conclusions*, 105). Such discussions of "human groupings" and not nation-states would draw the attention of evangelicals six years later at Lausanne 1974, when Ralph Winter spoke of "hidden peoples," later to become known as unreached people groups.
69. Hater, "Catholic Evangelization," 15.
70. Paul VI, *Evangelii nuntiandi*, 12, 13, 19.
71. Paul VI, *Evangelii nuntiandi*, 15, 16.
72. Paul VI, *Evangelii nuntiandi*, 18.

initiative. These elements may appear to be contradictory, indeed mutually exclusive. In fact they are complementary and mutually enriching."[73]

Building on such global developments, by 1983 John Paul II began to advocate a "new evangelization."[74] The term referred to the ministry needed in countries where the people have already heard the gospel.[75] Under the title "Evangelization 2000," John Paul II led the church to a "decade of evangelization" to prepare for the year 2000. An office for Evangelization 2000 was established in Rome with several regional offices throughout the world. The purpose was "to give Jesus Christ a more Christian world as the best two thousandth birthday gift possible."[76] Evangelization 2000 established training schools and sought to motivate Catholics for the new evangelization. Through prayer and the efforts of many people, the strategy was "to announce Christ to the world with a power that leads to conversion and transformation."[77]

Within Catholic thought regarding the new evangelization was the notion of inculturation, which was the "main goal" of such global engagement.[78] Protestants often equate the term *inculturation* with contextualization. Vatican II did not use the word in print, but John Paul II was the first pope explicitly to speak on the topic of inculturation. Given cultural shifts toward secularization and the need for a new evangelization, Catholic thought considered culture itself a target of the church in need of evangelization. The Jesuit Hervé Carrier stated that "the most promising aspect of the *new evangelization*" is that the church now views culture as "the decisive locus for evangelization."[79] While such is a noble notion, this language confuses rather than clarifies kingdom labors in post-Christianized contexts. How does one evangelize that which is nonsentient, without a soul, nonhuman, and nebulous as "culture"?[80] Evangelizing people who then live lives that reflect a kingdom ethic and transform business, military, arts, education, politics, finance, and law is biblically correct and strategically achievable, as opposed to speaking the gospel to that which has no mind, heart, ears, feelings, or ability to repent and place faith in Christ as Lord. Carrier attempts to clarify by noting that "inculturation is the effort to inject Christ's message into a given socio-cultural milieu, thereby summoning that milieu to grow in accordance with its own values, so long as they can be reconciled with

---

73. Paul VI, *Evangelii nuntiandi*, 19.
74. John Paul II was the first pope to use the term, but it was already in use in Latin America (Grogan and Kim, *The New Evangelization*, 5).
75. Boyack, introduction to Boyack, *New Catholic Evangelization*, 8.
76. Forrest, "Evangelization 2000," 215.
77. Forrest, "Evangelization 2000," 215.
78. Carrier, *Culture of Modernity*, 5.
79. Carrier, *Culture of Modernity*, 1.
80. It should be noted that some Protestants are guilty of this thought as well.

the Gospel message."[81] His approach, that it is people who are reconciled with the gospel, fails to make a distinction between preaching (i.e., evangelizing) the gospel to people and preaching (i.e., evangelizing) to an intangible social system. People may be redeemed by the gospel; culture may be transformed by redeemed people. This is a key matter of doctrine and evangelistic practice for the Roman Catholic Church. Unless the church clarifies the audience for evangelization, confusion reigns among both congregants and leaders and affects methods.

In 2007 the Congregation for the Doctrine of Faith published the "Doctrinal Note on Some Aspects of Evangelization." Building upon the works of Paul VI and John Paul II, the report states that it is necessary "to clarify certain aspects of the relationship between the missionary command of the Lord and respond for the conscience and religious freedom of all people."[82] It emphasizes that human rights are not to be violated and "non-Christians can be saved through the grace which God bestows in 'ways known to him.'"[83] Conversion is for both Christians and non-Christians.[84] Terms are clarified in that "*evangelization* is the *mission ad gentes* directed to those who do not know Christ. In a wider sense, it is used to describe ordinary pastoral work, while the phrase 'new evangelization' designates pastoral outreach to those who no longer practice the Christian faith."[85] Evangelization becomes everything the church does related to witness, and when this occurs, biblical evangelism takes a backseat to other matters.[86]

In 2010 Pope Benedict XVI established a new department in the Vatican Curia, the Pontifical Council for Promoting the New Evangelization.

The next apostolic exhortation that influenced Catholic evangelization was Pope Francis's publication *Evangelii gaudium* (*The Joy of the Gospel*). Building on the work of his predecessors, including the XIII Ordinary General Assembly of the Synod of Bishops in 2012, which gathered to discuss the theme "The New Evangelization for the Transmission of the Christian Faith," Francis repeated that the new evangelization was carried out in "ordinary pastoral ministry" to "*the baptized whose lives do not reflect the demands of Baptism*" and "first and foremost . . . to *those who do not know Jesus Christ or who have always rejected him.*"[87] Inculturation is driven by evangelizing zeal and not a

---

81. Carrier, *Culture of Modernity*, 67.
82. Congregation for the Doctrine of the Faith, *Doctrinal Note*, I.3.
83. Congregation for the Doctrine of the Faith, *Doctrinal Note*, II.7.
84. Congregation for the Doctrine of the Faith, *Doctrinal Note*, III.9.
85. Congregation for the Doctrine of the Faith, *Doctrinal Note*, IV.12.
86. Claudia Währisch-Oblau is correct in observing, "The Catholic perception of 'evangelization' is quite close to the evangelical and ecumenical understanding of 'mission'" ("Evangelism in *Evangelii gaudium*," 264).
87. Francis, *Evangelii gaudium*, 17, 18.

desire to force others into one's cultural preferences.[88] All Christians are to be "'missionary disciples' and actively engaged in evangelization."[89] Through the inner work of the Holy Spirit, the church is "constantly evangelizing itself."[90] Interreligious dialogue is important and involves remaining true to one's convictions, but "non-Christians, by God's gracious initiative, when they are faithful to their own consciences, can live 'justified by the grace of God,' and thus be 'associated to the paschal mystery of Jesus Christ.'"[91] However, the primary motivator for evangelizing is the love we have for Jesus.

Orthodox Church

In 1920 the Orthodox Ecumenical Patriarchate published an encyclical to all churches addressing their common witness and mission. While this work brought a reawakening to Orthodox churches, it would be almost a century before the first official statement on mission was published in 2016.[92] *The Mission of the Orthodox Church in Today's World* (*MOCTW*) built upon the WCC statement "Together Towards Life: Mission and Evangelism in Changing Landscapes"[93] and has been acknowledged as significant and worthy of placement alongside "The Cape Town Commitment" (2010), *Evangelii gaudium* (2013), and "Together Towards Life" (2012).[94] Throughout the twentieth and early twenty-first centuries, the WCC sought to engage the Orthodox churches to encourage cooperative missiological discussions.[95]

Though the word *evangelism* and its variants are not used in the document, related terms may be found. After referencing Matthew's Great Commission, *MOCTW* states, "This mission must be carried out not aggressively or by different forms of proselytism, but in love, humility and respect towards the identity of each person and the cultural particularity of each people." The document addresses the dignity of persons, freedom and responsibility, peace

---

88. Francis, *Evangelii gaudium*, 95 (emphasis in original).
89. Francis, *Evangelii gaudium*, 97.
90. Francis, *Evangelii gaudium*, 109. Later Francis states, "The Church does not evangelize unless she constantly lets herself be evangelized" (135).
91. Francis, *Evangelii gaudium*, 184, 186.
92. In 1958 the Pan-Orthodox Missionary Society was established and issued its first bulletin in 1959, titled *Porefthendes* ("Go ye"). James Stamoolis notes that despite a long history of missionary work, the first part of the twentieth century observed little work, but the second half "has been one of the most creative periods for missionary theology" in Orthodox history, with the Pan-Orthodox Missionary Society serving as a positive step toward a renewed interest (*Eastern Orthodox Mission*, 120).
93. Kariatlis, "Together Towards Life," ix–x.
94. Bargár, "Mission of the Orthodox Church."
95. Raiser, "Foreword," vii.

and justice, peace and the aversion of war, discrimination, and the mission of the church as a witness of love through service. It is in the latter section that the document notes, "In fulfilling her salvific mission in the world, the Orthodox Church actively cares for all people in need." Buried within this section is a reference to engage in "the proclamation of the Kingdom of God and the cultivation of a sense of unity among her flock."[96]

If such is a reflection of the church's thoughts on evangelism, then one must look elsewhere for guidance on the topic, as most of what is included is related to standing against injustices, secularization, and taking care of the poor and the environment.[97]

In 1974 Nikos Nissiotis published an Orthodox view of evangelism in which he defines the ministry as "first and foremost the presence, service, and witness of Christians, through their involvement in the transformation of the world for the sake of humanity."[98] Proclamation "is the heart of evangelism and is addressed to all men, while conversion represents the conscious answer of man before the revealed person God."[99] For Nissiotis, ecclesiology is the main difference between an Orthodox approach to evangelism and that of evangelicals and some Roman Catholics. The ecclesial basis "is a *sine qua non* for the Orthodox understanding and practice of evangelism" and "is lacking, though in different ways and for different reasons, from both the radical and the conservative evangelical theology of the non-Orthodox Church (and also in the works of certain radical Roman Catholic theologians)."[100] Practically, the church views itself as an island of Christ and kingdom in the sea of ungodliness. The world is invited to come to the island to experience God and know him, for "belief arises from encounter."[101] Without the corporate liturgy, it is difficult for the church to develop evangelism methods for the marketplace and the community beyond the church's physical property. The church and, more specifically, the liturgy must be present in a community for the community to

---

96. All quotations in this paragraph are from Holy and Great Council of the Orthodox Church, "Mission of the Orthodox Church."

97. Alexander Veronis notes, "Orthodox understand the Gospel as a message to the total person, physically as well as spiritually. They see Christ's teaching about healing the sick, feeding the hungry, caring for the widow and orphan, uplifting the disinherited, supporting the oppressed, fighting injustice, and making life in this world hospitable for all as part of the complete Gospel message" ("Orthodox Concepts," 46). While a biblical theology of evangelism would agree with this statement, one is still amazed to find the number of times such emphases are noted to the exclusion of repentance and faith in what constitutes the message preached. For a critique of the document's information on witness and evangelism, see Vassiliadis, "Short Comment," on *MOCTW*.

98. Nissiotis, "Modern Trends in Evangelism," 182.
99. Nissiotis, "Modern Trends in Evangelism," 183.
100. Nissiotis, "Modern Trends in Evangelism," 187.
101. Tibbs, *Eastern Orthodox Theology*, 22.

receive the gospel. Evangelism becomes difficult without complex structures in place. For Nissiotis, "It is not sufficient to preach Christ alone, lest he become the intellectualistic, monistic principle of an individual faith. Christ must be preached within His historical reality, His Body in the Spirit, without which there is neither Christ nor the Gospel. Outside the context of the Church evangelism remains a humanism or a temporary psychological enthusiasm."[102]

Ion Bria expresses it from another angle, noting that "a church without evangelism and without mission is one that has abandoned its fundamental calling to be the original and authentic witness of the Pentecost." He continues that the "Orthodox emphasize that no evangelism should take place outside the Church without a definite reference to its spiritual and sacramental existence, precisely because the Church is part of the message, or stated in another way, it is the new reality of that message incarnated into the historical condition. Evangelism is, in a way, the self-manifestation of the Church as a living witness of the communion between God and man in Christ."[103]

According to Bria, "In liturgical action, Jesus Christ himself is the 'Apostle' and invites the people to him. . . . Where Christ is present, there man is attracted, although one cannot prove the evangelistic force of the liturgical life of the Church."[104] While such theology and practice have some evangelistic merit, they remind one of the seeker-sensitive and seeker-driven movements of the late twentieth century in the United States, whereby seekers were extended invitations to come and experience an evangelical worship gathering.[105] One of the limitations of this evangelistic methodology is that it is dependent on unbelievers willing to come to a strange gathering of religious people to observe and hear (i.e., experience) the gospel. When they stop coming, evangelism dries up. It is also a method that tends to reach people who are culturally like Christians.

In the 1970s Orthodox discussion developed around the "liturgy after the liturgy." Bria developed this matter in his book *The Liturgy After the Liturgy*.

102. Nissiotis, "Modern Trends in Evangelism," 191.
103. Bria, "Church's Role in Evangelism," 245.
104. Bria, "Church's Role in Evangelism." 248. Georges Lemopoulos describes this as "the world [being] brought into the church in the forms of the natural elements, the cultural riches of the local community, or the everyday preoccupations of the faithful. . . . The church's mission is not literally throwing the gospel into the face of the world, but rather seeking first to understand what every human being longs for, and then seeing how, through the Word and the Sacrament, the church can respond to these needs or heal any infirmities" ("Come, Our Light," 324).
105. Of course, the Orthodox tradition long precedes that of evangelicals or the twentieth century. Alexander Veronis notes that this approach by the witness of the eucharistic community "has been the central way by which Orthodox missionaries have taught the gospel to the nations" ("Task of the Church," 441).

The notion was related to the extension of the church's witness beyond the gathering of the worshiping community. The liturgy is composed of two movements. The first is related to the gathering of the people for worship, preaching, and Eucharist, where they feed on the "food for missionaries"; the second movement involves the members being sent out to become "actors of mission."[106] By being part of the gathered community, members are "learning a language of communication in order to reach other people who are looking for faith."[107]

The twentieth and twenty-first centuries were marked by a large number of global gatherings and documents related to evangelism. Mainline Protestants, evangelicals, Roman Catholics, and Orthodox traditions all experienced much theological and practical discussions related to the global task. Each of these traditions observed church, agency, and denominational reorganizations to embrace developments in the areas of evangelism and mission.

— QUESTIONS TO CONSIDER —

1. Why do you think that the twentieth and twenty-first centuries saw frequent and large evangelism congresses as compared to previous centuries?
2. What surprising insights did you encounter reading about Catholic and Orthodox evangelization practices?
3. What were the main differences between the WCC and evangelical thoughts and approaches to evangelism after the mid-twentieth century?

---

106. Bria, *Liturgy*, 24.
107. Bria, *Liturgy*, 30.

— PART 4 —

CULTURE AND COMMUNICATION

The gospel is to be shared via the communication mediums that the Lord has provided his church. Such sharing has never occurred within a culturally neutral context. Neither the evangelist nor the recipient of the message is capable of suspending their worldviews, experiences in life, personalities, interests, and so on to step outside of themselves during the transmission or reception process. God has created people in his image (Gen. 1:27) to express themselves with cultural manifestations. Humans are social beings.

In this section, I draw attention to the importance of understanding how culture and context affect productive communication. While the gospel is a constant, all evangelism is not equal, and it lies on a cultural spectrum that must be understood. Throughout the twentieth century, evangelicals developed tools to assist with making the message clear (Col. 4:4). Related to culture and evangelism is apologetics. Though a defense for the faith is not the same as sharing the gospel, it is important for the church to be able to provide a reason for the hope she has received (1 Pet. 3:15). Here I address the value and methods of apologetics and the need to understand differing worldviews.

16

CROSSING CULTURAL GAPS

Evangelism has always been about crossing cultural gaps. The distance between the message of the kingdom and another worldview, belief system, ideology, and so forth is a cultural gap. Culture is not always based on ethnicity, language, or geography. A great gulf is found between the kingdom of light and the kingdom of darkness. When the gospel is shared with an invitation to respond, that is evangelism, no matter where it is done or with whom it is communicated. It is not evangelism in my neighborhood and *missions* when done overseas. Cultural distance between myself and the other person is where the challenge may be found. This chapter addresses some important matters related to making those cultural leaps to share the good news.

The gospel is a constant, a never-changing truth with divine origins. However, just as the Word is eternal and without shifting shadows (James 1:17), he became flesh and tabernacled among humanity (John 1:14). This incarnational act served as the ultimate means of contextualization and evangelization. The transcendent moved into the neighborhood in a way unlike anything Israel experienced with the tabernacle or temple. God's history of communication with his people built upon itself until in the fullness of time he sent the Son (Gal. 4:4). Divine communication reached the zenith. Being the exact imprint of God's being (Heb. 1:3), Jesus was able to state that those who had seen him had seen the Father (John 14:9).

Though Christianization spread for centuries throughout Europe and other countries, the faith finds its origins in first-century Jewish and ancient Fertile Crescent cultural contexts. It was birthed in the Middle East, not in Europe or North America. This is important for several reasons. First, such was God's plan and should cause us to seek and to understand these ancient societies to better understand the gospel we embrace. Second, God's approach to communicating his truth should cause the church to consider how to most effectively communicate it to others since individuals and societies are far removed from the ancients. Third, as we examine the spread of the gospel in the Scriptures, we observe that while some communication devices were adapted to various audiences, some elements of what was communicated were nonnegotiable. And to tamper with this universal truth leads the manipulator to a syncretized religious message that is not Christian at all.

Rethinking with the Apostolic Imagination

Prior to Jesus's ascension, his disciples needed an eschatological adjustment. Their imaginations were bound with a variety of interpretations of what the religious establishment had assumed would be characteristic of the Messiah's order of operations. The prophets foretold that once the Messiah arrived, judgment day would follow. He would reign and crush the enemies of God (and Israel) under his feet. The disciples knew that Jesus was the Messiah. Therefore, it was time for the kingdom of God to be established over the earth.

While the disciples were correct about the order of events, their timing was inaccurate. The last days would exist between Jesus's advent and parousia and would require an extended period of time. Their last question to Jesus was, "Lord, will you at this time restore the kingdom to Israel?" (Acts 1:6). The kingdom would come, but first the fulfillment of Joel's prophecy would take place, and they would be his witnesses "in Jerusalem and in all Judea and Samaria, and to the end of the earth" (Acts 1:8). God desired to see the earth filled with his image-bearers bringing glory to his name (Gen. 1:28; 9:1). The day of diversity would arrive (Rev. 7:9) but would first require the church to experience a theological and missiological paradigm shift.

The coming of the Spirit not only was the promised seal of God on his people but also empowered them to carry out a very dangerous and global task—one that was more dangerous than they probably realized and definitely larger than they would ever know. A source of comfort, guidance, and knowledge was necessary for the task at hand, for the outline of Acts 1:8 was much more than a geographical set of concentric circles emanating from Jerusalem. Rather, Jesus was preparing his disciples for their role in salvation history to see the earth filled with the knowledge of God and all nations—Jew and gentile—honoring the Creator (Hab. 2:14; Rev. 22:2). Distance would be the least of their concerns. The crossing of cultural gaps would rock their world as Jesus built his church.

For the most part, during the first seven chapters in Acts, the disciples engaged those who were Jewish and culturally like themselves. Centuries of Jewish diaspora had created enclaves of Jewish communities throughout the world. Assyrian, Babylonian, Persian, Greek, and Roman rule had contributed to the first-century reality on the day of Pentecost: "There were dwelling in Jerusalem Jews, devout men from every nation under heaven" (Acts 2:5). Though their homes were in distant lands, they were Jews at heart. The three thousand who came to faith that day had much in common with the disciples. The Spirit worked in an amazing way on that day, but a degree of expectation was present. God had said that this day would come when he would pour out his Spirit on his *sons and daughters*. Surely, this meant exclusively the Jews (Acts 2:17).

But strange things began to happen. Following Stephen's martyrdom (Acts 7:54–60), Philip fled to Samaria and "proclaimed to them the Christ" (Acts 8:5). When news spread that the Samaritans had embraced the Messiah, the Jerusalem church needed to investigate. Could it be that the Samaritans (who subscribed to Torah alone and denied Jerusalem as the proper place for worship) had been received by God like the Jews? Two of the most important leaders, Peter and John, traveled to the community and prayed and laid hands on them to receive the Spirit (Acts 8:14–17). Following this work of the Spirit, the apostles started preaching to many Samaritan villages. God had confirmed his reception of the Samaritans into his church.

The Lord drove Philip to a desert area where he encountered a God-fearing Ethiopian eunuch returning from worshiping in Jerusalem. Though eunuchs were prohibited from entering the sacred areas of the tabernacle/temple (Deut. 23:1), this one was about to have God come to him. On encountering this African, Philip "opened his mouth" and "told him the good news about Jesus" (Acts 8:35). The result was the eunuch's baptism and going on his way rejoicing (Acts 8:38–39).

Peter later experienced a dramatic vision of God. While the immediate implications were related to foods being considered clean, Peter fully understood the truth of "what God has made clean, do not call common" (Acts 10:15) when he was sent to Cornelius's home to find a house filled with "unclean" people ready to receive the gospel. Through his preaching, "the Holy Spirit fell on all who heard the word," leaving Peter's traveling companions shocked "because the gift of the Holy Spirit was poured out even on the Gentiles" (Acts 10:44–45). Again, just as God had confirmed Jewish and Samaritan believers, now even God-fearing gentiles were sealed with the Holy Spirit.

Peter's entrance into Cornelius's house would result in tension and conflict with Jewish Christians in Jerusalem (Acts 11:2–3). Using a lengthy discourse, the apostle convinced members of the church that God had granted repentance to the gentiles (Acts 11:18). And just when the early Jewish disciples probably thought they had experienced enough theological and missiological shifts related to the gospel spreading to differing cultural groups, conflict was to come that almost split the church.

Unnamed men who fled Jerusalem following Steven's death traveled three hundred miles north to Antioch. They preached the gospel to Greek-speaking gentiles (Hellenists), and a great number of them turned to the Lord (Acts 11:20–21). It was one thing for Jews, Samaritans, and God-fearers to receive the Holy Spirit and become part of God's people; it was a completely different matter for full-blooded gentiles to be received by God and considered equal to the aforementioned groups. When news arrived in Jerusalem, Barnabas (who took the recently converted Paul with him) was sent to investigate. Later, he and Paul would venture deep into gentile territory with stories to share of the power of the gospel (Acts 13–14).

A great dispute arose because Jewish Christians began teaching that no one could be saved apart from circumcision (Acts 15:1). Leaders gathered in Jerusalem to discuss the matter. Peter was called to give account, as well as Barnabas and Paul. James had the final word. After hearing the missiological evidence of what had occurred in Samaritan and gentile territory and among God-fearers, he directed everyone's attention to the book of Amos. God had promised to rebuild David's tent, and such was going to include "all the Gentiles who are called" by his name (Acts 15:16–17; cf. Amos 9:11–12). The truth had been recorded for centuries. However, it required the church to rethink with her apostolic imagination and shift her first-century theological and missiological paradigms to align with the eschatological work of the Spirit before the day of the Lord.

This mystery of Christ—God uniting Jew and gentile into one body—was scandalous (Eph. 3:6). The dividing wall of hostility (Eph. 2:14) had been present for centuries due to cultural biases and theological issues. Disciple-making among all the nations was more about crossing cultural gaps than geographical boundaries. Such was true in the first century; such remains true today.

REACHING THOSE IN FOLK ISLAM

In the following account, Yakup Korkmaz describes his encounter with a Kurdish man caught in much fear and superstition. Korkmaz notes how he used elements of the man's worldview and felt needs to bridge to gospel conversation.

> As I was writing this article, a young Kurdish man came into our office for tea. I had reached this section and asked him if I could ask him some questions about the Hodjas in his area. This led into a discussion of the evil eye and cursing. He then pulled a *muska* out of his pocket. Before he had gone to do his mandatory military service, a *eyh* (Muslim shaman) had given him a special *muska* for protection. This was to protect him against demons and the enemy. The *muska* had a bobby pin on it so it could be clipped to his clothing, and it was wrapped in a stylish camouflage cloth. This led me to explain from the scriptures that trusting in objects and people who prepare them takes allegiance off the one true God. I explained that I never have a need to wear a *muska* or go to a *Hodja/eyh* for help or protection, because as a child of God I have the privilege of always having protection from harm. I turned to Numbers 23:23 and read to him: "No spell can curse the descendants of Jacob. No magic can harm employing the people of Israel. Now it will be said of Jacob and Israel: 'See what God has done!'" I had been doing Qur'anic research evangelism (asking questions from Islamic theology and the Qur'an to find bridges to the gospel) with this man and had seen much fruit. He began to study the scriptures and compare the Qur'an with them. He has now renounced the practice of wearing muskas and understands that the Bible is the only true authority. In the summer of 2008, he was baptized and now joins us on mission trips throughout the Kurdish regions of Turkey. He is also active in one of our church plants in an Eastern province, sharing his faith with family and friends.
>
> Korkmaz, "Research Evangelism," n.p.

Questions

1. What are some of the bridges to the gospel that you observe in your context?
2. The Kurdish man came from a strong fear-power context. What worldview dichotomy best sums up your context?
3. What elements of the gospel are the most relevant to the felt needs of those in your context?

Intercultural Evangelization: The Greatest Need

Just as the members of the early church had problems with crossing cultural gaps to reach those who did not look, sound, talk, or smell like them, such remains generally the case today. People, no matter where in the world, like to become followers of Jesus without crossing racial, ethnic, or class barriers—and like to congregate with people like themselves. While such could be a manifestation of racism, ethnocentrism, or classism, social beings like familiarity. They like their cultures. Shared culture brings comfort and predictability. It allows for ease in communication. It unites and provides security and solidarity. However, cultural diversity makes things challenging at times, especially when it comes to evangelism.

Yet as disciples of Christ, the church is called into a multiethnic, multicultural world of sinners created in the image of God. The power of the gospel not only to save Jew and gentile (Rom. 1:16; Gal. 3:28) but also to unite such diversity into a family stronger than any biological family, or country, is a miracle. It is one thing to love one another as a witness to the world when people are culturally monolithic; it is another matter to a watching world when the Spirit brings diversity together. Every generation, in every location, must remember and apply Jesus's words to their lives: "By this all people will know that you are my disciples, if you have love for one another" (John 13:35).

Throughout history, evangelism and mission have been dichotomized to refer to kingdom labors done in different geographical locations. Evangelism was applied to the context of peoples who had been Christianized but were still in need of the gospel.[1] From the church's perspective, evangelism was done at home. Mission, or missions for some, was related to work done "overseas," among the unreached peoples.

Given the present global realities addressed in chapter 4, the greatest need is intercultural evangelism. Such requires members of the church to cross cultural gaps to take the gospel to people unlike themselves. Whether across the street or across the world, unless churches—wherever they may be found—move beyond themselves to engage those unlike themselves with the gospel, the unreached will remain unreached. This was a great challenge in the first century and haunts the church in every generation.

The International Congress on World Evangelization brought this matter to the forefront of evangelical thinking in 1974 when Ralph Winter gave his plenary presentation "The Highest Priority: Cross-Cultural Evangelism."[2] Not-

---

1. Bosch, *Transforming Mission*, 409–10.
2. Though Winter's vision helped mobilize evangelicals to cross significant cultural gaps throughout the world, those in the United States continued to view such work as "overseas."

ing the misconception held by many who believed that crossing cultural gaps with the gospel was no longer necessary because the church was planted in every country, Winter brought attention to the reality that nations consist of a variety of different peoples reflecting a wide array of worldviews and cultural expressions. Countries are not monolithic. Diversity is global. Winter, arguing that "most non-Christians in the world today are not culturally near neighbors of any Christians," said that "it will take a special kind of 'cross-cultural' evangelism to reach them."[3] In order to fulfill the Great Commission, "normal evangelism will not do the job."[4] Winter pointed out that there is a difference between geographical proximity to Christians and cultural proximity. For example, Indonesia, by far a Muslim-majority country, has a large Christian presence. Though Muslims and Christians live near one another, they remain culturally separated. Unless Indonesian Christians—or Christians from other countries—cross the cultural gaps to communicate the gospel, Indonesian Muslim people groups will remain hidden from view and unreached.[5]

For Winter, the gospel is a constant, but the means of evangelism are not universal. He advocated a spectrum that would distinguish evangelistic work according to culture, not geography or even language. Sharing the gospel in a Christian worship gathering is evangelism, and sharing the gospel among Bedouins in North Africa is also evangelism. However, such groups should not be approached with the same method or priority. Using Indian people groups as an example, Winter developed a typology that categorizes evangelism and clarifies that all evangelism is not equal.

> Let's give labels to those different kinds of evangelism. Where an Ao Naga won another Ao, let us call that *E-1 evangelism*. When an Ao went across a tribal language boundary to a sister language and won the *Santdam*, we'll call it *E-2 evangelism*. (The E-2 task is not as easy and requires different techniques.) But then if an Ao Naga goes to another region of India, to a totally strange language, for example, Telegu, Korhu or Bhili, his task will be considerably more difficult than E-1 or even E-2 evangelism. We will call it *E-3 evangelism*.[6]

While Winter in the early 1980s called churches in the United States to such labors in their backyards, it has been a long and slow process of the application of such thinking to this country. To date, intercultural evangelism is not practiced enough, though the United States is the third-largest country in the world and is home to the third-largest number of unreached peoples groups (see Payne, *Strangers Next Door*).

3. Winter, "Highest Priority," 213.
4. Winter, "Highest Priority," 214.
5. Winter spoke of a people blindness that exists as Christians do not see the "hidden" peoples of the world. This language would eventually become the language of "unreached" and "unengaged-unreached" peoples.
6. Winter, "Highest Priority," 215.

Later in his presentation, Winter described a fourth category as E-0 evangelism, "the winning of nominal Christians to personal faith and commitment.... But there is no cultural distance involved."[7]

In order for the majority of the world to hear the gospel from people who are culturally like themselves (E-1 evangelism), it is first necessary for other followers of Christ to cross cultural gaps to share the gospel with them (E-2 and E-3 evangelism). Winter stated,

> To go to the special efforts required by E-2 and E-3 evangelism is not to let down the standards and make the Gospel easy—it is to disentangle the irrelevant elements and to make the Gospel clear. Perhaps everyone is not able to do this special kind of work. True, many more E-1 evangelists will eventually be necessary to finish the task. But the highest priority in evangelism today is to develop the cross-cultural knowledge and sensitivities involved in E-2 and E-3 evangelism. Where necessary, evangelists from a distance must be called into the task. Nothing must blind us to the immensely important fact that at least *four-fifths* of the non-Christians in the world today will never have any straightforward opportunity to become Christians unless the Christians themselves go more than halfway in the specialized tasks of cross-cultural evangelism. Here is our highest priority.[8]

Since Lausanne I, a great deal of progress has been made to take the gospel to the unreached peoples, requiring E-2 and E-3 evangelism. However, E-2 and E-3 evangelism remain the greatest need in the United States, across the traditionally Western countries, and throughout Majority World contexts.[9] Unless the church, wherever she may be found in the world, crosses into different and radically different cultural groups, the unreached peoples will remain lost.

Tools Across Time

An awareness of the remaining task to make disciples of all nations resulted in a desire to communicate better the truth of the gospel. History is filled with examples where the church has engaged in her global task only to experience

---

7. Winter, "Highest Priority," 230–31.
8. Winter, "Highest Priority," 225.
9. For example, in the United States, predominantly Brazilian churches must reach the Yemenis who have also migrated to the country. Caucasian churches must reach the Saudi Arabian population. Japanese churches must reach the Chinese peoples. The evangelistic efforts of any local churches are not to be limited by cultural gaps represented by ethnicity, language, or worldview. The gospel must travel from everyone to everyone. However, what is E-2 or E-3 for one group may be E-1 for another group. Brazilian churches in the United States reaching the Chinese may be E-3, but for the Japanese it may be E-2. Chinese churches reaching other Chinese could possibly be E-1, but for most white churches it would involve E-3 efforts.

significant communication breakdown, accommodation, and syncretism. Developments in communication theory influenced missiologists who began to apply such matters to evangelistic practices. The twentieth century observed a number of such resources related to gospel communication beyond works on homiletics and personal evangelism.

Spiritual-Decision Process

While a student in the Wheaton Graduate School, Viggo Søgaard suggested a scale portraying a series of steps showing how people make a decision for Christ. James Engel later modified it and published it in *Church Growth Bulletin* in 1973. Two years later, in the book *What's Gone Wrong with the Harvest? A Communication Strategy for the Church and World Evangelism*, Engel and H. Wilbert Norton published it as "The Spiritual-Decision Process." This tool, which later become known as the Engel Scale, proceeds as follows:

- -8 Awareness of a supreme being, but no effective knowledge of the gospel
- -7 Initial awareness of the gospel
- -6 Awareness of the fundamentals of the gospel
- -5 Grasp of the implications of the gospel
- -4 Positive attitude toward the gospel
- -3 Personal problem recognition
- -2 Decision to act
- -1 Repentance and faith in Christ
- 0 New believer
- +1 Post-decision evaluation
- +2 Incorporated into the body
- +3 A lifetime of conceptual and behavioral growth in Christ[10]

Everything on the negative side is related to the unconverted state. Everything on the positive side represents growth in Christ. Engel and Norton noted that this diagram reveals both the divine elements and the evangelist's actions in the evangelizing process. Here both general and special revelation come together in conjunction with the unregenerate. This resource attempts to show that not everyone is at the same point in their spiritual journeys. Using "an appropriate combination of message and media," the Christian communicator

---

10. Adapted from Engel and Norton, *What's Gone Wrong?*, 45.

is "to cause them to *progress in their decision process toward initial commitment and subsequent growth*."[11] This process is to move people toward 0, or what would be conversion, and then begin teaching obedience to the claims of Christ.

Resistance/Receptivity Scale

Within a few years, Edward Dayton published the Resistance/Receptivity Scale as a means to assess how favorable a population (or even an individual), in general, is to the gospel. Whereas the Engel Scale attempts to discern a cognitive level related to the gospel so that the communicator would know where to begin in the communication, the Resistance/Receptivity Scale is an effective tool for measuring how someone feels about the gospel.

FIGURE 16.1
THE DAYTON RESISTANCE/RECEPTIVITY SCALE

Adapted from Wagner and Dayton, *Unreached Peoples '79*, 30.

Dayton was a mission strategist and wanted to understand a context to communicate the gospel effectively. His theory is that a people who are strongly favorable toward the gospel would respond positively toward almost any evangelistic method. However, those to the far right would need "a great deal of special care" and are unlikely to accept the gospel.[12] Those determined to exist somewhere between the two ends would require much contextualization of communication and the trying of a variety of evangelistic methods.

Søgaard Scale

Viggo Søgaard, whose early ideas were the foundation for the Engel Scale, recognized that effective communication of the gospel requires an understanding of someone's knowledge of the gospel and attitude toward the gospel. People are complex beings. Just because they have much knowledge of the gospel does not mean that they will respond favorably to an invitation to

---

11. Engel and Norton, *What's Gone Wrong?*, 46–47 (emphasis in original).
12. Dayton, "To Reach the Unreached," 30.

SØGAARD SCALE IN PRACTICE

Viggo Søgaard told the following of two examples where his scale was used in Asia and Europe.

> The model was used to illustrate the ministry of an organization in South India that has been producing evangelistic programs in the form of traditional Indian dances. The cognitive content of the dances was limited, but they affected change of attitudes. The Hindu audience was basically negative towards the gospel, but by presenting the gospel in Indian dress through Indian dances the gospel was seen as Indian. The organization also produced radio programs that provided biblical content and further understanding. The actual contact ministry was based on local church outreach, and in order to assist the churches in this ministry they produced a number of cassette tapes. . . .
>
> The audience has a very limited understanding of the gospel, and at the same time is quite negative. On the model their position would be at approximately -4 on the affective scale and 2 on the cognitive scale. Dance-drama aimed at affective changes, moving the audience from -4 towards -1 or even to a neutral position. Cognitive change was the goal of the radio programs that aimed at giving foundational Christian teaching. The bridge to the church, or we could say the actual "reaping" ministry, was provided by church members using cassette tapes as part of their personal witness.
>
> Another example can be taken from the ministry to a group of young people in Denmark. The group is located at approximately 7 on the cognitive dimension and -5 on the affective dimension. A church has established a youth club as a contact ministry. There is no preaching, but as the leaders spend time with the youth who come there a testimony is given, and a trust-relationship is established. This should provide a basis for affective changes from -5 and towards a neutral position. The leader of the club conducts a Bible study in his home and interested youth are invited to attend. Here basic Bible teaching is given to provide growth in knowledge.
>
> Søgaard, Media, 70–71.

Questions

1. What are some other methods that may bring about cognitive change and affective change in these South Asian and European contexts?
2. In general, where does your context fall on the scale? Consider charting a specific individual.

follow Christ. Also, just because someone has a favorable attitude toward the gospel and the church does not mean that they are ready to receive Christ.

FIGURE 16.2
TWO-DIMENSIONAL MODEL WITH COGNITIVE AND AFFECTIVE DIMENSIONS

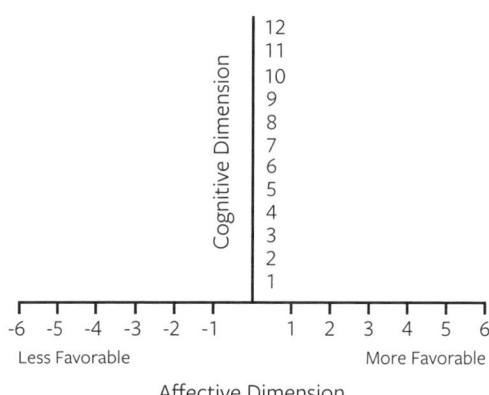

From Søgaard, *Media in Church and Mission*, 64.

As with the Engel Scale, the Søgaard Scale has been modified over the years.[13] However, this scale attempted to combine the Engel and the Resistance/Receptivity Scales into a single figure noting the cognitive and affective dimensions within the human heart.[14] Søgaard's scale is related to what he believed were limitations in Western evangelistic media. Much of what he observed "focuses on conversion, and few [media] concentrate on the 'sowing' or initial phase of the spiritual decision process. Evangelistic material produced in the West is often far too narrow in scope to reach the intended audience."[15] He noted, "For some people their spiritual journey begins with information and knowledge, but others will begin their spiritual journey as a result of a power encounter which has caused attitude change. For most people, there will probably be concurrent processes of cognitive and affective changes and these will continue after the decision or change in allegiance has been made."[16]

13. See Gray, "The Gray Matrix."
14. Early reflections of Søgaard's thoughts related to cognitive and affective elements may be found in his book *Everything You Need to Know for a Cassette Ministry: Cassettes in the Context of a Total Christian Communication Program*.
15. Søgaard, *Media*, 61.
16. Søgaard, *Media*, 63–64.

Søgaard stated that Engel followed a linear approach to decision-making but believed that a two-dimensional decision-making model was needed.[17] Instead of viewing conversion as a moment in time that follows a series of levels of cognitive development and progress, Søgaard noted that, in reality, people often come to faith with a low level of biblical knowledge.[18] Different audiences, and individuals, require different approaches to sharing the gospel. For examples of applying Søgaard's scale, see the sidebar "Søgaard Scale in Practice."

Receptor-Orientation

Building on communication and rhetorical theory and the works of scholars such as Eugene Nida, Marvin Mayers, Charles Kraft, Hendrik Kraemer, and James Engel, David Hesselgrave produced the monumental *Communicating Christ Cross-Culturally* in 1978. Hesselgrave drew attention to effective communication when he challenged readers to understand that evangelism is not as simple as broadcasting the message through a universal medium: "Missionaries must divest themselves forever of the naïve notion that the gospel message as decoded by respondents is the same irrespective of how it is conveyed to the world—whether by book, magazine, radio, television, film, sound recording, tract, chalk artistry, or drama. Perhaps no fiction has had wider currency in Western missions than the idea that if you put a gospel message into any of these media at one end, it will come out the other end as the same gospel message."[19]

Part of his response to communication breakdown was for communicators to be receptor-oriented in their approach to ministry.[20] Like a radio station that broadcasts a signal, and a receiver that accepts it, so is the communication act in evangelism. Someone preaches and someone hears.

17. Søgaard, *Media*, 63, 64.
18. Søgaard, *Media*, 64.
19. Hesselgrave, *Communicating Christ*, 50.
20. Numerous books were published in the twentieth and twenty-first centuries on the topic of gospel communication. Some of these are general in nature, while others are specific to worldviews. It is well beyond the scope of this book to offer a comprehensive list. However, here are some examples: Kraemer, *Communication of the Christian Faith*; Nida, *Message and Mission*; Weber, *Communication of the Gospel*; Mayers, *Christianity Confronts Culture*; Engel, *Contemporary Christian Communications*; Kraft, *Communication Theory*; Van Rheenen, *Communicating Christ*; R. Johnson, *How Will They Hear?*; Nazir-Ali, *Mission and Dialogue*; Shaw and Van Engen, *Communicating God's Word*; Steffen, *Reconnecting God's Story*; De Neui and Lim, *Communicating Christ*; Sanneh, *Translating the Message*; Dillon, *Telling the Gospel*; Mischke, *Global Gospel*; Georges and Baker, *Honor-Shame Cultures*; Dean et al., *Communication in Mission*.

However, two things must be kept in mind: interference and interaction. As the message of the gospel is communicated, it passes through an atmosphere of static and arrives at the receiver with a potential breakdown in understanding. Noise, distractions, preconceived ideals of Christians, and a person's background and experience are just a few of the elements that affect reception of the message. Interaction, unlike what happens between a radio transmitter and receiver, is necessary because it allows for discussion, questions and answers, and rebuttals. The one sharing enters a give-and-take with the recipient. This allows the evangelist to be receptor-oriented in communication as they attempt to discern, "How is this person hearing and understanding what is being shared?" Even in a context that does not allow for dialogue, the one sharing seeks to understand the audience beforehand, reads the room, and attempts to keep oneself in check. Effective evangelism requires the witness to understand not only the gospel but also their own cultural background and that of the hearers.

Christ at the Center

By the twenty-first century, evangelicals, particularly in the traditionally Western contexts, had regular conversations about worldview dichotomies. Centuries of global labors and anthropological and sociological study resulted in publications and conversations about societies predominantly concerned with guilt and justice, shame and honor, and fear and power. Darrell Whiteman was correct when he wrote, "Focusing on trying to convince people to change their behavior without the Holy Spirit fostering a deeper change in their values, beliefs, and worldview at best is superficial and at worst leads to nominal Christianity and hypocrisy."[21] In order to move toward more effective communication, missiologists began to examine how the gospel addresses such worldview categories. The beauty of what is found in the Scriptures is that the multifaceted gospel addresses soteriological issues that may be keenly felt in each of these perspectives. The good news of Christ addresses guilt and justice—a matter that most of us in the West are familiar with. However, the gospel also speaks much about overcoming shame and restoring honor and overcoming fear and experiencing true power.

21. Whiteman, *Crossing Cultures*, 97.

BARRIER TO THE GOSPEL AMONG NATIVE AMERICANS / FIRST NATIONS

Patrick Lennox writes the following to assist the church in rethinking her approach to reaching Native Americans. Numerous historical problems caused by poor ministry methods have influenced the present and should be understood. Contemporary barriers to the gospel often develop over a lengthy period of time, and Lennox draws attention to this reality in his work.

> Native pastors and ministry leaders with whom I serve consistently report confronting persistent resistance to the gospel. While some level of resistance is to be expected, historical factors have created formidable barriers between the church and her Native neighbors.
>
> Those can be traced back to the conquest and colonization of North America by a dominant culture in the US and Canada that espoused Christianity. But another dispossession followed the dispossession of land that occurred centuries ago. This time it was not the land, but the children. This had deep and far-reaching effects on Native communities for generations up to this very day.
>
> In the latter part of the nineteenth century through most of the twentieth century, both the US and Canadian governments, with participation from many Christian denominations, initiated and sustained the Indian boarding school movement. Native children, as young as four years old, were separated from their parents and tribe and sent to government schools far from home.
>
> The driving doctrine was "Kill the Indian, save the man." At the schools, children endured abuse of all kinds. Many died. The entire program was designed to strip Native children of all cultural influence, beginning with changing each child's Indian name to his or her new "Christian" name.
>
> Numerous Native children grew to reject the "white man's religion," deeming it as antithetical to Native culture. Yet by God's grace, many others did embrace the Savior. In both cases, Native communities, today, live with the fallout of this destructive government program in which a misguided church participated.
>
> Per capita, Native people in the US suffer with the highest rates of poverty, alcoholism, suicide, drug abuse, domestic violence, gang violence, mental illness, PTSD, human trafficking, high school dropout rates, teen pregnancy, and historical trauma. The statistics are nearly identical in Canada.
>
> Yet, these are not just statistics. They are people. Native people are also not historical curiosities trapped in the past or relics discovered through DNA kits. They are communities of families and individuals created in the image of God with a shared history, and a present reality. They are an integral part of God's continuing story of redemption.
>
> Lennox, "Rethinking Missions," 35.

> *Questions*
>
> 1. How do past experiences affect present realities for good or for bad? Give examples from your experience and context.
> 2. Explain the difference between civilizing, Christianizing, and evangelizing a society. Who determines the definition of what is civil, Christian, and evangelism?
> 3. How may the church communicate the gospel to others so that they will not think that the gospel is identified with one's race, ethnicity, or culture?

W. Jay Moon and W. Bud Simon recognize the need for a shift in the way the church conceptualizes her global task in their book *Effective Intercultural Evangelism: Good News in a Diverse World*. They reframe evangelism to be "intercultural" and to take into consideration different worldview dichotomies. They define their understanding of evangelism as "the process of putting Christ at the center of someone's worldview in order to initiate them into Christian discipleship through culturally relevant starting points."[22] Evangelism becomes an entry—or initiation—into the way of Jesus.

Building on the three worldview dichotomies (guilt/justice, shame/honor, fear/power), Moon and Simon add a fourth: indifference/belonging with purpose, which they believe to be found throughout much of the post-Christianized contexts of the world.

Worldview	Guilt/Justice	Shame/Honor	Fear/Power	Indifference/Belonging with Purpose
Typical location	West (N. America, Europe)	East (Middle East, N. Africa, Asia)	South (sub-Saharan Africa, tribal, Caribbean)	postreligious
Sin's result	guilt/separation	shame	fear/curse/bondage	indifference
Solution in Jesus	payment/ substitute	honor restored, cleansed	deliverance	belonging with purpose
Image of salvation	courtroom/ justice	relationship, cleansing	power, freedom	coming home
Relationship with God	Judge who declares, "Not guilty!"	Father who restores honor	Creator who protects and delivers	Family who welcomes you home

From Moon and Simon, *Effective Intercultural Evangelism*, 37.

22. Moon and Simon, *Effective Intercultural Evangelism*, 10.

For each of the worldview categories, Moon and Simon attempt to note the dominant way sin is felt in society and how the gospel addresses the matter. Corresponding biblical metaphors regarding salvation are noted and the connection with God. In each of these worldviews, sin's results and Jesus's solution may be found. However, as Craig Ott notes, "Although cultural understandings of any given metaphor will seldom be identical to the biblical understanding, choosing the appropriate biblical image as a starting point can open doors of understanding that will resonate with the audience."[23] Moon and Simon do not attempt to dilute the gospel, but rather to accentuate that which is already part of the gospel when evangelism occurs among diverse worldviews. Practically, this means no less than the church's need to understand cultures, societies, and individuals while avoiding a monolithic evangelistic package. The gospel is a constant, always to be proclaimed. People are diverse and require different approaches. The never-changing message must be clearly communicated (Col. 4:4) in ever-changing ways.

Evangelism has been about crossing cultural gaps. Beginning with the apostolic God who sent himself into creation to share a message of good news with finite beings and extending to our conversion experiences, the gospel has traveled across cultures. While the message of hope does not change, the means of communication is always in flux. As humans, we live in specific contexts and proclaim the gospel to other people in similar and different contexts. The church shares a message that may be embraced by those representing all the cultures of the world. Once embraced, the gospel will transform cultures, never leaving them the same. The good news is for men, women, and children, the educated and illiterate, the wealthy and poor. All may become one in Christ Jesus (Gal. 3:28).

— **QUESTIONS TO CONSIDER** —

1. Do you agree or disagree that every evangelism encounter is about crossing cultural gaps? Explain.
2. Is most of your evangelism E-0, E-1, E-2, or E-3? What about your church? If not E-2 and E-3, what needs to change to practice such evangelism?
3. What does being "receptor-oriented" in evangelism look like for your practice?

---

23. Ott, "Biblical Metaphors," 370.

17

APOLOGETICS AND WORLDVIEW

The church has always been engaged in providing a reason for the hope she has in Christ (1 Pet. 3:15). When questioned about the kingdom, Jesus pointed to the Scriptures and his miracles. The apostolic church was frequently called to provide a defense for her beliefs and behavior. From the beginnings of the early church to the twenty-first century, apologetics has been connected to evangelism.

Purpose of Apologetics

Apologetics has been described as having a twofold purpose: (1) responding to objections to the faith and (2) providing evidence for the faith. However, if apologetics is truly the "handmaiden to evangelism," a third purpose should be included: segueing to the gospel call. Apologetics should not be confused with evangelism, for it is possible that apologetical matters may be addressed without gospel sharing.

Apologetics that attempts to refute false teachings or objections to the faith is called negative or defensive apologetics. Examples of this approach include responding to the problem of evil and a good God or to the supposed incoherence of the human and divine nature of Christ. That which attempts to offer positive reasons for the faith is called positive or objective apologetics. For example, providing arguments for God's existence or the historicity of the resurrection would be considered within this category.[1]

1. Cowan, introduction to Gundry and Cowan, *Five Views on Apologetics*, 8.

Cautions

Relegation of Evangelism

Within the United States, churches and educational institutions seem to be elevating the place of apologetics well above evangelism and into a category of its own. This may be due to a fear of losing the culture wars or to the embarrassment of potentially being labeled fundamentalist. On the one hand, an apologist is perceived to be a thinker, and a rational one at that. An evangelist, on the other hand, is seen as a zealot, theologically anemic, culturally uncouth, and a holdover from yesteryear. Apologetics often seems to be pushed deeper into the local church context as a means of teaching ethics and strengthening believers. While a significant role of apologetics is that of equipping the saints, it is meant to build them up in the faith so that they may evangelize those apart from God. Christopher Brooks perhaps states it best: "Apologetics and evangelism act as two sides of the same coin. From a biblical perspective they are inseparable. In order for apologetics to have any virtue or spiritual value, it must be intentionally and eternally tied to evangelism. . . . Apart from evangelism, apologetics is aimless and potentially dangerous because it lacks the heart of the gospel, which is to bring people to Christ! Apologetics for purely academic purposes should be avoided at all costs."[2]

Limits

Apologetics is not the gospel. Apologetics does not save. No one has entered the kingdom of God because of a rational argument. God cannot be put into a test tube and proven to exist. The writer of Hebrews notes, "Without faith it is impossible to please him, for whoever would draw near to God must believe that he exists and that he rewards those who seek him" (Heb. 11:6). In the parable of the rich man and Lazarus (Luke 16:19–31), Jesus makes an important point about his resurrection, but the principle extends to the belief that a convincing argument or empirical miracle is sufficient to bring salvation. In the parable, the man in torment cries out to Abraham to resurrect someone from the dead to go tell his brothers about the horrors of Hades so they would believe and go to Paradise. Abraham's response is that his brothers have access to the Scriptures, and "if they do not hear Moses and the Prophets, neither will they be convinced if someone should rise from the dead" (16:31).

2. Brooks, *Urban Apologetics*, 40.

DEFEATERS OF THE DAY

One should be prepared for "defeater" beliefs or questions when seeking to provide a reason for the hope that is within. While the word defeater seems to be recent nomenclature in apologetics circles, every generation has had reasons to deny and oppose the gospel. Defeaters have been and remain universal and contextual. What is widespread in one setting may not be much of a concern in another. Below is a list of some contemporary defeaters found in many Western contexts. Resources, both in print and online, abound that provide guidance for how to respond to these, and their variations.*

- The Christian faith is irrational.
- Does God exist?
- Can the Bible be trusted?
- Science contradicts miracles.
- If God is omnipotent and omnibenevolent, why is there so much evil and suffering in the world?
- Is the Christian faith good for society?
- Jesus cannot be the only way.
- It is impossible for a man to be resurrected.
- Christianity is homophobic and oppressive to people.
- How can a loving God send people to hell?
- Religion is the cause of most of the world's problems.
- Faith is not based on evidence.
- How can God become a human being?
- Miracles do not happen.

*For examples of recent responses to select defeaters see Chamberlain and Price, *Everyday Apologetics*; McLaughlin, *Confronting Christianity*; Keller, *The Reason for God*; and Dodson and Watson, *Raised?* For examples of recent methods on how to respond to defeaters, see Chan, *Evangelism*, 241–77; Chatraw and Allen, *Apologetics at the Cross*, 251–89; Koukl, *Street Smarts*; J. Robinson, *Persuasive Apologetics*, 93–123.

Questions

1. Select three defeaters. How would you respond to them?
2. What defeaters have you encountered, or do you anticipate encountering in the future, that are not listed here? How would you respond to them?

Apologetics helps tear down cultural barriers before the gospel and builds bridges to the gospel. Coming to faith in Jesus is not a leap in the dark, hoping that one may be right. Rather, conversion is a matter of faith responding to evidence revealed in the cosmos, conscience, and Christ (Rom. 1–5). Jesus, the greatest apologist, experienced people who rejected his arguments and teaching. If some with whom he shared the gospel did not come to faith, then his disciples should rest in the fact that they will experience similar results, no matter how skilled they are in apologetics.

Humble Defense

The apostle Paul understood that much of the persecution he experienced was related to his ἀπολογία (*apologia*, "defense") of the gospel (Phil. 1:16). Within the church, he believed in destroying "arguments and every lofty opinion raised against the knowledge of God" (2 Cor. 10:5). On different occasions Luke uses the noun ἀπολογία or the verb ἀπολογέομαι to describe what the apostle was doing before various audiences (Acts 22:1; 24:10; 25:8; 26:1–2, 24). Peter stated that disciples should be "prepared to make a defense [ἀπολογία] to anyone who asks you for a reason for the hope that is in you," and that this apologetic is to be done "with gentleness and respect, having a good conscience, so that, when you are slandered, those who revile your good behavior in Christ may be put to shame" (1 Pet. 3:15–16). Many contemporary apologists should particularly heed the apostle's words related to demeanor and attitude, as some are prone to being impatient, brash, arrogant, and rude. Knowledge puffs up! (1 Cor. 8:1).

Consistent Lifestyle

Everyone expresses faith in something. This may be in scientism, Islam, secularization, hedonism, medicine, security systems, government, airplanes—the list is endless. The object of faith is significant. Worldviews are no exception. Whether it is deism, theism, atheism, or nihilism, a worldview involves a faith and a consistency component. If I hold to a certain worldview, am I consistent to that view in my belief *and* behaviors? Does the worldview have an internal consistency and not attempt to advocate truths that are inconsistent? Does the worldview best reflect the universe? Does the worldview "work" in such a universe? Apologetics is a means by which one is able to show the way of Christ as *the best way among all ways in the universe*. It allows for the apologist to reveal that they not only have thought deeply about the faith but also are consistent in practice. Jesus stated, "If you love me, you will keep my commandments" (John 14:15). The way of Christ involves the disciple in a journey of understanding and application that avoids contradiction. Apologetics is a segue to the gospel. Showing the love of Christ and his way by a consistent lifestyle and answering questions posed by the unbeliever is important but is not the gospel or evangelism. While it is a major component to evangelism, righteous behavior is only a display of the good news in action. A reasonable defense of the faith, in both words and actions, prepares the hearts of people for a hearing of the foundational truths on which such language and life are grounded.

Types of Apologetic Methods

Throughout history apologists have used rational arguments, pointing to the fulfillment of biblical prophecies, empirical evidence, personal experience, and morality in their defense of the faith. While apologists agree that apologetics is used to strengthen the faith of the church and assist in evangelism, the methods used differ among them. Two millennia have allowed for different approaches to be tested and developed. Each of these has its own strengths and limitations, and all should be used in their appropriate contexts.[3]

Classical

Many early apologists advocated for the classical method. It begins by using the created order to establish God's existence. In order to argue for miracles in history, a theistic context must be established. Following this, the classical method transitions to showing the historical evidence for the divinity of Christ and the trustworthiness of the Scriptures. It portrays the Christian faith as the best version of theism. Some contemporary expressions of this method may be found in the ministries of R. C. Sproul, William Lane Craig, Norman Geisler, and Richard Swinburne.

Evidential

The evidential method places more credence on human reason, advocating that historical evidence is sufficient to convince someone of the truth.

---

3. It is beyond the scope of this book to address the merits and limitations of apologetical methods. For an excellent discussion of this topic, see Gundry and Cowan, *Five Views on Apologetics*. In this chapter I follow Cowan's summary of classical, evidential, presuppositional, and cumulative case methods (introduction to Gundry and Cowan, *Five Views on Apologetics*, 15–19).

Miracles are believed to serve as one piece of evidence for God. Generally, the initial step is to argue for the historical fact of Jesus, resurrection, and the reliability of the Scriptures. Next, the resurrection is shown to be evidence for the Christian God. Finally, the resurrection reveals the incarnation and authority of Jesus. When comparing this method to the classical, Joshua Chatraw and Mark Allen note that "most evidentialists believe that the historical arguments contain enough firepower to make the case for theism and Christianity without having to turn to the first step in classical apologetics."[4] Gary Habermas notes that the evidential method provides a single step when it comes to evangelism, for "rather than necessarily having to make an additional, separate move by proving God's existence before moving to the claims of Jesus when time is often at a premium, evidentialism specializes in the one-step approach, arriving at a more direct presentation of the gospel by using data that are still very persuasive."[5] Some contemporary examples of this model may be found in the work of Gary Habermas, John Montgomery, and Michael Licona.

Presuppositional

The presuppositionalist desires to show how the faith is grounded not on probabilities but on assurance. This method argues that all meaning and truth presuppose the God of the Scriptures. A rejection of God and his revelation results in a failure to understand truth, experience, and meaning in its fullness. John Frame writes, "We should present the biblical God, not merely as the conclusion to an argument, but as the one who makes argument possible. We should present him as the source of all meaningful communication, since he is the author of all order, truth, beauty, goodness, logical validity, and empirical fact."[6] All worldviews are founded on presuppositions, including the Christian faith, and everyone uses a degree of circular reasoning to justify their presuppositions. Presuppositional apologetics attempts to show that other worldviews are inadequate, and that the Christian faith is the best approach not only to making sense of people's experiences but also in answering the big questions about life and meaning in the universe. Cornelius Van Til, Gordon Clark, James White, and Francis Schaeffer represent contemporary expressions of a presuppositional model.

4. Chatraw and Allen, *Apologetics at the Cross*, 116.
5. Habermas, "Evidential Apologetics," 121.
6. Frame, "Presuppositional Apologetics," 220.

THE WORD WORKS

Lutheran scholar David Valleskey writes of the power of God's word. Like a sword, its power is revealed when removed from the scabbard. Keeping it away is a mistake.

> The Christian needs only to get the Word out, to unsheathe its power. Knowing this helps to overcome timidity and feelings of inadequacy. The Word will produce its own results. The Word is the seed sown in the soil which springs up and sprouts of its own accord (Mark 4:26–29). It is the net cast into the sea by fishers of men (Luke 5:1–11). Evangelists are seed-sowers. Evangelists are net-casters. God makes the seed grow. God fills the net.
>
> Evangelists are witnesses telling the truth about what they have seen and heard (cf. Acts 1:8; 4:20). They are not lawyers who have to convince a jury. God does that. Christ's witnesses have a simple commission: Unsheathe the powerful Word of truth. . . .
>
> In one sense, apologetics has no place at all in evangelism. It may be possible to come up with rational, logical arguments that demonstrate the folly of unbelief, since the truth is neither irrational nor illogical. Such arguments, however, no matter how skillfully presented, will not have the effect of turning a person from unbelief to faith.
>
> Conversion is a supernatural work, brought about by the Holy Spirit. The only effective means of transforming an unbeliever into a believer, therefore, is to use the means by which the Holy Spirit works. That is why Christ's commission to his disciples was to preach repentance and forgiveness of sins (cf. Luke 24:47).
>
> Our call as Christians is not to *prove* the gospel but to *proclaim* it. The gospel by its very nature is self-authenticating. Apologetics cannot replace the preaching of law and gospel. It is not a substitute for the means of grace.
>
> On the other hand, apologetics can properly serve a helping role in evangelism. It can assist in clearing away misconceptions that may have resulted in a person being unwilling to listen seriously to what the Scriptures say.
>
> Valleskey, *We Believe*, 29, 111–12.

Questions

1. Do you agree or disagree with Valleskey on the relationship of apologetics to evangelism? Explain.
2. Since conversion is a supernatural work of the Spirit, who convinces the world, why does Peter state that believers should give a reason for the hope they have (1 Pet. 3:15)?

Cumulative Case

The cumulative case attempts to compile data into a theory that explains the data better than any alternative theories do. Christian theism is argued to be the most plausible explanation for all evidence. Much like an attorney builds a court case, the apologist attempts to show, with a variety of means, that the Christian faith makes the best sense when answering the questions of life. C. S. Lewis, C. Stephen Evans, Basil Mitchell, and Paul Feinberg are a few examples of apologists who emphasize this method.

Understanding Worldviews

An effective approach to apologetics, and evangelism, involves an understanding of *worldview*. From an academic and philosophical perspective, conversations may be traced to the eighteenth century with Immanuel Kant (1724–1804) and were further developed by Wilhelm Dilthey (1833–1911). Worldview would be identified as a philosophy, outlook, or way of life followed by either an individual or social group. By the twentieth century, all worldviews were deemed socially constructed, with none being true or false. Everything was relative.

Paul Hiebert describes worldview as "the fundamental cognitive, affective, and evaluative presuppositions a group of people make about the nature of things, and which they use to order their lives."[7] As experiences, beliefs, values, and feelings come together, people develop a worldview that results in behaviors.[8]

FIGURE 17.1
THE DIMENSIONS OF CULTURE

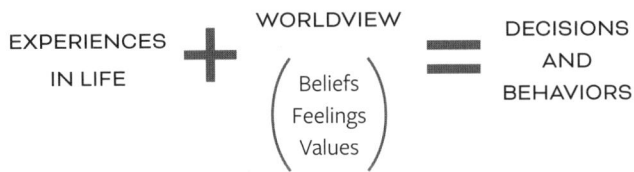

Adapted from Hiebert, *Transforming Worldviews*, 26.

James Sire takes a slightly different approach: "A worldview is a commitment, a fundamental orientation of the heart, that can be expressed as a story

7. Hiebert, *Transforming Worldviews*, 15.
8. Hiebert, *Transforming Worldviews*, 26.

or in a set of presuppositions . . . which we hold . . . about the basic constitution of reality, and that provides the foundation on which we live and move and have our being."[9] Perhaps a simple way of explaining worldview is that it is a set of lenses through which people filter information and understand the universe. N. T. Wright notes that a worldview attempts to answer basic, overarching questions about life, and "wherever we find the ultimate concerns of human beings, we find worldviews."[10] According to Wright, these ultimate concerns are expressed in questions such as:

- Who are we?
- Where are we?
- What is wrong?
- What is the solution?[11]

Wright's questions may be inserted into Hiebert's formula in figure 17.1. Societies, and individuals, tell themselves stories to help understand past, present, and future reality to answer such questions. They develop symbols to communicate important stories related to meaning and engage in cultural practices that teach proper societal functions. As addressed in the previous chapter, these take shape in categories such as fear/power, honor/shame, guilt/justice, and indifference/purpose.

Apologetics that results in effective evangelism takes into consideration the worldview of the individual or group. Every worldview attempts to make sense out of life and provide answers to the aforementioned four questions. Sire has done an excellent job tracing the historical development of the most prominent worldviews, in Western contexts, and summarizing their tenants. His work *The Universe Next Door: A Basic Worldview Catalog* is a must-read for those seeking to become more effective in evangelism. Understanding worldviews assists the witness in knowing how to speak the gospel clearly into the lives of people and answer the big questions they have about life and the universe.

Theism

The three major theistic traditions today are Judaism, Christianity, and Islam. Here an all-powerful, transcendent god created all and oversees all.

---

9. Sire, *Naming the Elephant*, 141.
10. N. T. Wright, *New Testament*, 122.
11. N. T. Wright, *New Testament*, 123. A closely related question also involves a people's time in history: "What time is it?"

> ## SEVEN STEPS IN CONVERSATION
>
> The following seven steps serve as a model for attempting to understand others and being understood during dialogue. These steps, and variations, may be found in the writings of various scholars including Joshua Chatraw (*Telling a Better Story*), Joshua Chatraw and Mark Allen (*Apologetics at the Cross*), Sam Chan (*Evangelism*), and Timothy Keller (*The Reason for God* and *Making Sense of God*).
>
> Step 1: Invite the other person to provide their explanations for reality and truth.
> Step 2: Seek to understand their view, particularly the presuppositions, from their perspective.*
> Step 3: Comment on points of agreement.
> Step 4: Ask them to explain the Christian perspective, on whatever topic is being discussed, as they view it.
> Step 5: Clarify where their explanation is correct and incorrect.†
> Step 6: Compare the two perspectives to make the case that the way of Christ makes the best sense of the truth of the world and offers the more excellent way.
> Step 7: Challenge them to follow Christ with the gospel message.
>
> * Joshua Chatraw describes this act as stepping into the other person's story—a necessary element before showing them the way out and into the better story of the gospel (*Telling a Better Story*, 63).
>
> † Sam Chan notes that once we are able to "describe, understand, and empathize with their presuppositions," then we can graciously "dismantle" their understanding of reality by showing "a deficiency or dissonance in their presuppositions" (*Evangelism*, 255).
>
> ### Questions
>
> 1. How would you summarize these steps in your own words?
> 2. What steps, if any, need to be added—especially ones specific to your context?

Deism

Deism has its origins in England and became popular in the United States. Deism is a theistic worldview with a god who is unconcerned with the universe he created. God and morality can be understood through reason. God established the cosmos and set it into motion to run on its own by physical laws. He is detached and distant from the world. People and the created order are bound to the mechanistic system that he created and started. Miracles do not exist. There is no fallen humanity.

Naturalism

In the naturalistic worldview, the material is all that exists. The universe is the cause for what exists. There is no God, supernatural, or spiritual realm. Everything has occurred by chance, over time, as matter came together. The laws that govern the universe are in motion, with it eventually ending on its own. Morality develops from experience. Knowledge is best understood through scientific method. There is no ultimate meaning or purpose in life as humanity is moving toward extinction. Everything that occurs is based on cause-and-effect events.

Nihilism

Some would argue nihilism is not a worldview. Matter is all that exists. Humans are complex machines that function based on chemical and physical properties. Nihilism is best defined as the negation of everything. All is meaningless. Humans do not have freedom, as the universe is a closed system of cause and effect. All human actions are determined by past events. Freedom is an illusion. Morality has no foundation, as such values are relative to one's cultural setting.

Existentialism

It is good to have purpose and meaning. People make actual choices that have consequences, as there is objectivity and subjectivity in the universe. Atheistic existentialism attempts to move beyond nihilism.[12] People are free regarding their destinies. They create their own value and worth and are responsible only to themselves. Science and logic are keys to understanding the objective world but are unable to address the subjective matters of life, such as value, meaning, and significance.

Pantheism

God is everything, as there is no distinction between god and matter. The universe is eternal; god is impersonal, unchangeable, and pure. Truth and morality are relative. Various expressions of pantheism may be found in Buddhism and Hinduism. Humanity's problems may be related to ignorance—or there are no problems because everything is an illusion—and karma is to be overcome in order to become one with Brahman or the Void after cycles of reincarnation.

---

12. Theistic existentialism attempted to move beyond dead Christian orthodoxy and theological liberalism.

Postmodernism

It has been argued that postmodernism is not a worldview but a mood. While truth exists, it cannot be discovered. Therefore, truth is socially created and experienced according to the individual in the societal context. Metanarratives are not universal but are relevant only to those who decide to embrace them. Morality and ethics are relative. Science is valuable but unable to address matters such as ethics, religion, and morality. Science failed to be the savior it promised to be, as it created problems and pain and, especially, unethical and immoral atmospheres in which people responded in harmful ways toward others. People seek power over other people often throughout metanarratives, rituals, and structures. Authoritative figures and texts that claim universal application of their metanarratives are not to be trusted.

Understanding worldview is critical to effective communication of the gospel. Whether evangelizing one person or a group, one must understand the general perspective of the hearers. This approach assists with becoming receptor-oriented in sharing and part of the process to become all things to all people to win some (1 Cor. 9:19–23). Coupled with understanding worldview is the value of apologetics. The church should be prepared to give a reason for her hope (1 Pet. 3:15), which involves a defense (Phil. 1:16) as well as persuasion (2 Cor. 5:11). While apologetics is not evangelism, the former assists the latter through effective, humble, loving, and winsome communication.

— **QUESTIONS TO CONSIDER** —

1. If the gospel is the power of God for salvation, why should apologetics be used by the church?
2. When doing apologetics, do you use a humble and respectful approach toward others?
3. How would you summarize Sire's major worldview categories in your own words?

— PART 5 —

CONTEMPORARY ISSUES

In this final section I address some contemporary issues related to evangelism. Whereas the previous sections include sidebars and questions in an attempt to move the reader toward practical application, this section contains fewer footnotes, more stories from my personal experience, and a different writing style. Evangelism is not meant to remain in the lofty atmospheres of theological and methodological inquiry but rather is to be accomplished in reality. This section considers tools such as the use of one's testimony and the Sinner's Prayer. A variety of practical questions related to personal matters are raised and answered as well as how to share the gospel with family and children. After nearly twenty years in pastoral ministry, I came to understand the significance of pastoral leadership in a church's evangelistic endeavors. Readers also will find a chapter related to this topic.

18

TESTIMONY

One of the most helpful and practical tools available when sharing the gospel is one's testimony. Throughout the Scriptures, testimony is related to legal matters. Witnesses were established when a significant transaction was involved. In an attempt to get to the truth, a testimony was expected (Deut. 19:15). New Testament authors draw from the Old Testament foundation, carrying on the necessity for witnesses in matters of disputes (Matt. 18:16; 2 Cor. 13:1). This chapter considers some of the biblical and practical matters related to the use of a testimony in evangelism.

Old Testament

The Old Testament uses עֵד (*'ēd*), translated as "testimony" or "witness." The related verb עוּד (*'ûd*) means "bear witness" or even "warn," as when God often warned Israel to not sin and to walk faithfully with him (Deut. 4:26; Jer. 11:7). A witness can be a person (Isa. 43:10) or an inanimate object (Gen. 31:52; Ps. 89:37). The book of the law was to serve as a witness of God before Israel (Deut. 31:26), as was the tabernacle (Exod. 38:21).

The giving of the Mosaic covenant included a witness between God and Israel (Deut. 4:26). False witnesses were despised because they misrepresent the truth and bring injustice into society (Exod. 20:16; 23:1; Deut. 5:20; Prov. 6:19; 25:18). The lying tongue and false witness comprise the "things that the Lord hates" (Prov. 6:16–19). Such evil was equated with murder, adultery, sexual immorality, theft, slander, and evil thoughts (Matt. 15:19). During the intertestamental period, the Septuagint used the μαρτ- (*mart-*) stem to translate such terms.[1]

1. G. Taylor, "Testimony."

EXPLAIN YOUR TERMS

For years, Christians have been accused of using *Christianese* when speaking to those who have not received the gospel. We frequently use insider language when speaking with outsiders. Below are several terms commonly used when sharing the gospel. Think through the most basic meaning of each one, recognizing that being receptor-oriented in your communication may mean avoiding the term and using the definition in your testimony.

1. Born again = moving from death to life
2. Repentance = turning, changing direction
3. Righteousness = being made right in God's eyes
4. Sin = anything that goes against God's commands
5. Gospel = good news
6. Grace = God's riches at Christ's expense
7. Faith = belief, trust, forsaking all to trust Christ
8. Mercy = withholding punishment and receiving grace
9. Forgiveness = overlooking wrongs and extending grace, mercy
10. Jesus = Son of God
11. God = Creator and sustainer of the universe
12. Holy Spirit = God's invisible presence
13. Sacrifice = taking on wrath/judgment on behalf of another
14. Love = unconditional affection that leads to sacrificial action
15. Belief = faith, trust
16. Eternal = forever
17. Christian = follower of Jesus
18. Death = separation from God
19. Glory = God's perfection/righteousness on display
20. Saved = rescued from separation from God
21. Redemption = from being a slave to sin to being free
22. Confess = admit
23. Lord = sovereign/leader/ruler over all
24. Condemned = assigned a place of separation because of sin
25. Resurrection = raised from the dead

> *Questions*
>
> 1. Select five words. How would you explain them in your context?
> 2. What words and meanings need to be added to this list for your context?
> 3. Would you consider sharing your testimony with someone who is not a follower of Jesus and allow them to discuss all the words that they did not understand?

New Testament

As was noted in chapter 1, throughout the New Testament the verb μαρτυρέω (*martyreō*) is found and translated as "bear witness." The nouns μαρτυρία (*martyria*) and μαρτύριον (*martyrion*), translated as "testimony," are present, with μαρτυρία also referring to the content of the testimony provided (John 1:19; Acts 22:18). A person who is a witness is referred to as a μάρτυς (*martys*).

Jesus's apostles were witnesses of the life, ministry, death, and resurrection of the Messiah (Luke 1:2; 1 John 1:1–4). They were to preach to the people and to "testify" (διαμαρτύρομαι, *diamartyromai*) that Jesus was the one appointed by God (Acts 10:42). John makes much use of testimony and bearing witness, as over one-third of the New Testament uses of μαρτυρέω and μαρτυρία are found in the Fourth Gospel.[2] Jesus, even though he is the faithful witness (Rev. 1:5), acknowledged the need for a testimony about himself (John 5:31).

The story of the gospel, and evangelism, is one that demands testimony. The use of one's testimony is intimately connected to the message and experience. Just as Israel was to bear witness to what they had experienced with their God, the disciples were expected to speak about what they had observed, heard, and touched (1 John 1:1).

Testimony as Evidence to the World

During a time when truth claims about religiosity and morality are socially constructed, stories are viewed as truth claims. I may not agree with your story and claim; however, it is powerful and truth to you. I may find your experience as strange and unpalatable, but I am unlikely to call you a liar. The

---

2. G. Taylor, "Testimony."

world may deny testimony as evidence regarding the Christ, but denial does not negate the truth.

Testimony as Story Told and Lived

The story experienced is the story to be shared. While the sharing of one's testimony is not the same as sharing the gospel, it is possible to incorporate an evangelistic message into the story (e.g., Acts 26:12–29).

If the story told is inconsistent with the life lived, the world will rightly see hypocrisy. What the church subscribes to in doctrine must be consistent with what is expressed in individual behaviors among her members. It is possible to bear false witness when the story shared is contrary to the life displayed. Not only is a false witness impotent in society when it comes to gospel impact and transformation, but also hypocrisy is deeply despised by God.

Testimony Developed

The classic model of sharing one's testimony is based on a tripartite structure. Elements of this may be found in Luke's record of Paul's story where he speaks of his life before encountering Christ, what the Lord did to bring him to faith, and his life after his conversion. Though ancient in expression, this is still a helpful way to communicate one's story. As the testimony is shared, look for particular circumstances that you experienced that connect with the listener(s).

- **What was life like before Christ?** What was life like before coming to faith? Attention may be given to personal desires, fears, loneliness, lack of purpose or peace. Even if raised in a Christian family, one should address the sin nature and acts that displease God. Here is where attention is placed on God's holiness and one's sinfulness, and how they were recognized. Emphasize God's grace during this time and not the sinful lifestyle.
- **What did God use to bring me to himself?** Were you raised in a Christian home? Did God use a crisis? Friend? Particular circumstance? Bible study? Describe the steps involved in your conversion process.
- **What practical difference does this relationship make in daily life?** The old adage "Christians are so heavenly minded that they are of no earthly good" should have no place in the church. Given the pragmatic nature of many people today, one should give serious thought about how to communicate the practical difference that one's salvation makes in day-to-day

life. If a story can point only to the blessings of life after death, then a return to the Scriptures to understand the implications of kingdom life in the present is necessary. How did Christ meet the need(s) from the "before" section of your story that you were unable to satisfy?

- **Have you ever experienced anything like this?** This simple question after sharing one's story allows for the dialogue to continue. It also shows interest in the other person and an openness to hear their stories. Such humility and kindness reveal qualities of kingdom life. Listening to others' stories also provides an understanding of what they are basing their present and eternal security on, if Jesus has been confessed as Lord, and if they are walking in the assurance of his presence and security and enjoying the fullness of joy and pleasures from him (Ps. 16:11).

One should never be embarrassed about the miracle of God's grace in their life. Neither should a person feel inadequate because their story is not as "exciting" as that of another believer. Whenever I hear of such concerns, I think about Paul and Barnabas. These were very different men with different backgrounds. When readers of the New Testament are introduced to Barnabas, he is a faithful member of the Jerusalem church; Paul, however, is Saul of Tarsus, seeking to destroy the church. We know of Paul's experience on the Damascus Road, but we have no such biblical record of Barnabas's experience. However, God used both of these men in powerful ways to advance the gospel. One's experience is a testimony to God's love and is to be embraced and used for his glory. Four particular characteristics make this tool a powerful resource in evangelism.

Personal

One's story is unique. Testimonies are as different as the people who embrace them. They are a gift from God and should be cherished (James 1:17). Whether a person was raised in a Christian home and has no memory of a time of separation from Christ, or instead came to faith after years of debauchery, both conversion stories are miraculous testimonies to the power of God. The transcendent God revels his immanency and intimacy with people on an individual level by providing personal testimonies. It is good theology to speak of a "personal Lord and Savior" who knows the number of hairs on his children's heads (Luke 12:7) and has written their names in heaven (Luke 10:20).

Powerful

A person's testimony is a powerful story. It is not a work of fiction or one that stretches the truth. A testimony is to be shared without embellishment, for it is in the simple telling that a powerful effect occurs in listeners' minds (Acts 7:54).

Provocative

One's story challenges listeners to enter God's story as well. It provokes them to action. Storytelling for the sake of itself has no place in evangelism. A testimony is told with a purpose: that others may believe it (2 Thess. 1:10). As Paul was giving his testimony, he acknowledged Agrippa's belief in the Old Testament prophets. When confronted with the official's rebuff, "In a short time would you persuade me to be a Christian?" (Acts 26:28), he acknowledged that his testimony was told to provoke a positive response to Jesus. "Whether short or long," Paul stated, "I would to God that not only you but all who hear me this day might become such as I am" (Acts 26:29).

Evangelism upholds the Old Testament practice that two or more witnesses were required for the legitimacy of a testimony in court (Deut. 19:15). The Spirit (John 15:26; 16:8–11) and the Word of God (John 5:39; Heb. 4:12–13), along with the messenger's experience (John 15:27; Acts 1:8), speak to the heart of the listener. Coupled with one's personal story is the testimony of the community of believers. As disciples show love for one another, they give evidence to the world that they are Christ's followers (John 13:34–35). Witness to the world is both personal and communal.

Practical

A testimony is not a theoretical tale or a story without a challenge. It is not a narrative with a moral. Regardless of one's theological tradition, a testimony should be told in such a way that hearers can relate and respond for themselves. Though salvation is not by works, tell them what *you* did when you heard the gospel and experienced the Spirit's conviction. Action phrases should be used when recalling one's experience: "I read the Bible," "I prayed to God, asking him to reveal himself to me," "I turned from my direction in life and confessed him as Lord."

Watch Your Language

As social beings, humans use words, phrases, and expressions that communicate within their community. For the insider, such terminology is clear, accepted, and understood. However, for one who is an outsider, communication often breaks down when confronted with the language of the tribe. The church is no exception to having her own language. "You must be born again," a believer declares. While such is biblical, if Nicodemus was confused when God the Son used it, how much more we should expect confusion from those with whom we speak. Common parlance such as "repent," "faith," "saved," and "Lord" needs to be explained. Even ubiquitous terms should be used with caution and definition. Take "God," for example. In a pluralistic context, which god is being referred to in the testimony? Is this another one of the numerous gods found in the Hindu pantheon? A kindly grandfather figure in the sky? A vengeful and fickle one like those found in Greek, Roman, and Norse mythologies? It should not be assumed that a listener will know the meanings understood by many in the biblical world. Of course, if such is the case when using the language of Scripture, imagine the confusion that arises when commonly used words from church culture are mixed into one's testimony. "I asked Jesus into my heart" and "I walked the aisle to be saved" are laden with long-standing church culture and are examples of colloquialism that often cause confusion rather than provide clarity (see the sidebar "Explain Your Terms").

One's faith story is a powerful tool used in the hands of the Holy Spirit. Though it is possible to share one's testimony in such a way that is not evangelistic, we would be wise to share our stories that others may clearly understand the gospel we believe and how they should respond too. It is easy to think that if one did not have a dynamic experience like others have had, then one's testimony is of little use. Every conversion experience is a miracle of God and should be leveraged for his glory.

— QUESTIONS TO CONSIDER —

1. How would you explain your testimony in thirty seconds or less?
2. Do you ever feel as if your story is not powerful and effective? Explain.
3. What are the Christian terms you use most often that you need to explain to others?

19

THE SINNER'S PRAYER

The Sinner's Prayer is a fairly recent development in the history of the church. With the rise of evangelicalism, particularly in the United States, the prayer developed as a tool for use in evangelism. In all likelihood, the theological and methodological roots may be traced to the nineteenth century, with Bill Bright and Billy Graham popularizing its present form in the twentieth.[1] While one could cite the cries of the ten lepers (Luke 17:13), the tax collector (Luke 18:13), and the thief on the cross (Luke 23:42) as examples of sinners' prayers (not to mention many others in the Bible), what the church has come to call the Sinner's Prayer looks much different.

The prayer is simply an expression of a heart repentant toward God, confessing that one is a sinner separated from God, is repenting of sin, and believing in Jesus's death, burial, and resurrection and his lordship over life.

Theology of Prayer

There is no standard set of words in the Scriptures used by the unconverted to come to faith. No pithy statement or memorized script is found. The church will not locate a prescriptive chant that brings the lost into the fold. However, the Bible is not void of references to faith declarations.

Portions of this chapter are adapted from J. D. Payne, *Evangelism: A Biblical Response to Today's Questions* (InterVarsity, 2011), 125–27.

1. For extensive study, see Chitwood, "The Sinner's Prayer."

The theology behind the Sinner's Prayer is related to Joel's statements about the day of the Lord. Although judgment would be poured out on the world before that terrible day, "everyone who calls on the name of the LORD shall be saved" (Joel 2:32). Peter later directs his audience to this text when they recognize that judgment day is upon them (Acts 2:21), and Paul cites it as a promise from God to the one who confesses Jesus as Lord (Rom. 10:9, 13).

Referencing Origen, Thomas Watson writes, "Confession is the vomit of the soul whereby the conscience is eased of that burden which did lie upon it."[2] The heart moved by the word of God and touched by the Spirit causes the body to declare God's praise and a petition for acceptance. The Sinner's Prayer is a cry for mercy. It is a proclamation that among all gods, Jesus is Lord.

Purpose of the Prayer

There is value with this tool. The prayer may assist someone in expressing the desires of their heart. Sometimes people desire to express themselves to God in ways that require assistance. A prayer of declaration allows for the person to have a moment where they clearly understand crossing over from being an enemy of God to being adopted into his family as a beloved child. The prayer may be used to help the individual recognize what they are doing: repenting, believing, and committing to Christ.

The Sinner's Prayer assists people in making a public declaration that marks the moment in time when they volitionally repent of their sin and confess Jesus as Lord of their lives. Just as the Israelites were commanded to erect pillars of rocks as memorials to the works of the Lord in their lives, this prayer serves a commemorative purpose. While the Holy Spirit possibly has worked regeneration in the life of the person before they pray, the prayer erects a spiritual memorial, a marker in time.

Cautions with the Prayer

The prayer is not a magical mantra or incantation that manipulates God into saving a person. It is simply a tool and not a universal in evangelism. This resource is so ubiquitous, having been popularized by high-profile evangelists, that many people have come to see it as synonymous with salvation. Thus, someone who has not "prayed the prayer" is not saved. Some treat the prayer as a sacrament, though it becomes more like an animistic practice. They

---

2. T. Watson, *Doctrine of Repentance*, 32.

attempt to relate a person's assurance of salvation to the words spoken. Such theology should greatly trouble the church, for if such were the case, then the only people who have been saved throughout history are those born after the prayer came into existence in the nineteenth or twentieth century!

I recall sharing the gospel with a young man and leading him through praying a sinner's prayer. Later, I began to rethink my conversation with him. I found myself worrying that I might have left out some important words in the prayer. This concern weighed heavily on me, for I felt that it was very possible that I had not led him to pray as he needed to in order to be saved. My soul found comfort only after I grew in a proper understanding that salvation is by grace alone through faith alone and in the power of the Holy Spirit.

No one is regenerated by repeating a set of words. Many people have declared the Sinner's Prayer but never declared Jesus as Lord from a repentant heart. A young church member once shared with me a "commitment card" signed by her father, which stated that he had "prayed to receive Christ" on a certain date. While I attempted to encourage her, I was well aware of her father's attitude and actions, which reflected a lack of fruit in his life and no desire for the things of the Lord. He may have prayed a prayer at one time, but I doubted his repentance.

The apostle never told the church to examine a person's commitment card for a legitimate signature or discern whether someone "prayed the prayer"; rather, the church is to examine the fruit displayed in a person's life (Matt. 7:15–20). If there is little to nothing there that aligns with kingdom values, then the church has every right to state that that person is likely not in the kingdom (Matt. 18:17–18; 1 Cor. 5:5, 12–13). Paul insisted, "As you received Christ Jesus the Lord, so walk in him" (Col. 2:6). If one's heart is not bent in the direction of imitating Christ (1 Cor. 11:1; 1 Pet. 2:21), then it is safe to say that this person is not one of his, regardless of words mumbled.

Variations of the Prayer

I have used various forms of prayer in guiding people to profess faith in Jesus. After sharing the gospel with someone who then wants to follow Jesus, I will ask the person to tell the Lord of this desire. All that is necessary for an individual to be saved is to believe in the Lord Jesus (Acts 16:31). However, guiding someone to express their desires to the Lord is a matter of pastoral care. If someone says that they would like to speak with the Lord, I invite them to use their own words. If they want me to lead in a prayer, I explain a few things. First, the prayer does not bring salvation (Eph. 2:8–9). Second, the prayer will contain an acknowledgment of being a sinner and turning from sin, that Jesus died for sin and rose from the dead, and that he is Lord. If these statements reflect the person's heart, then the person may follow my lead in reciting this prayer:

> *Thank you for loving me. I believe that Jesus died to pay for my sin and was raised from the dead. I am turning from my sin and placing my faith in you right now. I confess Jesus as Lord. Show me how to live and empower me to follow you always. In Jesus's name I pray. Amen.*

The Sinner's Prayer is a popular evangelistic tool. Though not to be viewed or used as a superstitious incantation that saves, this method is helpful when summarizing a gospel conversation or sermon and helping someone to verbalize their heart's desire to God. While there are variations of this tool, all should clearly express that Jesus is Lord.

— QUESTIONS TO CONSIDER —

1. Have you placed too much value in the Sinner's Prayer in the past? If so, how?
2. In your own words, can you explain the value and the abuse of the Sinner's Prayer?

20

PASTORAL LEADERSHIP

While the understanding and ministries of elders, bishops, overseers, priests, and pastors developed extensively throughout church history and came to be defined differently according to church and denominational traditions, the New Testament equates such titles with pastoral functions. Paul noted that leaders are a gift from the Lord (Eph. 4:7, 11) and are "to equip the saints for the work of the ministry, for building up the body of Christ" (Eph. 4:12).[1] At the turn of the twentieth century, John Mott noted that pastoral leaders are necessary to evangelize the world. He wrote, "It is essential that the leaders of the Church in the home lands . . . regard the evangelization of the world as a primary obligation and devote themselves to its accomplishment."[2] Mott acknowledged in 1900 that the general and widespread attitude of church leaders did not reflect a zeal for the global task. World evangelization had become a "side issue" and not "the chief object for which the Church exists."[3] His challenge to church leaders was clear: "While the call to evangelize was addressed to the whole Church a special responsibility rests upon the home pastor because he has been divinely appointed to lead the forces. He holds a key position. If he lacks the missionary spirit; if he is not fully persuaded that the cause of missions is the cause of Christ Himself, his church will not be missionary. As the pastor so the people, is generally true in relation to this

---

1. It is worth noting that this passage mentions not only pastors (i.e., shepherds) but also evangelists (Eph. 4:11) as leaders who were to equip the church for ministry.
2. Mott, *Evangelization of the World*, 190.
3. Mott, *Evangelization of the World*, 191.

subject."[4] In light of Mott's zeal and the biblical understanding of church leadership, this chapter addresses the topic in relationship to evangelism, regardless of the ecclesial titles used.

Pastoral Passion

Eighty-four years after Mott shared his convictions, Richard Stoll Armstrong reached similar conclusions based on his ministry and research of numerous churches: "One painful conclusion I reached long ago and have not had reason to modify, after many years of trying to help churches accept and fulfill their ministry of evangelism, is that the bottle neck in the process is often if not usually the pastor. It may be theoretically possible, but it is highly improbable that any congregation of a so-called mainline denomination will accept its corporate evangelistic responsibility without the active leadership, support, and involvement of the pastor."[5]

Evangelism is not the only activity in which pastors are to be engaged, but it must become a priority and be done with intentionality.[6] Church leaders have different strengths, gifts, interests, experiences in life, and personality types. Evangelism is easier for some church leaders than for others. One person's zeal for such ministry may be greater than that of another person. This pastor seems to eat, breathe, and sleep evangelism while another one not to such degree. While church leaders must be who God has called and equipped them to be, all need to manifest a pastoral passion for equipping the saints for the work of the ministry. Pastors are very busy. This includes preparing church members to take the gospel to the highways and hedges of life.

Leadership Must Value Evangelism Training

What church leaders elevate and talk about before others is what the church as a whole will embrace and value with significance. If leaders have little desire to train churches in how to share the gospel, then those churches will see little value in sharing the gospel in their social networks.

---

4. Mott, *Evangelization of the World*, 191–92. Mott was so convinced of the importance of the role of local church leadership about world evangelization that he published a 250-page book, four years later, titled *The Pastor and Modern Missions: A Plea for Leadership in World Evangelization*. The book was ahead of its time. In addition to describing the global status of evangelization, Mott addresses the pastor's role as an educational force, financial force, recruiting force, and spiritual force within the church.

5. Armstrong, *Pastor as Evangelist*, 13.

6. Henard, "Great Commission Leader," 277.

Leadership Must Set the Example

Peter's command to elders to set an example (1 Pet. 5:3) and the writer of Hebrews' command to believers to look to elders for an example (Heb. 13:7) underline the importance of serving as a model before churches. Pastors are not perfect, but they must take the initiative to lift the banner of evangelism before others. Mack Stiles notes that much value is found in just talking about evangelism. He stresses, "If you are a pastor, it's important that you set aside a place in staff meetings and elder meetings to talk about your personal efforts to share our faith."[7] When training events are offered, church leaders should be present. This action reveals a value and willingness to learn. Pastoral leadership should be involved in community outreach events. Those who are responsible for corporate preaching and teaching should extend an evangelistic invitation to listeners. Even when I was preaching on tithing and giving, the tabernacle, or genealogies, I challenged the hearer to repent and place faith in Jesus.[8]

Leadership Must Find Ways to Share Evangelism Stories

Armstrong warned that pastors must not delegate evangelism to others in a more specialized ministry area, thinking that they are off the hook. His concern about pastors was that "we affirm the message as central to our preaching, but that is as far as our evangelistic responsibility extends."[9] For him, pastors must have stories to share. Church members cannot always be with their leaders. Opportunities for sharing the gospel occur when church members are not nearby. Such experiences should be shared as stories. Leaders should find a way that communicates their encounters with the church. For those regularly at the pulpit, stories may be incorporated into sermon illustrations. Those leading the church in corporate prayer could make reference to their encounter and ask the church to pray for the unbeliever by first name. For others, it may be the use of videos, blog posts, or even a story night where both church members and leaders are allowed to share their evangelistic encounters with the congregation and to celebrate what God has been doing with their witness.

---

7. Stiles, *Evangelism*, 97.

8. A few books that specifically address evangelistic invitations in corporate gatherings are Whitesell, *Evangelistic Invitations*; Fish, *Giving a Good Invitation*; Street, *Effective Invitation*; Hawkins, *Drawing the Net*; Hawkins and Queen, *Gospel Invitation*.

9. Armstrong, *Pastor as Evangelist*, 52.

FROM PULPIT TO PEW

Nicholas Thompson raises the point that many Reformed churches appear to be healthy in a variety of areas but often fall short in the area of evangelism. His discussion below challenges pastors to remember the church's missional identity before it is forgotten in the pulpit and the pew.

What does a faithful church look like? Many of Reformed persuasion are bound to give an answer similar to the following: a faithful church worships according to the Book, feeds on consecutive expository preaching, cherishes confessional theology, practices church discipline, and is marked by love among its members. Such an answer is not wrong in what it says, but in what it fails to say. There is a harrowing silence concerning outreach, evangelism, and mission. It is not that the church doesn't believe it should evangelize, but somehow its outward orientation has become less than fundamental to its identity. Such a church, though marked by biblical fidelity in many regards, has largely disregarded its God-given responsibility to reach the watching world with the gospel.

The consequence of this is disastrous. Scottish Presbyterian Alexander Duff warns, "What is the whole history of the Christian Church, but one perpetual proof and illustration of the grand position—that an evangelistic or missionary church is a spiritually flourishing church; and, that a church which drops the evangelistic or missionary character, speedily lapses into superannuation and decay!" Tragically, such "superannuation and decay" are apt descriptions of not a few confessionally Reformed churches.

Reformed pastors must recognize that if their churches are not actively engaged in reaching their narrower community and broader world for Christ, they are on their way to the grave. Having the appearance of life, they may actually be long departed (Rev. 3:1). This is not an overstatement. . . . God has designed the church to be the instrument through which His saving message is published to all people (e.g., Matt. 28:19–20; Acts 1:8; 1 Pet. 2:9). In a very real sense, mission is the lifeblood of the church of Jesus Christ. Thus, a church not on mission is, at best, a church in decay.

When a pastor forgets the foundationally missional identity of the church, his congregation will almost certainly follow suit.

Thompson, "Evangelistic Church Culture," 142–43.

Questions

1. How would you define a "faithful church"? Is evangelism part of your definition?
2. Do you think that Thompson's concern applies only to Reformed churches? Explain.
3. Do you agree or disagree that a "church not on mission is, at best, a church in decay"? Explain.

Guidelines for Equipping the Local Church

Churches consist of individuals with different gifts, passions, abilities, personalities, and life experiences. Just as there is no one way for all pastors to model evangelism, there is no one way to equip every church. As leaders develop equipping opportunities for their congregations, they must take contextual realities into consideration. The following seven guidelines are an attempt to provide direction.

Training Must Be Biblically Grounded

Churches need to understand why they should engage in evangelism before being taught how to practice it. A proper foundation must be established that clearly articulates a biblical definition of evangelism and theological foundation. Church leaders should lead with the Word as they equip the saints for the work of the ministry.

Principles Must Be Taught

While there is a place for models to be followed, leadership should begin teaching biblical principles of evangelism. A return to the chapters on Jesus and the apostolic church's approach is a great place to begin the process. Churches need to understand that evangelism is not a modern concoction. By understanding evangelistic actions in the Scriptures, they are able to discern the difference between acceptable and unethical practices.

Principles Must Be Applied

It is insufficient to teach only principles without leading people through processes to consider how they may apply such principles in their areas of influence. Again, this process trains people to think contextuality and be led by the Spirit, as opposed to memorizing a script or a canned approach to sharing the faith. God did not create unbelievers as robots; they are in his image and have their own questions, concerns, hurts, and fears related to the claims of Christ. A portion of training should involve asking church members, "How do you see this principle applying in your life?" For example, it was noted in chapter 8 that one principle found in the New Testament is to begin with people where they are in their spiritual journeys. Assisting members may be as simple as asking, "Given what you know about that friend or family member, what are some things you may need to say—or avoid saying—that would allow you to connect with them on their spiritual path?" As people learn to think in terms of applying biblical principles, they slow down, learn to listen to others and the Spirit, and feel less anxious.

Models Must Be Provided

The church, especially in the North American context, has a history of evangelism training that, at times, was little more than teaching people how to clone models. Often church leaders found the tool that aligned with their gifts and overall personalities and expected members to use it just as effectively. For those of similar characteristics it worked well; for those of a different state, it usually did not work well, often leaving them feeling unable to do evangelism because said tool is how the church defined evangelism. Just as a toolbox should be full of tools for a variety of jobs, leaders need to help their members add a variety of evangelism models to their training. No home repair job always uses the same tool. Throughout a given year, churches should train members how to use a variety of tools.

Training Must Be Added to the Calendar

What church leaders add to the calendar is what the church will prioritize throughout the year. Evangelism training should not be left to the whims of church leaders. Rather, an annual schedule should be developed and shared with the congregation. One suggestion is to offer a different type of training each quarter of the year. This way, the church understands that evangelism training is of value to her leaders, there are several annual opportunities whenever someone is unable to attend, and a variety of models will resonate with a variety of people. Members will soon realize that there is a place for them when it comes to sharing the gospel.

Encouragement and Opportunities to Share Must Be Available

People need to be encouraged in their evangelism at two levels. The first is the *organic* level. Leaders teach, encourage, and model to others that as they go throughout life, they should be ready to share the gospel. The second level is the *organized* level. It is at this level that the church periodically engages in a more formal or structured time of evangelistic work. For some churches, this involves visiting homes in the community weekly. Other churches will schedule a series of nightly meetings with evangelistic music and messages. Some will annually engage in student outreach events, online engagement, food distribution, health clinics, vacation Bible schools, or sports camps.

Perennial opportunities may also involve sharing with others after weekly worship gatherings in an "information room." While churches are unable to provide hands-on opportunities to share the gospel at the organic level, they are able to offer opportunities at the organized level.

Stories of People Sharing Must Be Celebrated

It is a powerful example whenever churches hear of and observe leaders involved in evangelism. Yet leadership must understand the importance of allowing members to share their experiences with other members. When someone hears a story from a person in their small group, it is no longer a clergy-related tale but rather an example from "someone like me." Leaders need to consider how they can regularly communicate evangelism stories from the rest of the congregation. This may be as simple as having someone share from the pulpit on a Sunday or a midweek evening gathering to hear multiple stories of how the Spirit is using the church to advance the gospel across the community.

The Lord has established leaders over local expressions of his universal body. Among numerous functions, they are to set an example to the flock in belief and practice (1 Pet. 5:3). Though they may not be evangelists (Eph. 4:11), apart from their leadership churches will rarely emphasize evangelism. Every local church is a diverse community. Leaders must find ways to prioritize evangelism and equip the saints for the work of the ministry (Eph. 4:12). Challenging people through one's teaching and example and allowing them to share their stories of evangelism are ways a leader can develop the church in this global work.

— **QUESTIONS TO CONSIDER** —

1. What is your plan for modeling evangelism before others?
2. How can your church share evangelism stories?
3. What are three things you will do to become aware of different evangelism tools for your church?

21

REACHING CHILDREN

Whenever I teach a session related to sharing the gospel with children, I often begin with a simple survey. "Raise your hand if you came to faith before the age of eighteen." Almost everyone raises their hand. "Raise your hand if you came to faith before the age of fourteen." Approximately half of those present will raise their hands. Though I have conducted this unscientific study among seminary and college-aged students in the United States, the results have been consistent over the past two decades. While these findings are likely to change among this US demographic, it does raise the issue that many people today came to faith in Christ before adulthood. Clearly, there are exceptions in the West and throughout Majority World contexts, but the church would be wise to recognize that the Spirit frequently has worked among youth to bring them into the kingdom.

It's a Younger World Out There

When I wrote *Pressure Points: Twelve Global Issues Shaping the Face of the Church*, I noted that the numbers and the needs of children and youth are one of twelve major issues shaping the face of the church.[1] Many traditionally Western countries are aging and graying. Such is not the case throughout much of the Majority World, where sizable percentages of the population are children or youth. While there is no universally agreed-upon definition of *child*

---

1. Payne, *Pressure Points*.

or *youth* among governments, the church should prioritize ministering to a younger demographic and expect younger people to come to faith in Christ.

Receptivity in the United States

Studies have shown that the majority of believers in the United States come to faith as children. In an early twenty-first century study, George Barna notes that among those who came to faith in Jesus:

- 64 percent did so before eighteen years of age
- 34 percent did so before thirteen years of age[2]

God is not limited to statistics, but such numbers suggest that prioritizing evangelism with children and young people is strategically wise. While one cannot extrapolate from Barna's findings that such is also the case within other cultural contexts, it is at least something worth considering. Jesus was delighted to have children in his presence (Matt. 19:13–15). Some have argued for focused evangelistic attention on the "4/14 Window," the timeframe in a person's life between four and fourteen years of age.[3] Charles Spurgeon wrote, "Capacity for believing lies more in the child than in the man. We grow less rather than more capable of faith."[4] While God can perform a miracle on anyone at any age, a hardening of the heart usually comes as one grows older and becomes more worldly.

Jesus Loves the Little Children

Jesus often used children as living examples of how one comes into the kingdom and is expected to live in the kingdom. When adults attempted to remove children from Jesus's presence, he reminded them that the kingdom belongs to them and revealed his affection toward them (Matt. 18:1–6; Mark 10:13–16).

---

2. "Evangelism Is Most Effective Among Kids," Barna Group, October 11, 2004, https://www.barna.com/research/evangelism-is-most-effective-among-kids; Barna, *Transforming Children*, 33.

3. Child Evangelism Fellowship references a 2015 National Association of Evangelicals poll that found 63 percent of their members became disciples between the ages of four and fourteen. See "What is the 4 to 14 Window? Why Children's Ministry Is a Priority" (https://www.cefonline.com/articles/teach-kids-articles/the-4-to-14-window-why-childrens-ministry-is-so-important-cef/).

4. C. H. Spurgeon, "Jesus and the Children," sermon, October 17, 1886 (https://www.spurgeon.org/resource-library/sermons/jesus-and-the-children/#flipbook/).

No Junior-Size Gospel

The gospel is the same for all people. Children come to faith as adults do. Repentance and faith are necessary. A compromised gospel message is false and does not communicate God's truth to children. The message must be contextualized to the child. However, effective communication does not mean a watered-down presentation.

Keep It Simple

Evangelizing children forces the church to return to a biblical simplicity of gospel proclamation. Children process concepts literally and often fail to understand the abstract. Phrases such as "Ask Jesus into your heart" and "Pray the prayer" often miscommunicate biblical truth. The church must watch her language and share the gospel by clearly defining terms such as *repent*, *faith*, *resurrection*, *confess*, and *Lord*. Keeping it simple means sharing in a way that a child can understand.

Conversion Is Not Based on Age

I know of children who came to faith as older teenagers and some as young as four, five, and six years of age. There is no biblical age restriction on the Spirit's work. Do children understand their status before a holy God? Do they know who Jesus is and what he did on the cross? Do they believe in his resurrection? Are they willing to turn from their sin nature and put trust in Jesus as Lord? For some, the Spirit works at young ages, while for others it is later in life.

Create Evangelistic Atmospheres

Parents should be taught how to weave the gospel into routine activities and conversations with their families. Ancient Israel was told to teach their children when they got up in the morning, went to bed at night, and as they traveled together (Deut. 6:6–25). By encouraging children to follow Jesus throughout their daily lives and ask questions, an evangelistic atmosphere is created in homes. Questions asked by children may be extreme, unusual, or humorous to adults, but they should be taken seriously as they provide opportunities to share the gospel. When our evening family devotions addressed the topic of baptism, questions came from our children, such as "Why can't I be baptized?" Following the biblical example of baptism being a postconversion experience, we shared what it represented and that it was for believers. When our children observed our church participating in the Lord's Supper, we heard, "Why can't I partake?" Again, this allowed us to teach our children the meaning of the ordinance and the audience for the practice. One day, one of our children informed us that now was the time for baptism. "Why?" we asked. "Because I have become a follower of Jesus," was the reply. Ancient Israel was told to teach their children when they got up in the morning, went to bed at night, and as they traveled together (Deut. 6:6–25).

Timothy Beougher offers seven evangelism tips for parents that are helpful in creating evangelistic atmospheres within the home:

- You as a parent are responsible for the spiritual foundation of your child.
- Share your testimony with your children.
- Share the gospel with your children in an age-appropriate way clearly and often.
- Let your children see you share the gospel with those in your circles of influence.
- Keep the Bible as the source of authority in your home.
- Plan mission-oriented family activities.
- Be joyful about your walk with the Lord.[5]

Don't Expect a Crisis of Faith

I have seen children profess faith in Jesus while showing little to no emotion, and I have seen children weep profusely over their sin and joy of forgiveness. Sometimes adults, and even some church traditions, expect an emotional response to receiving the good news. From a biblical perspective, sometimes there is great emotion and other times we have no record of emotion. An emotional response is not a criterion for a conversion experience. While sometimes there is an outwardly emotional response from adults who have lived years apart from God and then experienced forgiveness, children often do not carry the weight of sin or feel its relief. For some children raised in a Christian home, they cannot cognitively recall a time when they did not know about God and love him. From a theological perspective, regeneration happened in that person's life at a moment in time based on repentance and belief but may not be retained within the brain. Such is no less a miraculous conversion experience as an adult with a "Damascus Road story" to share. While adults may be able to date their conversions, children raised in a context where the gospel is frequently shared and modeled sometimes have a different experience.

---

5. Beougher, *Invitation to Evangelism*, 279–81.

Use Open-Ended Questions Rather Than Leading Questions

Leading questions should not be used when speaking with children. "Do you want to go to heaven?" "Do you want to be forgiven of your sin?" "Do you believe what Jesus did?" Such questions are easily answered with a yes or no, and children may respond based on what they think adults desire for them. Ask questions that require a child to explain what they are thinking. "Why do you want to follow Jesus?" "Who is Jesus to you, and what did he do?" "What is sin?" "Why do you want to be forgiven?" Such questions invite children into a conversation. They show respect and interest in the child's thoughts and feelings. Open-ended questions not only communicate to the child that one cares but also allow for more effective communication. Children should never be pressured into making a false commitment to Christ. Having a conversation allows one to lead the child on a journey of discovery toward faith.

Closely related to such questioning is the use of high-pressure methods. While warnings of judgment must be shared, undue emphasis in an attempt to scare children is unhelpful. Getting children to make public acts that could be done because of peer pressure or desired adult affirmation, such as walking an aisle, standing up in a crowd, or raising a hand during a worship gathering, have a tendency to force a public declaration. Years ago, Oswald Sanders wrestled with appropriate methods for sharing the gospel with children. He told the following story after observing a minister's method: "One evangelist invites children present at his meetings, if they desire to receive Christ as Saviour, to go home and write their name in John 3:16 instead of 'the world' and 'whosoever,' and post it to him, or hand it to him the next day. This avoids the use of undue pressure and the danger of children responding because others are doing so."[6]

Sanders's point is well made. Children are very impressionable and sometimes follow the crowd for fear of being left out or valued less in the eyes of onlooking adults. During my first pastorate, I made the mistake described above and saw all of the children present for vacation Bible school come to the front of our worship area to "receive" Christ. For future events, I still shared the gospel and called children to turn from sin and place faith in Jesus. However, I then instructed them, "If you decided to follow Jesus, then come to me or one of your teachers during our snack or recreation time and let us know." This proved to be a more effective approach and allowed for helpful follow-up and conversations with individual children whose hearts had been changed.

6. Sanders, *Effective Evangelism*, 86–87.

Use Visual Tools

Because most children need visuals and do not always understand abstract concepts, drawings, colors, videos, booklets, pictures, and songs can be very effective at communicating the gospel.[7]

The church should not be hesitant to share the gospel with children. Jesus welcomed them with open arms. The gospel is simple enough for a child to embrace through repentance and faith. Just as there is no room in evangelism for manipulating adults, there is none when it comes to children. A basic gospel presentation that communicates at a child's level of maturity is necessary. One should anticipate questions (if speaking to a group) or allow for dialogue (if speaking to an individual). As long as the child believes what the Scripture teaches about their separation from the holy God, and why Jesus died and arose, and wants to turn from sin and confess Christ as Lord, then all that remains is the child's response to God's invitation.

— QUESTIONS TO CONSIDER —

1. Does your church give priority to disciple-making among children? Are children encouraged to follow Jesus? Are parents and caregivers encouraged to share the gospel with their children?
2. What needs to be done in your church to equip families for sharing the gospel with children?

---

7. Resources such as Awana's Gospel Wheel, Wordless Book, and EvangeCube have been effective and popular visual tools for sharing the gospel with children. My wife and I found Sally Lloyd-Jones's *Jesus Storybook Bible* to be a most helpful resource for sharing the gospel with our children. We took five minutes each night before bed to read from it and pray.

22

OVERCOMING PERSONAL CONCERNS

Personal preparation is critical when it comes to evangelism. Having an assurance of one's relationship with the Lord and walking in step with the Spirit are necessary for life in general, but definitely for evangelism. If one is grieving or quenching the Spirit with unconfessed sin (Eph. 4:30; 1 Thess. 5:19), evangelism will be hindered. The supernatural warfare experienced by those attempting to extract people from the kingdom of darkness is intense and challenging (Eph. 6:10–20). A daily dying to self (Rom. 12:1–2) and walking in the light (1 John 1:10) allow for the disciple to abide in Christ and bear much fruit (John 15:7–8). Evangelism is a spiritual matter that must involve much prayer as it is done on the front line of kingdom expansion where the battle rages (2 Cor. 10:3–6).

But some of the personal preparation matters involve practical questions related to evangelism. This chapter addresses several that I have encountered. Some are related to overcoming fears and excuses, past mistakes, and personal limitations. Regardless, these concerns should be considered and addressed. Pastors, if you have not asked yourself these questions, it is very likely that a church member will ask them in the future. This chapter is also written to better prepare you for providing counsel to the flock.

Portions of this chapter are adapted from J. D. Payne, *Evangelism: A Biblical Response to Today's Questions* (InterVarsity, 2011), 125–27.

What If I Do Not Have the Gift of Evangelism?

Over the years, I have heard many people refer to the gift of evangelism. I have seen evangelism listed on spiritual gifts inventories, and I have found myself (and many others) scoring high in the area of evangelism, meaning, in terms of the test, that we "have the gift."

But is there such a gift? Are gift inventories definitive, indicating who has and does not have certain gifts? When we examine the Scriptures, we find that there is no place in the Bible where a gift of evangelism is mentioned. In the most extensive lists of spiritual gifts, evangelism is not one of the gifts (Rom. 12:3–8; 1 Cor. 12; 14; 1 Pet. 4:10–11).

The word *evangelist* is used three times in the Bible. Luke referred to Philip as an evangelist (Acts 21:28), and Paul used the word twice. The Lord "gave the apostles, the prophets, the evangelists, the shepherds and teachers, to equip the saints for the work of ministry, for building up the body of Christ" (Eph. 4:11–12). He reminded Timothy to "always be sober-minded, endure suffering, do the work of an evangelist, fulfill your ministry" (2 Tim. 4:5). If there is a gift of evangelism, it makes sense that those most likely to have it would be evangelists. However, the Scriptures remain silent on the existence of such a gift—in spite of the claims of modern inventories.

The Gift to the Church Was Leadership

Christ gave evangelists to the early church for ministry in building up the body of Christ. While it is clear that evangelists were a gift to the church, it does not naturally follow that there is a gift of evangelism any more than it may be concluded that there are gifts of pastoring and apostling.

There are gifts of prophecy and teaching clearly listed in other passages. Based on this evidence, while it might be possible that unnamed gifts of apostling, pastoring, and evangelizing exist, to be fair, the gifts of prophecy and teaching are also listed in the same verses as other gifts for which there is no clear biblical office (e.g., serving, exhorting, giving).

If there is a gift of evangelism, the evangelist would be the person most likely endowed with that gift. But such thinking is speculation. There is textual evidence for the gift of the evangelist, but not enough information to make a strong case for the gift of evangelism.

According to Ephesians 4:11–12, a major responsibility of the evangelist was to prepare followers of Jesus for ministry. While there probably were many evangelists, Philip is the only one mentioned by name (Acts 21:28). If his actions were representative of all the evangelists, then, from what is recorded, they were involved in evangelism and church planting.

Apostolic Work Involved Evangelism

Paul reminded Timothy to set things in order in the church at Ephesus and teach faithful men to pass along the truths to others (2 Tim. 2:2). The church at Ephesus already had elders in place (Acts 20:17); Timothy was not a permanent pastoral fixture there but rather was completing work that had been left undone. Paul urged him to work as an evangelist while in Ephesus (2 Tim. 4:5).[1] This would involve preaching the good news to unbelievers and equipping the church for the work of the ministry.

All Believers Should Share the Gospel

Every believer is to be involved in sharing the gospel, regardless of giftedness. While not everyone is called to be an evangelist—as not everyone is called to be an apostle, prophet, or pastor-teacher—one thing is very clear: everyone in the body of Christ is to be involved in telling others of the risen Savior. People are brought into God's family to be a blessing to others (Gen. 12:1–3), to make disciples of all nations (Matt. 28:19), to preach repentance and forgiveness (Luke 24:47), to be a witness for him (Acts 1:8), and to proclaim his glories (1 Pet. 2:9).

What If I Am Wrong?

When I was in seminary, I had a professor who told the class that every time he took an inventory of spiritual gifts he scored a zero for the gift of mercy. While he might not have had the gift of mercy, he recognized that as a follower of Jesus he was called to be merciful.

If the gift of evangelism exists but I do not have the gift, would I then be excused for not being intentional about sharing the gospel with others? As a follower of Jesus, can one claim to be exempt from giving because they do not have the spiritual gift of giving (Rom. 12:8)? Or can we avoid helping (1 Cor. 12:28) simply because the Spirit has not graced us with this gift either? Not everyone is called to lead as a pastor, but there will be times when all of us shepherd and teach other brothers and sisters so they can grow in Christ.

— QUESTIONS TO CONSIDER —

1. Do you believe that there is a special gift of evangelism? If so, why? Can you support your belief from Scripture?
2. How does your belief about a gift of evangelism affect your personal witness?

---

1. For an interpretation of this text as being about not specifically evangelism but ministry in general, see Carson, "Work of an Evangelist."

Do I Have to Offend People When I Share the Gospel?

Few people like to cause trouble. Most of us are wired in such a way that we do not like to raise the ire of others. Two matters need to be kept in mind. First, we must realize that individuals confronted with Jesus do not all respond the same way. Second, allowing the cross of Christ to offend people and *being offensive as we talk to people* about the cross are not the same thing.

Allow the Gospel to Offend

The apostle Paul wrote, "For we are the aroma of Christ to God among those who are being saved and among those who are perishing, to one a fragrance from death to death, to the other a fragrance from life to life" (2 Cor. 2:15–16). To some, the messenger is a scent of delight, to others, the stench of death. The message of the cross is "a stumbling block" to some and "folly" to others (1 Cor. 1:23). Paul spoke of the "offense of the cross" (Gal. 5:11). As the Holy Spirit convicts individuals of sin, righteousness, and judgment (John 16:8), they begin to feel guilty before God, many times taking out their frustration on others. Though they are angry at God, they sometimes shoot the messenger—angry people crucified Jesus, stoned Stephen (Acts 7), and ran Paul out of synagogue after synagogue.

Some people will become offended at the message shared. Yet we must not react by cowering in fear and ceasing to share the love of God with others. Satan has tempted all to give in to the sin of fear. The church should repent of such sin and call on the Lord for empowerment, remembering that he has promised a spirit "not of fear but of power and love and self-control" (2 Tim. 1:7).[2]

Avoid a Combative Attitude

In all the years of sharing the gospel with people, I have had only a few times when people became extremely angry, and even then no one threatened me with bodily harm. When dialoguing with others, remember, "A soft answer turns away wrath, but a harsh word stirs up anger" (Prov. 15:1). Divine knowledge received should not lead to arrogance, pride, or disdain for those outside the kingdom of God. Conversations should not become bitter debates. Point others to Jesus. Seek to remain calm, speak the truth in

---

2. Books addressing the issue of fear in evangelism include Bright, *Witnessing Without Fear*; Fay, *Share Jesus Without Fear*; Schneider, *Evangelism for the Fainthearted*; Hildreth and McKinion, *Sharing Jesus*.

love, and show others respect, as they are created in the image of God and loved by him.

This does not mean that sharing the gospel should be done with a casual attitude. The message should be shared with urgency, poignancy, and with much sobriety. At times we might find ourselves with the self-righteous, like when Jesus encountered the religious leaders (Luke 13). Such conversations may need to be firm and blunt. Yet even during such tense exchanges there is no room for a mean spirit.

While writing this chapter at my favorite coffee shop, I was interrupted when a former student engaged me in conversation. A man standing nearby overheard our dialogue about a class, and after the student left he immediately started talking to me about my job as a professor. He inquired about my teaching and faith, and I asked about his profession. Shortly into the conversation, I asked if he had a faith tradition, and he responded that he was Baha'i. After he had made references to Jesus and quoted several Bible passages from memory, I inquired, "Could you please tell me what you believe about Jesus?" He responded by putting his hands together and bowed his head toward me, and said, "Oh, thank you for asking me to share with you what I believe."

Though I did not agree with many of the things he told me, by my applying Peter's words related to gentleness and respect (1 Pet. 3:15), the Lord opened up a great opportunity to share my personal story about Jesus and the gospel. I noted where we disagreed, but my attitude was not offensive to him. He did not come to place his faith in Christ during this conversation, but he was able to hear the good news in a manner that communicated gentleness, respect, and love. (See Case Study 2 at the end of this book on avoiding offense.)

— QUESTIONS TO CONSIDER —

1. How would you explain the difference between the gospel being an offense and Christ's followers being offensive?
2. When you share the gospel, are you serious, humble, and respectful toward others, or is your demeanor harsh, rude, and abrasive? Can you give an example?
3. Have you been passive about sharing the gospel out of fear of offending someone? Can you give an example? If so, would you share your fears with the Lord?

EVANGELISM: WESLEYAN WAY

Drawing from the influence of John Wesley, Henry Knight and Douglas Powe address how evangelism should be conducted in contemporary settings. The following gives particular attention to allowing one's lifestyle to reflect the truths of the kingdom.

> The Wesleyan way of evangelism requires that we live evangelistic lives by loving our neighbors. Wesley's relational approach to evangelism centers on the way in which we live out what it means to be a disciple of Christ in practice. The reason we want to be renewed into the image of God, to testify to God's goodness, to help others understand the length God goes to forgive us (acceptance), etc., is for us to be able to live transformed lives. Living an evangelistic life means daily we seek to love God and our neighbor with everything in us. There are no vacation days or time off from living a life that is truly given to loving God and neighbor. . . .
>
> The way in which we live out the love of God and neighbor is what distinguishes us as Christians. It therefore must distinguish our evangelistic efforts. As Christians we cannot pick who to love and who is acceptable to God; we must love all people and reflect God's love to them. . . .
>
> Congregations that are able to help individuals to love in this manner will become evangelistic and notice a difference in their parishioners. Congregations who are living evangelistic lives may not see a huge growth in church numbers, but the parishioners will be making a difference in the lives of people wherever they come in contact with them. If congregations do nothing else suggested in this book, the one thing they should do is to encourage people to live evangelistic lives—lives that demonstrate to others the true transforming power of loving God and neighbor.
>
> Knight and Powe, *Transforming Evangelism*, 99–100.

Questions

1. What is the relationship between a godly lifestyle and the gospel proclaimed? Can these be separated?
2. What are the problems if someone states that they want to only proclaim the gospel or to live a godly lifestyle before others?
3. Is it possible to love one's neighbor without verbally sharing the gospel? Explain.

What If I Can't Memorize All Those Bible Verses?

Because some methods require memorizing scripts and numerous verses, a common stereotype is that effective evangelism requires a great deal of memorization. Scripts are connected to tools, and it is true that we should learn as many methods as possible. However, it is false to assume that someone who is not good at rote memorization and regurgitation of lines should not be engaged in witnessing.

Scripture is integral to the lives of believers, for it is "profitable for teaching, for reproof, for correction, and for training in righteousness" (2 Tim. 3:16). God works through his Word to save us and to nourish believers in truth. His Word is daily bread, and the more the church memorizes his word (Ps. 119:11), the better she will be at sharing the gospel with others. There is no substitute for familiarity with and memorizing God's Word.

Who Said That You Must Memorize Leviticus?

While it is recommended that one should memorize a few verses, it is unnecessary to memorize large portions of the Bible to share the gospel. We must tell what we have experienced—as Peter and John noted, "We cannot but speak of what we have seen and heard" (Acts 4:20). God's Word is living, active, sharp, and more powerful than anything we could say about it (Heb. 4:12). It is important to share personal experiences and weave God's Word into our testimonies.

Most people are capable of memorization. They have already memorized email addresses, phone numbers, Social Security numbers, passwords, and birthdays. Scripture can be memorized as well. Most of the readers of this book have memorized John 3:16. That verse tells the gospel in a nutshell. Share it with others, challenging them to repent and place faith in Jesus.

Use an App on Your Phone or Marked New Testament

One excellent way to be prepared to share from the Scriptures is to use a Bible app. If you prefer a hard copy, keep a small New Testament with certain passages marked for ease of reference. For example, in the cover of the Bible write "Romans 3:23" along with the page number. After turning to Romans 3:23, underline the passage and write in the margin "Romans 6:23" along with that page number. Underline this passage and write "Romans 5:8" and its page number in the margin. Finally, after underlining Romans 5:8, write "Romans 10:9, 13" in that margin along with its page number. This marked New Testament will provide guidance to several significant verses of Scripture to use when sharing the good news with others. These verses in Romans are sometimes called the "Romans Road to Salvation." Even lacking a good memory, one may start small and set a personal goal to memorize these important passages.

Use a Tract

Consider getting a small booklet with a clear biblical presentation of the gospel. Many such tracts are high quality in design and contain excellent gospel presentations. Some may be downloaded to your mobile device. Outstanding websites and videos are available to share the gospel message with others. If someone will allow, a simple reading through or watching the presentation together is an excellent way to share the gospel that includes discussion.

— QUESTIONS TO CONSIDER —

1. Have you ever used the excuse that you cannot share your faith because you do not know enough Scripture?
2. What are some ways to keep significant verses accessible when you are sharing your faith?
3. If you have not already done so, will you make a plan to memorize the Romans Road to Salvation? If not, why not?

What If I Do Not Feel Like Sharing the Gospel?

I often do not feel like sharing the gospel with others—and I have a PhD in evangelism, teach evangelism courses, and write books about the subject! I am not supposed to feel this way, right? This matter is part of the fact that the flesh is at war with the spirit. What we know we should do, we do not do, and what we know we should not do, we do (Rom. 7:15–25). The good news is that there is grace from the Lord. Paul's words offer encouragement: "Wretched man that I am! Who will deliver me from this body of death? Thanks be to God through Jesus Christ our Lord!" (Rom. 7:24–25).

I remember sitting in my vehicle outside a hair salon, praying to the Lord for *desire* to walk through the open door and share my faith with the person about to cut my hair. I wish I could say that was a one-time occurrence, but it was not. Many times I have to stop and repent of my lack of desire to do what the Lord wants me to do. The Lord deals graciously with his children when the heart's desire is to serve him, but the desires of the flesh interfere.

When we make it a regular and intentional practice to share our faith with others, the desire often comes with the practice. The times I have made personal evangelism a regular part of my life are the times when I have found myself feeling motivated to witness. But when I am not witnessing regularly, I find motivation lacking in my life. The neglect of the spiritual discipline of sharing our faith extracts the moisture of zeal from the soul, leaving it like a desert.[3]

In addition, being faithful to the Lord does not always mean that we will have good feelings. Jesus was always faithful to the Father but was greatly grieved over going to the cross. He was so grieved that he asked for another option (Mark 14:36). Paul likely did not feel enthusiastic during imprisonments, stonings, beatings, shipwrecks, and a snake bite for the sake of gospel advancement.

I had a friend who was very excited about sharing his faith. "There is nothing like the *feeling* you get whenever you personally introduce someone to Jesus and they say yes," he told me. The Lord would later bless me with experiences like that; however, sometimes as the angels rejoiced (Luke 15:10), I waited for a feeling that never arrived. After feeling guilt for a lack of *feeling* related to evangelism, I decided I would be faithful to the Lord regardless of feelings.

Zeal is important. There are stories in the Old Testament of the zeal of the Lord coming upon specific individuals. Although many times the Spirit emotionally supercharges us to do his will, sometimes there is no emotional rush. The church cannot be driven by feelings to do what the Lord desires. Serving him is about faithfulness, not feelings.

— QUESTIONS TO CONSIDER —

1. Do you ever base your obedience to Jesus on feelings, or do you serve him regardless of your emotions in the moment? Can you give an example?
2. Why do you think that I find it more difficult to share my faith with others when it has been a lengthy period of time since I last shared the gospel? What is your experience?

---

3. Don Whitney (*Spiritual Disciplines*) is to be commended for including evangelism as a spiritual discipline that should be a regular part of the believer's life. Without it, sanctification is hindered. Jerry Root and Stan Guthrie (*Sacrament of Evangelism*) describe evangelism as a *sacrament* that God uses to grow and mature the believer.

What If I Make a Mistake When Sharing the Gospel?

The fear of making mistakes abounds. Whether related to a question that cannot be answered, offending people, or saying something that will cause someone to miss the grace of God and spend eternity in hell, fears can result in an evangelistic paralysis. Here are several considerations to help respond to the fear of making a mistake when sharing the gospel.

The Likelihood for Error Is Low

Unless a person is told that they do not need Jesus, or one refrains from sharing the good news, the likelihood of making a mistake is extremely low. Witnessing is about sharing what one has personally experienced with God. It is telling another person how to have an abundant life now and for eternity.[4]

Remember the First Believers

On this side of the cross, resurrection, and ascension, the church has more knowledge about Jesus and salvation than many first-century believers, who did not have the New Testament. An examination of their bold witness (with what they had) and how the Spirit greatly worked through their willingness is an encouragement when fearing mistakes.

Remember God's Love

The Lord loves the unbeliever more than the church does. The Spirit works through limitations and inadequacies (2 Cor. 2:15–16). The church's efforts will be honored when offered in faith. It is difficult to believe a sovereign God would send his Son to the cross for someone's salvation, only for that person to go to hell because a finite church member had a bad day.

Fear Is Sin

Fear should be confessed and repented of before God, who does not want his people to fear. Paul reminded the church to not be anxious, but instead to take such concerns to the Lord, who gives peace (Phil. 4:5–7). The Lord is with his people, for them, and works through them to accomplish his will. The church should rest in this truth and not fear mistakes.

---

4. In an encouraging article, Tom Steffen asks, "To what extent does the Holy Spirit compensate for our faulty evangelism and church planting?" ("Flawed Evangelism").

— QUESTIONS TO CONSIDER —

1. How does knowing that God loves the lost person more than you do affect your concerns about making a mistake?
2. Will you repent of any fear you have about sharing your faith with others?

What If My Behavior Wasn't Christlike When I Shared the Gospel?

At the beginning of this book, I described my first attempt to share the gospel with my teacher. I said little because my attitude and behavior were consumed with anger due to his reaction to my question. What should someone do if they later recognize that their lifestyle did not reflect the Jesus they tried to share?

There is a place for righteous indignation, but not personal agitation. My teacher acted and spoke as he did because he was lost. The church should *not* expect unbelievers to act, talk, and think like believers. A kingdom lifestyle stands up for truth but does not berate the person encased in darkness. Sin is to be named, but people need to hear a message and *see* a messenger of hope. Evangelism is difficult work, done in the dust and dirt of ordinary life.

When people find themselves in situations like mine, is all lost? No. Are our relationships forever severed? Maybe, but probably not. What is an appropriate response that may allow for future times to share the gospel with this person?

Repent

If the Lord has revealed sin, even when one is attempting to share the gospel, it is time to repent. Jesus still loves his people. His grace is sufficient. If he can use the scoundrels seen throughout the Bible, he can use humble sinners in the twenty-first century. Do not wallow in the mistake.

Confess

Return to the person and apologize. Confess the sin to them, sharing that your actions and words were not Christlike and that the Lord wants you to attempt to mend the relationship. This is another opportunity to bear witness to the gospel. Let the person know that believers are not perfect and that a mistake was made.

Attempt to Restore the Relationship

Ask for forgiveness. Transparency, honesty, humility, and brokenness are a powerful testimony to the gospel. If the person accepts the apology, the relationship continues. The person may spout blasphemy, refuse the apology, and claim hypocrisy. Regardless, an attempt will have been made to reconcile the relationship. God will use the effort for his purposes.

— QUESTIONS TO CONSIDER —

1. Have you ever acted inappropriately when you attempted to share your faith? Why did you act the way you did? Is there something you should do now because of past actions?
2. What are some things that have upset you when you have attempted to talk with unbelievers about Jesus? Is there something you can do now to better prepare for future situations that could involve frustrations?

Am I Disobedient if I Do Not Share the Gospel with Strangers?

"Cold-call evangelism" typically is understood as evangelism that is done with a complete stranger. Yes, it is disobedient to predetermine that you will *never* do cold-call evangelism. The expectation found in Scripture is that the church will evangelize strangers, if the Spirit provides the opportunity.

While all the details are not provided, most examples of evangelism in the New Testament involve encounters with strangers: Jesus and the Samaritan woman, Jesus and the Gerasene demoniac, Stephen and the religious leaders, Philip and the Ethiopian, Peter and Cornelius, Paul and Silas with Lydia, and Paul and Silas with the Philippian jailer. If we refrain from sharing with strangers whom God puts in our paths and share the gospel only with those with whom we have established relationships, then we fail to follow the dominant model used by Jesus and the apostolic church. If evangelism is based only on previously established relationships, then the gospel will be shared with few people. No one must "earn" the right to share the gospel with another person. Jesus earned the right for us. Here are two guidelines to assist with sharing the gospel with strangers.

Be Prepared

Disciples must be prepared to share the gospel with anyone, at any time, and at any location. Paul told Timothy to preach the word in times of convenience and in times when it was inconvenient (2 Tim. 4:1–5). If we share only with those close to us, we will quickly run out of people to witness to and miss out on many wonderful opportunities the Spirit brings our way. We must be open to a surprise by the Spirit. A great morning prayer is, "Please guide my conversations and interactions with others throughout this day. May I be able to share your gospel with others and witness them confessing Jesus as Lord."

Be Intentional

The missional life consists of joyful and delightful intentionality and regularity when it comes to evangelism. God is making his appeal to the world through the church, as Christ's ambassadors, as we implore others to be reconciled to God through Christ (2 Cor. 5:20). I have yet to hear of a national ambassador who is not intentionally and regularly engaged in hard work representing their country in international contexts.

In a New York taxicab, on my way to the airport, I started talking with the driver. A few minutes into our conversation, he asked if I was married.

"Yes," I replied. "For many years."

Looking at me in the rearview mirror, the driver then asked, "Do you still love your wife?"

"Oh, yes," I said.

"You didn't hesitate to answer my question," the driver said, glancing at me again in his mirror. "That's surprising. When I ask that question to most people, they usually take a moment or two before responding. What's the secret to staying in love with someone for that long?"

Wow! What an opportunity to talk about how Jesus is the reason my wife and I still love each other and how he has transformed our marriage.

"Well, since you asked," I replied, "I know this may sound strange, but my wife and I are followers of Jesus Christ." And so the dialogue continued with a wonderful opportunity to talk about my faith and challenge him to consider the claims of Christ.

Here was a complete stranger. I did not want to talk. I had just spent the day teaching a class and was tired. But here was a door of opportunity to share the good news. There were two options for consideration: I could think, *This guy is a total stranger. He doesn't trust me. We have no previous relationship. Spiritual matters are too personal to talk about with complete strangers. So, I'll just tell him that my wife and I work hard* [which we do] *at our marriage and make it work*; or I could use the opportunity to point to Jesus and allow the Holy Spirit to work with the gospel message.

— QUESTIONS TO CONSIDER —

1. Can you recall a time when you talked to a stranger about Christ? Describe it.
2. While it might not be your preferred way to evangelize, are you willing to share the gospel with total strangers if the Lord opens those doors? If not, why not?
3. If you have concerns about sharing the gospel with strangers, will you plan to talk to someone about this and seek the Lord for clarity and strength?

23

SHARING AND RESPONDING

In this final chapter on contemporary applications, the topic of starting and engaging in conversations is addressed. How do I begin the process of sharing the gospel with a person? What should I share? What if I am asked a difficult question? How do I share with friends and family? What do I do if someone rejects Jesus's invitation? What do I do if someone says they want to follow Christ? It is important to know how to respond to these practical questions and be able to lead others into healthy evangelistic practices when they ask for our counsel on them.

How Do I Begin Conversations About Spiritual Matters?

We need to overcome the difficulty of transitioning a conversation to the topic of spiritual matters. We will find it challenging at times to talk with some people, but the truth of the matter is that people are spiritual beings, and most are willing to share their spiritual experiences and beliefs if we let the Spirit lead us and if we approach people with respect.

When I first started sharing my faith on a regular basis, I was introduced to a book that promoted a high-pressure, psychologically manipulating, sales-oriented method for doing evangelism. I did not know that there was another way, so I devoured the book and immediately began applying the method to my practice. Several times when I was talking with someone, I recognized

---

Portions of this chapter are adapted from J. D. Payne, *Evangelism: A Biblical Response to Today's Questions* (InterVarsity, 2011), 125–27.

that the person did not want to discuss spiritual matters. Believing that the salvation process was dependent on my control of the situation—rather than trusting the Spirit—I tried to force people into discussion.

When I was a university student, I walked up to a girl crossing my campus. I introduced myself and my accompanying friend and stated that we were talking to students about spiritual matters, all the while continuing to walk alongside her. It was obvious that she had no desire to speak with us because she started walking faster and faster. The more I talked, the faster she walked. And the faster she walked, the faster we walked. Before we decided to let her go on her way, we were approaching jogging speed!

If we are intentionally attempting to share the gospel and the person clearly is not willing to talk about such matters, then we do not have to force open the conversation door. Remember, salvation is of the Lord. He can open doors that we cannot open. We simply need to be willing, available, and intentional in our efforts. Some of the best gospel presentations I have given have been those that flowed naturally from the conversation at hand. The following are some guidelines to assist in beginning conversations about spiritual matters.

Pray

Prayer must be an ongoing part of fellowship with the Father. It is a vital component to seeing a conversation transition from the mundane to the truths of Jesus. Paul wrote, "At the same time, pray also for us, that God may open to us a door for the word, to declare the mystery of Christ, . . . that I may make it clear, which is how I ought to speak" (Col. 4:3–4). We should pray before and during our interactions with others, that the Lord would guide conversations and provide opportunities to share the gospel in a way that allows others to understand and place faith in Jesus.

Look for Opportunities

If we are willing to look, we will find numerous opportunities to speak about spiritual matters. People will sometimes ask why we think or act the way we do, and that is an opportunity to share how the Lord affects daily life. Others might ask some of life's big questions, such as why tragic events happen. People talk about christenings, supernatural experiences, fate, luck, church, hope, peace, fear, and religion. Listen for points in the conversation that bridge to the good news.

People wear crosses on their necklaces; others wear religious symbols or have tattoos. These can be conversational bridges too. If people are bold enough to wear items for the world to see, let alone permanently paint them on their bodies, they probably are willing to talk about them.

I remember talking about names with a guy in a gourmet popcorn store. He wanted to know what my initials stood for. After telling him my name, he told me his first and middle name and the name that he wished that his parents had named him—Luke. I told him that I liked the name Luke and asked if he knew that there was a book in the Bible called Luke. He responded that he did—another conversational bridge.

Once I was getting a haircut when the stylist asked me if I heard about a plane crash that occurred that morning in which every passenger died. I acknowledged that I had caught the story on the news. "When it is time for a person to die, I believe there is nothing they can do to prevent it," she said, and then told me a story illustrating this point from her Muslim tradition.

Here was an opportunity! I could have simply said, "That's nice. Yeah, God's in control of everything." But realizing this was a divine moment *and that the Spirit had opened this door of conversation with her for me to talk with her about ultimate reality*, I asked, "Do you know where you are going when you die?"

Now, had I walked into her shop and opened with this question, she probably would have shut her ears and written me off as a religious nut. Yet here was a situation in which the conversation (super)naturally transitioned into the topic of spiritual matters.

"No, I do not know where I'm going when I die," she replied.

"Well, I'm a follower of Jesus, and I know how you can know for certain that you will go to heaven.[1] Do you mind if I share with you how you can know this information for certain?"

"Oh no, please do!" was her simple reply.

For the next several minutes, I was able to share the gospel with her, answering her questions and hearing her comments. She did not respond in a rage. It was a conversation, simple discussion, with nothing forced. The door opened, the conversation bridge was there, and thankfully I was able to cross it.

Be Natural

The best conversations I have had with others about Jesus have come when I did not try to force the conversation in a particular direction. For example, suppose you are walking down the street with a friend and say something like, "Wow, look at that tree! God created all trees. He loves you. And sent Jesus

---

1. I actually said "follower of Isa," as she was Muslim. *Isa* is the word used for *Jesus* in the Qur'an.

to die for the sins of the world. Now what do you think about that?" This is not what I describe as being natural. Guiding a conversation is one thing; forcing the conversation is another matter. Be intentional in communication, but do not oppose the natural direction of the exchange. Otherwise, people will feel that they have been sucker punched with religion.

Take the Step

Ultimately, we want to take the step of moving the conversation from the mundane to the hope of Jesus, and we want to do this lovingly and humbly and as the Spirit guides. Again, if people indicate that they are not interested in listening, then assume that the Lord is not opening the door at this time. We can make ourselves available for future conversations.

Share Your Story

I share my story of how I came to faith in Jesus and how he is at work in my life. People are interested in hearing of our experiences; they may not agree, but personal stories are very powerful.

After telling the story about my experience, I often ask, "Have you ever experienced anything like this?" The question allows others to feel respected and heard, assuming that they desire to share experiences. The responses I receive help me understand where individuals are in their spiritual journeys.

A word of caution is necessary: If you ask someone about their experiences, be prepared for what you might hear. After sharing my story with a woman and asking if she had ever experienced anything similar, she said, "Absolutely! Just last night I had a dream in which the devil was chasing after me!" Now, while God works through dreams, my story did not include anything about a dream. It did not have anything in it about the devil either. But somehow this woman was able to connect with me in dialogue over spiritual matters.

Let People Talk

People should be allowed to share their experiences. The title of Ron Johnson's book communicates a great truth: *How Will They Hear If We Don't Listen?*[2] Listening shows others that we value and respect them as people in the image of God and are interested in them and their experiences. Allowing people to share shows respect.

---

2. Johnson, *How Will They Hear If We Don't Listen?*

Allow people to ask questions. People learn by receiving answers to questions. Another word of caution is necessary: be prepared for what you will be asked. Refrain from laughter or mockery, given that the question comes from a sincere heart. William Fay asks questions and allows people to share what they believe about Jesus, heaven and hell, and salvation. Then he asks, "If what you said was not true, would you want to know?" If the answer is no, the conversation is over. If the answer is yes, they have invited him to share the gospel.[3]

Another approach I use when someone tells me about a spiritual experience is to ask, "What do you think God could be trying to tell you through that experience?" It is not always appropriate to ask this question. However, if the Spirit of God is at work in the world, drawing people to the truth, then the church must recognize that God works through natural revelation in the process of bringing people to encounter special revelation (Acts 10). For example, the following is a summary of what I recall of the woman's story about her dream of the devil:

> In my nightmare, there was a man who kept killing people, and I continued to run from him. Soon he started coming after me, but I could never see his face. Near the end of my dream, I was able to see his face—it was the devil. He was trying to kill me. It was then that I woke up, because I had rolled off the sofa and landed on the floor. I was terrified and was crying. I called my mother, because she is a religious woman, and told her my dream. She asked, "What have you done that is so bad the devil is after you?" I told my mother that I had no idea, because I could not figure out what I had done that was wrong.

It was at this moment the Lord provided the proper question to ask: "What do you think God could be trying to tell you through that experience?" She responded that she did not know. I said that I thought I knew and asked if I could explain. Of course, she was open to my words. I simply walked her through the gospel, beginning with the facts that all have sinned (Rom. 3:23), are presently in the kingdom of darkness, and the devil comes to kill and destroy (John 10:10).

Notice, first, that I did not say that God was definitely speaking to her through her dream. I could not know this for certain, but I could assume the possibility. Second, I did not put her experience on par with the Scriptures. Third, I looked for a way to use the open door, created by her experience, to connect her to the God who holds all dream interpretations (Gen. 40:8).

3. Fay, *Share Jesus Without Fear*.

— QUESTIONS TO CONSIDER —

1. Do you find it difficult to bridge conversations from the ordinary matters of life to the good news? If so, why?
2. Do you intentionally look for natural opportunities to transition conversations to the gospel? If not, pray that you will become more sensitive during conversations with unbelievers.

What Should I Share in an Evangelistic Situation?

Every encounter is unique because people and situations differ. Though I am a fan of learning different models for sharing faith with others, I am not a fan of being locked into a single standardized pattern. Remember methods are tools, and a variety of them should be used for evangelism. They were developed in specific contexts by specific individuals with certain personalities, gifts, passions, and talents. Listen and learn from their experiences, but do not get locked into one that does not match your personality and gifts and fit within the context. Regardless of the model of evangelism used, share at least three things: testimony, gospel, and challenge.

Personal Story

The person, group, or congregation to whom you are speaking needs to hear about your life before coming to Jesus, how you came to faith in Jesus, and how Jesus has transformed your life since then. (For more details, see chap. 18.)

Gospel Message

Testimonies are very important, but the gospel is the most important story shared in the encounter. It is the power of God that brings faith for salvation (Rom. 1:16–17). This message of the death and resurrection of Jesus speaks to the needs of people today. (For more details, see chap. 3.)

Challenge

Those listening need to be provided an opportunity to respond to the message shared. While not all situations will allow the entire gospel to be proclaimed, some challenge should still be extended. This might come in the form of asking the person to read the Bible, watch a video, talk with a pastor, give serious thought to what you said, or check out an evangelistic website.

NUDGE QUESTIONS

Samuel Chan recommends using "nudge questions" in conversations. These serve as a "catalyst" to move the conversation forward. He writes,

> Nudge questions are designed to give our friend permission to talk about their faith, spirituality, and religion. Here are some examples of nudge questions:
>
> - What are you looking for in life?
> - Why is this important to you?
> - What is the one thing you absolutely must have in this life?
> - What happens if you don't find what you're looking for?
> - What do you think it all means?
> - What do you believe about God?
> - What do you think God wants from you?
> - Do you have a faith?
> - What religion did you parents raise you with?
> - Do you pray?
> - What's the best thing about being a Muslim?
> - Tell me about some traditions, festivals, or celebrations that are important to you?
> - What do people get wrong about Islam?
>
> When we ask these questions, the goal is to *listen* and allow the other person to keep on talking. We're not trying to give them advice. We're not trying to have an argument. We're not trying to reason them into the faith. We're not trying to debate them. We're not asking them to defend their position. We are simply using the questions to give them our permission to take the conversation to the next level. It's an invitation, not an inquisition or interrogation.
>
> Chan, Talk About Jesus, 42–43.

Questions

1. What are some nudge questions that are specific to your context and relationships?
2. What is the difference between a conversation and an interrogation?

— QUESTIONS TO CONSIDER —

1. Have you ever been trained in personal evangelism? If not, consider going through the process, whether formally with a group or class or informally, such as reading a personal evangelism book.

2. What are the similarities and differences in how Jesus talked with Nicodemus (John 3), the Samaritan woman (John 4), and the demon-possessed man (Mark 5:1–20)?
3. Have you found a good online evangelistic resource to share with someone? If not, take a moment to locate a link and save it for the next time you speak with someone.

What If Someone Asks Me a Question I Can't Answer?

The thought of being asked a question and not knowing the answer causes many people much anxiety when it comes to witnessing. Early in my walk with the Lord, I believed that I had to have an answer to every question. I felt that showing my ignorance would embarrass the Lord, and I believed that others' salvation depended on how convincing I could be about the truth of Jesus.

It is important to study the Scriptures to understand the things God has revealed, and we should study Christian apologetics to learn how to respond appropriately to the tough questions people ask (see chap. 17). There is no excuse for remaining ignorant in our knowledge of the Scriptures and how to better respond to questions, but we must understand that no one knows *everything*.

Whenever someone asks a question you cannot answer, reply, "I don't know." Consider these truths regarding the importance of speaking out of knowledge, rather than giving an uninformed response:

- "Every prudent man acts with knowledge, but a fool flaunts his folly" (Prov. 13:16).
- "Do you see a man who is hasty in his words? There is more hope for a fool than for him" (Prov. 29:20).
- "Desire without knowledge is not good, and whoever makes haste with his feet misses his way" (Prov. 19:2).

God does not need the church to be his bodyguard and defender. When challenged with a question we cannot answer, simply respond, "That's a very good question. I don't have an answer for you right now, but I will find out. Let's get back together and talk about it."

When we respond to someone's question in a manner such as this, it reveals four important values for effective witnessing: honesty, humility, sincerity, and care.

Honesty

Admitting that we do not know something reveals honesty. We have the power to speak falsely, to make up something just to seem informed. But by admitting a lack of knowledge, you communicate that you are not a know-it-all and that the question has value.

I once shared the gospel with a man in my home. He had come by my house to activate our security system. I cannot recall exactly how the Lord opened up the opportunity for me to share the good news with him, but I do remember his question. After we talked about Jesus, sin, salvation, and God, he said, "J. D., why doesn't the Bible talk about life on other planets?"

That is not the typical question I normally receive after talking about Jesus! However, I could tell that this man asked in all sincerity and truly wanted to know the answer.

"You know, that is a very good question, simply because you are asking it," I responded. "I don't know why the Bible doesn't talk about life on other planets. I don't have an answer for you. I do know that the Bible says that God created everything, and if there is life on other planets, he created that life as well. Also, while I don't know why the Bible is silent on this topic, I do know what the Bible has to say about life on our planet." I was able to return the conversation to Jesus. It is important to respond to people's legitimate questions, but it is also important not to get sidetracked and to return as soon as possible to the gospel.

Humility

Admitting that we do not know the answer to a question reveals a humility that is a testimony to the power of the gospel. Humility communicates that omniscience is unnecessary for following Christ. It reveals a security in one's faith. It shows that followers of Jesus are learners and have open, inquiring minds. A humble response reveals a person who does not revile others when backed into an intellectual corner. A humble acknowledgment of ignorance shows that Jesus is bigger than the conundrums of life.

Sincerity

A sincere demeanor is revealed whenever one is willing to search for truth on behalf of another person. Rather than dismissing a question as nonsense or foolishness, this action communicates a sincerity and personal interest in the concerns of the person.

Care

Offering to find out the answer to a person's question provides an opportunity to set up another time for conversation. Care is revealed by a willingness to work on the other person's behalf. Such action reveals that one is more interested in the person than in simply making a point and moving on to the next topic.

— QUESTIONS TO CONSIDER —

1. Are you concerned about not knowing enough of the Bible to be an effective witness? If so, please share your concerns with the Lord, repenting of any fear.
2. Are you comfortable admitting that you do not know the answer to a question but will work to find an answer? If not, why not?
3. Are you honest, humble, sincere, and caring in your witnessing? What do you need to work on these four areas?

What Is the Best Way to Witness to Family Members or Close Friends?

Sometimes the closest relationships allow for the best evangelism. For example, the Samaritans came to believe in Jesus because of the testimony of one woman from their village (John 4:39). After Jesus called Levi (Matthew) to be a disciple, a party was thrown at his house. The guests included many friends and fellow tax collectors so they could meet the guest of honor (Luke 5:27–32). However, sometimes witnessing to close relatives and friends is most challenging. This has been part of my story. It seems strange, as they are in proximity to us and are people whom we know most intimately. Here are some matters to keep in mind and apply in practice.

Invite Them on the Journey

Jesus began his ministry by calling the twelve disciples (John 1:35–51). Andrew was among the first called. After coming to Jesus, he found Simon Peter, his brother, and invited him to meet Jesus. Later, Jesus called Philip. Philip found Nathanael and told him about Jesus, but Nathanael was doubtful: "Can anything good come out of Nazareth?" Those close to us will not come to faith without the gospel. We must share it with them. Much like Nathanael, family members and friends sometimes will question beliefs, but our humble response, like Philip's, should be to invite them to investigate Jesus for themselves: "Come and see."

Model the Transformed Life

A helpful passage related to witnessing to those in one's home is 1 Peter 3:1–2: "Likewise, wives, be subject to your own husbands, so that even if some do not obey the word, they may be won without a word by the conduct of their wives, when they see your respectful and pure conduct." Peter is not stating women should say nothing and simply live a good life before their husbands. The context must be taken into account. Later he addresses both men and women, saying, "But in your hearts honor Christ the Lord as holy, always being prepared to make a defense to anyone who asks you for a reason for the hope that is in you; yet do it with gentleness and respect, having a good conscience, so that, when you are slandered, those who revile your good behavior in Christ may be put to shame" (1 Pet. 3:15–16).

The unbelieving husbands were with their believing wives each day and had opportunities to see if their words about Jesus matched their lives with Jesus. These husbands needed to see changed lifestyles, faith in action, faith lived out. Their wives were to make certain that they walked the talk and were not to try to make every single conversation with their husbands about the gospel. Their lives adorned the gospel in real time.

Pray Without Ceasing

We must never underestimate the power of God. Sometimes it seems as if those nearest to our hearts are most resistant to his love. In addition to witnessing, pray for their salvation and keep praying for it. Do not give up. Years ago, I recall Chuck Lawless sharing about his father's conversion. The story was a great encouragement to me, not only because of the man's salvation but also because intercession occurred for over thirty years![4] At that time, I had been praying for a family member for two decades. Though I still have relatives far from God, ten years after reading Chuck's story, I had the joy of seeing my loved one make a profession of faith in Christ. Do not give up! Do not stop praying, even if it means continuing for decades.

— **QUESTIONS TO CONSIDER** —

1. Do you need to be more intentional when it comes to praying for and sharing the gospel with family and friends?
2. Are lifestyle changes needed that reflect the gospel you claim to believe?

---

4. Chuck Lawless, "Remembering My Dad," June 17, 2015, https://chucklawless.com/2015/06/remembering-my-dad/.

After I Have Shared the Gospel, Must I Bring It Up in All Future Conversations?

The church is to preach the message in season and out of season and proclaim that the gospel is the power of God for salvation (Rom. 1:16; 10:14; 2 Tim. 4:2). People will not come to faith unless they receive the message of hope. But must we become inept at carrying on conversations with others unless those conversations include discussions of their need for salvation? Do we have to become socially uncouth toward unbelievers, unable to function and communicate with them in ordinary ways? Must we share the plan of salvation with others in every future encounter we have with them until we know they are believers?

Ready to Share

Even after we have shared the gospel with someone, we should be prepared to talk with the person again in the future. New questions may arise in that person's mind; new doors might open. Continue praying and looking for those opportunities as the Lord arranges them.

Future Conversations

Humans are social beings. Life cannot function normally if the only spoken message between two people is the same message over and over again. After we have explained the gospel to someone, we should be encouraging conversations about topics other than repentance and faith in Jesus in order to build the relationship.

The gospel is the most important information anyone can hear, but unbelievers to do not know this fact. They will not appreciate someone appearing to be a playlist on repeat, speaking nothing but the same message over and over again. Good intentions will be perceived as insensitive and uncaring.

Old Testament Examples

Throughout the Old Testament we see examples of individuals who lived as witnesses for the Lord among unbelievers. The lives of Joseph, Daniel, Shadrach, Meshach, and Abednego, for example, provide insights for how we should live. They continued to contribute effectively to their society and lived and spoke words of witness whenever the opportunities arose. They were people who showed that they could function normally in a community while letting their lights shine.

Wise Words

Proverbs has much to say about words spoken at the right time and the need to use wisdom and discernment:

- "There is one whose rash words are like sword thrusts, but the tongue of the wise brings healing" (Prov. 12:18).
- "A word fitly spoken is like apples of gold in a setting of silver" (Prov. 25:11).

Wise Actions

Prior to sending the Twelve, Jesus instructed them to be "wise as serpents and innocent as doves" (Matt. 10:16). After sharing the gospel with an acquaintance, it is important to watch one's future behavior. Jesus drew attention to a lifestyle before a watching world.

> You are the salt of the earth, but if salt has lost its taste, how shall its saltiness be restored? It is no longer good for anything except to be thrown out and trampled under people's feet.
>   You are the light of the world. A city set on a hill cannot be hidden. Nor do people light a lamp and put it under a basket, but on a stand, and it gives light to all in the house. In the same way, let your light shine before others, so that they may see your good works and give glory to your Father who is in heaven. (Matt. 5:13–16)

Paul encouraged the use of wisdom when it came to sharing the gospel. He wrote to the Colossians, "Walk in wisdom toward outsiders, making the best use of the time. Let your speech always be gracious, seasoned with salt, so that you may know how you ought to answer each person" (Col. 4:5–6). A gentle spirit, compassion, pure conduct, a respectful attitude, and a consistent lifestyle provide a powerful witness to those who have heard from us the gospel message.

— QUESTIONS TO CONSIDER —

1. How can you be an ongoing, wise witness for Jesus to someone with whom you have already shared the gospel?
2. What do you think about the statement "The gospel is offensive, but we don't have to be"? Do you think that it is possible to share an offensive message without being an offensive person? Explain.

What Do I Do When Someone Says They Do Not Want to Follow Jesus?

When someone makes it clear they do not wish to follow Jesus, the appropriate response is to allow that person to have their way. The church cannot save anyone. Manipulation is unacceptable and false confessions are wrong. After sharing the gospel, one must rest in the work of the Word and the Spirit. Here are some practices for those times when people state they are uninterested in following Jesus.

They Are Not Rejecting You

When people do not respond positively to the gospel, they are rejecting Jesus. It must not be taken personally. If egos are more important than Jesus's will, we must repent of this pride. The church is an ambassador, representing the King, not herself or her message (2 Cor. 5:20).

Respect the Person

Delight should never be taken whenever someone rejects God's offer of salvation. However, the person must be respected and allowed that choice. They have the freedom to accept or reject the gospel. Much embarrassment and many problems would have been avoided if the church had followed this guide throughout history and been appalled at forced conversions and Christianization by the sword.

Keep the Door Open

It should not be assumed that since a person rejected Jesus today, they will do so tomorrow. There is both biblical and historical evidence of individuals and people groups who were resistant to the initial presentation of the gospel but later received the good news with gladness of heart. One should express an openness to continuing the discussion and engaging future questions.

Give a Reminder of the Consequences

James wrote that lives are like vapor, lasting for only a short duration of time (James 4:14). While it is not a pleasant matter to remind people of their mortality, they should be encouraged to make a positive decision for Christ while time remains. This must be done with grace, concern, and love in the tone of voice used.

Leave Something Behind

A video, online link, audio file, or evangelistic literature should be placed in the hands of the person.[5] Gospel tracts, for example, are best used in the context of a relationship or where one has already had the opportunity to share the gospel. After sharing with people who say they do not want to follow Jesus, I usually respond, "I would like to give you this little booklet that basically summarizes what we have been talking about." I hand it to them and encourage them to read it later and consider our discussion. I will often add my contact information so they may follow up if desired. The value of a piece of gospel literature, or online resource, is that it remains with the person and allows them to reconsider the details of the conversation.

Continue to Pray and Watch

Pray often for the person. The Spirit should be asked to work through the witness and resource left behind. It is also wise to pray that others would have future opportunities to share the gospel with the person. If permitted to have future interactions, pray and look for additional opportunities to share the faith.

— QUESTIONS TO CONSIDER —

1. If someone tells you they do not want to follow Jesus, do you feel they have rejected you? Explain.
2. When someone rejects Jesus, do you have a difficult time respecting that decision? Explain. What are some practical things you can do to keep the door open for future opportunities with this person?

What Do I Do When Someone Says They Want to Follow Jesus?

While in high school, I had been sharing the gospel with a friend over a period of time. A day arrived when she said she wanted to follow Jesus. "What must I do to be saved?" she asked. I froze, not knowing what to say. My response? I took her to meet one of the pastors of my church because I

---

5. Any resource shared must be appropriate for the context. It should be appealing in appearance and overall quality, well produced, with a biblical gospel presentation. It should include instructions about repentance and faith and provide steps to take after becoming a follower of Jesus.

wrongly assumed she needed "professional" help to get to the next level in the spiritual journey.

The following guidelines may assist in this simple endeavor.

Don't Panic, Relax

Do not fear that you will make a mistake. There is nothing you can do that will keep someone from the sovereign grace of God. No one's salvation depends on your perfection to win them.

Ask Questions

Make certain that the person with whom you are speaking understands the gospel message. I ask people if they understand that they are separated from God and why they are separated from him. Have them explain their understanding of Jesus's life and work, and whether they believe that he is the only Savior, who died for sins and arose from the dead. Last, I ask if they believe that Jesus is Lord, what this means for their lives.

Share What the Bible States

When Paul and Silas were confronted by the Philippian jailer's question, their response was simple: "'Believe in the Lord Jesus, and you will be saved, you and your household.' And they spoke the word of the Lord to him and to all who were in his house" (Acts 16:30–32). Paul's message to the Roman Christians was the same simple claim: "If you confess with your mouth that Jesus is Lord and believe in your heart that God raised him from the dead, you will be saved. . . . For 'everyone who calls on the name of the Lord will be saved'" (Rom. 10:9, 13).[6]

As noted throughout this book, belief is not simply an intellectual acknowledgment of Jesus and what he did. Even the demons believe in Jesus (Mark 1:24; cf. James 2:19). The call to believe is the call for repentance, and the call to repent is the call for belief—they are two sides of the same coin. People must agree with God that Jesus is Lord over the universe, he died for sin, and was raised from the dead to provide salvation.

As noted in chapter 19, the use of the Sinner's Prayer may be a helpful tool during this time. However, it must be noted in Scripture that no one is told

---

6. Peter's sermon to Cornelius's household contains the following instruction: "To him all the prophets bear witness that everyone who believes in him receives forgiveness of sins through his name" (Acts 10:43). John phrased it as follows: "But to all who did receive him, who believed in his name, he gave the right to become children of God (John 1:12).

to pray a prayer for salvation, speak to a pastor, be baptized,[7] go through a catechism class, walk an aisle, have an emotional experience, hear the audible voice of God, roll around on the floor, or anything beyond confessing Christ as Lord. And while confession to God is a likely and acceptable response, the Scripture does not command people to pray anything to God to be saved. Those who sincerely believe that Jesus is Lord of their lives are those who are saved and in God's kingdom.

What should someone be told after gaining a clear understanding of sin and God's plan of salvation? Simply, "Believe in Jesus. Turn from sin and declare him as Lord of your life."

Follow Up

After confession of Jesus as Lord, the journey begins. New believers should be encouraged to share the gospel immediately with friends or family. As soon as possible, they need to be baptized and learn to minister with their gifts and talents through a local church. They need to be taught how to pray and how to study the Scriptures. They need to understand the realities of spiritual warfare and how to live the victorious Christian life here and now.

The scope of this book does not permit me to address the important elements involved in "teaching them to observe all" Jesus commanded (Matt. 28:20), but it is extremely important to follow up with people after their conversions and ensure that their journey is in a healthy direction. Someone is needed to disciple and mentor them, especially during the early days of their new lives in Christ.

— **QUESTIONS TO CONSIDER** —

1. How will you respond to the person who tells you they want to follow Jesus?
2. Will you commit to teach and mentor someone you see come to faith in Jesus?

---

7. Some have taken Peter's words (Acts 2:37–38) as evidence for baptismal regeneration, but such is not the case. Rather, the evidence that someone is following Jesus and has received forgiveness of sins and the Spirit is that they will be baptized. Throughout the Bible and in Peter's future preaching (see Acts 10:43), salvation is by grace alone through faith alone.

CONCLUSION

This book attempts to address a variety of important topics related to an understanding of evangelism. Its contents are not exhaustive, but they are critical to a student's academic introduction to the subject. Without a biblical and theological foundation, contemporary motives and methods are in danger of falling short of God's glory and misrepresenting the gospel. Overlooking history is likely to result in a failure to learn from the strengths and limitations of those who have gone before us. We stand on their shoulders, just as subsequent generations (Lord willing) will stand on ours. Faith comes through effective communication, and the minister must always be seeking to make the gospel clear, which is how we ought to speak (Col. 4:4).

Evangelism is about crossing cultural gaps with a clear message of the good news of Jesus. The present status of global evangelization reveals that billions still have never heard the gospel, let alone been taught to obey all that Christ commanded. The highest priority for the church, wherever she may be found on the planet, is intercultural evangelism. Whether at home or throughout the world, the call to preach the gospel and make disciples is a ministry of crossing cultural gaps.

Evangelism and missions have been taught in the academy for many years. However, most North American schools of theological education offer little instruction in evangelism and missions—the requirement is one course, maybe two. Given the need, both at home and abroad, one would think that such would not be the case.[1] We must do better. It is my prayer that this book will assist in developing others in evangelism, who will then multiply their ministry by equipping others in evangelism.

---

1. The founding dean of Fuller Theological Seminary's School of World Mission, Donald McGavran, bemoaned this fact with his 1988 publication *Effective Evangelism: A Theological Mandate*. Though dated, this work is well worth one's time. Progress has been made in some North American institutions, but most curricula remain evangelistically anemic.

One of the dangers of studying evangelism, especially in the academy and from a textbook on the topic, is that evangelism remains in theory. It is easy to discuss definitions, theological conundrums, historical problems, and contemporary methods, while never sharing the gospel with others. I know, from experience, this to be the case. I am as guilty of apathy, neglect, and silence as others. We must do better, by God's grace.

It is my prayer that this book not only stimulates your learning in evangelism but also warms your heart (if such is possible via a textbook) and motivates you to action. Our generation stands between Psalm 67 and Revelation 7. We read the psalmist's desire for all the nations to praise God and John's declaration that such will occur. God's mission will be accomplished. The question we must ask is, Will we be part of the fulfillment of that mission? Could John have seen people who were the result of our evangelism?

The faithfulness of women and men, crossing cultural gaps, across the ages, eventually resulted in us hearing and believing in the gospel. May we be faithful stewards in our day, to grow in understanding evangelism and share with others what we have received.

CASE STUDY 1

GROUP CONVERSION

Decision-making varies throughout the world. While some societies tend to be more individualistic, others tend to be more communal. The following story reveals the surprise and concerns of two missionaries as they observed how one group considered the claims of Christ.

> Mark looked at the chief and elders before him and at the more than two hundred men, women, and children crowding behind them. "Have they all really become Christians? I can't baptize them if they don't each decide for themselves!" he said to Judy, his wife.
> Mark and Judy Zabel had come to Borneo under the Malay Baptist Mission to start a new work in the highlands. They spent the first year building a thatched house, learning the language, and making friends with the people. The second year they began to make short treks into the interior to villages that had never heard the gospel. The people were respectful, but with a few exceptions none had shown any real interest in the gospel.

Disease had spread throughout the region. One village that had been resistant to the gospel reached out to Judy and Mark, now interested in hearing about their God. Upon arrival, they realized that the village had been in discussion about the gospel for some time. All the men had gathered privately and invited Mark to share the gospel with them. They spent a good deal of time in discussion with Mark and among themselves.

This case study is from Hiebert and Hiebert, *Case Studies in Missions*, 159–60.

The arguments died down, and then the leaders from the various lineages gathered with the chief. Again there was a heated discussion. Finally the chief came to Mark and said, "We have all decided to follow the Jesus Way. We want to be baptized like Woofak and Tarobo."

Although it was late, neither Mark nor Judy could sleep after the meeting. The decision of the village, especially the way it was made, had caught them totally by surprise. They knew that tribal people often made important decisions, such as moving their villages or raiding neighboring tribes, by discussion and group consensus. But they never dreamed that people might use this method to choose a new god. All their theological training in their church and Bible College had taught the young missionaries that people had to make personal decisions to become followers of Christ. Here the group leaders had decided for all. What did that mean? Was it a valid decision, especially when it was clear from the debates that some had opposed the choice? How could they baptize the whole village when not all were agreed? . . .

As Mark and Judy searched for an answer, suddenly the great spirit gong in the men's long house rang out. Hurrying over to find out what was going on, Mark found the chief and asked him why they were summoning the tribal spirits, now that they had become Christians. "Don't worry," the chief said. "We are calling them to tell them to go away because now we have a new God."

Judy and Mark were still uncertain as they finally fell asleep, bone-tired and knowing that they would have to give the chief and the village an answer in the morning.

— QUESTIONS TO CONSIDER —

1. Did the villagers' decision-making process surprise you as it did Judy and Mark? Why?
2. Do you think that the people of the community repented of their sin and placed faith in Jesus? Explain.
3. What did the "summoning of the tribal spirits" indicate?
4. If you were Judy or Mark, what would you do the following morning?

CASE STUDY 2

NOT BEING OFFENSIVE

During their time ministering in Austria, Floyd and Christine Schneider became convinced that they did not have to be offensive. Though there is an offense of the cross and conviction of the Spirit, they were not to be the stumbling block. Reflecting on their time, Floyd writes,

> Through our Bible reading with Karl and Brigitta, Christine and I learned another very important lesson pertaining to friendships with unsaved people. Karl and his girlfriend had been brought up to honor their religion, but this meant simply the outward form of religion: that is, going to church, paying their church taxes, doing a good deed now and then, and not committing any major crimes against society. Their religion had nothing to do with either their philosophy of life or their private lives. How they chose to live morally did not matter, as long as they were not openly living in adultery. Fornication, however, was quite acceptable for a number of reasons.
>
> First, everybody did it. Once a person moved away from home and either went to university or got a job, it was more or less expected that he or she would find a suitable partner with whom to live until they both determine that they were suited for one another. A trial period was not only the normal practice but also encouraged by many parents and priests. In their view, divorce was a major sin, but fornication, if done "in love," was not.
>
> Then, between three and five years later, they would get married. During the time they lived together before the wedding, they would have one or two children. The Austrian government paid them more social housing allowance

---

This case study is from Schneider, *Evangelism for the Fainthearted*, 88–91.

to live together unmarried, and the woman was given a substantial sum for having children out of wedlock. . . . A couple would benefit financially by staying together but unmarried for a few years first.

Karl and his girlfriend fit this normal pattern. When we first met and I discovered the situation, I was shocked, but I tried not to express this shock. Instead, I began asking them questions, and I came to realize how "normal" they saw themselves. I also began to see how "abnormal" my biblical views were as opposed to the social and religious norms.

At this point, I decided that I could not fight their whole immoral system all at once; I would have to handle it a step at a time. I asked myself how Jesus reached immoral but "good, religious" people. I reread the gospel of John, and when I came to chapter 4, I had my answer. He made the Samaritan woman curious by first showing Himself friendly to her, and then pointing out her sin. The order of these approaches seemed important, so I decided to try it in our Bible study each week.

My whole emphasis centered on the person of Christ. During our first few sessions together, I must have asked the question a hundred times, "Who is this person, Jesus?"

When we came to John 1:29, I still do not point out their immoral lifestyle. I simply asked them the following questions.

"What is *sin*?"

They answered, "Everybody defines sin according to their own viewpoint."

"Correct. Does God have a viewpoint of sin, and if He does, is His viewpoint different from the human viewpoint?"

They had never thought of that. They did not know.

"If God does have a viewpoint, should we consider His viewpoint more important than our own or anyone else's?"

"Yes, that makes logical sense," they concluded. . . .

"If the Bible is from God, wouldn't it make sense to read it to find out God's standard of right and wrong?"

Agreed.

"There is a second question, however. What if we read the Bible and discover that we don't agree with God's viewpoint? What if we discover that we, according to God's viewpoint, are living in sin?"

I did not tell them that they were living in sin. I did not say, "In my opinion, you are living in sin." My opinion would have been worthless at this time. Their whole culture spoke against my opinion, and there was absolutely no reason why they should accept my opinion, compared with everything they had been raised to believe.

After we finished John 4, then I could say, "The Bible teaches that it is sin for a man and a woman to live together and not be married." I still did not tell them my own opinion. At one point, they attacked me about this view, and I simply said that they would have to argue with Jesus about that. . . . Then I asked them, "Do you have the right to tell Jesus what is right and wrong? If He is really God, as He claimed and demonstrated, doesn't He have the right to tell you how to live? I'm not going to tell you how to live! I'm not God. But what about Jesus? Is He God or isn't He?"

I have related this conversation to illustrate an important aspect of the friendship principle. When you start a friendship with someone who does not know the Lord, do not overreact to their sin. Do not condemn them on the spot for their immoral lifestyle. Let the Holy Spirit do that through their reading of God's Word. If you condemn them, you will be labeled a prude, and your friends will probably stop listening to you. It could spell the end of your verbal evangelism.

Some of our friends have stopped reading the Bible with us after the Holy Spirit convicted them of their sin in their lives. Although we were sad to see this reaction, we do not believe that we chased them off. We have come to expect some people to reject the conviction of the Holy Spirit. We keep the door of friendship open to them. We have not rejected them. They have stopped wanting to spend time with us.

— QUESTIONS TO CONSIDER —

1. Do you think that it was a good or a bad idea to not "fight the whole immoral system all at once"? Explain.
2. What was the benefit of allowing others to discover in Scripture what God said about morality as opposed the Schneiders simply stating the truth?
3. When sharing the gospel, how can you make it clear to others that you are not communicating your opinions but rather are expressing God's words to humanity?

BIBLIOGRAPHY

Abraham, William J. *The Logic of Evangelism*. Eerdmans, 1989.

Adams, Charles. *Evangelism in the Middle of the Nineteenth Century*. Peirce, 1851.

Adeney, Frances S. *Graceful Evangelism: Christian Witness in a Complex World*. Baker Academic, 2010.

Ahn, Ché. *Spirit-Led Evangelism: Reaching the Lost Through Power and Love*. Chosen Books, 2006.

Akers, John N., William W. Conard, and Marie Coutu. *Amsterdam 2000: Proclaiming Peace and Hope for the New Millennium: A Pictorial Report*. Billy Graham Evangelistic Association, 2001.

Akin, Daniel L., Benjamin L. Merkle, and George G. Robinson. *40 Questions about the Great Commission*. Kregel Academic, 2020.

Aldrich, Joseph C. *Gentle Persuasion: Creative Ways to Introduce Your Friends to Christ*. Multnomah Books, 1988.

Aldrich, Joe. *Lifestyle Evangelism: Learning to Open Your Life to Those Around You*. Multnomah Books, 1993.

Allen, Roland. "Pentecost and the World." In *The Ministry of the Spirit: Selected Writings of Roland Allen*, edited by David M. Paton. Eerdmans, 1960.

Allison, Gregg R. *Historical Theology: An Introduction to Christian Doctrine*. Zondervan, 2011.

"Amsterdam 2000. The Amsterdam Declaration: A Charter for Evangelism in the 21st Century." *Evangelical Review of Theology* 25, no. 1 (2001): 5–16.

"The Amsterdam Declaration: A Charter for Evangelism in the 21st Century." *Christianity Today*, August 1, 2000. https://www.christianitytoday.com/2000/08/amsterdam-declaration/.

Anderson, Tawa J., W. Michael Clark, and David K. Naugle. *An Introduction to Christian Worldview: Pursuing God's Perspective in a Pluralistic World*. IVP Academic, 2017.

Appleton, Mark. "We Are All Digital Missionaries." *Mission Frontiers* (May–June 2023): 13–15.

Archibald, Arthur C. *New Testament Evangelism: How It Works Today*. Judson, 1946.

Arias, Mortimer, and Alan Johnson. *The Great Commission: Biblical Models for Evangelism*. Abingdon, 1992.

Arminius, James. *The Writings of James Arminius*. Vol. 1. Translated by James Nichols. Baker, 1977.

Armstrong, Richard Stoll. *The Pastor as Evangelist*. Westminster, 1984.

Autrey, C. E. *Basic Evangelism*. Zondervan, 1959.

Bacon, Francis. *New Atlantis*. Clarendon, 1915.

Bargár, Pavol. "Pondering 'The Mission of the Orthodox Church in Today's World.'" *International Review of Mission* 106, no. 2 (2017): 389–99.

Barna, George. *Transforming Children into Spiritual Champions*. Regal, 2003.

Barrett, David B. *Evangelize! A Historical Survey of the Concept*. New Hope, 1987.

Barrett, David B., and Todd M. Johnson. *World Christian Trends AD 30–AD 2200: Interpreting the Annual Christian Megacensus*. William Carey, 2001.

Barrett, David B., and James W. Reapsome. *Seven Hundred Plans to Evangelize the World: The Rise of a Global Evangelization Movement*. New Hope, 1988.

Barrs, Jerram. *Learning Evangelism from Jesus*. Crossway, 2009.

Bartlotti, Leonard N., ed. *People Vision: Reimagining Mission to the Least Reached Peoples*. William Carey, 2024.

———. "Reimagining and Re-envisioning People Groups." *Evangelical Missions Quarterly* 56, no. 4 (2020): 46–50.

Bashford, Robert. *Mission and Evangelism in Recent Thinking, 1974–1986*. Latimer House, 1990.

Bassham, Rodger C. *Mission Theology, 1948–1975: Years of Worldview Creative Tension—Ecumenical, Evangelical, and Roman Catholic*. William Carey, 1979.

Beaver, R. Pierce. *American Protestant Women in World Mission: History of the First Feminist Movement in North America*. Eerdmans, 1968.

Bediako, Kwame. "Translatability and the Cultural Incarnations of the Faith." In Scherer and Bevans, *Faith and Culture*.

Beougher, Timothy K. *Invitation to Evangelism: Sharing the Gospel with Compassion and Conviction*. Kregel Academic, 2021.

———. *Richard Baxter and Conversion: A Study of the Puritan Concept of Becoming a Christian*. Mentor, 2007.

Beougher, Timothy, and Alvin Reid. *Evangelism for a Changing World*. Harold Shaw, 1995.

Bevans, Stephen B., and Roger P. Schroeder, *Constants in Context: A Theology of Mission for Today*. Orbis Books, 2004.

Birdsall, S. Douglas, and Lindsay Brown. Foreword to *The Cape Town Commitment: A Confession of Faith and a Call to Action*. https://lausanne.org/statement/ctcommitment#foreword.

Blauw, Johannes. *The Missionary Nature of the Church: A Survey of the Biblical Theology of Missions*. McGraw-Hill, 1962.

Borchert, Gerald L. *Dynamics of Evangelism*. Word, 1976.

Borthwick, Paul. *Stop Witnessing . . . and Start Loving*. NavPress, 2003.

Bosch, David J. "Evangelism: Theological Currents and Cross-Currents Today." In Chilcote and Warner, *The Study of Evangelism*.

———. *Transforming Mission: Paradigm Shifts in Theology of Mission*. Orbis Books, 1991.

———. *Witness to the World*. Marshall, Morgan & Scott, 1980.

Boyack, Kenneth. Introduction to Boyack, *The New Catholic Evangelization*.

———, ed. *The New Catholic Evangelization*. Paulist Press, 1992.

Braaten, Carl E. "The Meaning of Evangelism in the Context of God's Universal Grace." In Chilcote and Warner, *The Study of Evangelism*.

Brennan, J. Patrick. *Re-imagining Evangelization: Toward the Reign of God and the Communal Parish*. Crossroad, 1995.

Bria, Ion. "The Church's Role in Evangelism." *International Review of Mission* 64, no. 255 (1975): 243–50.

———. *The Liturgy After the Liturgy: Mission and Witness from an Orthodox Perspective*. WCC Publications, 1996.

Briggs, John A. Y. "Accra Conference." In Moreau, *Dictionary of World Missions*.

———. "Jerusalem Conference (1928)." In Moreau, *Dictionary of World Missions*.

——— "World Council of Churches Conferences." In Moreau, *Dictionary of World Missions*.

Bright, Bill. *Witnessing Without Fear*. Nelson, 1993.

Brooks, Christopher W. *Urban Apologetics: Why the Gospel Is Good News for the City*. Kregel, 2014.

Broomhall, Benjamin. *The Evangelisation of the World: A Missionary Band; A Record of Consecration, and an Appeal*. Morgan & Scott, 1889.

Bruce, A. B. *The Training of the Twelve; or, Passages Out of the Gospel Exhibiting the Twelve Disciples of Jesus Under Discipline for the Apostleship*. T&T Clark, 1871.

Brueggemann, Walter. *Biblical Perspectives on Evangelism: Living in a Three-Storied Universe*. Abingdon, 1993.

Brunner, Emil. *The Word and the World*. Student Christian Movement Press, 1931.

Burt, Robert L. *Affirming Evangelism: A Call to Renewed Commitment in the United Church of Christ*. United Church Board for Homeland Ministries, 1993.

Calkins, Raymond. *How Jesus Dealt with Men*. Abingdon-Cokesbury, 1942.

Calvin, John. *Institutes of the Christian Religion*. Translated by Henry Beveridge. Hendrickson, 2008.

Cameron, Kirk, and Ray Comfort. *The Way of the Master: Seek and Save the Lost the Way Jesus Did*. Genesis, 2006.

Carrier, Hervé. *Evangelizing the Culture of Modernity*. Orbis Books, 1993.

Carson, D. A. "Do the Work of an Evangelist." *Themelios* 39, no. 1 (2014): 1–4.

———. *The Gospel According to John*. Inter-Varsity; Eerdmans, 1991.

Carwardine, Richard. "The Second Great Awakening in Comparative Perspective: Revivals and Culture in the United States and Britain." In *Modern Christian Revivals*, edited by Edith L. Blumhofer and Randall Balmer. University of Illinois Press, 1993.

Chafer, Lewis Sperry. *True Evangelism: Winning Souls by Prayer*. Zondervan, 1919.

Chamberlain, Paul, and Chris Price, eds. *Everyday Apologetics: Answering Common Objections to the Christian Faith*. Lexham, 2020.

Chan, Sam. *Evangelism in a Skeptical World: How to Make the Unbelievable News About Jesus More Believable*. Zondervan, 2018.

———. *How to Talk About Jesus (Without Being That Guy): Personal Evangelism in a Skeptical World*. Zondervan Reflective, 2020.

Chatraw, Joshua D. *Telling a Better Story: How to Talk About God in a Skeptical Age*. Zondervan Reflective, 2020.

Chatraw, Joshua D., and Mark D. Allen. *Apologetics at the Cross: An Introduction for Christian Witness*. Zondervan Academic, 2018.

Chilcote, Paul W., and Laceye C. Warner, eds. *The Study of Evangelism: Exploring a Missional Practice of the Church*. Eerdmans, 2008.

Chitwood, Paul. "The Sinner's Prayer: An Historical and Theological Analysis." PhD diss., Southern Baptist Theological Seminary, 2001.

Church of England. "The Evangelistic Work of the Church." In *Reports of the Archbishops' Committees of Inquiry*. Society for Promoting Christian Knowledge, 1919.

Cocoris, G. Michael. *Evangelism: A Biblical Approach*. Moody, 1984.

Coleman, Robert E. *The Heart of the Gospel: The Theology Behind the Master Plan of Evangelism*. Baker Books, 2011.

———. *The Master Plan of Evangelism*. Revell, 1963.

———. *The Master's Way of Personal Evangelism*. Crossway, 1997.

"Conference on World Mission and Evangelism Report." *International Review of Mission* 107, no. 2 (2018): 547–60.

Congregation for the Doctrine of the Faith. *Doctrinal Note on Some Aspects of Evangelization*. Vatican, 2007.

Conn, Harvie M. *Evangelism: Doing Justice and Preaching Grace*. Zondervan, 1982.

Costas, Orlando E. *Christ Outside the Gate: Mission Beyond Christendom*. Orbis Books, 1982.

———. "Evangelism and the Gospel of Salvation." In Chilcote and Warner, *The Study of Evangelism*.

———. *Liberating News: A Theology of Contextual Evangelization*. Eerdmans, 1989.

Courson, Jim, and Wilson S. Geisler IV. "The Changing Landscape of Lostness: Why Global Shifts Are Driving the Need for New Engagement Indices." *Great Commission Baptist Journal of Missions* 1, no. 2 (2022): 1–15.

———. "Status of the Task and State of the Church: International Mission Board's Multi-Indicator Engagement Scales for Peoples and Places." *Great Commission Baptist Journal of Missions* 1, no. 2 (2022): 1–13.

Cowan, Steven B. Introduction to Gundry and Cowan, *Five Views on Apologetics*.

Coxe, A. Cleveland. "Introductory Note to Clement of Alexandria." In vol. 2 of Roberts and Donaldson, *Ante-Nicene Fathers*.

———. "Introductory Note to Irenaeus Against Heresies." In vol. 1 of Roberts and Donaldson, *Ante-Nicene Fathers*.

———. "Introductory Note to the First Apology of Justin Martyr." In vol. 1 of Roberts and Donaldson, *Ante-Nicene Fathers*.

———. "Introductory Notice." In vol. 1 of Roberts and Donaldson, *Ante-Nicene Fathers*.

Crabtree, Charles. "Disciples Are Our Number One Goal." In *Equipping for Evangelism: NACIE 94*, by North American Conference of Itinerant Evangelists. World Wide Publications, 1996.

Cruse, C. F., trans. *Eusebius' Ecclesiastical History*. Updated ed. Hendrickson, 1998.

Cust, Robert Needham. *Essay on the Prevailing Methods of the Evangelization of the Non-Christian World*. Luzac, 1894.

Datema, Dave, and Leonard N. Bartlotti. "The People Group Approach: A Historical Perspective." *Evangelical Missions Quarterly* 56, no. 4 (2020): 8–11.

Dawson, Scott, ed. *The Complete Evangelism Guidebook: Expert Advice on Reaching Others for Christ*. Baker Books, 2006.

———. *Evangelism Today: Effectively Sharing the Gospel in a Rapidly Changing World*. Baker Books, 2009.

Dayton, Edward R. "To Reach the Unreached." In *Unreached Peoples '79*, edited by C. Peter Wagner and Edward R. Dayton. Cook, 1978.

Dean, Marcus, Scott Moreau, Sue Russell, and Rochelle Scheuermann, eds. *Communication in Mission: Global Opportunities and Challenges*. William Carey, 2022.

De Neui, Paul, and David Lim, eds. *Communicating Christ in the Buddhist World*. William Carey, 2006.

DiFransico, Lesley. "Repentance" In *Lexham Theological Wordbook*, edited by Douglas Mangum, Derek R. Brown, and Rachel Klippenstein. Lexham, 2014.

Dillon, Christine. *Telling the Gospel Through Story: Evangelism That Keeps Hearers Wanting More*. IVP Books, 2012.

Dodd, C. H. *The Apostolic Preaching and Its Developments.* Willett, Clark, 1937.

Dodson, Jonathan K., and Brad Watson. *Raised? Finding Jesus by Doubting the Resurrection.* Zondervan, 2014.

Dorsett, Lyle W. *A Passion for Souls: The Life of D. L. Moody.* Moody, 1997.

Douglas, J. D., ed. *Let the Earth Hear His Voice: International Congress on World Evangelization Lausanne, Switzerland.* World Wide Publications, 1975.

———, ed. *Proclaim Christ Until He Comes: Calling the Whole Church to Take the Whole Gospel to the Whole World.* World Wide Publications, 1990.

Douglass-Chin, Richard J. *Preacher Woman Sings the Blues: The Autobiographies of Nineteenth-Century African American Evangelists.* University of Missouri Press, 2001.

Doyle, Tom, and JoAnn Doyle. *Women Who Risk: Secret Agents for Jesus in the Muslim World.* Nelson, 2021.

Drummond, Lewis A. *Evangelism—the Counter-Revolution.* Marshall, Morgan & Scott, 1972.

———. *Leading Your Church in Evangelism.* Broadman, 1975.

———. *The Word of the Cross: A Contemporary Theology of Evangelism.* Broadman, 1992.

Dulles, Avery. "Evangelizing Theology." *First Things* 61 (March 1996): 27–32.

Dunelm, Handley. "Election." In vol. 2 of *The International Standard Bible Encyclopaedia*, edited by James Orr. Howard-Severance, 1915.

Dzubinski, Leanne M., and Anneke H. Stasson. *Women in the Mission of the Church: Their Opportunities and Obstacles Throughout Christian History.* Baker Academic, 2021.

Earley, Dave, and David Wheeler. *Evangelism Is . . . : How to Share Jesus with Passion and Confidence.* B&H Academic, 2010.

Easley, Jordan, and Ernest Easley. *Resuscitating Evangelism.* B&H, 2020.

Elwell, Walter A., and Barry J. Beitzel. "Elect, Election." In *Baker Encyclopedia of the Bible*, edited by Walter A. Elwell. Baker, 1988.

Engel, James F. *Contemporary Christian Communications: Its Theory and Practice.* Nelson, 1979.

Engel, James F., and H. Wilbert Norton. *What's Gone Wrong with the Harvest? A Communication Strategy for the Church and World Evangelism.* Zondervan, 1975.

Epstein, Barbara Leslie. *The Politics of Domesticity: Women, Evangelism, and Temperance in Nineteenth Century America.* Wesleyan University Press, 1986.

Erdmann, Martin. "Mission in John's Gospel and Letters." In Larkin and Williams, *Mission in the New Testament.*

Evangelical Lutheran Church in America. "Evangelism." https://elca.org/evangelism.

Everts, Don. *The Reluctant Witness: Discovering the Delight of Spiritual Conversations*. IVP Books, 2019.

Everts, Don, and Doug Schaupp. *I Once Was Lost: What Postmodern Skeptics Taught Us About Their Path to Jesus*. InterVarsity, 2008.

Fackre, Gabriel, Ronald H. Nash, and John Sanders. *What About Those Who Have Never Heard? Three Views on the Destiny of the Unevangelized*. InterVarsity, 1995.

Fay, William. *Share Jesus Without Fear*. Broadman & Holman, 1999.

Fernando, Ajith. *Sharing the Truth in Love: How to Relate to People of Other Faiths*. Discovery House, 2001.

Fish, Roy. *Giving a Good Invitation*. Broadman, 1974.

Ford, Leighton. "An Evangelism Adequate for Today." In *Evangelism: Mandates for Action*, edited by James T. Laney. Hawthorn Books, 1975.

———. "Proclaim Christ." In Douglas, *Proclaim Christ*.

Forrest, Tom. "Evangelization 2000: A Global View." In Boyack, *The New Catholic Evangelization*.

Frame, John M. "Presuppositional Apologetics." In Gundry and Cowan, *Five Views on Apologetics*.

Francis. *Evangelii gaudium: The Joy of the Gospel*. The Dynamic Catholic Institute, 2014.

Frost, Michael, and Alan Hirsch. *The Shaping of Things to Come: Innovation and Mission for the 21st Century Church*. Hendrickson, 2003.

Fung, Raymond. *Evangelistically Yours: Ecumenical Letters on Contemporary Evangelism*. WCC Publications, 1992.

Georges, Jayson, and Mark D. Baker. *Ministering in Honor-Shame Cultures: Biblical Foundations and Practical Essentials*. IVP Academic, 2016.

Ghering, Roger W. *House Church and Mission: The Importance of Household Structures in Early Christianity*. Hendrickson, 2004.

Gill, Brad. "A Church for Every People: A Retrospect on Mapping Peoples." *Evangelical Missions Quarterly* 56, no. 4 (2020): 43–45.

Gitari, David. "Kenya: Evangelism Among Nomadic Communities." In *One Gospel—Many Clothes: Anglicans and the Decade of Evangelism*, edited by Chris Wright and Chris Sugden. The Evangelical Fellowship in the Anglican Communion and Regnum Books, 1990.

Glasser, Arthur F. "International Conferences for Itinerant Evangelists (Amsterdam 1983, 1986)." In Moreau, *Dictionary of World Missions*.

———. "World Congress on Evangelism (Berlin 1966)." In Moreau, *Dictionary of World Missions*.

———. "World Council of Churches Assemblies." In Moreau, *Dictionary of World Missions*.

Goheen, Michael W. *A Light to the Nations: The Missional Church and the Biblical Story*. Baker Academic, 2011.

González, Justo L. *The Reformation to the Present Day*, vol. 2 in *The Story of Christianity*. HarperCollins, 1985.

Goodall, Norman, ed. *The Uppsala Report 1968: Official Report of the Fourth Assembly of the World Council of Churches, Uppsala, July 4–20, 1968*. World Council of Churches, 1968.

Gorski, John F. "From 'Mission' to 'Evangelization': The Latin American Origins of a Challenging Concept." In *The New Evangelization: Faith, People, Context and Practice*, edited by Paul Grogan and Kirsteen Kim. Bloomsbury T&T Clark, 2015.

Graham, Billy. *A Biblical Standard for Evangelists*. World Wide Publications, 1984.

Gray, James. "The Gray Matrix—Tracking Its History (1977–2015) ver1.0." https://thegraymatrix.org/wp-content/uploads/2019/10/GrayMatrix_Tracking-its-History.pdf.

Green, Michael. *Evangelism in the Early Church*. Eerdmans, 1970.

———. *Evangelism: Learning from the Past*. Eerdmans, 2023.

———. *Evangelism Through the Local Church: A Comprehensive Guide to All Aspects of Evangelism*. Nelson, 1992.

Grogan, Paul, and Kirsteen Kim. *The New Evangelization: Faith, People, Context and Practice*. Bloomsbury T&T Clark, 2015.

Grudem, Wayne. *Systematic Theology: An Introduction to Biblical Doctrine*. Zondervan, 1994.

Guder, Darrell L., ed. *The Missional Church: A Vision for the Sending of the Church in North America*. Eerdmans, 1998.

Guinness, Os. *Fool's Talk: Recovering the Art of Christian Persuasion*. InterVarsity, 2015.

Gulley, Norman R. "Regeneration." In *The Anchor Yale Bible Dictionary*, edited by David Noel Freedman. Doubleday, 1992.

Gundry, Stanley N., and Steven B. Cowan, eds. *Five Views on Apologetics*. Zondervan, 2000.

Gustafson, David M. *Gospel Witness: Evangelism in Word and Deed*. Eerdmans, 2019.

Habermas, Gary R. "Evidential Apologetics." In Gundry and Cowan, *Five Views on Apologetics*.

Handley, Joseph W., Jr. "Reflection on the Fourth Lausanne Congress," *Evangelical Review of Theology* 48, no. 4 (2024): 293–301.

Harnack, Adolf. *The Expansion of Christianity in the First Three Centuries*. Translated by James Moffatt. 2 vols. Arno, 1904–5.

Harvey, John D. "Mission in Matthew." In Larkin and Williams, *Mission in the New Testament*.

Hater, Robert J. "Distinctive Qualities of Catholic Evangelization." In Boyack, *The New Catholic Evangelization*.

Havlik, John F. *People-Centered Evangelism: Christian Love and Understanding as the Basis for Witnessing*. Broadman, 1971.

Hawkins, O. S. *Drawing the Net: 30 Practical Principles for Leading Others to Christ Publicly and Personally*. Broadman, 1993.

Hawkins, O. S., and Matt Queen. *The Gospel Invitation: Why Publicly Inviting People to Receive Christ Still Matters*. Nelson, 2023.

Heath, Elaine A. *The Mystic Way of Evangelism: A Contemplative Vision for Christian Outreach*. Baker Academic, 2008.

Henard, William D. "The Great Commission Leader: The Pastor as Personal Evangelist." In *The Great Commission Resurgence: Fulfilling God's Mandate in Our Time*, edited by Chuck Lawless and Adam W. Greenway. B&H Academic, 2010.

Henry, Carl F. H. *Evangelicals at the Brink of Crisis: Significance of the World Congress on Evangelism*. Word, 1967.

Henry, Carl F. H., and W. Stanley Mooneyham, eds. *One Race, One Gospel, One Task: Official Reference Volumes; Papers and Reports*. 2 vols. World Wide Publications, 1967.

Hesselgrave, David. *Communicating Christ Cross-Culturally: An Introduction to Missionary Communication*. 2nd ed. Zondervan, 1991.

———. *Paradigms in Conflict: 10 Key Questions in Christian Missions Today*. Kregel Academic, 2005.

Hiebert, Paul G. *Anthropological Reflections on Missiological Issues*. Baker, 1994.

———. *Transforming Worldviews: An Anthropological Understanding of How People Change*. Baker Academic, 2008.

Hiebert, Paul G., and Frances F. Hiebert. *Case Studies in Missions*. Baker, 1987.

Hildreth, D. Scott, and Steven A. McKinion. *Sharing Jesus Without Freaking Out: Evangelism the Way You Were Born to Do It*. 2nd ed. B&H Academic, 2020.

Hinson, E. Glenn. *The Evangelization of the Roman Empire*. Mercer University Press, 1981.

Hobbes, Thomas. *Leviathan*. Crooke, 1651.

Hobbs, Herschel H. *New Testament Evangelism: The Eternal Purpose*. Convention Press, 1960.

Hoekstra, Harvey T. *The World Council of Churches and the Demise of Evangelism*. Tyndale House, 1979.

Hoke, Donald, and Paul Little. Introduction to Douglas, *Let the Earth Hear His Voice*.

Holleman, Heather, and Ashley Holleman. *Sent: Living a Life That Invites Others to Jesus*. Moody, 2020.

Holy and Great Council of the Orthodox Church. "The Mission of the Orthodox Church in Today's World." https://www.holycouncil.org/mission-orthodox-church-todays-world.

House, H. Wayne. *Charts of Christian Theology*. Zondervan, 1992.

Hunter, George G., III. *The Celtic Way of Evangelism: How Christianity Can Reach the West . . . Again*. Abingdon, 2000.

———. *How to Reach Secular People*. Abingdon, 1992.

Hvalvik, Reidar. "In Word and Deed: The Expansion of the Church in the Pre-Constantinian Era." In *The Mission of the Early Church to Jews and Gentiles*, edited by Jostein Ådna and Hans Kvalbein. Mohr Siebeck, 2000.

Hybels, Bill, and Mark Mittelberg. *Becoming a Contagious Christian*. Zondervan, 1996.

Innes, Dick. *I Hate Witnessing: A Handbook for Effective Christian Communication*. Regal Books, 1983.

International Missionary Council. *The Life of the Church: International Missionary Council Meeting at Tambaram, Madras, December 12th to 29th, 1938*. Oxford University Press, 1939.

Jambrek, Stanko. "Christian Witness in a Multi-Religious World in the Light of God's Word." *Kairos* 8, no. 2 (2014): 187–215.

Jauncey, James H. *Psychology for Successful Evangelism*. Moody, 1972.

Jenkins, Philip. *The Lost History of Christianity: The Thousand-Year Golden Age of the Church in the Middle East, Africa, and Asia—and How It Died*. HarperOne, 2008.

Johnson, Ben Campbell. *An Evangelism Primer: Practical Principles for Congregations*. John Knox, 1983.

———. *Rethinking Evangelism: A Theological Approach*. Westminster, 1987.

———. *Speaking of God: Evangelism as Initial Spiritual Guidance*. Westminster John Knox, 1991.

Johnson, Ronald W. *How Will They Hear If We Don't Listen? The Vital Role of Listening in Preaching and Personal Evangelism*. Broadman & Holman, 1994.

Johnson, Samuel. *A Dictionary of the English Language*. Strahan, 1755.

Johnston, Arthur P. *The Battle for World Evangelism*. Tyndale House, 1978.

Johnston, Thomas P. *Charts for a Theology of Evangelism*. B&H Academic, 2007.

———. *Commission, Practice, and Follow-Up*, vol. 2 in *Evangelizology: A Biblical-Historical Perspective on Evangelism*. Evangelism Unlimited, 2011.

———. *A History of Evangelism in North America*. Kregel Academic, 2021.

———. *Motivation and Definition*, vol. 1 in *Evangelizology: A Biblical-Historical Perspective on Evangelism*. Evangelism Unlimited, 2011.

Johnstone, Patrick, and John Robb. "Track 310—Unreached Peoples." In Douglas, *Proclaim Christ*.

Jones, E. Stanley. *Conversion*. Abingdon, 1959.

Jones, Peyton. *Reaching the Unreached: Becoming Raiders of the Lost Art*. Zondervan, 2017.

Joshua Project. "How Many People Groups Are There?" https://joshuaproject.net/resources/articles/how_many_people_groups_are_there.

Kallenberg, Brad J. *Live to Tell: Evangelism for a Postmodern Age*. Brazos, 2002.

Kanyoro, Musimbi R. A. "Called to One Hope: The Gospel in Diverse Cultures." In Scherer and Bevans, *Faith and Culture*.

Kariatlis, Philip. "'Together Towards Life': A New World Council of Churches Affirmation on Mission and Evangelism: An Orthodox Reflection." *Phronema* 34, no. 1 (2019): ix–xix.

Keathley, Kenneth. *Salvation and Sovereignty: A Molinist Approach*. B&H Academic, 2010.

Keller, Timothy. *Making Sense of God: Finding God in the Modern World*. Penguin Books, 2016.

———. *The Reason for God: Belief in an Age of Skepticism*. Penguin Books, 2008.

Kelley, Charles S., Jr. "Ethical Issues in Evangelism: A Pyramid of Concerns." *The Theological Educator* 46 (Fall 1992): 33–40.

Kennedy, D. James. *Evangelism Explosion*. 4th ed. Tyndale House, 1996.

———. "Evangelism Explosion: 'Reaching All the Nations.'" *Evangelical Missions Quarterly* 33, no. 3 (1997): 298–301.

Kidner, Derek. *Genesis: An Introduction and Commentary*. InterVarsity, 1967.

Kilpatrick, T. B. *New Testament Evangelism*. Hodder & Stoughton, 1911.

Kittel, Gerhard, Gerhard Friedrich, and Geoffrey W. Bromiley. *Theological Dictionary of the New Testament: Abridged in One Volume*. Eerdmans, 1985.

Klaiber, Walter. *Call and Response: Biblical Foundations of a Theology of Evangelism*. Translated by Howard Perry-Trauthig and James A. Dwyer. Abingdon, 1997.

Kling, David W. *A History of Christian Conversion*. Oxford University Press, 2020.

Knight, Henry H., III, and F. Douglas Powe, Jr. *Transforming Evangelism: The Wesleyan Way of Sharing Faith*. Discipleship Resources, 2006.

Kolb, Robert. *Speaking the Gospel Today*. Rev. ed. Concordia, 1995.

Korkmaz, Yakup. "Research Evangelism Among Folk Muslims: A Call to Missionaries to Christian Cultural Anthropology." *Evangelical Missions Quarterly* 45, no. 4 (2009): 430–37.

Köstenberger, Andreas J. *The Missions of Jesus and the Disciples According to the Fourth Gospel*. Eerdmans, 1998.

Koukl, Gregory. *Street Smarts: Using Questions to Answer Christianity's Toughest Challenges*. Zondervan Reflective, 2023.

Kraemer, Hendrik. *The Communication of the Christian Faith*. Westminster, 1956.

Kraft, Charles. *Communication Theory for Christian Witness*. Abingdon, 1983.

Kuiper, R. B. *God-Centered Evangelism: A Presentation of the Scriptural Theology of Evangelism*. Baker, 1963.

Larkin, William J., Jr. "Mission in Luke." In Larkin and Williams, *Mission in the New Testament*.

Larkin, William J., Jr., and Joel F. Williams, eds. *Mission in the New Testament: An Evangelical Approach*. Orbis Books, 1998.

Larsen, David L. *The Evangelism Mandate: Recovering the Centrality of Gospel Preaching*. Kregel, 1992.

Latin American Episcopal Council. *Conclusions*, vol. 2 in *The Church in the Present-Day Transformation of Latin America in the Light of the Council*. 2nd ed. General Secretariat of Celam, 1973.

———. *Position Papers*, vol. 1 in *The Church in the Present-Day Transformation of Latin America in the Light of the Council*. General Secretariat of Celam, 1970.

Latourette, Kenneth Scott. *A History of Christianity: Beginnings to 1500*. Rev. ed. Prince, 1975.

Lausanne Movement. "The Cape Town Commitment: A Confession of Faith and a Call to Action." https://lausanne.org/statement/ctcommitment#capetown.

———. "Great Commission Discipleship." https://lausanne.org/report/great-commission-discipleship.

Lawless, Chuck. "Remembering My Dad," June 17, 2015, https://chucklawless.com/2015/06/remembering-my-dad.

Lawrence, J. B. *The Holy Spirit in Missions*. Home Mission Board, Southern Baptist Convention, 1966.

Leavell, Roland Q. *Evangelism: Christ's Imperative Commission*. Broadman, 1951.

Lemopoulos, Georges. "Come, Our Light, and Illumine Our Darkness!" *International Review of Mission* 87, no. 346 (1998): 322–30.

Lennox, Patrick. "Rethinking Missions in Native America." *Evangelical Missions Quarterly* 60, no. 2 (2024): 33–39.

Lewis, R. W. "Clarifying the Remaining Frontier Mission Task." *International Journal of Frontier Missiology* 35, no. 4 (2018): 154–68.

Liefeld, Walter L. "Women and Evangelism in the Early Church." In Chilcote and Warner, *The Study of Evangelism*.

Linn, Jan G. *Reclaiming Evangelism: A Practical Guide for Mainline Churches*. Chalice, 1998.

Liptak, Yeong Woo. "Bible Women: Evangelism and Cultural Transformation in the Early Korean Church." PhD diss., Southern Baptist Theological Seminary, 2015.

Little, Paul E. *How to Give Away Your Faith*. 2nd ed. InterVarsity, 1988.

Lloyd-Jones, Sally. *Jesus Storybook Bible*. Zonderkidz, 2007.

Lovell, Arnold B. *Evangelism in the Reformed Tradition*. CTS, 1990.

Lovett, C. S. *Soul Winning Made Easy*. Personal Christianity, 1980.

MacGregor, Kirk R. "Regeneration." In *The Lexham Bible Dictionary*, edited by John D. Barry et al. Lexham, 2016.

MacMullen, Ramsay. *Christianizing the Roman Empire (A.D. 100–400)*. Yale University Press, 1984.

Malherbe, Abraham J. *Social Aspects of Early Christianity*. 2nd ed. Fortress, 1983.

Martin-Achard, Robert. *A Light to the Nations: A Study of the Old Testament Conception of Israel's Mission to the World*. Translated by John Penney Smith. Oliver & Boyd, 1962.

Matthews, Kenneth A. *Genesis 11:27–50:26*. Broadman & Holman, 2005.

Mayers, Marvin K. *Christianity Confronts Culture: A Strategy for Cross-Cultural Evangelism*. Zondervan, 1974.

McCloskey, Mark. *Tell It Often–Tell It Well: Making the Most of Witnessing Opportunities*. Here's Life Publishers, 1986.

McGavran, Donald A. *The Bridges of God: A Study in the Strategy of Missions*. Friendship Press, 1955.

———. *Effective Evangelism: A Theological Mandate*. Presbyterian and Reformed, 1988.

———. *Momentous Decisions in Missions Today*. Baker, 1984.

———. *Understanding Church Growth*. Rev. ed. Eerdmans, 1980.

McGrath, Alister E. *Christian Theology: An Introduction*. Blackwell, 1994.

McLaughlin, Rebecca. *Confronting Christianity: 12 Hard Questions for the World's Largest Religion*. Crossway, 2019.

McMahan, Alan. "Ferment in the Church: Missions in the 4th Era." *Evangelical Missions Quarterly* 56, no. 4 (2020): 36–38.

Medders, J. A., and Doug Logan, Jr. *The Soul-Winning Church: Six Keys to Fostering a Genuine Evangelistic Culture*. The Good Book Company, 2024.

Meeking, Basil, and John Stott, eds. *The Evangelical-Roman Catholic Dialogue on Mission 1977–1984: A Report*. Eerdmans, 1986.

Miles, Delos. *Evangelism and Social Involvement*. Broadman, 1986.

———. *How Jesus Won Persons: Fifteen Case Studies from the Gospels*. Broadman, 1982.

———. *Introduction to Evangelism*. Broadman, 1983.

———. *Master Principles of Evangelism*. Broadman, 1982.

———. *Overcoming Barriers to Witnessing*. Broadman, 1984.

Mischke, Werner. *The Global Gospel: Achieving Missional Impact in Our Multicultural World*. Mission One, 2015.
Mong, Ambrose. *Guns and Gospel: Imperialism and Evangelism in China*. Clarke, 2016.
Moon, W. Jay, and W. Bud Simon. *Effective Intercultural Evangelism: Good News in a Diverse World*. InterVarsity, 2021.
Moreau, A. Scott, ed. *Evangelical Dictionary of World Missions*. Baker Books, 2000.
Morris, Leon. *The Apostolic Preaching of the Cross*. 3rd ed. Eerdmans, 1965.
Mott, John R. *The Evangelization of the World in This Generation*. Student Volunteer Movement for Foreign Missions, 1900.
———. *The Larger Evangelism*. Abingdon-Cokesbury, 1944.
———. *The Pastor and Modern Missions: A Plea for Leadership in World Evangelization*. Student Volunteer Movement for Foreign Missions, 1904.
Mounce, R. H. "Kerygma." In vol. 3 of *The International Standard Bible Encyclopedia*, edited by Geoffrey W. Bromiley. Eerdmans, 1986.
Mugambi, J. N. K. "A Fresh Look at Evangelism in Africa." In Chilcote and Warner, *The Study of Evangelism*.
Mulholland, Ken. "Whitby Conference (1947)." In Moreau, *Dictionary of World Missions*.
———. "Willingen Conference (1952)." In Moreau, *Dictionary of World Missions*.
Muncy, W. L., Jr. *Evangelism in the United States*. Central Seminary Press, 1945.
Murray, James, ed. *A New English Dictionary on Historical Principles*. Clarendon, 1891.
Nazir-Ali, Michael. *Mission and Dialogue: Proclaiming the Gospel Afresh in Every Age*. SPCK, 1995.
Neill, Stephen. *Creative Tension*. Edinburgh House, 1959.
———. *A History of Christian Missions*. Rev. ed. Penguin Books, 1986.
Newbigin, Lesslie. *Foolishness to the Greeks: The Gospel and Western Culture*. Eerdmans, 1986.
———. *One Body, One Gospel, One World: The Christian Mission Today*. International Missionary Council, 1958.
Newell, Marvin J. *Commissioned: What Jesus Wants You to Know as You Go*. ChurchSmart Resources, 2010.
———. *A Third of Us: What It Takes to Reach the Unreached*. William Carey, 2021.
Newman, Randy. *Bringing the Gospel Home: Witnessing to Family Members, Close Friends, and Others Who Know You Well*. Crossway, 2011.
———. *Questioning Evangelism: Engaging People's Hearts the Way Jesus Did*. Kregel, 2004.

Nguyen, Minh Ha. "Globalization, Urbanization, Migration, and Rethinking the People Groups Concept." *Evangelical Missions Quarterly* 56, no. 4 (2020): 32–35.

Nida, Eugene A. *Message and Mission: The Communication of the Christian Faith.* Rev. ed. William Carey, 1960.

Niles, D. T. *That They May Have Life.* Harper & Brothers, 1951.

Nissiotis, Nikos "An Orthodox View of Modern Trends in Evangelism." *The Ecumenical World of Orthodox Civilization* 3 (1974): 181–92.

Nolland, John. *Luke 9:21–18:34.* Word, 1993.

Nuelsen, J. L. "Conversion." In vol. 2 of *The International Standard Bible Encyclopaedia*, edited by James Orr. Howard-Severance, 1915.

Olson, Roger E. *Arminian Theology: Myths and Realities.* IVP Academic, 2006.

Osiek, Carolyn, and David L. Balch. *Families in the New Testament World: Households and House Churches.* Westminster John Knox, 1997.

Osmer, Richard R. *The Invitation: A Theology of Evangelism.* Eerdmans, 2021.

Ott, Craig. "The Power of Biblical Metaphors for the Contextualized Communication of the Gospel." *Missiology* 42, no. 4 (2014): 357–74.

Packer, J. I. *Evangelism and the Sovereignty of God.* InterVarsity, 1961.

———. "Justification." In *Evangelical Dictionary of Theology*, edited by Walter A. Elwell. Baker, 1984.

———. "Report of Theologians Task Group." In *The Mission of an Evangelist: Amsterdam 2000.* World Wide Publications, 2001.

Paul VI. *Evangelii nuntiandi: On Evangelization in the Modern World.* United States Catholic Conference, 1975.

Paulsen, Judith. *A New and Ancient Evangelism: Rediscovering the Ways God Calls and Sends.* Baker Academic, 2024.

Payne, J. D. *Apostolic Imagination: Recovering a Biblical Vision for the Church's Mission Today.* Baker Academic, 2022.

———. "Eight Principles of New Testament Evangelism." Lausanne World Pulse Archives, May 2007. https://lausanneworldpulse.com/themedarticles-php/700/05-2007.

———. *Evangelism: A Biblical Response to Today's Questions.* InterVarsity, 2011.

———. *Kingdom Expressions: Trends Influencing the Advancement of the Gospel.* Nelson, 2012.

———. *Pressure Points: Twelve Global Issues Shaping the Face of the Church.* Nelson, 2013.

———. *Strangers Next Door: Immigration, Migration and Mission.* IVP Books, 2012.

———. *Theology of Mission: A Concise Biblical Theology.* Lexham, 2021.

Peace, Richard V. *Conversion in the New Testament: Paul and the Twelve.* Eerdmans, 1999.

Peifen, Jiang. "Women and Evangelism in the Chinese Church." *Missiology* 15, no. 3 (1987): 365–69.

Peters, George W. *Saturation Evangelism.* Zondervan, 1970.

Pickerd, Stephen K. *Liberating Evangelism: Gospel Theology and Dynamics of Communication.* Trinity Press International, 1999.

Pickering, Ernest. *The Theology of Evangelism.* Baptist Bible College Press, 1974.

Pippert, Rebecca Manley. *Out of the Saltshaker and into the World: Evangelism as a Way of Life.* InterVarsity, 1979.

Poe, Harry L. *The Gospel and Its Meaning: A Theology for Evangelism and Church Growth.* Zondervan, 1996.

Polhill, John B. *Acts.* Broadman, 1992.

Pope-Levison, Priscilla. *Building the Old Time Religion: Women Evangelists in the Progressive Era.* New York University Press, 2013.

———. *Evangelization from a Liberation Perspective.* Lang, 1991.

———. *Models of Evangelism.* Baker Academic, 2020.

———. *Turn the Pulpit Loose: Two Centuries of American Women Evangelists.* Palgrave Macmillan, 2004.

Posterski, Donald C. *Reinventing Evangelism: New Strategies for Presenting Christ in Today's World.* InterVarsity, 1989.

Presbyterian Church (U.S.A.). *Turn to the Living God: A Call to Evangelism in Jesus Christ's Way.* PC(USA) Office of the General Assembly, 1991.

Queen, Matt. *Recapturing Evangelism: A Biblical-Theological Approach.* B&H Academic, 2023.

Rainer, Thom S. *Sharing the Gospel with Ease: How the Love of Christ Can Flow Naturally from Your Life.* Tyndale Momentum, 2022.

Raiser, Konrad. Foreword to *Orthodox Perspectives on Mission*, edited by Petros Vassiliadis. Regnum, 2013.

Reid, Alvin. *Evangelism Handbook: Biblical, Spiritual, Intentional, Missional.* B&H, 2009.

———. *Introduction to Evangelism:* Broadman & Holman, 1998.

Richardson, Rick. "From the Will to Power to the Power of Weakness: Toward a Post-Christendom Evangelism." *Post-Christendom Studies* 5 (2020–21): 94–95.

———. *Reimagining Evangelism: Inviting Friends on a Spiritual Journey.* InterVarsity, 2006.

———. *You Found Me: New Research on How Unchurched Nones, Millennials, and Irreligious Are Surprisingly Open to Christian Faith.* IVP Books, 2019.

Robert, Dana L. *American Women in Mission: The Modern Mission Era, 1792–1992*. Mercer University Press, 1997.

Roberts, Alexander, and James Donaldson, eds. *Ante-Nicene Fathers: The Writings of the Fathers Down to A.D. 325*. 10 vols. Reprint, Hendrickson, 1994.

Robinson, Darrell W. *People Sharing Jesus: A Natural, Sensitive Approach to Helping Others Know Christ*. Nelson, 1995.

Robinson, Jeffrey M. *Persuasive Apologetics: The Art of Handling Tough Questions Without Pushing People Away*. Kregel Academic, 2023.

Root, Jerry, and Stan Guthrie. *The Sacrament of Evangelism*. Moody, 2011.

Rudnick, Milton L. *Speaking the Gospel Through the Ages: A History of Evangelism*. Concordia, 1984.

Sanders, J. Oswald. *Effective Evangelism: The Divine Art of Soul-Winning*. STL Books, 1982.

Sanneh, Lamin. *Translating the Message: The Missionary Impact on Culture*. Rev. ed. Orbis Books, 2009.

Scarborough, L. R. *How Jesus Won Men*. Baker, 1972.

———. *With Christ After the Lost*. Broadman, 1952.

Scharpff, Paulus. *History of Evangelism: Three Hundred Years of Evangelism in Germany, Great Britain, and the United States of America*. Translated by Helga Bender Henry. Eerdmans, 1966.

Scherer, James A., and Stephen B. Bevans, eds. *Basic Statements 1974–1991*, vol. 1 in *New Directions in Mission and Evangelization*. Orbis Books, 1992.

———, eds. *Faith and Culture*, vol. 3 in *New Directions in Mission and Evangelization*. Orbis Books, 1999.

Schirrmacher, Thomas. "The Code: 'Christian Witness in a Multi-Religious World'—Its Significance and Reception." *Evangelical Review of Theology* 40, no. 1 (2016): 82–89.

Schneider, Floyd. *Evangelism for the Fainthearted*. 2nd ed. Kregel, 2000.

Scribner, Dan. "The Making of Lists." *Evangelical Missions Quarterly* 56, no. 4 (2020): 39–42.

Scroggins, Jimmy, and Steve Wright. *Turning Everyday Conversations into Gospel Conversations*. B&H, 2016.

Shah, Rebecca Samuel. "Saving the Soul of India: Christian Conversion and the Rise of Hindu Nationalism." In *Christianity in India: Conversion, Community Development, and Religious Freedom*, edited by Rebecca Samuel Shah and Joel Carpenter. Fortress, 2018.

Shaw, R. Daniel, and Charles E. Van Engen. *Communicating God's Word in a Complex World: God's Truth or Hocus Pocus?* Rowman & Littlefield, 2003.

Sire, James W. *Naming the Elephant: Worldview as a Concept*. 2nd ed. IVP Academic, 2015.

———. *The Universe Next Door: A Basic Worldview Catalog.* 6th ed. IVP Academic, 2020.

Sjogren, Steve. *Conspiracy of Kindness: A Unique Approach to Sharing the Love of Jesus.* Bethany House, 2008.

Smith, Ebbie. "Introduction to the Strategy and Methods of Missions." In *Missiology: An Introduction to the Foundations, History, and Strategies of World Missions,* edited by John Mark Terry, Ebbie Smith, and Justice Anderson. Broadman & Holman, 1998.

Smith, Thomas. "Introductory Notice to the Recognitions of Clement." In vol. 8 of Roberts and Donaldson, *Ante-Nicene Fathers.*

Smither, Edward L. *Missionary Monks: An Introduction to the History and Theology of Missionary Monasticism.* Cascade Books, 2016.

Søgaard, Viggo. *Everything You Need to Know for a Cassette Ministry: Cassettes in the Context of a Total Christian Communication Program.* Bethany Fellowship, 1975.

———. *Media in Church and Mission: Communicating the Gospel.* William Carey, 1993.

Sohn, Lydia. "Rethinking What We Mean When We Talk About Evangelism." https://www.umc.org/en/content/rethinking-what-we-mean-with-evangelism.

Springer, Craig. *How to Revive Evangelism: 7 Vital Shifts in How We Share Our Faith.* Zondervan Reflective, 2021.

Sproul, R. C. *Grace Unknown: The Heart of Reformed Theology.* Baker, 1997.

Spurgeon, C. H. *The Soul Winner; or, How to Lead Sinners to the Saviour.* Revell, 1895.

Stamoolis, James J. *Eastern Orthodox Mission Theology Today.* Wipf & Stock, 1986.

Steffen, Tom. "Flawed Evangelism and Church Planting." *Evangelical Mission Quarterly* 34, no. 4 (1998): 428–35.

———. *Reconnecting God's Story to Ministry: Cross-Cultural Storytelling at Home and Abroad.* Rev. ed. Authentic Media, 2005.

———. "Why Communicate the Gospel Through Stories?" *Mission Frontiers,* November–December 2013, 6–9.

Stewart, George, and Henry B. Wright. *Personal Evangelism Among Students: Studies in the Practice of Friendship in School and College.* Association Press, 1920.

Stiles, J. Mack. *Evangelism: How the Whole Church Speaks of Jesus.* Crossway, 2014.

Stone, Bryan. *Evangelism After Christendom: The Theology and Practice of Christian Witness.* Brazos, 2007.

———. *Evangelism After Pluralism: The Ethics of Christian Witness.* Baker Academic, 2018.

Stott, John R. W. *Christian Mission in the Modern World.* InterVarsity, 1977.

———. *The Cross of Christ.* InterVarsity, 1986.

———. *Motives and Methods in Evangelism*. Inter-Varsity, 1962.

Stowe, David M. *Ecumenicity and Evangelism*. Eerdmans, 1970.

Strack, Jay, and Robert G. Witty. *Do the Work of an Evangelist*. Broadman, 1990.

Street, R. Alan, *The Effective Invitation*. Revell, 1984.

Stromberg, Jean, ed. *Mission and Evangelism: An Ecumenical Affirmation; A Study Guide for Congregations*. National Council of Churches of Christ in the U.S.A., 1983.

Sweazey, George E. *Effective Evangelism: The Greatest Work in the World*. Harper & Brothers, 1953.

Taylor, G. D. "Testimony." In *Lexham Theological Wordbook*, edited by Douglas Mangum, Derek R. Brown, and Rachel Klippenstein. Lexham, 2014.

Taylor, Mark. *1 Corinthians*. B&H, 2014.

Taylor, Mendell. *Exploring Evangelism: History, Methods, Theology*. Beacon Hill, 1964.

Templeton, Charles B. *Evangelism for Tomorrow*. Harper & Brothers, 1957.

Terry, John Mark. *Evangelism: A Concise History*. Broadman & Holman, 1994.

Terry, John Mark, and Robert L. Gallagher. *Encountering the History of Missions: From the Early Church to Today*. Baker Academic, 2017.

Terry, John Mark, and J. D. Payne. *Developing a Strategy for Missions: A Biblical, Historical, and Cultural Introduction*. Baker Academic, 2013.

Thiessen, Elmer John. *The Ethics of Evangelism: A Philosophical Defense of Proselytizing and Persuasion*. IVP Academic, 2011.

———. *The Scandal of Evangelism: A Biblical Study of the Ethics of Evangelism*. Cascade Books, 2018.

Thomas, M. M. "The Christian Witness in Society and Nation." In *The Ghana Assembly of the International Missionary Council, 28th December, 1957 to 8th January, 1958*, edited by Ronald K. Orchard. Edinburgh House, 1958.

Thompson, Nicholas J. "Developing an Evangelistic Church Culture." *Puritan Reformed Journal* 13, no. 1 (2021): 143–53.

Tibbs, Eve. *A Basic Guide to Eastern Orthodox Theology: Introducing Beliefs and Practices*. Baker Academic, 2021.

Tuttle, Robert G., Jr. *The Story of Evangelism: A History of the Witness to the Gospel*. Abingdon, 2006.

United Methodist Church. "Glossary: *evangelism*." https://www.umc.org/en/content/glossary-evangelism.

Uzzell, Lawrence A. "Don't Call It Proselytism." *First Things* 146 (October 2004): 14–16.

Valleskey, David J. *We Believe, Therefore We Speak: The Theology and Practice of Evangelism*. Northwestern Publishing House, 1995.

Van Rheenen, Gailyn. *Communicating Christ in Animistic Contexts*. William Carey, 1991.

Vassiliadis, Petros. "A Preliminary Short Comment." *International Review of Mission* 105, no. 2 (2016): 352–55.

Veronis, Alexander. "Orthodox Concepts of Evangelism and Mission." *Greek Orthodox Theological Review* 27, no. 1 (1982): 44–57.

———. "The Task of the Church to Evangelize the World." *Greek Orthodox Theological Review* 42, nos. 3–4 (1997): 435–44.

Visser 't Hooft, W. A., ed. *The New Delhi Report: The Third Assembly of the World Council of Churches, 1961*. SCM, 1962.

Wagner, Peter, and Edward R. Dayton, eds. *Unreached Peoples' 79*. David C. Cook, 1978.

Währisch-Oblau, Claudia. "Evangelism in *Evangelii Gaudium*, *The Cape Town Commitment*, and *Together Towards Life*." *International Review of Mission* 104, no. 2 (2015): 255–67.

Ward, Charles G. *Equipping for Evangelism: North American Conference for Itinerant Evangelists*. World Wide Publications, 1996.

Wardle, Terry. *One to One: A Practical Guide to Friendship Evangelism*. Christian Publications, 1989.

Warner, Laceye C. *Saving Women: Retrieving Evangelistic Theology and Practice*. Baylor University Press, 2007.

Watson, David. *I Believe in Evangelism*. Eerdmans, 1976.

Watson, Thomas. *The Doctrine of Repentance*. Banner of Truth Trust, 1988.

Webber, Robert E. *Ancient-Future Evangelism: Making Your Church a Faith-Forming Community*. Baker Books, 2003.

Weber, H. R. *The Communication of the Gospel to Illiterates: Based on Missionary Experience in Indonesia*. Translated by Olga Pilpel. Christian Literature Society, 1960.

Wells, David F. *God the Evangelist: How the Holy Spirit Works to Bring Men and Women to Faith*. Eerdmans; Paternoster, 1987.

———. *Turning to God: Biblical Conversion in the Modern World*. Paternoster; Baker, 1989.

Wesley, John. *The Works of John Wesley*. 3rd ed. 14 vols. in 7. Baker Books, 2007.

Westerhoff, John H. "Evangelism, Evangelization, and Catechesis: Defining Terms and Making the Case for Evangelization." In Chilcote and Warner, *The Study of Evangelism*.

Whiteman, Darrell L. *Crossing Cultures with the Gospel: Anthropological Wisdom for Effective Christian Witness*. Baker Academic, 2024.

Whitesell, Faris D. *Basic New Testament Evangelism*. Zondervan, 1949.

———. *65 Ways to Give Evangelistic Invitations*. 4th ed. Zondervan, 1945.

Whitney, Donald S. *Spiritual Disciplines for the Christian Life*. NavPress, 2014.

Wilmoth, Rodney E. *How United Methodists Share Their Faith*. Abingdon, 1999.

Wimber, John. *Power Evangelism*. Chosen Books, 1986.

Winter, Ralph D. "The Highest Priority: Cross-Cultural Evangelism." In Douglas, *Let the Earth Hear His Voice*.

World Council of Churches. "The Challenge of Proselytism and the Calling to Common Witness: A Study Document of the Joint Working Group." *The Ecumenical Review* 48, no. 2 (1996): 212–21.

———. "Christian Witness in a Multi-Religious World: Recommendations for Conduct." https://www.oikoumene.org/sites/default/files/Document/ChristianWitness_recommendations.pdf.

———. "Common Witness and Proselytism: A Study Document." *The Ecumenical Review* 23, no. 1 (1971): 9–20.

———. *Minutes of the Assembly of the International Missionary Council: Ghana*. World Council of Churches, 1958.

———. "Report from the Ecumenical Conference on World Mission and Evangelization." In Scherer and Bevans, *Faith and Culture*.

———. "Together Towards Life: Mission and Evangelism in Changing Landscapes." n.d. https://www.oikoumene.org/sites/default/files/Document/Together_towards_Life.pdf.

———. "Together Towards Life: Mission and Evangelism in Changing Landscapes: A New WCC Affirmation on Mission and Evangelism." *International Review of Mission* 101, no. 2 (2012): 250–80.

———. "Towards Common Witness: A Call to Adopt Responsible Relationships in Mission and to Renounce Proselytism." *International Review of Mission* 86, no. 343 (1997): 463–73.

World Missionary Conference. *The History and Records of the Conference*. Oliphant, Anderson & Ferrier; Revell, 1910.

Wright, Christopher J. H. *The Mission of God: Unlocking the Bible's Grand Narrative*. IVP Academic, 2006.

Wright, N. T. *The New Testament and the People of God*. Fortress, 1992.

Wynkoop, Mildred Bangs. *Foundations of Wesleyan-Arminian Theology*. Beacon Hill, 1967.

Zurlo, Gina A. *Global Christianity: A Guide to the World's Largest Religion from Afghanistan to Zimbabwe*. Zondervan Academic, 2022.

———. *Women in World Christianity: Building and Sustaining a Global Movement*. Wiley Blackwell, 2023.

Zurlo, Gina A., Todd M. Johnson, and Peter F. Crossing. "World Christianity and Mission 2021: Questions About the Future." *International Bulletin of Mission Research* 45, no. 1 (2021): 15–25.

SCRIPTURE INDEX

Old Testament

Genesis
1:1 65, 93
1:27 39, 66, 189
1:28 192
1:28–30 66
2:15–23 66
3:6 66
3:15 67
3:19 120
9:1 66, 192
12:1–3 95, 249
12:3 9, 67
21:30 35
22:18 67n3
26:4 67n3
31:44 35
31:52 35, 223
40:8 265

Exodus
4:12 9
6:6 112
15:18 94
19:5–6 68, 69
20:16 35, 223
23:1 35, 223
33:19 96
38:21 223

Leviticus
1:4 107

Numbers
23:23 195

Deuteronomy
4:5 9
4:6 69
4:26 35, 223
4:30 115
4:37 96
5:20 223
6:6–25 243, 244
6:7–9 146
7:6 95
7:6–8 96
9:4–6 96
11:19 9
14:2 95, 96
15:15 112
19:15 223, 228
23:1 193
28:25 70
29:29 100
30:6 120
30:19 35
31:26 223
32:3 10
32:21 66
33:5 94

1 Samuel
12:5–6 35
20:12 35
31:9 9

2 Samuel
4:10 11
6:21 96
7:1–17 69, 78
7:12–16 94
18:19 9
18:22 11n16

1 Kings
3:8 96
8:41–43 70
8:60 70
10:7 9

2 Kings
19:15 94

1 Chronicles
12:32 43
16:8 9
16:23–24 9
16:24 8, 50
29:11 94

2 Chronicles
19:8–10 10
36:22–23 70, 71

Ezra
1:1–11 70
6:26–27 115

Nehemiah
9:6 93

Psalms
2:12 94
8:6 94
9:11 9
16:11 32, 227
19:1 8, 35
19:4–5 66
22:27 115
22:27–28 71
22:28 94
40:9 10
47:2 94
47:4 96
47:8 94
51 116
67 50, 280
67:1–3 71
78:4 8
89:9 94
89:37 223
96:2–3 9
96:10 71, 94
97:1 94
103:19 94
105:1 9
106:23 96
115:3 95
119:11 253
119:46 9
130 116
135:4 96

309

145:1 94
145:11 10

Proverbs

6:16–19 223
6:19 223
11:30 89
12:18 273
13:16 268
14:5 35
14:25 35
15:1 250
16:18 54
19:2 268
19:28 35
21:28 35
25:11 273
25:18 223
29:20 268

Isaiah

2:2–3 71
6:9–10 10
6:10 115
10:21 115
12:4 9
19:23–25 71
40:3 65
40:9 9
42:1 96
42:1–7 71, 96
43:10 35, 223
43:12 35
43:21 8
44:8–9 35
44:22 112
45:22 119
48:3–5 95
49:1–7 71
49:6 68
50:4–9 71
52:7 9, 10, 17, 24, 94
52:13–15 71
53:1–12 71
55:1–9 115
55:7 115
56:7 71
60:6 10
61:1 10, 11
61:1–2 9, 10, 65
65:1 66, 96

66:18–23 68
66:19 9

Jeremiah

3:1–4 115
3:12 116
3:12–13 115
3:12–24 116
4:1–4 115
11:7 223
18:1–12 96
20:15 9
24:7 115
26:3 115
29:4–7 70
31:31–34 120
31:31–40 71
31:34 9
32:36–41 71
32:39–40 120

Lamentations

5:19 94
5:21 115

Ezekiel

11:19–20 120
16:1–14 96
18:4 94
18:23 101
33:9 10
36:22–32 71
36:25–27 120
36:27 120

Daniel

2:44–45 78
4:34–37 94
4:35 93, 95
7:13–14 65, 78, 94

Hosea

5:15–6:5 116

Joel

2:12 115, 116
2:28–32 65
2:32 103, 117, 231

Amos

4:6–13 116
9:11–12 xi, 66, 194

Jonah

1:2 10
1:9 10
3:2 10

Micah

4:7 94
6:8 28

Nahum

1:15 9

Habakkuk

2:14 50, 193

Zechariah

1:3 115
8:23 71

Malachi

4:5–6 71

New Testament

Matthew

2:2 94
3:2 78
3:7–10 118
4:17 78, 118
4:19 75, 78
4:23 11
5:12 35
5:14 37
5:16 37
6:10 85, 94
7:13–14 32
7:15–20 232
7:21 54
9:35 12
10:7 7
10:18 35
11:5 11
11:19 56
11:20–24 115
11:28 103

12:15–21 96
12:28 94
12:41 13
12:48–50 113
13:1–9 95
13:45–46 90
13:52 13n25, 78n13
15:19 223
16:16 75
16:18 30, 50, 52, 94
16:24–25 55
18:1–6 242
18:3 119
18:16 223
18:17–18 232
18:18 77n10
19:13–15 242
19:16–30 54
20:28 112
21:5 94
23:15 116
24:14 5, 11
24:22 97
25:18 43
25:31–32 94
26:13 12, 76
27:57 13n25, 78n13
28:16–20 7n6
28:18 94
28:18–20 56, 65, 75, 77
28:19 13, 75n5, 78n13, 90, 249
28:19–20 237
28:20 30, 75n5

Mark

1:1–9 65
1:14 11, 12
1:14–15 33
1:15 71, 117, 118–19
1:17 75
1:24 276
2:5 94
2:10–12 94
4:26–29 214
4:39 94
5:1–20 268
5:19 91
5:20 91
6:12 12

Scripture Index

10:13–16 242
10:17–31 54
10:21 54, 90
10:22 55
10:29–31 55
10:45 112
13:9 35
13:10 11, 75, 75n6, 76
13:13 76
13:20 97
13:24–27 76
13:32–36 76
14:3–6 76
14:9 11, 75, 75n6, 76
14:36 255
16:15 75n6
16:20 13nn22–23

Luke

1:2 225
1:4 23n26
1:16 115
1:19 11
2:10 11
3:3 118
3:7–9 118
3:18 11
4:17–19 65
4:18 11, 12, 85
5:1–11 214
5:27–32 270
6:13 96
7:22 7n7
7:34 56, 90
7:50 117
8:1 7n7, 11
9:2 12
9:22 50
9:23 55, 79
9:23–24 90
9:35 96
9:62 55, 79, 118
10:9 94
10:20 227
11:28 79
11:32 13
12:7 227
12:42–48 42
12:48 42
12:51 79

13 251
13:3 79, 90
14:25–33 55, 79, 90
15:2 56
15:7 52
15:10 52, 79, 255
15:11–32 119
16:16 11
16:19–31 209
17:13 230
17:20–21 85
18:13 230
18:18–30 54
19:7 90
19:9 90
19:10 79
19:38 94
21:13 35
22:32 120
23:35 96
23:42 230
24:44–49 79
24:46 37
24:47 37, 79, 214, 249
24:49 79

John

1:7 12, 35
1:12 110, 117, 129, 276n6
1:14 75, 191
1:15 35
1:19 225
1:29 284
1:32 35
1:34 35
1:35–51 270
1:43 75
1:49 94
3 84, 268
3:3 88, 111
3:3–7 120
3:5 93
3:5–8 111
3:16 34, 75, 77, 103, 125, 245, 253
3:18 34, 111
3:28 35
4 84, 268, 284
4:4 84
4:10 88

4:17–18 90
4:39 270
4:39–42 84
5:31 225
5:36 35
5:37 35
5:39 35, 228
6:37 102, 103
8:18 35
8:31–36 77
8:32 112
8:34 112, 121
8:44 113
9:4 50
10:10 34, 110, 265
10:16 50
10:25 35
10:28 119
11:25 110
12:1–8 76
13:34–35 228
13:35 196
14:6 84, 117
14:9 191
14:15 50, 212
14:27 111
15:1–5 75
15:1–11 7n6
15.7–8 247
15:15 111
15:16 96
15:26 35, 228
15:27 35, 228
16:8 54n3, 86, 250
16:8–11 228
16:13 86
17:6 96
17:21 168n7
20:21 76
20:21–23 76
20:23 76, 77n10

Acts

1:2 96
1:5–8 66
1:6 192
1:8 12, 37, 81, 85, 192, 214, 228, 237, 249
1:21 120
2–4 33

2:5 193
2:11 57, 115
2:16–21 65
2:17 193
2:20 85
2:21 103, 231
2:22–41 119
2:23 95
2:32 12, 37
2:37 53
2:37–38 277n7
2:38 53, 79
2:40 37
2:41 75
2:41–42 119
2:43 86
3:15 12, 37
3:19 118, 119
3:25 67n3
4:4 119
4:12 84, 117
4:13 85
4:20 214, 253
4:28 95
4:31 85
4:33 85
4:34 81
5:31 79, 121
5:32 12, 37
6:1 75, 81
6:5 57n9, 115
6:7 75
7 250
7:54 228
7:54–60 193
7:55–56 85
8 84
8:4–8 86
8:5 12, 193
8:5–25 119
8:14–17 193
8:26 86
8:26–40 119
8:29 86
8:35 88, 193
8:36–39 91
8:38–39 193
9:1–19 119
9:2 81
9:31 75
9:35 119
9:42 119

10 84, 123, 265
10:1–11:18 119
10:15 193
10:19–20 86
10:36 10, 11
10:39 37
10:42 4, 225
10:43 35, 276n6, 277n7
10:44–45 194
10:44–48 119, 123
11:2–3 194
11:18 121, 123, 194
11:20–21 194
11:21 118, 119, 120
11:26 81
13–14 91, 194
13:1–3 86
13:14–43 51
13:38–39 112
13:43 115
13:47 66
13:48 52, 95
13:52 52
14:15 119
14:17 35
14:21 13, 78n13
14:23 91
15:1 194
15:3 118n6
15:7 96
15:13–19 66
15:15–17 116
15:16 xi
15:16–17 194
15:19 117
16:14–15 121
16:30 14n30
16:30–32 276
16:31 232
17:16–34 89
17:22 86
17:22–33 51
17:22–34 84
17:23–28 179
17:28–29 87
17:30 119
17:30–31 116
19:8–10 75
19:9 81
19:23 81
20:17 249

20:21 6, 13, 27, 84, 104, 117, 118
20:24 11
20:28 112
20:29–30 15
20:32 112
21:8 11
21:28 248
22:1 211
22:4 81
22:6–16 119
22:15 35
22:18 225
24:5 134
24:10 211
24:14 81
24:16 57
24:24 117
25:8 211
26:1 87
26:1–2 211
26:12–18 119
26:12–29 226
26:16 12, 35
26:18 112, 117, 119
26:20 114, 118, 119
26:24 211
26:28 228
26:29 228
28:31 12, 81

Romans

1–5 211
1:15 14n27
1:16 37, 196, 272
1:16–17 266
2:4 119
3:21 12, 35
3:21–26 119
3:23 34, 107, 253, 265
3:24 112
3:25 111
3:26 112
3:35 107
4:2–5 112
4:25 34
5:8 253
5:10 111
5:19 113
6:18 119
6:23 120, 253

7:15–25 254
7:24–25 254
8:14–17 113
8:19–23 66
8:29–30 95
8:30 113
8:31–38 119
9–11 97
9:10–24 96
9:11 97
10:9 35, 75, 103, 231, 253, 276
10:10 35, 112
10:13 35, 103, 117, 231, 253, 276
10:14 15, 272
10:17 xv, 37
10:18–20 66
11:1–6 96
11:5 97
11:7 97
11:28 97
12:1–2 247
12:3–8 248
12:8 249
14:11 94
16:13 96
16:25 13

1 Corinthians

1:2 119
1:18–29 51
1:21 13, 32
1:23 12, 38, 40, 84, 250
1:26–31 96
2:1 42n5
2:4 13, 86
2:7 42n5
2:13 86
3:5–17 42
3:9 52, 103
4:1–2 42
4:2 42
4:16–17 42
5:5 232
5:12–13 232
6:11 112, 117
6:20 119
8:1 211
9:12 57

9:19–23 219
9:22–23 40
10:31 50
11:1 54, 83, 232
11:26 6
12 248
12:4–7 xiv
12:28 249
14 248
14:24–25 14, 14n30, 39
15:1 7, 14n27, 32
15:1–2 23
15:1–4 84
15:3–4 32
15:5–7 32
15:8–10 119
15:11 32
15:14 13
15:15 12
15:25 94

2 Corinthians

1:22 74
2:15–16 250, 256
2:17 50, 57
4:2 40, 57
4:4 11
4:6 50
5:10–11 52
5:11 219
5:14 50
5:17 121
5:18–19 111
5:19 107
5:20 111, 259, 274
5:21 112
6:2 85
7:4 52
7:9–10 119
7:10 54n3
10:3–6 247
10:5 211
10:14 11
13:1 223

Galatians

1:8 14n27
2:15–3:29 112
3:8 67n3
3:26–29 114

Scripture Index

3:28 196, 207
4:1–7 129
4:4 65, 191
4:5 112
4:6–7 113
4:9 119
5:11 250

Ephesians

1:3 110
1:4 93, 97
1:4–5 96, 113
1:11 96
1:13 11, 74
2:1 111, 121
2:1–22 121
2:3 113
2:8–9 111, 113, 119, 232
2:10 96
2:14 194
2:16 107, 111
3:6 194
3:21 50
4:4–6 30
4:7 234
4:11 11, 234, 234n1, 240
4.11 12 xiv, 248
4:12 240
4:30 74, 120, 247
6:10–20 247
6:12 56
6:15 11
6:19–20 95

Philippians

1:15 50
1:16 211, 219
1:17 50
2:11 50
3:5–8 119
4:5–7 256
4:6–7 90

Colossians

1:5–7 75
1:13 54, 112, 120
1:13–14 94
1:15–17 94
1:22 111

2:6 232
2:11–12 117
2:15 94
3:12 97
4:3 xii
4:3–4 16, 27, 262
4:3–5 95
4:4 xv, 189, 207, 279
4:5–6 273
4:13 12

1 Thessalonians

1:4 97
1:4–5 93
1:4–9 119
1:5 86
1:8–10 75
1:9 114
2:9 12
2:20 52
5:19 247
5:23 112

2 Thessalonians

1:8 11
1:10 228
2:13 97
2:13–14 93
3:1 75

1 Timothy

2:3–4 101
2:7 12
5:21 96
6:15 94

2 Timothy

1:7 85, 250
1:9 97
1:11 12
2:2 249
2:10 57, 97
2:25 119
3:12 55
3:16 253
4:1–5 40, 259
4:2 7, 272
4:5 11, 248, 249
4:17 13

Titus

1:3 13
1:5 91
2:1 40
2:14 112
3:5 121
3:5–7 120

Hebrews

1:3 93, 191
2:17 111
4:12 253
4:12–13 228
6:4–6 119
9:22 113
9:27 53, 85
10:10 120
10:14 120
10:36–39 119
11:6 117, 209
11:13 129
13:7 236

James

1:17 191, 227
1:18 93
1:27 28
2:19 117, 276
4:12 94
4:14 85, 274
5:19–20 115, 120

1 Peter

1:1–2 96
1:3 111, 121
1:12 86
1:23 121
2:4–6 96
2:9 11, 69n4, 96, 237, 249
2:11 129
2:21 232
2:25 115
3:1–2 271
3:15 56, 189, 208, 214, 219, 251
3:15–16 xiii, 211, 271
4:10–11 248
4:17 11
5:3 236, 240

2 Peter

1:3 50
1:10 97
2:5 12
3:9 101, 119
3:12–13 93

1 John

1:1 225
1:1–3 35
1:1–4 225
1:5–10 119
1:9 120
1:10 247
2:2 111
2:3 23n26
2:29 120
3:1 114
3:10 113
4:7 120
4:10 111
4:18 52, 111
5:4 120
5:13 23n26

2 John

4 52

Revelation

1:5 35, 225
2:4–5 120
2:13 35
2:20 15
3:1 237
3:19 120
6:9 35
7:9 52, 192
7:9–10 94, 103
11:15 94
13:8 93, 103
17:8 103
17:14 94
21 93
22:2 193

AUTHOR INDEX

Abraham, William, 21, 21n18, 25, 25n31
Adams, Charles, 18n6
Adeney, Frances S., 20n14
Akers, John N., 177n40
Akin, Daniel, 75n6
Allen, Mark D., 210, 213, 213n4, 217
Allen, Roland, 85, 85n6
Allison, Gregg R., 97nn4–5, 98, 98n7, 99, 99n15
Arminius, Jacob, 98, 98n11, 159
Armstrong, Richard Stoll, 235, 235n5, 236, 236n9

Bacon, Francis, 18, 18n3
Baker, Mark, 203n20
Bargár, Pavol, 185n94
Barna, George, 242, 242n2
Barrett, David B., 5n3, 7, 7n7, 8, 8n11, 14, 14n28, 18, 18n3, 18n7, 19n10, 20n13, 41, 41nn1–2, 42n3, 43, 48, 146n53, 155n15
Barrs, Jerram, 83n1, 88, 88n13
Bartlotti, Leonard N., 46n10, 46n12
Bassham, Rodger C., 167n5, 169n11, 169n15, 170n16, 170n19
Beaver, R. Pierce, 147n2
Bediako, Kwame, 37, 37n9
Beitzel, Barry, 96n3, 100n24
Beougher, Timothy K., 8n9, 85, 85n5, 122n12, 123n13, 138, 244, 244n5
Bevans, Stephen B., 166n1, 168n9, 174n34
Birdsall, S. Douglas, 178n45
Blach, David L., 146n50
Blauw, Johannes, 67, 67n2, 76, 76n7, 77n9
Bosch, David J., 22, 22n26, 23nn26–27, 196n1
Boyack, Kenneth, 183n75

Braaten, Carl E., 67n2
Brennan, J. Patrick, 22n20
Bria, Ion, 23, 23n30, 187, 187nn103–4, 188nn106–7
Briggs, John A. Y., 167n6, 169n12, 171n21
Bright, Bill, 25, 25n33, 230, 250n2
Bromiley, Geoffrey W., 10n15, 11n17, 12nn20–21
Brooks, Christopher W., 209, 209n2
Broomhall, Benjamin, 19
Brown, Lindsay, 178n45
Bruce, A. B., 83n1
Brunner, Emil, 73, 74, 74n2, 75
Burt, Robert, 26n38

Calkins, Raymond, 83n1
Calvin, John, 97, 98, 98n6, 98n8, 156
Carrier, Hervé, 183, 183nn78–79, 184n81
Carson, D. A., 77n10, 249n1
Carwardine, Richard, 158n8
Chamberlain, Paul, 210
Chan, Sam, 56, 56n7, 89, 210, 217, 267
Chatraw, Joshua D., 210, 213, 213n4, 217
Chilcote, Paul W., 20, 20n15
Chitwood, Paul, 230n1
Coleman, Robert E., 83n1, 110, 111, 111n13, 121
Conard, William W., 177n40
Courson, Jim, 46n12
Coutu, Marie, 177n40
Cowan, Steven B., 208n1, 212n3
Coxe, A. Cleveland, 133, 133n1, 142, 142nn31–32, 145, 145n45, 145n47
Crabtree, Charles, 80

Crossing, Peter F., 29n1, 47, 47nn17–18
Cust, Robert Needham, 19

Datema, Dave, 46n10
Dayton, Edward R., 200, 200n12
Dean, Marcus, 203n20
De Neui, Paul, 203n20
DiFransico, Lesley, 116n3
Dillon, Christine, 203n20
Dodd, C. H., 13, 13n24, 32–34, 33nn3–5
Dodson, Jonathan K., 210
Donaldson, James, 135n5, 136n14, 137n17, 139n21, 140nn23–24, 141nn26–27, 142n30, 143nn35–39, 145n44, 145n46, 145nn48–49, 146n52
Dorsett, Lyle W., 163n15
Douglas, J. D., 60n25, 175n35, 177n42
Douglass-Chin, Richard, 147n2
Doyle, JoAnn, 147n2
Doyle, Tom, 147n2
Drummond, Lewis A., 8n9, 95, 95n1, 104, 104n28
Dulles, Avery, 181, 181n62
Dunelm, Handley, 101, 101n26
Dzubinski, Leanne M., 147n2

Elwell, Walter, 96n3, 100n24
Engel, James F., 199–200, 199n10, 200n11, 202–3, 203n20
Epstein, Barbara Leslie, 147n2
Erdmann, Martin, 77, 77n11
Everts, Don, 127, 127n20

Fay, William, 250n2, 265, 265n3
Fernando, Ajith, 56, 56n8
Fish, Roy, 236n8
Ford, Leighton, 176, 177n41
Forrest, Tom, 183nn76–77
Frame, John, 213, 213n6
Francis (pope), 22, 22nn24–25, 184, 184nn87–91
Friedrich, Gerhard, 10n15, 11n17, 12nn20–21
Frost, Michael, 124n15

Gallagher, Robert L., 152, 152n12
Geisler, Wilson S., IV, 46n12
Georges, Jayson, 203n20
Ghering, Roger W., 146n50
Gill, Brad, 46n12
Glasser, Arthur F., 173n30, 174n31, 175n39
Goheen, Michael W., 69, 69n6, 70, 70n7
González, Justo L., 156, 156n2, 159n9

Goodall, Norman, 174n32
Gorski, John F., 4n2, 21n19, 181n67
Graham, Billy, 60, 60nn22–24, 164, 173, 175, 177, 230
Gray, James, 202n13
Green, Michael, 34n7, 50, 50nn1–2, 71n8, 84n1, 88n12, 102, 133, 133nn2–3, 147n1, 163n15
Grogan, Paul, 22n23, 183n74
Grudem, Wayne, 98, 98n9, 108n3
Guder, Darrell L., 87n11, 124n15
Guinness, Os, 39, 39n12
Gundry, Stanley N., 208n1, 212n3
Gustafson, David M., 86, 86n10
Guthrie, Stan, 255n3

Habermas, Gary R., 213, 213n5
Handley, Joseph W., Jr., 180n60
Harnack, Adolf, 135, 136n11
Harvey, John D., 77, 78n14
Hater, Robert J., 181n61, 182n66, 182n69
Havlik, John F., 34n8
Hawkins, O. S., 236n8
Henard, William D., 235n6
Henry, Carl F. H., 173, 173nn28–29
Hesselgrave, David, 76n7, 203, 203n19
Hiebert, Frances F., 281
Hiebert, Paul G., 124, 124n14, 125–26, 126nn17–18, 215, 215nn7–8, 216, 281
Hildreth, D. Scott, 250n2
Hinson, E. Glenn, 136n12, 144, 144n40
Hirsch, Alan, 124n15
Hobbes, Thomas, 18, 19n8
Hobbs, Herschel H., 83, 84, 84n4
Hoekstra, Harvey T., 168n8, 169n14, 170n18, 172, 172n27
Hoke, Donald, 175n35
House, H. Wayne, 108, 108n2
Hunter, George G., III, 127n20
Hvalvik, Reidar, 135, 135n10, 136, 146, 146n51

Jambrek, Stanko, 59, 60n21
Jenkins, Philip, 148, 148n4, 150n7
Johnson, Ronald W., 203n20, 264, 264n2
Johnson, Samuel, 18, 18n4
Johnson, Todd M., 29n1, 47, 47nn17–18, 146n53, 155n15
Johnston, Arthur P., 168n8, 170n20, 171n24
Johnston, Thomas P., 7n7, 8, 8n8, 8n10, 9, 9n13
Johnstone, Patrick, 45, 45nn7–8
Jones, E. Stanley, 124, 124n16

Kanyoro, Musimbi R. A., 38, 38n10
Kariatlis, Philip, 185n93
Keathley, Kenneth, 98, 99, 99nn13–14, 99n16
Keller, Timothy, 210, 217
Kelley, Charles S., Jr., 51
Kennedy, D. James., 44
Kidner, Derek, 67n3
Kilpatrick, T. B., 19, 19n11, 20, 20n12
Kim, Kirsteen, 22n23, 183n74
Kittel, Gerhard, 10n15, 11n17, 12nn20–21
Klaiber, Walter, 8n9, 14n27
Kling, David W., 116n4, 122, 122n11
Knight, Henry H., III, 252
Korkmaz, Yakup, 195
Köstenberger, Andreas J., 76n8, 77n10
Koukl, Gregory, 210
Kraemer, Hendrik, 203, 203n20
Kraft, Charles, 203, 203n20
Kuiper, R. B., 100n25

Larkin, William J., Jr., 79n16
Larsen, David L., 74n3, 122, 122n9
Latourette, Kenneth Scott, 136, 136n13, 137n16, 150n5, 150n9, 151n10, 154n13
Lawless, Chuck, 271, 271n4
Lawrence, J. B., 86, 86n8
Leavell, Roland Q., 79n15
Lemopoulos, Georges, 187n104
Lennox, Patrick, 205
Lewis, R. W., 47n16
Liefeld, Walter L., 147n2
Lim, David, 203n20
Linn, Jan G., 23, 23n28
Liptak, Yeong Woo, 147n2
Little, Paul, 176n35
Lloyd-Jones, Sally, 246n7
Logan, Doug, Jr., 90n15
Lovett, C. S., 90n15

MacMullen, Ramsay, 135, 135nn6–7, 135n9, 136, 142, 142n34
Malherbe, Abraham J., 134n3
Martin-Achard, Robert, 68
Matthews, Kenneth A., 67n3
Mayers, Marvin K., 203, 203n20
McCloskey, Mark, 88, 88n14, 104, 104n29, 109, 109n11, 110, 110n12
McGavran, Donald A., 75n5, 128, 128nn22–25, 129n26, 174, 174n33, 279n1
McGrath, Alister E., 108n4, 109n8
McKinion, Steven A., 250n2
McLaughlin, Rebecca, 210

McMahan, Alan, 46n12
Medders, J. A., 90n15
Meeking, Basil, 58, 59n16
Merkle, Benjamin L., 75n6
Miles, Delos, 8n9, 83n1, 91, 91n17
Mischke, Werner, 203n20
Moon, W. Jay, 206–7, 206n22
Mooneyham, W. Stanley, 173, 173n29
Morris, Leon, 112n14
Mott, John R., 19, 167, 234, 234nn2–3, 235, 235n4
Mugambi, J. N. K., 86n9
Mulholland, Ken, 170, 170n17, 170n19
Murray, James, 19n9

Nazir-Ali, Michael, 203n20
Neill, Stephen, 74, 74n3, 150n6, 150n8
Newbigin, Lesslie, 87, 87n11
Newell, Marvin J., 75n6, 77, 77n12
Nguyen, Minh Ha, 46n12
Nida, Eugene A., 203, 203n20
Niles, D. T., 25, 25n32, 164, 164n19, 169
Nissiotis, Nikos, 23, 23n29, 186, 186nn98–100, 187, 187n102
Nolland, John, 42, 42n6
Norton, H. Wilbert, 199, 199n10, 200n11
Nuelsen, J. L., 114, 115, 115n2

Olson, Roger E., 99n18, 100n21, 109, 109n19
Osiek, Carolyn, 146n50
Ott, Craig, 207, 207n23

Packer, J. I., 21, 21n17, 101, 101n27, 105, 112, 112n15, 169n13
Paul VI (pope), 4n2, 22, 23, 58, 182, 182nn70–72, 183n73
Paulsen, Judith, 5n4, 84n1
Payne, J. D., 47n15, 74n4, 84n3, 87n11, 133, 197n2, 230, 241n1, 247, 261
Peace, Richard V., 118n7, 122, 122n8
Peifen, Jiang, 147n2
Poe, Harry L., 13n24, 34, 34n6
Polhill, John B., 79n17, 81n18
Pope-Levison, Priscilla, 17, 17n1, 18n5, 90, 91n16, 147n2
Powe, Douglas F., Jr., 252
Price, Chris, 210

Queen, Matt, 8n9, 236n8, 295

Raiser, Konrad, 185n95
Reid, Alvin, 8n9, 288

Richardson, Rick, 89n15
Robb, John, 45, 45nn7–8
Robert, Dana L., 147n2
Roberts, Alexander, 135n5, 136n14, 137n17, 139n21, 140nn23–24, 141nn26–27, 142n30, 143nn35–39, 145n44, 145n46, 145nn48–49, 146n52
Robinson, George G., 75n6
Robinson, Jeffrey M., 210
Root, Jerry, 255n3
Rudnick, Milton L., 148n3, 152n11, 157, 157n3, 158n8, 168n8

Sanders, J. Oswald, 245, 245n6
Sanneh, Lamin, 203n20
Scarborough, L. R., 83n1
Scharpff, Paulus, 156, 156n1, 159n12, 162, 163, 163n16
Schaupp, Doug, 127, 127n20
Scherer, James A., 166n1
Schirrmacher, Thomas, 59, 59n19
Schneider, Floyd, 250n2, 283, 285
Scribner, Dan, 46n12
Shah, Rebecca Samuel, 114n1
Shaw, R. Daniel, 203n20
Simon, W. Bud, 206–7, 206n22
Sire, James W., 215–16, 216n9
Smith, Thomas, 140, 141n25
Smither, Edward L., 6n5, 152n11
Søgaard, Viggo, 199, 200–203
Sohn, Lydia, 25n35
Sproul, R. C., 108, 108n5, 212
Spurgeon, C. H., 90n15, 242, 242n4
Stamoolis, James J., 185n92
Stasson, Anneke H., 147n2
Steffen, Tom, 149, 203n20, 256n4
Stewart, George, 20n14
Stiles, J. Mack, 236, 236n7
Stone, Bryan, 23n26, 24, 55n4
Stott, John, 12, 12n19, 17, 18, 18n2, 58, 59n16, 107, 299
Stowe, David M., 15, 15n31, 16
Street, R. Alan, 236n8
Stromberg, Jean, 122n10

Taylor, G. D., 223n1, 225n2
Taylor, Mark, 42n5
Terry, John Mark, 47n15, 84n2, 152, 152n12, 154n14, 157n4, 161n13, 163nn17–18
Thiessen, Elmer John, 55, 56, 56nn5–6, 57n11
Thomas, M. M., 167, 171, 171n23
Thompson, Nicholas J., 237
Tibbs, Eve, 186n101

Uzzell, Lawrence A., 59, 59nn17–18

Valleskey, David J., 214
Van Engen, Charles E., 203n20
Van Rheenen, Gailyn, 203n20
Vassiliadis, Petros, 186n97, 302
Veronis, Alexander, 186n97, 187n105
Visser 't Hooft, W. A., 172nn25–26

Wagner, Peter, 200, 291
Währisch-Oblau, Claudia, 184n86
Wardle, Terry, 128n21
Warner, Laceye C., 20, 20n15
Watson, Brad, 210
Watson, David, 8n9
Watson, Thomas, 116n5, 231, 231n2
Webber, Robert E., 14, 14n26, 85, 85n7
Weber, H. R., 203n20
Wells, David F., 126, 127n19
Wesley, John, 99, 99n17, 100, 100nn19–20, 100nn22–23, 108, 109, 109nn6–7
Whiteman, Darrell L., 204, 204n21
Whitesell, Faris D., 236n8
Whitney, Donald S., 255n3
Wimber, John, 142n33
Winter, Ralph D., 45, 182n68, 196–98
Wright, Christopher, J. H., 69, 69n5
Wright, Harry B., 20n14
Wright, N. T., 216, 216nn10–11
Wynkoop, Mildred Bangs, 109, 109n10

Zurlo, Gina A., 29n1, 30, 47, 47nn17–18, 147n2

SUBJECT INDEX

Abraham, 9–10, 67, 69, 95, 111, 115, 209
Ad Gentes, 181n61
adoption, 31, 96, 113
African Methodist Episcopal Church, 161
Against Celsus, 139n21, 140n24, 142, 142n30, 143n35, 145n44
Against Heresies, 142, 142nn31–32, 143n36
Agapius, 137
Allen, Mark, 213, 217
Ambrose of Milan, 151
American Bible Society, 158
American Board of Commissioners for Foreign Missions, 158
Anabaptists, 156–57
Ansgar, 153
Anthony the Great, 155
antinomy, 101, 105
anxious benches, 161
apologetics, xiii, xv, 4, 39, 135, 189, 208–9, 211, 213–19, 268
  dealing with defeaters, 210
  limits, 209, 214
  methods, 212–13, 215
atonement, vii, ix, 63, 84, 101, 107–11, 113, 117, 170
Armenia, 134, 150, 150n6
Arminian, 99n18, 100n21, 101–2, 106, 107, 108–10, 121
Arminianism, 98–99, 159, 161
Arminius, Jacob, 98, 159
Augustine of Canterbury, 153
Augustine of Hippo, 97, 108, 109, 151, 154
awakenings, 86, 131, 158, 158n5, 158nn–8, 159
  First Great, 158, 160
  Second Great, 158

Third Great, 159
Fourth Great, 159

Baptist World Alliance, 165
Barth, Karl, 100
Barrett, David, 5n3, 7, 7n7, 8n11, 14, 14n28, 18, 18n3, 18n7, 19n10, 20n13, 41, 41nn1–2, 42n3, 43, 48, 146n53, 155n15
Barrows, Cliff, 164
belief, 6, 14n30, 28, 35, 78, 108, 110, 111, 115–19, 121, 122, 124, 128, 224, 244, 276
Benedict XVI (pope), 184
Benedict of Nursia, 152
Billy Graham Evangelistic Association, 36, 164, 175
Bohemians, 157
Boniface of England, 153
born again, 4, 88, 111, 120–21, 123, 125, 129, 148, 224, 229
Bria, Ion, 23, 187

Caecilius, 140
Calvin, John, 97, 98, 156
Calvinism, 98, 99, 107, 108, 161
Calvinist, ix, 99, 101, 102, 108, 109, 110, 121, 159, 160
Calvinist Methodists, 160
camp meeting, 158, 161
Catholic, 5, 6, 7, 17, 18, 21, 22, 49, 57, 154, 156, 166, 166n1, 179, 181, 182, 184, 186, 188
  dialogue, with evangelicals on mission, 58–59
  evangelization, xiii, 4n2, 181n61, 182n66
  new evangelization, 22, 22n25, 182–84
  reevangelization, 14, 14n29, 181, 182n68
Celsus, 139, 140, 142, 143n35, 144, 145n44

Ceylon, 150n5, 164
Chan, Sam, 56, 89, 217
Chatraw, Joshua, 217
Child Evangelism Fellowship, 242n3
children, 241–46
　EvangeCube, 246n7
　Gospel Wheel, 246n7
　parents of, 243–44
　Spurgeon and, 242, 242n4
　Wordless Book, 246n7
Christianese, 224, 228–29
Christianity Today, 164, 177
Christianization, xiv, 6n5, 148, 148n3, 155, 167, 181n61, 191, 274
"Christian Witness in a Multi-Religious World: Recommendations for Conduct," 59
Chrysostom, John, 151
Church of England, 20, 159, 159n11
circuit riders, x, 158, 162
Clement, 137, 140, 143, 145
Clovis, 148n3, 152
"Code of Ethics for the Christian Evangelist," 60
Coleman, Robert, 83n1, 110, 111, 121
Columba, 152
Columbanus, 152–53
Commission of World Mission and Evangelism, 168, 168n7
Congregation for the Doctrine of Faith, 184
Constantine, 135n6, 136
contextualization, xv, 34, 183, 191, 200
conversation in evangelism, 195, 217, 232, 233, 243, 250–51, 261
　content to share, 266, 268
　difficult questions, 268–70
　guidelines, x, 261–66, 271–72
　nudge questions, 245, 267
　prayer for guidance, 259
　response to rejection, 274–75
conversion
　beginning of sanctification, 129
　group conversion, 128, 128n24, 281–82
　set theory, 123–26
cross, 34, 38, 51, 55, 79, 90, 102, 107, 230, 243, 250, 255, 256, 283
cultures, xv, 38n11, 39–40, 57, 83, 86, 124, 196, 207
　bounded center set, ix, 125
　cultural text, 89
　Dayton Resistance/Receptivity Scale, ix, 200
　digital, ix, 36
　dimensions of, ix, 215
　extrinsic fuzzy set, ix, 125–26
　gospel-cultural hermeneutics, ix, 89
　Søgaard Scale, x, 200–203
Cyprian, 134
Cyril, 153

Dayton, Edward, 200
Decision (magazine), 164
decision cards, 163
decision making, 55, 115, 118, 128, 199–203, 274, 275, 281–82
de Molina, Luis, 98
Diognetus, 137, 145
Diognetus, Epistle to, 137, 145
"Doctrinal Note on Some Aspects of Evangelization," 184
Dodd, C. H., 13n24, 32–34
double predestination, 96n2
Duff, Alexander, 166, 237

"Ecumenical Conference on World Mission and Evangelization" (report), 38n11
Edessa, 150
Edwards, Jonathan, 158
election, 67, 93, 95–100, 100n20, 101–6, 110
Engel, James, 199–200, 202–3, 203n20
Engel Scale, 199–200, 202
Ethiopia (Abyssinia), 150
euangelizo, 7, 7n7, 9–10
Eusebius, 137, 139, 141, 144
evangelicals, 15, 40, 58–60, 74, 142n33, 169n13, 171–75, 181n60, 182n68, 186, 187n105, 188–89, 196n2, 204, 242n3
Evangelii gaudium, 22, 184, 184n86, 185
Evangelii nuntiandi, 4n2, 21, 58, 182
evangelism
　audience, 13–16, 18, 38, 39, 78, 82, 83, 87, 89, 127, 129, 149, 156, 181, 184, 192, 201, 202, 203, 204, 207, 211, 231, 244
　biblical terms, 7, 8–13, 32, 33, 78
　categories for defining, 20–23, 25–27
　cold-call, 258
　congresses. *See* World Missionary Conferences/Congresses
　crusade, 14n30, 127, 163, 164
　cultural gaps, viii, 37, 40, 45, 175, 191, 193–94, 196–98, 198n9, 207, 279–80
　definitions, vii, 1, 4, 16, 17, 20, 20n13, 25, 28, 74, 280
　door-to-door, xiii, 4, 161
　E-0, E-1, E-2, E-3, 197–98, 198n9

Subject Index

ethics, vii, 5, 49, 51, 55–56, 57n11, 60–61, 175
fear of, 15, 24, 209, 247, 250, 250n2, 251, 256–57, 270, 276
global status of evangelization, vii, 1, 41, 43, 45, 47, 235n4
greatest need, 196–98
importance of pastors, xiv, 44, 163, 234–36, 234n1, 247
innovation in, 150, 159, 165
intercultural, xv, 196, 197n2, 206, 279
invitation, 275–77
location, xiii, 4, 6, 13–14, 16, 30, 41, 43, 49, 69, 133, 134, 196, 258
message shared, 13, 30, 32, 34, 169, 250, 266
models, 6, 238, 239, 266
motives, vii, 1, 49–51, 53–55, 61, 136, 177, 279
not a gift, 248–49
reevangelization, 14
signs and wonders, 85, 142, 142n33, 143
principles, xiii, xv, 6, 22n26, 63, 80, 83, 84n3, 92, 163, 238–39
training, 44, 80, 83n1, 149, 157, 159, 164, 175, 183, 235–36, 238–40, 253, 282
with strangers, 3, 258–60
Evangelism and the Sovereignty of God, 101
Evangelism Explosion, ix, 44
evangelistic syncretism, 27–28
evangelists, ix, 5n4, 11, 15, 44, 51, 60, 80, 86–87, 90, 91, 104, 141, 144, 147–49, 157, 159–62, 175–77, 182n66, 198, 214, 231, 234n1, 240, 248
Evangelization 2000, 183
e word, ix, 24
Exhortation to the Heathen, 145

faith, 110, 114–129
Far East Broadcasting Company, 165
Finney, Charles, 161, 163
folk Islam, x, 195
forgiveness, 9, 27, 31, 33, 37, 65, 76–77, 79, 81, 84, 109, 113, 116, 121, 123, 129, 214, 224, 244, 249, 258, 276n6, 277n7
4/14 Window, 242
Francis (pope), 184
Francis of Assisi, 154
Francke, August Hermann, 157
free will, 98, 99
Frelinghuysen, Theodore, 160
Frisians, 153

Georgia, 150
Global Research Department (IMB), 42, 45, 46, 47n19
gospel
biblical terminology, 11–12
comprehensive nature, 30–32
content, 32–35
contextualization of, 38–40
definition, 30
irreducible minimum, 32, 40
offense of, 40, 51, 250, 251, 283–85
translatability, 37–38
Goths, 150, 151
grace, 11, 28, 31, 63, 67, 96, 97–99, 103, 107–13, 116, 119, 120, 121, 143, 144, 157, 176, 184, 185, 205, 214, 224, 226, 227, 232, 254, 256, 257, 274, 276, 277, 280
common, 108, 109
efficacious, irresistible, 108, 110
prevenient, 109
Graham, Billy, 60, 164, 173, 175, 177, 230
Great Commission, xiii, 6, 13, 29, 30, 41, 44, 56, 59, 63, 73, 75, 75nn5–6, 77, 78, 82, 88, 90, 91, 104, 121, 129, 135, 138, 162, 166, 169, 170, 180, 185, 197
Green, Michael, 50, 84n1, 88n12, 102, 133, 147n1
Gregory I (pope), 153
Gregory II (pope), 153
Gregory Thaumaturgus, 150

Halle, University of, 157
Harald Klak (king), 153
heaven, 31, 54, 76, 82, 93, 95, 96n2, 100n23, 110, 138, 227, 245, 263, 265
hell, 31, 49, 55, 96n2, 100n23, 114, 173, 210, 256, 265
Hellenization, 71, 134
hermeneutics, ix, 89
Hesselgrave, David J., 76n7, 203
Communicating Christ Cross-Culturally, 203
receptor-oriented, xv, 15, 203–4, 207, 224
Hiebert, Paul, 124, 125, 126, 215, 281
Holiness Movement, 161
Holy Spirit, 20, 21, 22, 33, 48n19, 85–86, 123, 142, 173, 174, 176, 185, 193–94, 204, 214, 224, 229, 231–32, 250, 256n4, 259, 285
humanization, 168, 174
Huntingdon, Selina (countess), 160
Hus, Jan, 154
Hussites, 154

inculturation, 183–84
International Conference for Itinerant Evangelists, 60, 175, 177
  Amsterdam Declaration, 177, 177n40
International Missionary Council, 167
  merger into World Council of Churches, 171
inquirers' room, 163
Irenaeus, 142, 143
Israel, ix, 8, 9, 10, 33, 66, 68, 69, 70, 71, 75, 79, 95, 96, 112, 115, 116, 118, 121, 191, 192, 195, 223, 225, 243, 244

Jesus Movement, 159
John Paul II (pope), 22n23, 183, 183n74
Joshua Project, 42, 45, 45n9, 46, 47
judgment, 10, 27, 31, 46, 52, 53, 54n3, 55, 65, 66, 67, 70, 77, 81, 82, 85, 86, 96, 97, 100, 115, 116, 137, 145, 149, 192, 231, 245, 250
justification, 34, 112–13, 114
Justin Martyr, 145

Keller, Timothy, 210, 217
Kim, Billy, 164–65
kingdom, 5, 11, 31, 33, 34, 42, 43, 65, 74, 78–81, 86, 89, 94, 103–4, 111–13, 120, 123, 148, 186, 191, 192, 208–9, 227, 242, 257, 277
  of darkness, 34, 53–54, 94, 112, 114, 120, 123, 191, 247, 265
  ethic, 1, 27, 28, 53, 55–56, 59, 68, 147n1, 172–73, 183, 232
Knox, John, 156

Lausanne, 175, 177
Lausanne Congress on World Evangelization, 45, 164
  Cape Town, 60, 177–78
  Cape Town Commitment, 60, 178, 185
  Lausanne Covenant, 27, 175, 178
  hidden peoples, 45, 175, 182n68, 197n5
  Manilla, 45, 177
  Manilla Manifesto, 60, 177
  Seoul-Incheon, 131, 180
  Seoul Statement, 180
  "Track 310—Unreached Peoples," 45
Lectures on Revivals of Religion, 161
libertarianism, 99
Liturgy After the Liturgy, The, 187–88
Lollards, 154
Louis the Pious, 153
Luther, Martin, 97, 156, 156n1
Lutheran Church, 25, 157

Majority World, 5, 29, 30, 40, 128, 147, 161, 168, 171, 175, 198, 241
Marrant, John, 160
Martin of Tours, 150
martyrdom, 136–37, 140, 193
Martyrdom of the Holy Martyrs, The, 146
matheteuo, 13, 78
McGavran, Donald A., 75n5, 128, 174, 279n1
McGready, James, 158
Methodists, xiii, 159, 159n10, 160, 162
Methodius, 153
middle knowledge, 99, 99n14
Minucius Felix, 140
Mission of the Orthodox Church in Today's World, The, 185
Molinism, 98–99, 99n14
Molinist, 101
monasteries, 153, 155
Monica, 151
Moody, Dwight L., 163, 163n15
Moody Bible Institute, 163
Moon, W. Jay, 206–7
Moravians, 157
multicultural world, vii, 29, 39, 40, 196

nations, x, 5, 9, 10, 37, 44, 50, 65, 67, 68–71, 76, 76n7, 93–95, 134, 144, 174, 187n105, 198, 205, 249, 280
neoorthodoxy, 170, 172
Niles, D. T., 25, 164, 169
Nissiotis, Nikos, 23, 186, 187
Norton, H. Wilbert, 199–200

Oberlin College, 161
Octavius, 140
Octavius of Minucius Felix, The, 140
Ordinary General Assembly of the Synod of Bishops, 22, 184
Origen, 139, 140, 142, 150, 231
Orthodox Church, 23, 185, 186, 186n96
Osei-Mensah, Gottfried, 164

Packer, J. I., 21, 101, 105, 112, 169n13
Paeon, 146
Palmer, Phoebe, 161, 161n14
Pan-Orthodox Missionary Society, 185n92
Pantaenus, 141
pastor, 38, 123n13, 156, 158, 160, 161, 164, 165, 249, 266, 277
  example in evangelism, 235n4, 236
  priority for evangelism, 237
  responsibility for evangelism, 234
  zeal for evangelism, 235

Subject Index

Patrick of Ireland, 151, 152n11
Paul VI (pope), 4n2, 21, 22, 58, 182
pax Romana, 71, 133
Pelagius, 97
Persia, 70, 71, 134, 148, 150
Pia Desideria, 157
Pietism, 156, 157, 159, 160, 165
Polycarp, 142
Pontifical Council for Promoting the New Evangelization, 184
Porefthendes, 185n92
prayer, xii, 15, 27, 39, 45, 69–71, 102, 124, 143, 156, 161, 168, 183, 221, 230–32, 236, 242, 243, 247, 259, 262, 276, 277, 279, 280
preaching, ix, 4, 5, 7, 10, 12, 14n30, 20, 65, 85, 86, 102, 134, 141, 153, 157, 158, 159, 169, 176, 187, 214, 225, 249, 258, 272, 279
predestination, 95, 96, 97, 98, 99
propitiation, 107, 111
proselytism, 18, 57, 57n10, 57n11, 58, 59, 61, 179, 185
proselytization, 60
protevangelium, 66, 67, 72
protomissio, 66, 72

Reapsome, Jim, 5n3, 41, 48
receptor-oriented communication, xv, 15, 203, 204, 207, 224
Recognitions of Clement, 140, 143
reconciliation, 23, 23n27, 58, 84, 100, 111, 120, 172, 179
redemption, 53, 54, 70, 74, 112, 113, 121, 149, 172, 173, 205, 224
  general, 107
  particular, 107
Reformation, 6, 154, 156, 156n1
regeneration, xv, 22n25, 48n19, 75, 91, 104, 108, 111, 114, 115, 120, 121, 122, 123, 129, 148n3, 231, 244, 277n7
repentance, 14n30, 26, 33, 37, 54n3, 70, 79–81, 84, 104, 108–9, 114–29, 179, 186n97, 199, 214, 224, 232, 244
Reports of the Archbishops' Committees of Inquiry, 20
reprobation, 95–100, 100n20, 100n22
Resistance/Receptivity Scale, 200, 202
resurrection, 11, 31, 33, 39, 76, 79, 103, 117, 208, 209, 213, 225, 230, 243, 256, 266
revivals, 158, 158n6, 158n7, 161
  Cane Ridge, 158
  Pyongyang, 158
  revivalism, 158
Romans Road, 254

sanctification, 54, 75, 82, 91, 112, 120, 125, 129, 255n3
Sankey, Ira, 163
Second Apology, 145
Second General Conference of Latin American Bishops, 181
Simon, W. Bud, 206–7
Singh, Bakht, 163
sinner's prayer, viii, 221, 230, 230n1, 231, 276
  cautions with, 231–32
  model, 233
  purpose of, 231
  theology of, 230–31
Sire, James, 215, 216
Slavs, 153
Smith, Amanda Berry, 161
social justice, 28, 170, 172
Søgaard, Viggo, x, 199–203
soul-winning, 44, 90n15, 163
sovereignty, vii, 10, 63, 93–95, 98–102, 104–5, 176
Spener, Philipp Jakob, 156, 157
Successus, 134
Sunday, Billy, 163

Tennent, Gilbert, 160
Tertullian, 136, 136n14
testimony, viii, 4, 12, 35, 81, 137, 160, 201, 221, 223, 224, 225, 228–29, 244, 258, 266, 269, 270
  development of, 226–27
Thomas Aquinas, 97, 154
Tibetans, 150
"Together Towards Life," 26, 178, 179, 179n49, 185
Turks, 150

Ulfilas, 150
Universe Next Door, The, 216
unreached people groups, 46, 47n15, 164, 182n68, 197n2
  "hidden peoples," 45, 175, 182n68, 197n5
  unengaged, 48, 76n7, 197n5

Valdes. *See* Waldo, Peter
Vatican II, 18, 181, 181n61, 183
vikings, 153
von Zinzendorf, Count Ludwig Nickolaus, 157

Waldenses, 154
Waldo, Peter, 153
  "Poor in Spirit," 154
  "Poor Men of Lyon," 154

Wesley, Charles, 159, 159n11
Wesley, John, 99, 100, 100n20, 110n23, 108, 109, 159, 160, 162, 252
Wesleyan, x, 101, 252
Wesleyan-Arminianism, 108, 159
Whitefield, George, 159, 160
Winter, Ralph D., 45, 182n68, 196, 197, 197n2, 197n5, 198
wisdom, xii, 9, 63, 83, 86, 95, 100n23, 145, 273
witness, 12, 22n26, 23, 35, 37, 51, 56, 57, 58–59, 70, 81–82, 87n11, 99n14, 147n1, 151, 170–72, 176, 178–79, 186n97, 201, 214, 223, 225, 226, 228, 255, 256, 259, 272–73, 276n6
  to family and friends, 270–71
World Christian Database, 45n9
World Christian Encyclopedia, 41
World Congress on Evangelism, 173
World Council of Churches, 25, 26, 38, 38n11, 57, 57n10, 58, 59, 164, 168, 168n7, 168n8, 169n13, 171, 173, 174, 178, 179, 185, 188
  Commission on World Mission and Evangelism, 38, 122, 174, 179
World Missionary Conferences/Congresses, 166
  Accra (1958), 171
  Arusha (2018), 179–80
  Berlin (1966), 173, 174
  Crete (2012), 178–79
  Edinburgh (1910), 131, 167, 168n8, 173
  Jerusalem (1928), 168
  Lausanne (1974, 1989, 2010, 2024). *See also* Lausanne Congress on World Evangelization
  Liverpool (1860), 167
  London (1854, 1878), 166–67
  New Delhi (1961), 171
  New York (1854, 1900), 166–67
  Tambaram (1938), 169
  Uppsala (1968), 174
  Willingen (1952), 170, 170n19
  Whitby (1947), 170
worldview, 206
  deism, 217
  existentialism, 218
  naturalism, 218
  nihilism, 218
  pantheism, 218
  postmodernism, 219
  theism, 216
Wright, N. T., 216
Wycliffe, John, 154
Wynfrith, 153

YMCA, 163

Zwingli, Huldrych, 156